DOCTORAL PROGRAMS IN BUSINESS & MANAGEMENT IN THE USA 2000

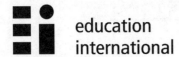
education international

EI Education International Ltd.
205 - 5325 Cordova Bay Road
Victoria, BC V8Y 2L3 Canada
Internet: http://www.eiworldwide.com
email: educate@eiworldwide.com

Copyright © 2000 by EI Education International Ltd.

All rights reserved. No part of this book may be reproduced, stored or
transmitted in any form by any means without prior written permission
of the publisher.

Canadian Cataloguing in Publication Data

Guide to doctoral programs in business and management in the USA

ISBN 1-894122-61-5

  1. Management--Study and teaching (Graduate)--United States--
Directories. 2. Business schools--United States--Directories. I. Education
International (Organization)
HF1131.G835   650'.071'173

Printed in Canada by Quebecor Jasper Printing
Researched in Victoria, Canada by EI Education International Ltd.

The publisher has made every effort to ensure the accuracy and completeness of
the information contained in this book; however, no responsibility can be taken
for any errors or omissions.

DOCTORAL PROGRAMS IN BUSINESS & MANAGEMENT IN THE USA  2000

▼

more than 40 in-depth profiles
provide complete information

▼

covers all types
of doctoral-level programs

▼

feature article on
management education

education
international

Contents

Welcome	1
Opportunities & Challenges in Management Education	3
Graduate Management Admissions Test® (GMAC®)	5
Map of the USA	8
Notes on Reading the Profiles	11
List of Profiled Doctoral Business & Management Programs by State	13
Program Quick Facts	14

Profiled Doctoral Business & Management Programs   21

AACSB Listing of Accredited Institutions in the USA	187
AACSB Listing of Accredited International Institutions	204
AACSB Candidate Institutions	205
AACSB Member Institutions	211
Destination USA	215
Additional Resources	219
Glossary	224
Index	227

Welcome

Management education in the USA is evolving so rapidly that each year there are more exciting and diverse program options from which to choose. For prospective students, selecting the ideal program to further their individual career training, to meet their unique interests and accommodate their personal responsibilities and schedules is one of the most important decisions they will make. Pursuing doctoral management education is also a major investment. Annual program costs for full-time doctoral programs in the USA — at public and private institutions — average $12,100 for in-state students and $15,800 for out-of-state and international students. EI's *Guide to Doctoral Programs in Business & Management in the USA - 2000*, published in cooperation with AACSB - The International Association for Management Education, is an indispensible tool to help potential students narrow down their choices and make the most informed program investment possible.

Students using this guide should keep some special features in mind:

- **In-Depth Coverage ...** Programs are profiled on four pages and include all the pertinent information for selecting a program, including admission requirements, expenses, program overview, international student support, and university information. *No other guide provides such in-depth and comparable program coverage.*

- **Objective, Accurate and Current ...** This guide is professionally researched and written. All information is verified by program managers and academic deans. *The information is so current that the guide is often the only published source.*

- **All-Encompassing, Authoritative Information ...** Additional articles address the most important concerns potential students may have. Everything from the many options in US business education to different methods of applying (including online application) is covered in this *unique, stand-alone resource.*

EI's *Guide to Doctoral Programs in Business & Management in the USA - 2000* equips students to make educated, intelligent choices regarding their management studies and future career goals. This informative tool is a crucial step for anyone who wants to pursue a fulfilling career in management.

Good luck in your search.

David Boag, President
EI Education International Ltd.

Milton R. Blood, Managing Director
AACSB–The International Association for Management Education

Take the Next Step!
EI's Reader Response Card Service

Now that you've begun to explore the range of doctoral programs in business and management available, your next step is to determine which program is right for you.

> AIR MAIL
>
> You can also fax the other side of this card to us at 1-250-658-6285
>
> ATTACH AIR MAIL POSTAGE
>
> **EI EDUCATION INTERNATIONAL LTD**
> PTSGE CORP./5000 Columbia Center, 701 5th Ave.
> Seattle, Washington USA 98104-7078

> **ei education international**
>
> TO RECEIVE INFORMATION ON ALL THE SCHOOLS THAT ARE PROFILED IN THIS GUIDE, CHECK THE APPROPRIATE BOX BELOW, COMPLETE THE FORM AND SEND THE CARD TO THE ADDRESS ON THE BACK. YOU CAN ALSO FAX THIS CARD TO EI AT 1-250-658-6285.
>
> - ☐ Arizona State University
> - ☐ Cornell University
> - ☐ Drexel University
> - ☐ Duke University
> - ☐ Florida International University
> - ☐ Florida State University
> - ☐ Illinois Institute of Technology
> - ☐ Kent State University
> - ☐ Ohio State University, The
>
> Last Name _____ First Name _____ Age ____ Sex ____
> Address _____
> _____ Zip Code _____ Country _____
> Telephone (___) _____ Fax (___) _____ Email _____
> Area Code   Area Code
> DBM '00

The Reader Response Cards in this guide provide a quick, convenient way for you to request program information from specific universities or colleges. You will find two kinds of Reader Response Cards: general Education International cards and institution-specific cards. The following guidelines will help you use EI's Reader Response Card Service to make an informed, educated decision!

1. If the school has an institution-specific Reader Response Card, you should fill this out and return it directly to the university, college or institute.

2. If the school does not have an institution-specific card, fill out a general EI card and return this to us. We will make your request and the school will return the information directly to you. By completing EI's Reader Response Cards, you will provide the institutions that interest you with clear contact information.

3. Be sure to print clearly and to affix the proper postage to the cards—you want your request to be addressed as quickly and as efficiently as possible. This will speed up your request for catalogues, brochures, application forms and financial aid.

Opportunities & Challenges in Management Education

College and university faculty enjoy many work and life-style privileges not typically available to those in other walks of life. Substantial professional and intellectual autonomy permits a large measure of freedom in defining work arrangements and areas of academic activity. Nine-month contracts often enable faculty to travel and undertake alternate teaching, research and consulting assignments, if they so desire. Opportunities to teach highly motivated students and develop satisfying relationships with colleagues within the country and abroad are virtually without parallel in other professions. Professors have the where-with-all to pursue knowledge and techniques that improve the practice of management and contribute to the greater good; that is, professors have the chance to impact individual lives as well as larger society.

Business school faculty often have substantially higher salaries than their counterparts in other academic fields. An annual survey by AACSB – The International Association for Management Education, found that in 1999-2000 the average starting salary for new doctorates teaching nine months of the year ranged from US$61,500 to US$91,900, depending on the field. More than half earned more than $70,000. Average salaries for full professors of business ranged from US$89,900 to US$105,000, depending on the field. Top faculty typically received salaries of more than $100,000 over a nine-month period. With additional compensation for summer teaching and research activities, consulting assignments, executive program teaching, textbook writing, and sponsored papers and speeches, business faculty salaries look very attractive.

The employment climate for faculty in the business disciplines, though not as vibrant as in the early nineties (when there were three position openings to every one doctoral graduate), has remained healthy. In contrast to prospects within other academic fields, in which the supply of new doctoral graduates exceeds the number of position openings, those graduating with a doctorate in business enjoy a favorable hiring environment. In addition to faculty posts, a range of opportunities in industry have emerged. Many companies have opened their own executive education centers, requiring some full-time faculty, and maintain their own research and development units. Similarly, consulting firms have opened to provide companies with strategic planning, human resource management, economic forecasting and financial services expertise. Indeed, few careers today offer the rich intellectual and personal challenge, monetary reward and flexibility that business school faculty have available.

The Dynamics of Management Education

It may be surprising to discover that many business doctoral students have academic backgrounds in fields such as psychology, sociology, mathematics and political science. Some students have never taken a business course prior to entering the doctoral program! This seeming contradiction is better understood when the breadth and complexity of business school curricula is considered. Topics range from:

- the international monetary system to the pricing of a computer chip

- the effectiveness of different management methods within large corporations to the nature of nascent entrepreneurial ventures

- financial portfolio theory to the art of managing an opera company

- the complex psychology of consumer demand to the subtlety of interpersonal relationships

- establishing and maintaining production processes to effective financial controls and information systems, in private and public sectors.

Faculty members are a critical resource within an academic institution. They are experts on current knowledge in their field and dedicated to furthering the pursuit of new ideas through research and consulting, as well as interpreting and implementing innovative approaches to teaching and learning.

Regardless of one's field of specialization, study in business and management takes place in a professional setting and is interdisciplinary and applied. Intellectual rigor and professional relevance are equally important and a professional education demands that the apparent line between theory and practice is traversed easily and often. Business faculty must have their feet planted firmly in substantive theory, as well as in current business practice.

Increasingly, business schools are restructuring their curricula to emphasize interdisciplinary and problem/issue-oriented teaching and research groups. Faculty members seek to strike a balance

between loyalty to their specific field and the importance of cross-disciplinary work with colleagues. This tension between specialization and interdisciplinary work makes for an exciting intellectual climate. The primary difference between business study and that of other disciplines, then, lies not so much in their theoretical roots or disciplinary content, but in the types of issues addressed, the potential for professional application and the multi-disciplinary nature of research and instruction.

Choosing a School

Doctoral education emphasizes self-directed learning and close relationships with faculty in the student's area of specialization. Faculty "mentors" play a crucial role in helping students define a course of study and prepare for qualifying examinations and in providing guidance through the dissertation process and the steps needed to secure a first faculty position. The demanding course of doctoral study requires that students select a program carefully.

Even among the leading doctoral programs at renowned research institutes, there will be significant variation in the areas in which they have national and international recognition for research and instruction. It pays to invest time looking into the characteristics of faculty and their research interests, no matter which school you are considering. Means to obtain information about a school include:

- consult faculty to obtain a list of potential state, regional or national programs available

- consult research journals to identify scholars doing research and writing in your field of interest

- visit the campus to meet with doctoral program officials and faculty with whom you might want to study

- use the visit to ask about teaching and research assistantships, as well.

Other Considerations

The two principal degree designations offered by business doctoral programs are the PhD (Doctor of Philosophy) and DBA (Doctor of Business Administration). In an earlier era of management education, popular opinion held that the DBA provided more general exposure to business topics, while the PhD focused more on research in a given business specialty. Over the years, the distinction between these degrees has become blurred. The PhD is more commonly offered than the DBA. Contact schools directly to find out which approach they have taken to the doctoral business degree.

Another factor to consider is accreditation. Virtually all colleges and universities have standing with a regional accrediting agency, comprised of peers representing a number of educational institutions. This agency ensures that all of its members offer programs that meet regional standards for faculty composition and development, curriculum content, instructional resources, students and intellectual contributions in accord with its mission. Within business and management fields, accreditation is conferred by AACSB — The International Association for Management Education. The recent proliferation of diploma offerings in business and other fields has made it imperative that prospective students exercise care in selecting a school. Those considering a doctoral program in business from a US institution that is not accredited by AACSB should obtain a job placement record of that school's graduates.

It is never too early to devise strategies for negotiating the rigorous requirements of a doctoral program. In addition to contacting faculty, other doctoral students and recent graduates are an invaluable resource when it comes to weighing your options for pursuing study at a doctoral level.

Contributed by AACSB - The International Association for Management Education

The Graduate Management Admission Test® (GMAT®)

Graduate
Management
Admission
Council®

First offered in 1954, the GMAT has been taken by more than six million individuals; more than 200,000 candidates register for the exam each year. And, more than 1,300 management programs throughout the world use the GMAT to make admission decisions.

The GMAT, which is administered by the Educational Testing Service® (ETS®) on behalf of the Graduate Management Admission Council® (GMAC), is a standardized test of general verbal, mathematical and analytical skills:

- the quantitative component of the GMAT evaluates basic mathematical skills as well as the ability to reason quantitatively, solve quantitative problems and interpret graphic data
- the verbal section tests comprehension of standard written English
- the analytical writing section determines the ability to think critically and communicate complex ideas

As of October 1997, the paper-and-pencil format of the GMAT was replaced throughout most of the world with the GMAT Computer-Adaptive Test (CAT), a change that affects approximately 95 per cent of all GMAT registrants.

The Computer-Adaptive GMAT

The basic structure and content of the GMAT have not changed. The computer-adaptive test, however, determines which questions to ask based on responses to previous questions. Therefore, the CAT adjusts to each test taker's aptitude, administering few questions that are too easy or too difficult for the test taker. The analytical writing section has not changed, although essays are now keyed into the computer rather than handwritten.

The Benefits of the GMAT CAT

GMAC committed to changing the GMAT to a computer-adaptive mode in 1995. Changes in graduate management programs paralleled greater diversity in the student population; executives and single parents, among others, were attracted to academic programs that accommodated their career and personal obligations. The GMAT—and preparation for it—did not fit as readily into their schedules. In particular, the test was held only four times each year. Its inflexibility

> ...the CAT adjusts to each test taker's aptitude, administering few questions that are too easy or too difficult for the test taker.

did not match the flexibility of the academic realm.

The CAT accommodates candidates' schedules by enabling them to take the exam when it is convenient for them. It is offered three weeks per month, six days a week and 10 hours a day at approximately 600 computer-based testing centres in North America, Europe, Asia and Latin America.

Once candidates have completed the exam, they can receive unofficial test scores on the verbal and quantitative sections immediately. An official score report is sent to them within 10 days of testing. Scores may be sent to five institutions, the cost of which is covered by the test fee.

GMAT test takers are automatically included in the Graduate Management Admission Search Service℠ (GMASS℠) unless a candidate notifies ETS in writing otherwise. The results of GMASS searches are now available on-line, enabling schools to access the names of approximately 98 percent of those who write the GMAT, 24 hours a day, seven days a week.

Strategies for Taking the GMAT CAT

The exam strategies used in the past may not be applicable to the GMAT CAT. In particular, there are concerns regarding the inability to omit questions or change answers once they have been entered. These restrictions are related to the computer-adaptive algorithm, which relies on the sequential nature of questions asked and answers given. If a candidate were able to return to a question and change a correct response to one that is incorrect, the process upon which the candidate's score had been determined would be destroyed. Likewise, the level of difficulty of each question is based on previous responses; if a question were left unanswered, the algorithm could not proceed to the next question.

Minimal computer skills are required to complete the GMAT CAT, although the effects of computer literacy on the ability of individuals to take the exam are a legitimate concern. A mandatory tutorial ensures that test takers have enough competency with the mouse and word processing systems to complete the test.

Graduate Management Admission Council®

The transition from a paper-and-pencil format to a computer-adaptive test has been seamless. In a comprehensive study, GMAC found that the two tests are indeed comparable. Furthermore, the question difficulty and number of questions answered correctly are comparable across all GMAT CAT scores.

Preparing to Take the GMAT CAT

For many, the computer-adaptive format of the GMAT CAT will be different, and traditional study methods and test-taking strategies may not be applicable. There are, however, a number of steps that candidates can take to prepare themselves for the test and increase their chances for success.

First, students should ensure that they are comfortable using a mouse and a conventional keyboard on a computer; this could ease some of their worries while taking the exam. Second, they should review practice tests. GMAC publishes The Official Guide for GMAT Review, a study guide with real GMAT® questions. Another tool, Powerprep® Software published in conjunction with ETS contains two computer adaptive tests. Powerprep® can also be downloaded from the MBA Store℠ on the MBA Explorer® website. Third, they could benefit from meeting with a friend or acquaintance who successfully completed the GMAT, gaining an understanding of the exam from the perspective of one who has taken it and possibly acquiring some helpful hints.

When taking the test, examinees should answer all of the questions; they are advised to provide a guess if they do not know an answer. It takes about one and three quarter minutes to respond to verbal questions, and approximately two minutes to respond to quantitative questions. Candidates should make every effort to pace themselves in order to answer all of the questions.

Scheduling an Appointment

Candidates in the US and Canada can

> There are a number of steps that candidates can take to prepare themselves for the test and increase their chances for success.

schedule an appointment by calling 1-800-GMAT-NOW. Candidates outside the US and Canada can call one of 12 regional registration centres; local testing centres and regional registration centre phone numbers are provided in the GMAT *Information Bulletin* and through GMAC's website MBA Explorer® (http://www.gmat.org). Those who would like to retake the CAT can do so once each month.

GMAT candidates are required to present two forms of signed identification, at least one with a photo. A digital photograph is taken at the test site and stored with biographical information in the central archive at ETS. In order to ensure the security of the GMAT CAT, the testing area is monitored by proctors, as well as video and audio systems.

The Cost of the GMAT CAT

It costs US$165 to take the GMAT CAT in the US and US$210 to take it in other countries. Individuals rescheduling their exams at least seven days in advance of their testing appointments will be charged an additional US$40 in the US, US territories and Puerto Rico, and US$48 outside of the US. If they reschedule fewer than seven days in advance, they must pay the full fee for a new appointment. A refund of US$66 in the US and US$84 outside of the US will be granted to those who cancel at least seven days in advance of their appointment; otherwise, no refund will be given.

The Future of the GMAT CAT

In the future, questions that address cognitive areas beyond verbal and quantitative reasoning, as well as those that address leadership and listening skills, could potentially be integrated into the GMAT, due to the conversion of the GMAT to computer delivery. And, assessments customized to the various selection and diagnostic needs of schools with different missions may also be offered through the CAT. For more information on the GMAT CAT investigate the Graduate Management Admission Council's (GMAC) website, *MBA Explorer,* at http://www.gmat.org.

Contributed by the Graduate Management Admission Council.

★ ★ ★ ★ **THE PATH TO GREATNESS IS FORGED, NOT FOLLOWED.**

Greatness is not the easy choice. It requires that you make your own way. By choosing to earn a PhD at Olin, you will have chosen to forge your path at a business school committed to excellence in teaching and research. You will make a commitment to pushing yourself harder than you may have thought possible through a curriculum grounded in economics and quantitative methodology. And you will empower yourself with the skills it takes to succeed in today's business education marketplace. Upon completion of your Olin PhD, you will have done something very few can do. Forge your own path.

WASHINGTON·UNIVERSITY·IN·ST·LOUIS

★ OLIN IS RANKED IN THE TOP TWENTY BY BUSINESS WEEK MAGAZINE
★ FOR MORE INFORMATION CALL (314) 935-6340
★ www.olin.wustl.edu

MANAGEMENT EDUCATION • LIFETIME ACHIEVEMENT

United States of America

GraduateBusiness.com

the website of graduate management programs

GraduateBusiness.com is designed exclusively for students who are searching for master's- and doctoral-level business and management programs.

Check out the website to

Search for a wide range of programs, from MBAs and EMBAs to accounting, specialized management and executive development programs

Find in-depth information for each program on admission requirements, program options, student services, tuition and more

Link directly to school websites and other useful websites

Request application packages from each school online via an automated email system

GraduateBusiness.com has the most up-to-date and accurate information available on business and management programs. All information is verified and approved by program directors from the schools.

education international

Guiding Students to Success

EI Education International Inc. (USA)
5000 Columbia Center, 701-5th Ave., Seattle, Washington, 98104-7078, USA
EI Education International Ltd. (Canada)
205, 5325 Cordova Bay Road, Victoria, British Columbia, Canada V8Y 2L3
Phone: 250-658-6283   Fax: 250-658-6285
Email: info@educationinternational.com

Notes on Reading the Profiles

The goal of this guide is to provide as much relevant information as possible in as comparable a format as possible. To facilitate comparison between universities and colleges, all the profiles follow a standard format. Statistics used in the profiles are based on the most recent figures available from each institution. Within the profiles, "n/a" is used to indicate statistics that are not applicable to the program or university in question. The words "not available," "not tracked," or "-" indicate that the item *is* applicable to the program or institution, but the corresponding statistic is not regularly compiled.

The *Program Quick Facts* chart, which follows all of the profiles, is designed to provide a quick reference of some of the more important facts compiled.

For style standard guidance, EI uses both the *Chicago Manual of Style* and *NAFSA Style: A Manual for Writers and Editors*.

Current trends in writing are to a simplified style: less use of capitalization, punctuation and hyphenation. Where practicable, EI has adopted this approach (e.g., postsecondary, coursework, groupwork, videoconferencing, US, MBA)

Currencies are indicated in the following way:

US$ – US dollars
C$ – Canadian dollars

Dollar amounts given reflect the information available at the time of writing. Prices are liable to increase for coming years, and EI makes no guarantee about tuition or fee costs. Statistics included in the profiles are based on the most recent figures available for each university.

Throughout the guide, the words "international," "foreign" and "overseas" are used interchangeably in reference to students who study in a nation other than their own.

The information provided under *Admissions Criteria & Procedures* and in the *Admissions at a Glance* sidebar is not intended to be comprehensive, but rather to provide general guidelines. Students should contact the program directly before submitting their applications to be sure that they will meet the most current application requirements and deadlines.

Information provided under *Student Profile* typically shows the statistics for the most recent school year unless indicated otherwise. Information on the number of students applying and enrolling in the program is given on a per year basis. Where possible, EI has provided a range for class sizes; where only one number appears, this figure indicates an average.

The *Expenses & Financial Assistance* section is intended to provide a general breakdown of the costs individuals should expect to encounter during the program, and some guidance to the financial assistance programs offered by the schools. Interested students are encouraged to contact the institution directly for more detailed information.

The goal of this guide is to provide as much relevant information as possible in as comparable a style as possible. Generally, all the profiles follow a similar format; however, exceptions have occasionally been made in cases where the information usually included in the profile would not accurately reflect the nature of a specific program.

The information used to compile these profiles was obtained through program promotional literature and consultation with program representatives. Although all information is believed to be accurate, prospective students should contact the program directly for further information.

Although this guide offers general guidelines for individuals who are preparing for international study, it is not intended as a complete reference to immigration and visa procedures. Potential students should consult the appropriate embassy or consulate to obtain advice and the materials necessary to prepare for overseas study.

USEducationFairs.com

the website to education fairs on US study opportunities

USEducationFairs is designed exclusively for students who want to attend education fairs that feature US academic institutions.

Check out the website to

- **Find** out when the next education fair is being held in your area

- **View** profiles on participating universities, colleges and language schools who are promoting their degree and diploma programs as well as short courses

- **Link** directly to school websites and other useful websites

- **Request** further information from each school online via an automated email system

USEducationfairs.com puts you in touch with study opportunities in the USA.

education international

Guiding Students to Success

EI Education International Inc. (USA)

5000 Columbia Center, 701-5th Ave., Seattle, Washington, 98104-7078, USA

Phone: 1-250-658-6283   Fax: 1-250-658-6285

Email: info@USEducationFairs.com

List of Profiled Doctoral Business & Management Programs by State

Arizona
Arizona State University — 23

Arkansas
University of Arkansas — 83

California
Stanford University — 67
University of California – Irvine — 87

Connecticut
University of Connecticut — 103

Florida
Florida International University — 39
Florida State University — 43
University of Central Florida — 91
University of Florida — 107

Georgia
University of Georgia — 111

Illinois
Illinois Institute of Technology — 47
University of Chicago — 95
University of Illinois at Chicago — 115
University of Illinois at Urbana-Champaign — 119

Indiana
Purdue University — 63

Kansas
University of Kansas — 123

Maryland
University of Maryland - College Park — 127

Massachusetts
University of Massachusetts, Amherst — 131

Michigan
University of Michigan - Ann Arbor — 135

Minnesota
University of Minnesota, Twin Cities — 139

Mississippi
University of Mississippi — 143

Missouri
Washington University — 183

New York
Cornell University — 27
Syracuse University — 71

North Carolina
Duke University — 35

Ohio
Kent State University — 51
Ohio State University, The — 55
University of Cincinnati — 99

Oklahoma
University of Oklahoma — 147

Pennsylvania
Drexel University — 31
Pennsylvania State University, The — 59
Temple University — 75

Rhode Island
University of Rhode Island — 151

South Carolina
University of South Carolina — 155

Tennessee
University of Tennessee at Knoxville — 159
Vanderbilt University — 179

Texas
Texas A & M University — 79
University of Texas at Austin, The — 163

Utah
University of Utah — 167

Washington
University of Washington — 171

Wisconsin
University of Wisconsin – Madison — 175

Program Quick Facts

	Page	Student/Faculty			Entry Requirements			
		# of Full-time Students	# of Part-time Students	# of Faculty	Minimum GMAT	Average GMAT	Minimum TOEFL Paper paper-based test/computer-based test	Minimum GPA
Arizona State University	23	80		168	no set min	665	550	3.0
Cornell University	27	32		46	n/a	700	600 (pbt) 250 (cbt)	n/a
Drexel University	31	42	9	63	no set min	580	570	3.0-3.3
Duke University	35	47		75	no set min	721	550	no set min
Florida International University	39	3	4	12	560	620	570	3.0
Florida State University	43	68		100	550	640	600 (pbt) 250 (cbt)	3.0-3.5
Illinois Institute of Technology	47	5	14	12	600	620	550	3.5
Kent State University	51	62		54	—	614	600 pbt 250 cbt	—
Ohio State University, The	55	70		111	600	656	600	no set min
Pennsylvania State University, The	59	70 f/t & p/t	incl with f/t	149	no set min	690	585	3.3
Purdue University	63	112		85	≥80th percentile	690	575	3.5
Stanford University	67	99		88	no set min	—	n/a	no set min
Syracuse University	71	32		55	600	660	600	3.5
Temple University	75	50–60		125	600	—	600	3.5
Texas A&M University	79	81		146	570	658	600	3.0-3.25

KEY

[-] - not available
bef – before
cbt – computer-based test
cr – credit
dom - domestic

ft - full time
grad – graduate
hr – hours
incl – included
min – minimum

n/a – not applicable
pbt – paper-based test
pref – preferred
pt – part-time
sem – semester

spr – spring
sum - summer
win – winter
yr - year

Application Fee	Applications		Annual Research Funding	Tuition per yr (unless shown otherwise)		
	Application Deadlines	(US = domestic Int'l = International)		Tuition In-State	Tuition Out-of-State	Tuition International
$45	Jan 15 (application) Feb 1 (supporting documents)		US$1,843,793	US$2,188	US$9,340	US$9,340
$150	Jan 15		—	US$27,600	US$27,600	US$27,600
$35	Feb 1 (fall of odd-numbered years)		US$1,300,000	US$13,797	US$13,797	US$13,797
$65-75	Dec 31 (fall)		US$500,000	US$18,000	US$18,000	US$18,000
$20	Mar 1		—	US$144.96 per cr hr	US$505.69 per cr hr	US$506.69 per cr hr
$20	US: May 1 Int'l: Feb 1		varies	US$5,830	US$15,210	US$15,210
$50	Aug 1 (fall)		—	US$1,800 per course	US$1,800 per course	US$1,800 per course
$30	US: Feb 1 Int'l: Aug 1 (one yr prior to entry)		—	US$5,334	US$10,238	US$10,238
$30 (dom) $40 (int'l)	Jan 15		US$236.3 million	US$5,730	US$14,865	US$14,865
$40	Feb 1		US$4,000,000	US$3,267 per sem	US$6,730 per sem	—
$30	Feb 15		—	US$320 per sem	US$320 per sem	US$320 per sem
$55	Jan 2, 2001		—	US$27,243	US$27,243	US$27,243
$50	Feb 15 (fall)		—	US$14,000	US$14,000	US$14,000
40	Mar 15 (fall)		—	US$348 per cr hr	US$488 per cr hr	US$488 per cr hr
$35 (dom) $75 (int'l)	US: Mar 15 (fall), Oct 15 (spr), Nov 1 (sum) Int'l: Mar 1 (fall), Aug 1 (spr), Nov 1 (sum)		US$1,081,432	US$72 per cr hr	US$285 per cr hr	US$285 per cr hr

Program Quick Facts

	Page	Student/Faculty			Entry Requirements			
		# of Full-time Students	# of Part-time Students	# of Faculty	Minimum GMAT	Average GMAT	Minimum TOEFL Paper paper-based test/computer-based test	Minimum GPA
University of Arkansas	83	45		91	no set min	619	550 (pbt) 213 (cbt)	no set min
University of California, Irvine	87	31		42	no set min	680	600	no set min
University of Central Florida	91	9		101	500	605	577	3.0
University of Chicago	95	96		132	630	693	600	3.5
University of Cincinnati	99	35		70	600	650	600 (pbt) 250 (cbt)	3.0
University of Connecticut	103	40		50	no set min	640	550	3.0
University of Florida	107	80		97	550–600	665	550-600	3.0
University of Georgia	111	—		102	no set min	—	—	3.0
University of Illinois at Chicago	115	24	22	89	no set min	640	600	4.00
University of Illinois at Urbana–Champaign	119	43		60	no set min	660	600	3.0
University of Kansas	123	27		48	500	641	570	n/a
University of Maryland - College Park	127	87		100	no set min	697	575	3.0
University of Massachusetts, Amherst	131	55		44	600	653	590	3.0
University of Michigan	135	80		130	no set min	710	600	no set min
University of Minnesota - Twin Cities	139	81		93	600	697	600	3.0-3.5
University of Mississippi	143	56	7	49	550	565	550-600	3.0
University of Oklahoma	147	36		59	640	681	550 (pbt) 213 (cbt)	3.5
University of Rhode Island	151	43		55	60%	625	575 (pbt) 233 (cbt)	2.8-3.2

Application Fee	Application Deadlines (US = domestic Int'l = International)	Annual Research Funding	Tuition per yr (unless shown otherwise)		
			Tuition In-State	Tuition Out-of-State	Tuition International
$40	Feb 1 (int'l) Mar 1 (dom)	US$880,049	US$3,717	—	US$8,820
$40	Jan 15	—	US$5,178	US$15,200 (1st yr)	US$15,200
$20	May 15 Feb 1 for fellowships/assistantships	—	US$146 per sem hr	US$507 per sem hr	US$507 per sem hr
$65	US: Jan 15 Int'l: Jan 1 pref	—	waived with admission	waived with admission	waived with admission
$30	Feb 15	US$300,000	US$8,000	US$14,800	US$14,800
$40 (dom) $45 (int'l)	Feb 1	—	US$5,272	US$13,696	US$13,696
$20	Feb 1	US$1,291,094	US$1,729 per sem	US$6,060 per sem	US$6,060 per sem
$30	Jan 14 (for financial aid) Mar 1 (fall)	—	US$3,516	US$12,204	US$12,204
$40 (dom) $50 (int'l)	Feb 1	US$362,733	US$1,820 per sem	US$5,138 per sem	US$5,138 per sem
$40 (dom) $50 (int'l)	Acc: Jun 15 (fall); Fin: Feb 1 (fall) Bus Admin: first Monday in Feb (fall)	US$1,600,000	US$4,242	US$11,752	US$11,752
$50	Jan 15	US$530,000	US$103 per cr hr	US$338 per cr hr	US$338 per cr hr
$50	US: Feb 1 (fall-pref), Aug 1 (fall-final deadline) Int'l: Feb 1 (fall)	—	US$272 per cr hr	US$415 per cr hr	US$415 per cr hr
$25 (Mass) $40 (other)	Feb 1	US$200,000	US$2,640	US$9,018	US$9,018
$55	Jan 15	—	US$21,574 per two terms	—	—
$50 (dom) $55 (int'l)	Jan 15 for early consideration Mar 31 final deadline	US$1,000,000	waived with admission	waived with admission	waived with admission
$25	Apr 1 (fall) Oct 1 (spring)	—	US$170 per cr hr	US$342 per cr hr	US$342 per cr hr
$25 (dom) $50 (int'l)	Apr 1 (fall)	—	US$2,058	US$5,460	US$5,460
$30 - $45	Rolling admissions before Jun 1 First cut-off Mar 1	—	US$3,446	US$9,850	US$9,850

Program Quick Facts

	Page	Student/Faculty			Entry Requirements			
		# of Full-time Students	# of Part-time Students	# of Faculty	Minimum GMAT	Average GMAT	Minimum TOEFL Paper paper-based test/computer-based test	Minimum GPA
University of South Carolina	155	54	11	105	570	660	570-625	3.2
University of Tennessee at Knoxville	159	75	40	104	no set min	—	550	2.7
University of Texas at Austin	163	110		110	no set min	716	no set min	no set min
University of Utah	167	34		56	n/a	677	500	3.0
University of Washington	171	65		77	no set min	700	600	3.0
University of Wisconsin-Madison	175	73		80	no set min	680	600	3.0
Vanderbilt University	179	12		45	no set min	709	620	3.0
Washington University	183	32		73	no set min	upper 600s	600	no set min

ei's guide to doctoral programs in business & management in the usa - 2000

| Application Fee | Applications | | Annual Research Funding | Tuition per yr (unless shown otherwise) | | |
	Application Deadlines (US = domestic Int'l = International)			Tuition In-State	Tuition Out-of-State	Tuition International
$35	Feb 1		US$550,000	US$2,007 per sem	US$4,264 per sem	US$4,264 per sem
$35	Mar 1		US$1,257,000	—	—	—
$50 (dom) $75 (int'l)	Dec 1 (MSIS); Jan 15 (Fin) Feb 1 (Mgmt, Mktg); late Feb/early Mar (Acc)		—	US$2,800	US$6,700	US$6,700
$40 (dom) $60 (int'l)	Jan 15		US$300,000	waived with admission	waived with admission	waived with admission
$50	Feb 1		—	US$7,191	US$15,480	US$15,480
$45	Feb 1 (fall), Oct 15 (spring) Jan 2 (fellowship consideration)		US$1.5 million	US$5,406	US$17,109	US$17,109
$40	Jan 15		—	US$22,900	US$22,900	US$22,900
$75	Feb 15, Jan 25 (Chancellor Fellowship), Feb 1 (OlinFellowship)		US$930,000	waived with admission	waived with admission	waived with admission

Got a Mind for Business?

Get your Ph.D. in Business Administration from the University of Rhode Island. Our small, highly selective program prepares you for a career in academics or research and offers:

- a high level of student–faculty interaction
- opportunities for significant independent research and publication
- college-wide research seminars in all business disciplines, and
- an emphasis on developing University teaching skills.

Concentrations offered in:
- Finance
- Management
- Management Science
- Marketing

For more information, visit our Web site at http://www.cba.uri.edu/ or contact:

Shaw K. Chen,
Director,
Ph.D. Program
College of Business Administration
University of Rhode Island
Ballentine Hall,
7 Lippitt Road
Kingston, RI
02881-2011

Phone: 401-874-4339
Fax: 401-874-7047
E-mail: chenshaw@uri.edu

UNIVERSITY OF RHODE ISLAND

PROFILED DOCTORAL BUSINESS & MANAGEMENT PROGRAMS

ARIZONA STATE UNIVERSITY
PhD IN BUSINESS ADMINISTRATION

Program Highlights

- *Research is supported by several outstanding centers, including the Center for Services Marketing & Management*
- *Six concentration areas to choose from*
- *Students benefit from close interaction with outstanding, award-winning faculty*
- *Accredited by AACSB*

CONTACT INFORMATION
College of Business,
Doctoral Program Office
PO Box 874906
Tempe, Arizona USA 85287-4906
PH: 1-480-965-3368
FAX: 1-480-727-6625
EMAIL: asucobphd@asu.edu
INTERNET: http://www.cob.asu.edu

ARIZONA STATE UNIVERSITY, PhD IN BUSINESS ADMINISTRATION

PROGRAM OVERVIEW

Arizona State University's (ASU) College of Business (COB) offers a full-time PhD program in business administration with concentrations in accountancy, computer information systems, finance, management, marketing and supply chain management. The program is accredited by AACSB – The International Association for Management Education.

The PhD program requires a minimum of 84 semester hours of graduate study consisting of independent research, advanced coursework, seminars and a dissertation. Students typically complete the program in four to five years. The program allows for flexibility and encourages innovative thinking and excellence in research. All doctoral students must successfully complete a comprehensive written examination and a dissertation as part of their program requirements.

Accountancy

The accountancy program prepares students to conduct high-quality research and to teach in the fields of financial and managerial accounting, auditing, information systems, and taxation. Faculty members are engaged in progressive research.

Computer Information Systems

The computer information systems program allows students to pursue studies in specialized areas such as decision support systems, database management systems, artificial intelligence in business systems analysis and design, distributed information systems, data mining, and IT infusion and human interface. Students have access to computer facilities equipped with the latest technology available.

Finance

The finance program prepares students for careers as professors in leading institutions around the globe, or careers in industry and government. Research in areas such as financial derivatives, futures and equity markets, corporate finance, organizational structure, international finance, financial institutions, and asset pricing has made the department one of the top 20 finance departments in the world, according to leading business journals.

Management

Individuals interested in the management program benefit from a faculty consisting of 30 full-time professors with a range of expertise and professional experience. Students select from a series of course modules in organizational behavior, human resources management and strategic management. The program emphasizes independent research and teaching experience through fieldwork and interaction with faculty members.

Marketing

The Department of Marketing at ASU specializes in research and innovative approaches to marketing issues. The program includes five seminars in marketing research design, management, theory, consumer behavior and advanced research. The department is home to the Center for Services Marketing and Management, the leading university-based services marketing institution in North America.

Supply Chain Management

ASU is one of the few universities to offer a program in supply chain management. Designed for individuals with an interest in operations management, purchasing or logistics, the program provides students with the research, analytical and theoretical skills needed for careers as educators in leading business schools. The department is supported by two research institutions.

SELECTED RESEARCH AREAS

- Advertising
- Behavior decision theory
- Business law
- Business to business marketing
- Change management
- Channels management
- Consumer behavior
- Corporate governance
- Database management systems architecture
- Decision analysis
- Degree of price resolution & equity trading costs
- Design of computer networks
- Empirical examination of information
- Equilibrium pricing under parameter uncertainty
- Globalization
- High-technology management
- Human resource management practices
- Information systems
- International marketing
- Leadership structure
- Management communication
- Materials management & acquisition
- Modelling of internal control systems
- Organizational identity
- Partnership taxation
- Process & product management
- Real asset risk of determinants of systematic risk
- Real estate
- Selling & sales management
- Service marketing
- Small business & entrepreneurship
- Strategic marketing management
- Supply chain management
- Tax planning models
- Vendor evaluation

ARIZONA STATE UNIVERSITY, PhD IN BUSINESS ADMINISTRATION

ADMISSIONS CRITERIA & PROCEDURES

The COB seeks applicants who have the professional experience, leadership skills and academic potential necessary to excel in management studies at the doctorate level. Applicant credentials are evaluated using undergraduate and graduate transcripts, GPAs, GMAT scores, statement of career objectives, letters of recommendation, and employment history. Completion of a master's-level program is typically expected. Individuals must have completed college-level calculus and be competent computer users. Since admission decisions are made by reviewing a wide range of criteria, there are no set minimum GPA and GMAT requirements. Letters of recommendation should be submitted by individuals who are familiar with the candidate's recent academic or professional performance.

Admission to the doctoral program is granted for the fall term only. The deadline for applications is January 15. Supporting documents must be received by February 1. Candidates are encouraged to apply as early as possible. For online application, students should visit the website (http://www.asu.edu/graduate).

In addition to the above, international applicants who are non-native speakers of English must submit adequate TOEFL scores (a paper-based score of approximately 600). The COB also requires scores from the Test of Spoken English. All documents not originally in English must be accompanied by official translations.

EXPENSES & FINANCIAL ASSISTANCE

The approximate annual tuition fee for the PhD program is US$2,188 for Arizona residents and $9,340 for all other students. On-campus residence fees range from US$2,905 to $3,505 per year. Private accommodation is also available.

There are several forms of financial assistance available to PhD students, including assistantships, scholarships and loans. Teaching or research assistantships offer a stipend of approximately US$11,000 per year. Assistantships require 20 hours of work per week as determined by supervising faculty. Every effort is made to provide all qualified students with a minimum of one year of research assistantship support. Most students hold a teaching assistantship for at least one year during their studies. Graduate academic scholarships are awarded on the basis of academic merit. Information on scholarships and other merit-based awards can be obtained by contacting the Student Financial Assistance Office or Graduate College. US citizens and landed immigrants may be eligible for need-based loans.

INTERNATIONAL STUDENT SUPPORT

International students at ASU represent more than 120 countries. Of the 2,800 international students on campus, 54 percent are graduate students and approximately 18 percent are studying in the College of Business.

ASU's international students are supported through the International Student Office and 19 student organizations representing different countries and regions of the world. These groups organize airport pickup, temporary and permanent housing arrangements, assist with initial grocery shopping, and help with registration and social activities.

ADMISSIONS AT A GLANCE

Minimum GMAT:	no set minimum
Minimum GPA:	3.0
Minimum TOEFL (paper):	550
Minimum TOEFL (computer):	213
Application Fee:	US$45
Application Deadline:	
Jan 15 (application)	
Feb 1 (supporting documents)	

EXPENSES AT A GLANCE

Tuition:
- In State: US$2,188 per year
- Out-of-State: US$9,340 per year
- Int'l Students: US$9,340 per year

Books & Supplies: n/a
Health Insurance: US$725 per year
Accommodation:
- University Residences: US$2,905-3,505 per year
- Family Housing: n/a
- Private: US$500-700 per month

* Posted expenses are minimum estimates for the current year (1999-2000)

PROGRAM FACTS

# of Full-time Students:	80
# of Part-time Students:	none
# of Applications per year:	150 (approx)
# Accepted per year:	12-16
# Enrolled per year:	12-16 (entering)
Average GMAT Score:	665
Average Age:	34
% Men/Women:	66%/34%
Work Experience (avg yrs):	n/a
# of Faculty:	168
% Faculty with Doctoral Degree:	92%
Annual Research Funding:	US$1,843,793

ARIZONA STATE UNIVERSITY, PhD IN BUSINESS ADMINISTRATION

UNIVERSITY AND LOCATION

Since its founding in 1885 as the Territorial Normal School, Arizona State University has grown from a 20-acre campus with 33 students to become the fifth largest university in the country. ASU, an internationally recognized Research I university, serves 49,000 students at three campus locations (Main, East and West) and at various extended campus locations in the Phoenix area. The COB is the second largest college at ASU. College facilities include an auditorium, lecture halls, seminar rooms, faculty and administrative offices, a television studio and several computer labs. Computers at facilities around the campus support instruction, learning and research at ASU and in the COB. The COB has more than 300 Ethernet connections and many multimedia classrooms. The ASU Computing Commons is a comprehensive assembly of advanced academic computing technology.

Library facilities include six campus libraries, which collectively have more than 3.1 million volumes of periodical subscriptions, microfilm and bound texts. The library's business and economic holdings are strong in all areas of business, but have particular breadth in management and marketing.

Spacious walkways, subtropical landscaping and modern architecture characterize the ASU campus. Located in the Phoenix suburb of Tempe, the university provides activities catering to virtually any interest. Perpetual sunshine and an arid climate have earned the Phoenix metropolitan area the nickname "The Valley of the Sun." The valley holds many of the same attractions associated with large metropolitan areas throughout the country.

FACULTY
- Bitner, M.J. PhD, Washington
- Cardy, R.L. PhD, Virginia Tech
- Carter, J.R. DBA, Boston
- Carter, P.L. DBA, Indiana-Bloomington
- Coles, J. PhD, Stanford
- Glick, W. PhD, California at Berkeley
- Goul, M. PhD, Oregon State
- Hutt, M.D. PhD, Michigan State
- Kaufman, H. PhD, Pennsylvania State
- Keats, B. PhD, Oklahoma State
- Kulkarni, U.R. PhD, Wisconsin-Milwaukee
- McPheters, L. PhD, Virginia Polytech Institute
- Mokwa, M. PhD, Houston
- Penley, L. PhD, Georgia
- Reckers, P.M. PhD, Illinois
- Smith-Daniels, V. PhD, Ohio State
- Vinze, A.S. PhD, Arizona

City Population:	158,229
Cost of Living:	medium
Climate Range:	64° to 106°F
Campus Setting:	urban
Total Enrollment:	49,000 (approx)
Graduate Enrollment:	11,000 (approx)
Students in Residence:	–

CORNELL UNIVERSITY
JOHNSON GRADUATE SCHOOL OF MANAGEMENT

Program Highlights

- *The program has an interdisciplinary focus*
- *Eight major areas of study to choose from*
- *Small program allows interaction with faculty members in an informal setting*
- *Most PhD students receive research assistantships and fellowships that include tuition waivers and stipends*
- *Every PhD student is provided with a computer*
- *Accredited by AACSB*

CONTACT INFORMATION

Doctoral Admissions

Johnson Graduate School of Management

111 Sage Hall

Ithaca, New York USA 14853 - 6201

PH: 1-607-255-3669

FAX: 1-607-255-0065

EMAIL: js_phd@cornell.edu

INTERNET: http://www.johnson.cornell.edu

CORNELL UNIVERSITY, JOHNSON GRADUATE SCHOOL OF MANAGEMENT

PROGRAM OVERVIEW

The Johnson Graduate School of Management (Johnson) at Cornell University (Cornell) offers a Doctor of Philosophy (PhD) degree program in management.

Students learn practical and theoretical approaches to the solution of managerial problems and graduates are prepared for careers in teaching and research. Each student chooses a major and two minors. Johnson offers majors in accounting, behavioral sciences, finance, managerial economics, marketing, organizational behavior, production and operations management, or quantitative analysis. Behavioral sciences, managerial economics and quantitative analysis are usually taken as minors.

The Johnson PhD program has an average enrollment of 30 students. Seminars and workshops are personalized and active participation is encouraged and course selection, reading and research are tailored to students' specific needs. With the director's approval, students can choose one or both minors in areas offered outside the school. Common choices are economics, environmental engineering, industrial and labor relations, operations research, psychology, sociology and statistics.

Students spend their first two years taking courses, attending seminars, and participating in joint research with faculty and fellow students. Most fields include a weekly workshop in which faculty and students discuss research ideas and meet with faculty from other colleges and universities. When coursework is complete, students must demonstrate competency in their major and minors by completing an examination, consisting of oral and written components. Following the exam, research begins and when the thesis is complete, students defend their work in an oral examination.

Three years is the minimum length of time needed to satisfy PhD requirements; most students take four or five years.

Accounting
Scholars in the field of accounting focus on understanding the way financial data is used. For example, PhD students majoring in accounting may examine how earnings information relates to changes in share prices of reporting companies or on the role of accounting data in the motivation and evaluation of managers.

Finance
Students majoring in finance might examine the way specialists on the New York Stock Exchange set prices, investigate the pricing of various derivative securities, or explore market microstructure and option prices.

Marketing
Research topics in marketing range from analysis and modeling of consumer behavior to research into the decision-making processes of marketing organizations. Students and faculty approach marketing from both a psychological, behavioral perspective and a quantitative, empirical one.

Organizational Behavior
Research in organizational behavior covers subjects such as the evolution of firms and industries, innovation and organizational learning, growth and decline processes, procedural and distributive justice, the social structure of firms and markets, corporate governance, organizational culture, and power and politics in organizations.

Production and Operations Management
Research in productions and operations management addresses problems in scheduling production, managing complex distribution systems, locations for production facilities and maintaining the quality of goods and services. Students in this major work with faculty and students in Cornell's College of Engineering School of Operations Research and Industrial Engineering.

SELECTED RESEARCH AREAS
- Analysis of public-investment and economic-policy decisions
- Analytical models for marketing research and strategy
- Behavioral economics
- Behavioral finance
- Capital markets
- Characteristics of firms reporting large discretionary losses
- Combined effects of individual cognition and social context on negotiation performance
- Corporate and capital-market finance
- Credit risk
- Data-based marketing
- Derivatives
- Design and management of service operations
- Discretionary disclosure of information by firms
- Emotional responses to advertising
- Experimental economics
- Financial statement analysis
- Global strategies for knowledge management
- Group dynamics
- Impact of accounting standards on rate-regulated enterprises
- Influence of affect on social interaction, thought processes and decision making
- Interaction between capacity and inventory in manufacturing systems
- Inventory management
- Investor behavior and stock valuation
- Laboratory markets
- Market microstructure
- Mathematical models of consumer choice behavior
- Mental models and their impact on reasoning and decision-making
- Negotiation and conflict
- Option pricing
- Portfolio theory
- Quantitative approaches to decision making
- Structures of the securities market
- Supply-chain integration
- Uses of digital imaging and computer graphics

CORNELL UNIVERSITY, JOHNSON GRADUATE SCHOOL OF MANAGEMENT

ADMISSIONS CRITERIA & PROCEDURES

The Cornell doctoral program is research-oriented and does not require applicants to have a degree in business. Johnson is interested in attracting people with strong undergraduate backgrounds in economics, mathematics, engineering, sociology, psychology or physical sciences, in addition to business.

The admission decision is primarily based on GRE or GMAT scores, the applicant's statement of purpose, letters of recommendation and prior academic records. The average GMAT score of students accepted over the past five years is approximately 700 (the top two percent of those tested). Cornell is highly selective and only about one in every 20 applicants is granted admission.

To be considered for admission, applicants must submit a completed application form, two letters of reference, transcripts from all postsecondary institutions attended and a copy of GMAT or GRE scores.

Students whose native language is not English are required to submit TOEFL scores unless they have completed at least one year of study at an American institution of higher education.

EXPENSES & FINANCIAL ASSISTANCE

Students enrolled in Cornell's PhD in management program pay tuition fees of US$23,760 per year. Other expenses include US$822 a year for health insurance, US$650 a year for books and other materials and a US$48 activity fee. Students should also expect to pay approximately US$825 per month for on- or off-campus room and board.

The Johnson School offers fellowships and research assistantships to most doctoral students. These fellowships and assistantships cover tuition and fees and include a stipend of approximately US$20,000 for 12 months. The continuation of financial aid is contingent upon satisfactory academic performance.

To apply for financial aid, students should check the appropriate box on the application form and ensure that the application is submitted before January 15.

INTERNATIONAL STUDENT SUPPORT

The International Students and Scholars Office (ISSO) is the campus center for Cornell's extensive international student community, which comprises more than 2,500 students from 118 countries. The ISSO acquaints students with Cornell and its services and helps them make the adjustment to life and study in the US. The office can advise students about immigration regulations and forms and refer them to various campus services for academic, family and personal counseling, financial matters, medical care and housing.

Many organizations on campus focus on international students including the Chinese Students and Scholars Association, the Korean Students Association, the Russian Society and the Society for India.

ADMISSIONS AT A GLANCE

Minimum GMAT:	n/a
Minimum GPA:	n/a
Minimum TOEFL (paper):	600
Minimum TOEFL (computer):	250
Application Fee:	US$150
Application Deadline:	Jan 15

EXPENSES AT A GLANCE

Tuition:	
In State:	US$27,600
Out-of-State:	US$27,600
Int'l Students:	US$27,600
Books & Supplies:	US$650
Health Insurance:	US$822
Accommodation	
University Residences:	–
Family Housing:	–
Private:	–

PROGRAM FACTS

# of Full-time Students:	32
# of Part-time Students:	n/a
# of Applications per year:	379
# Accepted per year:	20
# Enrolled per year:	10
Average GMAT Score:	700
Average Age:	27
% Men/Women:	62%/38%
Work Experience (avg yrs):	–
# of Faculty:	46
% Faculty with Doctoral Degree:	100%
Annual Research Funding:	–

CORNELL UNIVERSITY, JOHNSON GRADUATE SCHOOL OF MANAGEMENT

UNIVERSITY AND LOCATION

Cornell University, one of eight members of the prestigious Ivy League, is an ideal setting for academic pursuits. It consists of 13 colleges and schools and the campus has many ivy-covered buildings and shaded quadrangles.

The university library system, made up of 19 libraries, is one of the 12 largest academic research libraries in the US, housing nearly six million books, periodicals and academic journals, 7.2 million microforms, 75,700 sound recordings and a dozen outstanding research collections. The Herbert F. Johnson Museum of Modern Art contains over 27,000 works of art and the Center of Theater Arts presents six to 10 productions a year. Athletic fields and recreational facilities provide students with plenty of opportunities for recreation.

Sage Hall, the historic building that houses the Johnson School, is equipped with an advanced infrastructure with teleconferencing capabilities, high-bandwidth fiber-optic cable and a wide selection of computer equipment. It is home to the Parker Center for Investment Research, which includes an innovative trading room equipped with more than US$1.5 million worth of sophisticated stock analysis software. The Johnson School has recently adopted a policy of providing each PhD student with a computer. Sage Hall's Business Simulation Laboratory is equipped with hardware and software, affording opportunities in state-of-the-art experimental research in behavioral science, experimental economics and other disciplines.

The university's 736-acre campus is located in the city of Ithaca, New York, on the southern tip of Cayuga Lake. Ithaca is a small, lively city approximately 60 miles south of Syracuse. Surrounded by open fields, farmland and lakeshores, Ithaca is in New York's wine-producing region and is filled with bookstores, shops, clubs, theatres and restaurants. It is five hours by car from New York City and Toronto and direct flights to most major east coast cities are available.

City Population:	29,541
Cost of Living:	high
Climate Range:	13° to 80°F
Campus Setting:	suburban
Total Enrolment:	19,000
Graduate Enrolment:	5,772
Students in Residence:	7,000

FACULTY

- Babbes, G.S. PhD, California - Berkeley
- Bailey, W.B. PhD, UCLA
- Ben Daniel, D.J. PhD, MIT
- Bhojraj, S. PhD, Florida
- Bierman, Jr., H. PhD, Michigan
- Bloomfield, R.J. PhD, Michigan
- Bradley, J.R. PhD, Stanford
- D'Souza, J. PhD, Northwestern
- Dyckman, T.R. PhD, Michigan
- Elliot, J.A. PhD, Cornell
- Frank, R.H. PhD, California - Berkeley
- Greenberg, D.P. PhD, Cornell
- Gukhal, C.R. PhD, Columbia
- Hass, J.E. PhD, Carnegie-Mellon
- Hilton, R.W. PhD, Ohio State
- Isen, A.M. PhD, Stanford
- Jarrow, R.A. PhD, MIT
- Kadiyali, V. PhD, Northwestern
- Kumar, P. PhD, SUNY - Buffalo
- Lee, C.M.C. PhD, Cornell
- Li, H. PhD, Yale
- Libby, R. PhD, Illinois
- Lind, R.C. PhD, Stanford
- Lojo, M.P. PhD, MIT
- Mannix, E.A. PhD, Chicago
- McAdams, A.K. PhD, Stanford
- McClain, J.O. PhD, Yale
- Michaely, R. PhD, New York
- Nelsen, B.J. PhD, Cornell
- Nelson, M.W. PhD, Ohio State
- O'Connor, K.M. PhD, Illinois
- O'Hara, M. PhD, Northwestern
- Orman, L. PhD, Northwestern
- Peterson, R.S. PhD, California - Berkeley
- Rao, V.R. PhD, Wharton
- Robinson, L.W. PhD, Chicago
- Russo, J.E. PhD, Michigan
- Sally, D.F. PhD, Chicago
- Smidt, S. PhD, Chicago
- Stayman, D.M. PhD, California - Berkeley
- Swaminathan, B. PhD, UCLA
- Swieringa, R.J. PhD, Illinois
- Tasker, S. PhD, MIT
- Thomas, L.J. PhD, Yale
- Waldman, M. PhD, Pennsylvania

DREXEL UNIVERSITY
LEBOW COLLEGE OF BUSINESS

Program Highlights

- *Seven primary areas of specialization*
- *Secondary specializations in statistics and international business*
- *Small program means greater faculty interaction*
- *College accredited by AACSB*

CONTACT INFORMATION

Jeffrey H. Greenhaus

Dept of Management, Drexel University

Philadelphia, Pennsylvania USA 19104

PH: 1-215-895-2139

FAX: 1-215-895-2891

EMAIL: greenhaus@drexel.edu

INTERNET: http://www.lebow.drexel.edu/phd

DREXEL UNIVERSITY, LEBOW COLLEGE OF BUSINESS

PROGRAM OVERVIEW

Drexel University (Drexel) offers a Doctor of Philosophy (PhD) degree in business administration with specializations in accounting, decision sciences, economics, finance, marketing, organizational sciences and strategic management through the LeBow College of Business (LCOB).

Completion of the program requires a minimum of 57 quarter credits beyond the master's degree. During the first year of post-master's, students take core requirements which consist of three courses in quantitative methods, two in research design and methodology and two in the conceptual foundations of business and administration. Students are then examined to determine readiness to proceed to areas of specialization.

Students select a primary field of specialization with a minimum of seven courses, and a secondary field. Secondary specializations are available in each of the primary fields and in international business and statistics. Students take written and oral candidacy examinations to test their preparation for dissertation research.

The doctoral dissertation results from original research that contributes to the student's chosen discipline. The completed dissertation must be defended in a final oral examination.

Areas of Specialization

Students specializing in accounting must complete doctoral seminars in accounting theory, financial accounting, managerial accounting, auditing and accounting research methodology, and three courses in the financial accounting, managerial accounting, auditing, accounting systems or taxation subfields. They are also required to participate in the accounting department's research workshop/lecture series.

The specialization in decision sciences provides students with competence in management information systems (MIS), operations management and management science, and a concentration in either MIS or operations management. Students must complete three decision sciences core courses and four courses in MIS or operations management.

Students in economics complete courses in advanced microeconomic and macroeconomic theory and econometrics and five additional courses in monetary theory, international economic theory, mathematical economics, public finance, managerial economics and other topics.

Required courses for the specialization in finance cover the foundations of finance theory, corporate finance theory, macro finance theory, quantitative financial analysis and research methodology in finance. Students also choose three of the four PhD seminars in corporate finance, investments, international finance and financial markets.

The primary specialization in marketing requires the completion of seven courses in topics such as the conceptual foundations of buyer behavior, marketing models, the development of marketing theory and thought, strategic marketing planning, international marketing, the development of marketing channel systems and the conceptual foundations of marketing promotion.

Students in organizational sciences are exposed to topics at the individual, group and organizational levels of analysis. Students complete courses in individual behavior and performance in organizations, the dynamics of interpersonal and group behavior and the design and structure of organizations, as well as four additional courses.

Strategic management students complete four courses in industrial organization and market structure, strategy formulation, strategy implementation and control, and technology and innovation. They choose three courses from mergers and acquisitions, business conditions and forecasting, organization change and development, marketing strategy and planning and manufacturing strategy.

SELECTED RESEARCH AREAS
- Biomedical investigation
- Cash flow analysis
- Consumer choice models
- Dividend policy
- Energy economics
- Entrepreneurial management
- Environmental monitoring
- Experimental economics
- Expert systems and artificial intelligence
- Financial accounting
- Financial reporting policies
- Foreign trade
- Global market strategies
- Human resource planning
- Information system design
- Internal accounting control system adequacy
- International channel management decisions
- International economics
- Management information systems
- Management of diversity
- Managerial accounting systems
- Manufacturing strategy and control
- Measurement of customer satisfaction
- Multi-objective programming
- Multivariate data analysis of market variables
- Portfolio theory
- Product development and strategic planning
- Professional and personal selling
- Promotional strategies
- Quality control
- Real estate
- Risk measurement
- Software life cycle
- Statistical process control
- Strategic management
- Taxation
- Technology and strategy
- Transportation and distribution
- Work-family relationships
- Work stress
- Working capital management

DREXEL UNIVERSITY, LEBOW COLLEGE OF BUSINESS

ADMISSIONS CRITERIA & PROCEDURES

Admission to the PhD program is competitive. Applicants must specify their proposed area of specialization. A master's degree is not a requirement, but most admitted students have completed a master's.

The LCOB faculty examine all prior coursework, paying particular attention to the specific courses completed. Applicants should have a minimum GPA of 3.0 (on a scale of 4.0) for all undergraduate coursework and a 3.3 GPA for graduate coursework. In some specializations, the faculty may expect a higher level of accomplishment. Scores from the GMAT are required.

Each applicant must submit a personal statement outlining the educational and personal experiences that influenced the decision to pursue a PhD and explaining future career plans and goals. Faculty are especially interested in applicants' prior research experience and commitment to future research in the primary area of specialization. Two letters of recommendation from academics or other professionals who can assess the applicant's likelihood of success in a research-oriented PhD program are also required.

Applicants whose native language is other than English and who have not already received a degree from a US university must submit a TOEFL score.

The doctoral program admits new students in alternate odd-numbered (e.g., 2001-2, 2003-4). PhD students are admitted in the fall term only. To be considered for fall admission, the completed application must be received by February 1.

EXPENSES & FINANCIAL ASSISTANCE

The LCOB awards a limited number of graduate assistantships to outstanding applicants. Assistants may be assigned supervised teaching responsibilities or assigned to a faculty research project. They receive a stipend and 27 credits of tuition remission per year in exchange for 20 hours of service per week. PhD students making satisfactory progress towards the degree may have their assistantship renewed for a maximum of three years.

Other available forms of financial aid include the Drexel Fellow teaching assignment for an advanced doctoral student and various need-based state and federal loan programs.

INTERNATIONAL STUDENT SUPPORT

The International Students and Scholars Office (ISSO) provides international students with a three-day orientation before classes begin. The orientation includes tours of the campus and the surrounding community, workshops on American culture and US education as well as information sessions about immigration requirements and employment restrictions. The ISSO also provides students with academic advising and provides assistance with US federal documents.

All international students attending Drexel must purchase health insurance. Drexel offers a low-cost group health insurance plan at approximately US$600 a year.

Each spring the ISSO sponsors the International Festival where students meet to exchange culture with the Drexel community and sell samples of international cuisine.

ADMISSIONS AT A GLANCE

Minimum GMAT: no set minimum
Minimum GPA:
   3.0 (undergraduate); 3.3 (graduate)
Minimum TOEFL (paper): 570
Minimum TOEFL (computer): –
Application Fee: US$35
Application Deadline:
   The doctoral program admits students in the fall of odd-numbered years. The application deadline is Feb 1

EXPENSES AT A GLANCE

Amounts showns are for the 1999-2000 academic year
Tuition:
   In State: US$13,797 per year
   Out-of-State: US$13,797 per year
   Int'l Students: US$13,797 per year
Books & Supplies:
   US$1,500 per year
Health Insurance: US$600 per year
Accommodation:
   University Residences:
      US$900–970 per month
Family Housing: –
Private: US$600–900 per month

PROGRAM FACTS

# of Full-time Students:	42
# of Part-time Students:	9
# of Applications per year:	94
# Accepted per year:	43
# Enrolled per year:	17
Average GMAT Score:	580
Average Age:	34
% Men/Women:	61%/39%
Work Experience (avg yrs):	–
# of Faculty:	63
% Faculty with Doctoral Degree:	98%
Annual Research Funding:	US$1.3m

DREXEL UNIVERSITY, LEBOW COLLEGE OF BUSINESS

UNIVERSITY AND LOCATION

Founded by Philadelphia financier and philanthropist Anthony J. Drexel in 1891 as the Drexel Institute of Art, Science and Industry, Drexel University assumed its current name in 1970. A private institution with a reputation for advanced technology and research, Drexel is made up of six colleges and three schools offering 50 degree programs at the bachelor's, master's, and doctoral levels to over 7,500 undergraduate and 2,500 graduate students from the US and around the world.

The university supports the second-oldest and third-largest cooperative education program in the US, with students employed in 2,500 businesses from 22 states and 11 countries.

The LeBow College of Business is housed in Matheson Hall and the Academic Building. Several fully equipped computer labs, utilize both Macintosh and IBM hardware and the latest in business software. A unique facility devoted to enhancing finance-oriented courses allows students to develop expertise in capital markets trading and risk management through the use of financial software simulations of stock trading, applied risk management and portfolio diversification.

Drexel's W.W. Hagerty Library has a collection of more than 1.2 million books, periodicals, microforms and government documents, with a focus on the fields of business, technology, science, design and information studies. Students can use the library's electronic network to access other library collections in Philadelphia and around the world.

Drexel is located on 50 acres within Philadelphia's University City neighborhood, one of the top academic communities in the US, in the heart of the eastern seaboard between Washington, D.C. and New York. The university is only minutes away from downtown Philadelphia, which is one of the country's major urban centers for industry, commerce and the arts.

The city's many attractions include Independence Hall, the Liberty Bell, the Philadelphia Museum of Art, the Rodin Museum and Penn's Landing, a recreational development along the Delaware River.

City Population:	4,900,000
Cost of Living:	high
Climate Range:	32° to 76°F
Campus Setting:	urban
Total Enrollment:	11,617
Graduate Enrollment:	2,715
Students in Residence:	1,535

FACULTY

- Aggarwal, L.K. PhD, Pennsylvania
- Agoglia, C. PhD, Massachusetts
- Anandarjah, M. PhD, Drexel
- Anderson, R.E. PhD, Florida
- Andras, T.L. PhD, Texas
- Arinze, B. PhD, London School of Economics
- Banerjee, A. PhD, Ohio State
- Brown, K. PhD, Case Western Reserve
- Burton, J.S. PhD, Texas Tech
- Chiang, T.C. PhD, Pennsylvania State
- Cremers, E. PhD, Minnesota
- Curatola, A.P. PhD, Texas A&M
- DeCarolis, D. PhD, Temple
- Gefen, D. PhD, Georgia State
- Goh, J. PhD, Washington U, St. Louis
- Gombola, M.J. PhD, South Carolina
- Govindarajulu, C. PhD, Mississippi
- Greenhaus, J.H. PhD, New York
- Hammoudeh, S. PhD, Kansas
- Hatfield, R. PhD, Florida
- Higgins, E. PhD, Florida State
- Hindelang, T.J. DBA, Indiana
- Jaenicke, H.R. PhD, Pennsylvania
- Jensen, P.E. PhD, Pennsylvania State
- Jeon, B.N. PhD, Indiana
- Keidel, R. PhD, Pennsylvania
- Kim, S.L. PhD, Pennsylvania State
- Koziara, E.C. PhD, Wisconsin

- Kritz, G.H. PhD, Indiana
- Laessig, R.E. PhD, Cornell
- Lester, B. PhD, Pennsylvania
- Lewis, P. PhD, Tennessee
- Linnehan, F. PhD, Temple
- Long, M. PhD, CUNY-Baruch College
- Mackie, J.J. PhD, Texas A&M
- Madan, V. PhD, Michigan State
- Maragah, H. PhD, Southwestern Louisiana
- Mason, J.R. PhD, Illinois
- McCain, R. PhD, Louisiana State
- McWilliams, T. PhD, Stanford
- Ndubizu, G. PhD, Temple
- Nelling, E. PhD, Pennsylvania
- Parasuraman, S. PhD, SUNY - Buffalo
- Partovi, F. PhD, Pennsylvania
- Pryor, A. PhD, North Texas
- Richards, M. PhD, Indiana
- Rosenbloom, B. PhD, Temple
- Schaubroeck, J. PhD, Purdue
- Siegel, S.R. PhD, Drexel
- Silver, M. PhD, Columbia
- Soller-Curtis, E. PhD, Indiana
- Song, W. PhD, Michigan State
- Suri, R. PhD, Illinois
- Swaminathan, S. PhD, Texas
- Szewczyk, S.H. PhD, Pennsylvania State
- Tang, L. PhD, Syracuse
- Trewin, J. PhD, Michigan State
- Tsetsekos, G.P. PhD, Tennessee
- Wang, Y. PhD, Pennsylvania
- Webb, K.L. PhD, North Carolina
- Wentzel, K. PhD, Texas
- Wu, D. PhD, Tsinghua
- Yan, C.S. PhD, Purdue

DUKE UNIVERSITY
PhD IN BUSINESS ADMINISTRATION

Program Highlights

- *Decision sciences, finance, management, marketing and operations management areas*
- *All PhD students in program receive assistantship/fellowship support and tuition/registration fee waivers for up to 10 semesters*
- *Less than one-to-one student-faculty ratio optimizes professional relationships*

CONTACT INFORMATION

The Graduate School

127 Allen Building Box 90065

Durham, North Carolina USA 27708-0065

PH: 1-919-684-3913

FAX: 1-919-684-2277

EMAIL: grad-admissions@acpub.duke.edu

INTERNET: http://www.gradschool.duke.edu

or http://www.fuqua.duke.edu

DUKE UNIVERSITY, PhD IN BUSINESS ADMINISTRATION

PROGRAM OVERVIEW

Duke University (Duke) offers a Doctor of Philosophy (PhD) degree in business administration with specializations in decision sciences, finance, marketing, management and operations management.

The program emphasizes independent inquiry, competence in research methodology and the communication of research results. Courses are individualized in consultation with the faculty in their area, based upon background, goals and interests. Most students take two years of coursework.

Students are also required to take a comprehensive examination in their area, usually in the third year of residence, and to propose, complete and defend a dissertation based upon original research.

The program usually requires 4 to 5 years of study.

Decision Sciences

The PhD program in decision sciences is an interdisciplinary program in methodological, foundational and applied issues. It includes graduate courses in operations research, statistics, economics, mathematics and/or psychology. Decision sciences students pursue broad interests and become experts in disciplines that complement their major area expertise, such as financial theory, risk management and marketing strategy.

Finance

Students in finance participate in weekly finance seminars, complete four semesters of graduate-level courses centered around six core modules that provide an overview of modern finance theory and empirical methodology, and complete independent research projects during each summer of residence.

Management

Management faculty have strong disciplinary roots in cognitive psychology and behavioral decision theory, social psychology, sociology and economics. Research and PhD training focus on judgment and decision making, organizational relationships and interpersonal processes and organizational forms.

Courses provide in-depth training in one primary research field and breadth in others. Students work with individual faculty on research projects and are required to complete a first-year research paper, a fifth-semester research paper and a PhD dissertation.

Marketing

Marketing coursework is in marketing areas such as consumer behavior, marketing models, marketing strategy and planning and marketing measurement and analysis. Additional degree requirements include first- and second-year research papers, a comprehensive exam normally taken at the start of the sixth semester, and a dissertation. Students participate in research seminars and work with faculty on original research projects.

Operations Management

Students in the operations management program take courses in mathematical programming, statistics, stochastic processes and simulation. Within the required seminars, students also study operations management topics encompassing strategic, tactical and operational decision making, including facility location and layout, capacity management, production planning and control, operations scheduling, quality management, automated production systems, service operations and manufacturing strategy.

SELECTED RESEARCH AREAS

- Advertising processing and management
- Banking
- Bargaining
- Behavioral decision theory
- Consumer behavior
- Corporate finance
- Decision analysis
- Defense economics
- Design of organization and market structure
- Ecnometrics
- Economic reform in China, Eastern Europe and the former Soviet Union
- Eliciting and representing brand associations
- Emperical asset pricing
- Executive compensation
- Financial accounting and reporting
- Foreign exchange rates
- Franchising
- Game theory
- Industrial marketing
- Industrial organization
- Interactive home shopping
- International finance
- Investments
- Judgment and choice
- Labor contracts
- Leasing and selling
- Negotiation
- Nonlinear dynamics in economics and finance
- Occupational attainment
- Operations mangement
- Pricing and channels
- Regulation of the securities market
- Regulatory economics and incentives
- Sequential analysis
- Social capital
- Social perception and management decision
- Stock options
- Supplier relations

DUKE UNIVERSITY, PHD IN BUSINESS ADMINISTRATION

ADMISSIONS CRITERIA & PROCEDURES

Applicants are not required to have a business administration background. However, prerequisite coursework may be required to pursue specific areas of specialization.

Applications must include three letters of evaluation written by persons qualified to judge the applicant's capacity for graduate work and official scores from the GRE general test or the GMAT. One official transcript, including degree certification and date awarded, is also required from each college or university previously attended and must be submitted to Duke either directly from the issuing institution or in unopened envelopes bearing the signature of the registrar across the seal. If official transcripts are not available, exact copies verified as certified true copies by the appropriate institutional official must be submitted. All documents in a language other than English must be accompanied by official English translations bearing an original ink signature and seal.

TOEFL results are required from all applicants whose native language is not English. A minimum score of 550 on the paper-based test or 213 on the computer-based version is required. International students must submit evidence of adequate financial resources to cover the costs of graduate study at Duke.

Applications must be accompanied by the application fee of US$65 for applications submitted before December or US$75 for those submitted afterwards.

EXPENSES & FINANCIAL ASSISTANCE

Annual tuition for PhD study is US$18,000. Students will need approximately US$1,000 per year for books and supplies and US$685 for health insurance, unless they have comparable coverage. Rental rates in the university-operated apartment facilities for graduate and professional students range from US$3,251 to $5,012 per academic year for single students.

The Fuqua School of Business provides research assistantships, fellowships and tuition and registration fee waivers to all new PhD students and for up to 10 semesters of study as long as students make satisfactory progress toward the PhD. The financial support package includes a stipend of US$975 a month for the first three years of doctoral study. This stipend is extended for the fourth and fifth years, provided the major field examination has been passed.

INTERNATIONAL STUDENT SUPPORT

Duke's International House (IH) helps students adjust to life and work at an American university. At the beginning of the academic year, IH provides a four-day orientation for international graduate and professional students that includes both academic and social activities. IH also sponsors an International Friends Program.

The university's International Office (IO) helps students with visa and immigration regulations and international students are required to report to the IO within 30 days of arrival.

A limited number of spaces are reserved for international graduate students in the Central Campus apartments and Townhouse apartments located between the East and West campuses.

ADMISSIONS AT A GLANCE

Minimum GMAT:	no set minimum
Minimum GPA:	no set minimum
Minimum TOEFL (paper):	550
Minimum TOEFL (computer):	213
Application Fee:	US$75 (US$65 before Dec 1)
Application Deadline:	Dec 31 (fall admission)

EXPENSES AT A GLANCE

Tuition per year:	
In State:	US$18,000
Out-of-State:	US$18,000
Int'l Students:	US$18,000
Books & Supplies:	US$1,000 per year
Health Insurance:	US$685 per year
Accommodation:	
University Residences:	US$3,251–5,012 per year
Family Housing:	–
Private:	–

PROGRAM FACTS

# of Full-time Students:	47
# of Part-time Students:	0
# of Applications per year:	245
# Accepted per year:	26
# Enrolled per year:	13
Average GMAT Score:	721
Average Age:	29
% Men/Women:	48
Work Experience (avg yrs):	–
# of Faculty:	75
% Faculty with Doctoral Degree:	100%
Annual Research Funding:	US$500,000

DUKE UNIVERSITY, PhD IN BUSINESS ADMINISTRATION

UNIVERSITY AND LOCATION

Duke University traces its origins to the Union Institute, established by Methodists and Quakers in 1838. In 1892, it moved to its current location in Durham, where it subsequently expanded and became Duke University in 1924.

A comprehensive research institution composed of nine schools, Duke is strategically located at the apex of North Carolina's Research Triangle Park, one of America's largest planned research areas. The university's library holdings are the eighth largest among private universities in the US and the Triangle Research Library Network gives students access to the libraries of the University of North Carolina - Chapel Hill and North Carolina State University.

Duke's athletic facilities include gyms, outdoor and indoor pools, tennis courts, dance studios, a large recreation building for basketball, handball, racquetball and squash, a golf course, weight training rooms, a cross-country course and acres of athletic and recreation fields.

The Duke University Museum of Art is a showcase for major traveling exhibitions each year. The museum also hosts music, lecture and film events tied to exhibits.

Duke is located in Durham, North Carolina, a city with a population of nearly 200,000 people located at the center of North Carolina. Durham is home to the Durham Bulls Triple A baseball team, a farm team of the major league's Tampa Bay Devil Rays. The city of Chapel Hill is located 20 minutes southwest by car and the state capital of Raleigh is located 25 minutes to the east. North Carolina's Atlantic coastline and the Blue Ridge Mountains are both less than a three-hour drive away.

City Population:	200,000
Cost of Living:	medium
Climate Range:	37° to 77°F
Campus Setting:	urban
Total Enrollment:	12,662
Graduate Enrollment:	5,878
Students in Residence:	7,900

FACULTY

- Anton, J.J. PhD, Stanford
- Ashton, A.H. PhD, Texas
- Ashton, R.H. PhD, Minnesota
- Baligh, H.H. PhD, Minnesota
- Banks, D.T. PhD, Pennsylvania
- Bansal, R. PhD, Carnegie Mellon
- Bellieveau, M.A. PhD, Berkeley
- Bercovitz, J.E.L. PhD, Berkeley
- Bettman, J.R. PhD, Yale
- Boulding, W.F. PhD, Pennsylvania
- Bradley, M. PhD, Chicago
- Brav, A. PhD, Chicago
- Breeden, D.T. PhD, Stanford
- Brodt, S.E. PhD, Stanford
- Burton, R.M. DBA, Illinois
- Cachon, G.P. PhD, Pennsylvania
- Carmon, Z. PhD, Berkeley
- Clemen, R.T. PhD, Indiana
- Cohen, K.J. PhD, Carnegie Mellon
- Coleman, W.J. PhD, Chicago
- Das Varma, G. PhD, Northwestern
- Desai, P.S. PhD, Carnegie Mellon
- DeSanctis, G. PhD, Texas Tech
- Dumas, B. PhD, Columbia
- Edell, J.A. PhD, Carnegie Mellon
- Fischer, G.W.. PhD, Michigan
- Forsyth, J.D. DBA, Illinois
- Fox, C.R. PhD, Stanford
- Francis, J. PhD, Cornell
- Gigone, D. PhD, Colorado
- Graham, J.R. PhD, Duke
- Harvey, C.R. PhD, Chicago
- Heath, C. PhD, Stanford
- Hsieh, D.A. PhD, Northwestern
- Huber, J. PhD, Pennsylvania
- Keller, T.F. PhD, Michigan
- Kornish, L.J. PhD, Stanford
- Kyle, A.S. PhD, Chicago
- Lariviere, M.A. PhD, Stanford
- Laughhunn, D.J. DBA, Illinois
- Levine, C.N. PhD, Carnegie Mellon
- Lewin, A.Y. PhD, Carnegie Mellon
- Li, W.. PhD, Michigan
- Lind, E.A. PhD, North Carolina
- Linville, P. PhD, Duke
- Lynch, J.G. PhD, Illinois
- Mahajan, S. PhD, Pennsylvania
- Maug, E.G. PhD, London School of Economics
- McCann, J.M. PhD, Purdue
- Mela, C.F. PhD, Columbia
- Moore, M.C. PhD, UCLA
- Moore, M.J. PhD, Michigan
- Moorman, C. PhD, Pittsburgh
- Mrkaic, M. PhD, Carnegie Mellon
- Nau, R.F. PhD, California
- Patterson, S.S. PhD, MIT
- Payne, J.W. PhD, California -Irvine
- Pekec, A. PhD, Rutgers
- Purohit, D. PhD, Carnegie Mellon
- Quadrini, V. PhD, Pennsylvania
- Regenwetter, M. PhD, California - Irvine
- Rossiensky, N. PhD, London Business School
- Schipper, K. PhD, Chicago
- Sheppard, B. PhD, Illinois
- Sitkin, S.B. PhD, Stanford
- Smith, J.E. PhD, Stanford
- Smith, M.J. PhD, Stanford
- Staelin, R. PhD, Stanford
- Staudenmeyer, N. PhD, MIT
- Vettas, N. PhD, Pennsylvania
- Viswanathan, S. PhD, Northwestern
- Wang, J.J.D. PhD, Utah
- Whaley, R.E. PhD, Toronto
- Willis, R.H. PhD, Chicago
- Winkler, R.L. PhD, Chicago
- Zipkin, P.H. PhD, Yale

FLORIDA INTERNATIONAL UNIVERSITY
PhD IN BUSINESS ADMINISTRATION

Program Highlights

- Carnegie Foundation for the Advancement of Teaching classifies FIU as a Doctoral I University
- Concentrations available in marketing and management information systems
- Accredited by AACSB

CONTACT INFORMATION
College of Business Administration
Ryder Business Building
Miami, Florida USA 33199
PH: 1-305-348-3322
FAX: 1-305-348-3792
EMAIL: phd@fin.edu
INTERNET: http://www.fiu.edu/~cba/phd/

FLORIDA INTERNATIONAL UNIVERSITY, PhD IN BUSINESS ADMINISTRATION

PROGRAM OVERVIEW

The College of Business Administration (CBA) at Florida International University (FIU) offers a PhD in business administration with concentrations in management information systems and marketing. The program provides students with the methodological and analytical tools required for conducting research and prepares them for an academic career. Students acquire the skills to formulate, conduct and communicate research and to teach effectively.

The PhD program generally requires four years of full-time study that involves two-and-a-half years of coursework and summer projects and one-and-a-half years of research. Students complete a minimum of 16 courses, including at least six in the area of concentration. They also conduct summer research projects under faculty supervision.

General degree requirements for PhD in business administration students include successful completion of required coursework, a comprehensive examination and a doctoral dissertation.

Management Information Systems

All students are required to complete a minimum of 15 graduate courses and the college colloquium series. Students in the management information systems concentration must take the seven seminars offered by the Decision Sciences and Information Systems Department, a two-course sequence in research methods and two to four statistics courses, depending upon their level of statistical knowledge. Other courses are selected by students in consultation with the department's PhD committee. Students must maintain a GPA of 3.3 or higher to remain in the program.

Marketing

Marketing students must complete 15 graduate courses, the college colloquium series and all seven seminars offered by the Marketing Department. A two-course sequence in research methods and two to four courses in statistics, depending upon the student's level of statistical knowledge, are also required. Additional coursework will be chosen by students with the advice and consent of the department's PhD committee. Students must achieve a minimum GPA of 3.5 in the seven courses that make up the marketing concentration and a GPA of 3.3 in other coursework.

Research Projects

PhD students complete research projects under the supervision of a faculty member during the summer semesters following their first and second years. The primary objective of the first summer project is to enhance students' research skills. Rather than develop a new research hypotheses, the student selects a previously tested hypothesis and develops and implements a study for testing that constitutes a meaningful methodological contribution to existing literature. The second summer research project requires the development of an original research hypothesis.

Students submit written papers based on the projects and make presentations to the faculty. Papers should be suitable for submission to a conference or an academic journal.

Comprehensive Examination

Upon completion of the required coursework, students must pass a comprehensive examination designed to assess their level of preparation for dissertation research. The examination consists of the student preparing a proposal that develops an original hypothesis or hypotheses in an area of substantive performance and describes a methodology for testing it. The proposal is evaluated by the department's PhD committee.

SELECTED RESEARCH AREAS

- Advertising
- Business ethics
- Channels of distribution
- Competitive use of information technology
- Consumer behavior
- Corporate ethics
- Database analysis and design
- Decision support systems
- Economic development in Latin America and the Caribbean
- Environmental management
- Export marketing
- International marketing
- International trade
- Logistics
- Management of the information services function
- Management science
- Marketing
- Marketing channels
- Marketing management
- Marketing research
- Marketing strategy
- Microcomputer simulations
- Multicriteria decision support systems
- Networking
- Operations management
- Opinion elicitation for conflict resolution and group consensus
- Persuasion
- Polls and surveys
- Production and operations management
- Productivity and quality management
- Project management
- Statistical applications
- Strategy and policy
- Systems analysis and design
- Use of information technology to support individual and organizational decision-making
- Visual languages

FLORIDA INTERNATIONAL UNIVERSITY, PhD IN BUSINESS ADMINISTRATION

ADMISSIONS CRITERIA & PROCEDURES

Applications are accepted from prospective students with a range of educational backgrounds, including business, liberal arts and sciences. Students accepted into the PhD program must demonstrate strong evidence of ability, scholarly interest and the likelihood to succeed.

Applications should include a completed application form (available from the PhD program office or on the Internet at http://www.fiu.edu/orgs/admiss/application/html), the processing fee, three letters of recommendation, official transcripts from all institutions at which the applicant completed undergraduate or graduate coursework, a GMAT score report, and a formal statement of purpose for seeking the doctoral degree and the reasons for applying to FIU. Applicants must have a minimum GPA of 3.0 in their graduate coursework and a minimum GMAT score of 560.

International applicants whose native language is not English must submit TOEFL scores. A minimum score of 570 on the paper-based test or 230 on the computer based test is required. All international applicants must meet the FIU admissions requirements as well as requirements for acceptance into the CBA's PhD program. The FIU admissions requirements for international students are described at http://www.fiu.edu/orgs/admiss/international.html. International students must also meet the Immigration and Naturalization Service's and State of Florida Board of Regents' requirements, outlined at www.fiu.edu/~isss.

The CBA admits doctoral students in the Fall semester of even numbered years. Completed applications must be received by March 1 for consideration.

EXPENSES & FINANCIAL ASSISTANCE

Tuition and fees vary every year. In 1999-2000, Florida residents paid US$144.96 per credit hour and non-Florida residents paid US$509.69 per credit hour. Students must also pay required student and health fees, which generally total less than US$100 for domestic students.

Applicants to the doctoral program may request financial aid by completing the appropriate form and submitting it with their applications. Assistantships carry a stipend of US$17,000 per year and involve teaching and research duties. A tuition waiver may be provided to outstanding applicants.

INTERNATIONAL STUDENT SUPPORT

The Office of International Student and Scholar Services (OISSS) assists international students and visiting professors and researchers by providing advice and services relating to immigration, legal, personal, academic, cultural, social, and financial concerns. The staff advises and consults with the university community on matters pertaining to individual international students and scholars and serves as a resource to the university community in matters of cross-cultural concern.

ADMISSIONS AT A GLANCE

Minimum GMAT:	560
Minimum GPA:	3.0
Minimum TOEFL (paper):	570
Minimum TOEFL (computer):	230
Application Fee:	US$20
Application Deadline:	Mar 1

EXPENSES AT A GLANCE

Tuition per credit hour:	
In State:	US$145
Out-of-State:	US$510
Int'l Students:	US$510
Books & Supplies:	US$1,000 (approx.)
Health Insurance:	US$600 (int'l students)
Accommodation:	
University Residences:	–
Family Housing:	–
Private:	–

PROGRAM FACTS

# of Full-time Students:	3
# of Part-time Students:	4
# of Applications per year:	100
# Accepted per year:	6-8
# Enrolled per year:	7
Average GMAT Score:	620
Average Age:	30
% Men/Women:	50%/50%
Work Experience (avg yrs):	6
# of Faculty:	12
% Faculty with Doctoral Degree:	100%
Annual Research Funding:	–

FLORIDA INTERNATIONAL UNIVERSITY, PhD IN BUSINESS ADMINISTRATION

UNIVERSITY AND LOCATION

Established by the Florida legislature in 1965, Florida International University held its first classes in 1972. It is a member of the State University System of Florida. FIU comprises nine schools — Accounting, Architecture, Computer Science, Hospitality Management, Journalism and Mass Communication, Music, Nursing, Policy and Management and Social Work — and the colleges of Arts and Sciences, Business Administration, Education, Engineering, Health Sciences, Urban and Public Affairs and the Honors College. Together, these academic units offer baccalaureate, master's and doctoral degree programs in more than 280 major areas of study.

FIU is the largest public university in Southern Florida, with campuses in western Miami-Dade County and on Biscayne Bay and academic sites in Davie, Fort Lauderdale and Homestead. The University Park campus occupies 342 acres and features apartment-style and traditional residence halls, a new eight-story library and an environmental preserve. The North Campus includes a natural mangrove preserve, and facilities such as apartment-style housing, a library, an aquatic center, and the Roz and Cal Kovens Conference Center, which accommodates up to 500 people.

The University Park and North Campus libraries have a combined collection of more than 1.3 million volumes and substantial holdings of state, federal, local and international documents, maps, microfilms, institutional archives and curriculum materials. The libraries subscribe to approximately 9,100 journals and serials and offer a variety of online resources.

FIU's intercollegiate athletic teams compete in the NCAA Division I and the Sun Belt Conference in sports such as basketball, track and cross-country, golf, tennis, soccer, softball and volleyball. The university has intramural programs in bowling, basketball, flag football, golf, soccer, softball and volleyball. Fitness centers at both campuses are equipped with Nautilus and Universal equipment and free weights. The aquatic center at the North Campus features an Olympic-sized pool and diving well and other athletic facilities include the 4,500-seat Golden Panther arena, the community stadium, and lighted baseball and soccer fields. Southern Florida's tropical weather enables students to enjoy outdoor recreational activities ranging from boating and water sports to tennis and golf throughout the year.

Miami-Dade County is a vibrant, multicultural area that links the two Americas. It is a major center for finance and international commerce, travel and tourism, international banking and real estate, entrepreneurial technology firms, cable television and the entertainment industry.

City Population:	2,100,000
Cost of Living:	high
Climate Range:	59° to 98°F
Campus Setting:	suburban
Total Enrollment:	30,500
Graduate Enrollment:	6,354
Students in Residence:	1,600

FACULTY

- Batra, D. PhD, Indiana
- Elam, J.J. PhD, Texas
- Greenberg, B. PhD, Texas
- Hogner, R.H. PhD, Pittsburgh
- Koulamas, C.P. PhD, Texas Tech
- Mandakovic, T. PhD, Pittsburgh
- Miniard, P.W. PhD, Florida International
- Nicholls, J.F.A. DBA, Indiana
- Ortiz-Buonafina, M. PhD, Miami
- Paul, K. PhD, Emory
- Seaton, B. PhD, Washington
- Zanakis, S.H. PhD, Pennsylvania State

FLORIDA STATE UNIVERSITY
COLLEGE OF BUSINESS

Florida State University

Program Highlights

- *Seven areas of concentration offered*
- *Interaction with students sharing similar interests balanced with personal attention from faculty members*
- *Classified as a Research I institution by the Carnegie Foundation*
- *Accredited by AACSB*

CONTACT INFORMATION
College of Business
Tallahassee, Florida USA 32306-1110
PH: 1-850-644-6458
FAX: 1-850-644-0915 (use cover sheet)
EMAIL: smartin@cob.fsu.edu
INTERNET: http://www.cob.fsu.edu/grad

FLORIDA STATE UNIVERSITY, COLLEGE OF BUSINESS

PROGRAM OVERVIEW

The Florida State University (FSU) College of Business (COB) offers a Doctor of Philosophy (PhD) degree in business administration with concentrations in accounting, finance, information and management sciences, marketing, organizational behavior, risk management and insurance, and strategic management.

The PhD program is large enough to ensure a stimulating environment for students with similar research interests yet intimate enough to offer personal attention. Faculty members are committed to teaching and research within the framework of developing future business teachers and researchers. Informal meetings contribute significantly to student learning and professional development

Analytical tools and research coursework directly support the research methodologies pertinent to the primary and support areas of study selected by each student. Students take six courses from the disciplines of economics, mathematics and/or statistics to acquire the skills necessary to understand and conduct research in functional business areas.

Areas of Concentration

The accounting program offers research seminars covering a wide range of topics in financial reporting, capital markets and behavioral and auditing research. Research interests of faculty are in areas such as time-series analysis, auditing, decision making, financial reporting, information systems, government, earnings management and capital markets. Common support areas for accounting majors include finance, psychology, econometrics and statistics.

The concentration in finance covers the foundations and theories of finance. Students complete courses in investment management and analysis, problems in financial management, micro- or macro-economics, and an econometrics or accounting elective. Finance majors usually choose a support area in econometrics, economics, accounting, quantitative methods, statistics, real estate or risk management and insurance.

The information and management sciences program focuses extensively on the organizational and behavioral aspects of management information systems. Courses and seminars provide opportunities for in-depth study of organizational, managerial and behavioral issues in information systems.

The organizational behavior program offers courses in human perception, attitudes, personality, stress, leadership, group dynamics, motivation, organization design, human resource management and labor relations. Support areas consist of three or four courses in business disciplines or in fields such as anthropology, psychology, public administration or sociology.

Students in the risk management and insurance concentration complete courses on employee benefit plans, risk management in business enterprises, the theory of risk and insurance, life and health insurance, and property and liability insurance. Typical support areas are finance, real estate and statistics.

Strategic management courses cover topics such as strategy formulation, management of strategic change, organization design, competitive dynamics and managerial cognition and decision-making. Common support areas for students pursuing this concentration include business or interdisciplinary disciplines such as international business or sociology.

Students in the marketing concentration complete six courses and two research colloquia in areas such as marketing history and systems, consumer behavior, marketing models, research methodology and marketing management. The support area may be chosen from another department within the COB or from outside the college.

SELECTED RESEARCH AREAS
- Accounting expertise
- Auditing
- Business law
- Business marketing
- Capital markets
- Commodity trading
- Consumer and economic psychology
- Consumer behavior
- Corporate finance
- Customer satisfaction
- Data quality
- Descision making process
- Design and use of information systems
- Earning forecasts
- Employee benefits
- Entry strategy in Japan
- Fashion orientation and expenditure patterns on the behavior of black consumers
- Financial and regulatory aspects of insurer operations
- Financial modeling
- Financial statement disclosure for firm value
- Human information processing
- Human information processing limitations on decisions under risk and uncertainty
- Impression management
- Insurance ethics
- Insurance regulation
- International marketing and business
- Investments
- Lease type choice for firms in financial distress
- Life insurance company structure and operation
- Management of multinationals
- Market planning
- Marketing on the Internet
- Materials management
- Portfolio management
- Psychometrics
- Real estate
- Research design
- Service quality
- Social responsibility issues confronting corporate managers
- Unions as organizations

FLORIDA STATE UNIVERSITY, COLLEGE OF BUSINESS

ADMISSIONS CRITERIA & PROCEDURES

Admissions decisions are made by the COB doctoral admissions committee based on grades, GMAT scores, letters of recommendation, the statement of purpose, the number of qualified applicants, current enrollment in the program and the COB's ability to offer financial assistance.

Applicants must have at least a 3.0 undergraduate and 3.5 graduate GPA and a 550 GMAT score balanced between verbal and quantitative areas. Students whose native language is not English must achieve a minimum score of 600 on the paper-based TOEFL or 250 on the computer-based version. International students applying for financial assistance must submit an acceptable TSE score.

The application process involves separate applications to the university and the college. The university portion includes an application form, the Florida resident affidavit, if applicable, the application fee, two official transcripts from all postsecondary institutions attended and an official TOEFL score report, if necessary. Application to the college requires an application form, an official GMAT score, three letters of recommendation from former professors or employers, a brief statement of purpose and a resume.

Admission occurs in the fall semester only. Application deadlines are May 1 for domestic students and February 1 for international students but the majority of decisions are made several months earlier. Financial assistance deadlines may be as early as January 1.

EXPENSES & FINANCIAL ASSISTANCE

The COB awards assistantships and fellowships to students whose application materials reflect high academic and professional performance, maturity and a strong ability to teach and communicate with students. Financial assistance is available for four years, conditional to the maintenance of a satisfactory level of academic and work performance.

Graduate, research and teaching assistantships offer stipends US$10,000 per year plus tuition waivers. The college teaching fellowship is for two semesters per academic year and is awarded only to new graduate students. It includes a tuition waiver and a US$6,300 stipend.

University fellowships are awarded annually and include matriculation waivers, out-of-state tuition waivers, if applicable, and a US$15,000 stipend. Applicants must submit applications by January 1 to be considered for university fellowships.

INTERNATIONAL STUDENT SUPPORT

The International Students Center (ISC) provides orientation to school and community. ISC offers various services such as counseling, referrals, and visa and immigration assistance

Through the ISC, students can participate in international organizations and social and cultural functions. Some of the programs offered include the International Friends program, which matches international students with a local FSU student for cultural exchange, and the Small World Speakers Bureau, which organizes talks by international students on campus and in the community. There are organizations for, among others, Asian, Caribbean, Chinese, Japanese, Korean, Turkish students.

The ISC holds an annual International Festival, a week long series of cultural expositions and educational events, and organizes Global Gatherings, a weekly series on international topics of interest.

ADMISSIONS AT A GLANCE

Minimum GMAT:	550
Minimum GPA:	3.0 undergrad; 3.5 grad
Minimum TOEFL (paper):	600
Minimum TOEFL (computer):	250
Application Fee:	US$20
Application Deadline:	US: May; Int'l: Feb 1

EXPENSES AT A GLANCE

Tuition per year:	
In State:	US$5,830
Out-of-State:	US$15,210
Int'l Students:	US$15,210
Books & Supplies:	US$2,000 per year
Health Insurance:	US$500 per year
Accommodation:	
University Residences:	US$2,400 per year
Family Housing:	–
Private:	US$500-700 per month

PROGRAM FACTS

# of Full-time Students:	68
# of Part-time Students:	–
# of Applications per year:	95-100
# Accepted per year:	20
# Enrolled per year:	15
Average GMAT Score:	640
Average Age:	29
% Men/Women:	53%/47%
Work Experience (avg yrs):	7
# of Faculty:	100
% Faculty with Doctoral Degree:	100%
Annual Research Funding:	varies

FLORIDA STATE UNIVERSITY, COLLEGE OF BUSINESS

UNIVERSITY AND LOCATION

Founded in 1857, Florida State University currently has 16 major divisions including the colleges of Arts and Sciences, Business, Communication, Education, Engineering, Human Sciences, Law and Social Science and the schools of Criminology and Criminal Justice, Film, Information Studies, Music, Nursing, Social Work, Theatre, and Visual Arts and Dance. The colleges and schools offer courses of study in 25 major disciplines.

FSU is one of 88 doctoral degree-granting research institutions in the US classified as a Research I university by the Carnegie Foundation.

The university's Robert Manning Strozier Library, one of six libraries on campus, holds over two million books and periodicals and is a depository for United Nations documents. The library has more than 300 computers with access to the Internet and hundreds of electronic databases including LEXIS-NEXIS.

The Charles A. Rovetta building, which has 76,000 square feet of classroom space, offices and support facilities, is the home of the COB. There are 17 classrooms in the building with a new presentation system that offers a video projector, Pentium III 500 MHz computers with Ethernet Internet access, a document camera, VCR and cable TV, laptop computer connection cables and AMX control panels.

The COB technology center offers students three labs with a total of 52 computers with Intel 200 MMX processors, full multimedia capabilities, CD–ROM, headphones, and each lab has two laser printers and two scanners. The lab for PhD students has similar equipment and 16 workstations.

FSU's location in Tallahassee, the capital city of Florida, provides

students the opportunity to interact with local government and federal agencies for research and possible employment. Offering its residents all amenities normally found in major metropolitan centers, Tallahassee enjoys a tropical climate and the surrounding landscape features many lakes, natural springs and underwater caves for swimming and exploration. Beautiful beaches on the Gulf of Mexico are located only a 30-minute drive away.

FACULTY
- Ang, J.S. PhD, Purdue
- Anthony, W.P. PhD, Ohio State
- Ahuja, M. PhD, Pittsburgh
- Bathke, A.W. PhD, Florida State
- Benesh, G.A. PhD, Virginia Tech
- Billings, B. PhD, Pennsylvania State
- Braswell, R.C. PhD, Florida State
- Brown, S.L. PhD, Florida
- Brusco, M. PhD, Florida State
- Celec, S.E. PhD, North Carolina
- Choudhury, V. PhD, UCLA
- Christiansen, W.A. PhD, Utah
- Clark, J.A. PhD, Illinois
- Coats, P.K. PhD, Nebraska
- Corbett, R. PhD, Georgia State
- Cradit, J.D. PhD, Iowa
- Cronin, J.J. PhD, Ohio State
- Downs, P.E. PhD, North Carolina
- Dumm, R.E. PhD, Georgia
- Dunn, C.L. PhD, Michigan State
- Durtschi, C. PhD, Arizona
- Dusenbury, R. PhD, Arizona
- Eastman, K.L. PhD, Pennsylvania
- Fennema, M. PhD, Illinois
- Fiorito, J. PhD, Illinois
- Flint, D. PhD, Tennessee
- Flynn, L. PhD, Alabama
- Freiden, J.B. PhD, Oklahoma

City Population:	125,000
Cost of Living:	medium
Climate Range:	38° to 90°F
Campus Setting:	urban
Total Enrollment:	31,193
Graduate Enrollment:	5,600
Students in Residence:	–

- George, J. PhD, California-Irvine
- Gerard, G. PhD, Michigan State
- Giunipero, L. PhD, Michigan State
- Goldsmith, R.E. PhD, Alabama
- Hillison, W.A. PhD, Florida
- Hofacker, C.F. PhD, California
- Hult, G.T.M. PhD, Memphis
- Humphrey, D.B. PhD, Berkeley
- Icerman, R.C. PhD, Florida State
- Kacmar, K.M. PhD, Texas A&M
- Karahana, E. PhD, Minnesota
- Ketchen, D. PhD, Pennsylvania State
- Knight, G. PhD, Michigan State
- Lamont, B.T. PhD, North Carolina
- Maroney, P.F. JD, Florida
- Marshall, R.A. PhD, Pennsylvania
- Martinko, M.J. PhD, Nebraska
- Mason, R. PhD, Georgia Tech
- McIntyre, E.V. PhD, North Carolina
- McKnight, H. PhD, Minnesota
- Morton, R. PhD, Pennsylvania State
- Nast, D.A. PhD, Pennsylvania State
- Nosari, E.J. PhD, Kentucky
- Osteryoung, J.S. PhD, Georgia State
- Paterson, J. PhD, Georgia
- Perrewe, P.L. PhD, Nebraska
- Peterson, D.R. PhD, North Carolina
- Peterson, P.P. PhD, North Carolina
- Rai, A. PhD, New York
- Reimers, J. PhD, Michigan
- Sabherwal, R. PhD, Pittsburgh
- Scott, E. PhD, Florida State
- Showalter, M. PhD, Ohio State
- Simmonds, P.G. PhD, Temple
- Stepina, L.P. PhD, Illinois
- Stith, M.T. PhD, Syracuse
- Turner, R.G. PhD, Kentucky
- Voich, Jr., D. PhD, Illinois
- Wilson, D. PhD, Ohio State
- Zenz, G. PhD, Wisconsin

ILLINOIS INSTITUTE OF TECHNOLOGY
PhD IN MANAGEMENT SCIENCE

Stuart
GRADUATE SCHOOL OF BUSINESS
Illinois Institute of Technology

Program Highlights

- *Full- and part-time programs*
- *Concentrations in operations and finance available*
- *Students benefit from proximity to Chicago's financial district and from interactions with Stuart's experienced faculty*
- *Quantitative Research Lab provides an interactive computer-based learning environment featuring real-time market feeds, a simulated trading environment and industry software*
- *Accredited by AACSB*

CONTACT INFORMATION

PhD in Management Science
Stuart School of Business
565 West Adams Street
Chicago, Illinois USA 60661-3691
PH: 1-312-906-6515
FAX: 1-312-906-6549
EMAIL: degrees@stuart.iit.edu
INTERNET: http://www.stuart.iit.edu

ILLINOIS INSTITUTE OF TECHNOLOGY, PhD IN MANAGEMENT SCIENCE

PROGRAM OVERVIEW

The Stuart Graduate School of Business (Stuart) at the Illinois Institute of Technology (IIT) offers a full- or part-time PhD program in management science with concentrations in operations and finance.

The program emphasizes analysis and synthesis in management science. Courses provide the tools to analyze problems into their component parts and then to synthesize new systems or new solutions. Dissertation work involves identifying a problem in the area of operations or finance, gathering data and applying the methodologies of management science to arrive at a solution.

The program is small and selective with a high degree of faculty/student interaction and a mentor relationship with a faculty adviser whose area of expertise matches the student's interests.

Degree Requirements

The PhD program typically requires the equivalent of three to four years of full-time study. Students complete 94.6 quarter credit hours beyond the master's degree, of which 32.4 are devoted to dissertation research. Seventeen quarter courses must be completed, including six core courses, eight electives in the area of concentration, three adviser-approved open electives and, for students planning an academic career, a single credit practicum.

Upon completion of core coursework, a written qualifying examination is required. After completion of elective coursework, a written comprehensive examination is required. This examination is a rigorous review of the level of competency achieved as a result of the entire program of graduate study except for the dissertation. The comprehensive examination may include an oral component.

The research project must be an original investigation of high quality with the results submitted in the form of a dissertation and a related publishable paper. An oral defense of the thesis must be completed before a committee.

Operations

Candidates in the operations concentration learn how the optimization of resources – people, technology, finance and information – can be effectively integrated for competitive advantage. Participants are trained in advanced operations integration tools and the application of the latest technologies.

Areas of research include design of quality systems, strategic management, forecasting, materials management, scheduling, economics of FMS and CIM, manufacturing strategy, management of technology-based businesses and strategic management of manufacturing firms.

Finance

The concentration in finance emphasizes the application of the techniques of management science to the area of finance.

The finance concentration is based on the core competencies of the PhD program in economics, simulation, optimization and data analysis. Elective courses focus on the application of these disciplines for financial forecasting, modeling and the valuation of financial instruments. Participants benefit from the school's proximity to the Chicago financial district and from interactions with faculty who work in the financial services industry.

Academic and Technological Resources

The Information Center contains the holdings of the Stuart Business Library and important collections of the European Union, the International Monetary Fund and the International Labor Organization. It provides access to IIT's networked computing facilities, including local and remote online research systems and CD-ROM databases.

Computer labs at the downtown campus contain 70 workstations linked to the Internet and networked with IIT libraries. The PC lab has spreadsheet, word processing and database programs used in business and the quantitative research lab features simulated trading, investment analysis software and industry databases.

SELECTED RESEARCH AREAS

- Assembly systems
- Business cycle theory and economic growth
- Development economics
- Economics and finance
- Effective organizations
- Energy economics
- Finance
- Forecasting
- Forecasting methods
- Futures and options markets
- Game theory
- Interest rate models
- International business
- International finance
- Inventory policy
- Investments
- Management science
- Mathematical programming and its application
- Models and techniques for options pricing
- Optimal control of queuing systems
- Production and operations management
- Production planning and control
- Productivity improvement
- Quality control
- Quality improvement
- Quantitative research models in finance
- Quantity discounts in inventory planning
- Queuing theory
- Risk management
- Statistical modeling and computer programming for manufacturing processes
- Statistics
- Strategic planning

ILLINOIS INSTITUTE OF TECHNOLOGY, PhD IN MANAGEMENT SCIENCE

ADMISSIONS CRITERIA & PROCEDURES

To be considered for admission to the PhD in management science program, applicants must have an outstanding academic record, a demonstrated ability for research and teaching, and a commitment to making a contribution to the profession of management. Successful applicants will usually have completed a master's degree and the business core at either the graduate or undergraduate level. Applicants who have a master's degree but have not completed the business core will be required to complete some business prerequisite courses after admission.

Applicants must submit a formal application for admission, three letters of recommendation, copies of all postsecondary transcripts and a recent GMAT or GRE score report.

International applicants must submit a financial affidavit for an I-20 or IAP-66 visa to be issued. Applicants from non-English speaking countries must also submit a score of at least 550 on the paper-based TOEFL, taken within the last two years, unless they have a postsecondary degree from an accredited institution in the US.

Admission takes place in the fall quarter only. The application deadline is August 1.

EXPENSES & FINANCIAL ASSISTANCE

Students in Stuart's PhD in management science program pay tuition fees of US$1,800 per course. The approximate cost of books and supplies is US$1,500 and on-campus housing is available for US$9,000 per year. Off-campus room and board can be expected to cost approximately US$650 to $800 per month.

Stuart offers partial tuition scholarships on a competitive basis to full-time students. Students should indicate their interest in such scholarships on their applications. IIT alumni may receive a one-third reduction in tuition for one course each quarter under the ALUMED program.

Several low-interest federal loan programs – the Stafford Loan, the Supplemental Loan for Students and the Perkins Loan – may be available to qualified US citizens and permanent residents.

INTERNATIONAL STUDENT SUPPORT

The International Center (IC) provides support services to international students and scholars on matters related to orientation, personal, visa, and immigration concerns. Social, cultural and educational events are planned by the center and open to all students. The IC organizes workshops on topics of interest to international students such as income tax requirements and off-campus employment opportunities.

The International Student Organization (ISO) provides resources for international students and helps them adjust to life in the US and the American education system. It also organizes community, pre-college and college outreach programs to encourage international students to attend IIT.

There are a number of student-run organizations at IIT including associations of students from countries such as Hong Kong, Turkey, India, Korea, Malaysia and Pakistan.

ADMISSIONS AT A GLANCE

Minimum GMAT:	600
Minimum GPA:	3.5
Minimum TOEFL (paper):	550
Minimum TOEFL (computer):	–
Application Fee:	US$50
Application Deadline:	Aug 1 (fall semester)

EXPENSES AT A GLANCE*

Tuition per course:
- In State: US$1,800
- Out-of-State: US$1,800
- Int'l Students: US$1,800

Books & Supplies: US$1,500
Health Insurance: –
Accommodation:
- University Residences: US$9,000 per year
- Family Housing: –
- Private: US$650–800 per month

*Expenses are for 1999–2000

PROGRAM FACTS

# of Full-time Students:	5
# of Part-time Students:	14
# of Applications per year:	27
# Accepted per year:	14
# Enrolled per year:	7
Average GMAT Score:	620
Average Age:	30
% Men/Women:	75%/25%
Work Experience (avg yrs):	10
# of Faculty:	12
% Faculty with Doctoral Degree:	100%
Annual Research Funding:	–

ILLINOIS INSTITUTE OF TECHNOLOGY, PhD IN MANAGEMENT SCIENCE

UNIVERSITY AND LOCATION

Established in 1890, IIT is a private, degree-granting university with programs in engineering, science, psychology, architecture, business, design and law. One of 17 elite institutions in the Association of Independent Technological Universities (AITU), IIT offers exceptional preparation for professions that require technological sophistication. Through a committed faculty and close personal attention, IIT provides challenging academic programs focused on practical concerns. The university's 6,000 students come from every state in the US and 80 other countries. IIT is accredited by the North Central Association of Colleges and Secondary Schools, the primary accreditation body for universities in its region.

IIT offers bachelor's, master's, doctorate, and law degrees, as well as certificate programs, through six colleges and schools: Armour College, the College of Architecture, the Stuart Graduate School of Business, the Institute of Design, the Institute of Psychology, and the Chicago-Kent College of Law.

IIT has five campuses in the Chicago area. The 120-acre main campus, located at 33rd and State in Chicago, and many of its buildings were designed by Ludwig Mies van der Rohe, former director of the IIT architecture program. In 1976, the American Institute of Architects recognized the campus as one of the 200 most significant works of architecture in the US. The 10-story downtown campus at 565 West Adams Street houses the Chicago-Kent College of Law, the Master of Public Administration Program, and the Stuart Graduate School of Business. The Institute of Design, an international leader in teaching systemic, human-centered design, is located in Chicago's Near North neighborhood. The 19-acre Daniel F. and Ada L. Rice Campus in Wheaton offers graduate programs, upper-level undergraduate courses, and continuing professional education. The five-acre Moffett Campus in Bedford Park houses the National Center for Food Safety and Technology, a consortium that seeks to improve the quality of our nation's food supply.

Located on the shores of Lake Michigan in the heart of the US and of the midwest, Chicago is a city with a diverse population and an impressive array of cultural and entertainment facilities. There are more than 40 museums, 200 theaters and 7,000 restaurants in the city of Chicago and it is home to the Sears Tower, the Amoco Building and the John Hancock building, three of the tallest man-made structures in the world. Outdoor amenities include 29 miles of lakefront, 552 parks and 18 miles of lakefront bicycle paths. The Art Institute of Chicago is the site of the largest collection of Impressionist paintings outside of the Louvre and the Harold Washington Library Center, with more than two million books, is the world's largest public library.

City Population:	2,783,726
Cost of Living:	medium
Climate Range:	15° to 85°F
Campus Setting:	urban
Total Enrollment:	5,906
Graduate Enrollment:	1,801
Students in Residence:	–

FACULTY
- Bilson, J.F.O. PhD, Chicago
- Boonstra, B.K. PhD, Michigan
- Hassan, M.Z. PhD, Illinois Institute of Technology
- Imam, S.A. PhD, Illinois Institute of Technology
- Knowles, T.W. PhD, Chicago
- Kumiega, A. PhD, Illinois at Chicago
- LaHaye, L. PhD, Chicago
- Moffitt, S.D. PhD, Texas at Houston
- Prabhaker, P.R. PhD, Rochester
- Thomopoulos, N.T. PhD, Illinois Institute of Technology
- Tourk, K.A. PhD, Berkeley
- Zabinsky, H. PhD, Rochester

KENT STATE UNIVERSITY

PhD in Business Administration

Program Highlights

- *Four major and eight minor areas of study offered*
- *Fellowships carry nine-credit-hour tuition waivers each semester and an annual stipend of US$12,000*
- *Accredited by AACSB*

CONTACT INFORMATION
Graduate School of Management
PO Box 5190
Kent, Ohio USA 44242 - 0001
PH: 1-330-672-2282 Ext. 235
FAX: 1-330-672-7303
EMAIL: gradbus@bsa3.kent.edu
INTERNET: http://business.kent.edu

KENT STATE UNIVERSITY, PhD IN BUSINESS ADMINISTRATION

PROGRAM OVERVIEW

The Graduate School of Management (GSM) at Kent State University offers a Doctor of Philosophy (PhD) in business administration degree. This program is designed to prepare qualified candidates for positions in university teaching and research, or administrative and research careers with government and private organizations. PhD students can major in accounting, finance, management systems or marketing and are required to complete a minor program of study in accounting, finance, management systems, marketing, economics, international economics, international business, applied statistics or another area approved by the advisor. The PhD is a full-time program with admission in the fall term. Kent State University Graduate School of Management is accredited by AACSB — the International Association for Management Education.

Coursework Requirements

Students must complete up to nine proficiency courses, five courses in the major area, up to four courses in the minor area and six courses of supportive and other coursework.

Proficiency courses ensure that all PhD students have a level of understanding of general business with the breadth and depth of an AACSB-accredited Master of Business Administration (MBA) program. These include courses in accounting, administrative science, economics, finance and marketing as well as one course each in international business and business strategy. Students who hold an MBA from an AACSB-accredited institution can expect to have most of these proficiency courses waived, provided they were completed with a minimum grade of B or better in each. Students with a Bachelor of Business Administration (BBA) degree from an AACSB-accredited school may also have some proficiency coursework waived. Six to nine undergraduate credit hours with grades of B or better are normally required to waive one three-credit-hour graduate-level course. Students complete the proficiency requirements in the first year of the PhD program.

Coursework in the major involves five courses, followed by a required comprehensive examination. The minor may be satisfied either by the completion of three courses and a comprehensive examination or by the completion of four courses, depending on the area.

Students must complete three courses in research methods and economics and three research methodology courses designed to enhance the area of concentration. Graduate courses in other departments may be substituted with the instructor's consent and approval by the associate dean of the GSM.

Each student must satisfy a residency requirement of at least 18 credit hours in two consecutive semesters, either fall to spring, or spring followed by fall. Summer semesters cannot be used to fulfill the residency requirement. A student must complete a minimum of nine hours in each semester to be counted toward the residency requirement, which must be fulfilled within two years of the start of the program.

Coursework takes a minimum of two years to complete and students are then eligible to take the comprehensive examinations.

Dissertation and Defense

The dissertation must demonstrate the student's ability to conduct research in a discriminating and original manner and should represent a contribution to the field significant enough to warrant adaptation for publication in a professional journal. The oral defense of the dissertation is open to the university community and a candidate passes if there is no more than one dissenting vote from the examining committee.

SELECTED RESEARCH AREAS

- Accounting history and regulation
- Advertising effects
- Applied microeconomics
- Auditing
- Automated systems development
- Consumer and marketing ethics
- Consumer satisfaction
- Corporate finance
- Decision theory
- Electronic commerce
- Financial reporting
- Housing and mortgage markets
- Human resource management and organizational behavior
- Information systems and competitive advantage
- Insurance and risk
- International asset pricing
- Labor economics
- Leadership
- Macro-organization theory
- Market anomalies
- Marketing research
- Marketing strategy and entrepreneurship
- Monetary theory
- Networks and services
- Neural networks and optimization
- Operations management
- Personality and consumer behavior
- Policy implications of equal employment opportunity
- Poverty
- Quantitative methods
- Regional economics
- Scheduling theory
- Strategic information systems
- Strategies for high-performance organizations and total quality management
- Tax

KENT STATE UNIVERSITY, PHD IN BUSINESS ADMINISTRATION

ADMISSIONS CRITERIA & PROCEDURES

The GSM welcomes applications from individuals with backgrounds in business and in other areas such as liberal arts or engineering. Every application is considered individually, with admission decisions based on the applicant's abilities and motivation to complete the program. Quantitative measures are important, as are work experience, demonstrated leadership, entrepreneurship, extracurricular and volunteer activities, and letters of recommendation.

Admission to the program is limited to persons with outstanding potential for doctoral study and for later professional achievement. Most students have masters degrees in business or related fields and many have prior teaching and business experience.

Admission decisions are based on of scholarly accomplishment in undergraduate and graduate coursework, the GMAT score, letters of recommendation, the applicant's resume, and a statement of educational and career objectives.

Competence in written and verbal English is expected of all students. International students whose native language is not English must achieve a minimum score of 600 on the paper-based TOEFL.

PhD applications are reviewed once a year in the spring for fall admission.

EXPENSES & FINANCIAL ASSISTANCE

PhD students who are residents of Ohio pay tuition fees of US$5,334 per academic year. Out-of-state and international students in the PhD program pay tuition fees of US$10,238 per academic year. The university's medical insurance plan costs US$498 per year and students should expect to pay US$600 to $800 for books and supplies. On-campus housing is available for graduate students at an average cost of US$600 per month, including meal plan.

The GSM offers teaching fellowships to most Ph.D. students on a competitive basis. Departments usually provide students with four years of funding. Appointments are based on academic standing and departmental needs. These positions carry stipends of about US$9,000 per academic year plus a tuition waiver to cover fees for nine hours of credit each semester. All appointees must carry at least eight semester hours of graduate credit per semester. Doctoral students perform a variety of teaching and research duties. Most teaching fellows provide about 20 hours of teaching and research service per week.

Doctoral students have the option of accepting summer teaching assignments that provide an additional US$3,000 stipend. Summer tuition for up to six credit hours is waived for doctoral assistants.

INTERNATIONAL STUDENT SUPPORT

The Office of International Student Affairs (OISA) is the central resource for international students seeking assistance with academic advising, cultural adjustment and emergency support, and is responsible for matters related to immigration and visa status. The OISA works closely with the Center for International & Comparative Programs (CICP), the Office of Campus Life (OCL) and other university offices to facilitating the international enrichment academic environment.

Special programs sponsored by the OISA include the International Awards Program, periodic immigration updates, a shuttle bus service from the airport to the campus before the beginning of each semester and orientation programs for new international students.

Admissions at a Glance
Minimum GMAT:	not available
Minimum GPA:	not available
Minimum TOEFL (paper):	600
Minimum TOEFL (computer):	250
Application Fee:	US$30
Application Deadline:	
US: Feb 1;	
Int'l: Aug 1 (one year prior to desired entry)	

Expenses at a Glance
Tuition:
In State:	US$5,334 per year
Out-of-State:	US$10,238 per year
Int'l Students:	US$10,238 per year

Books & Supplies: US$800 per year
Health Insurance: US$498 per year
Accommodation
University Residences:	US$600 per month
Family Housing:	–
Private:	–

Program Facts
# of Full-time Students:	62
# of Part-time Students:	0
# of Applications per year:	44
# Accepted per year:	18
# Enrolled per year:	10
Average GMAT Score:	614
Average Age:	39
% Men/Women:	70%/30%
Work Experience (avg yrs):	–
# of Faculty:	54
% Faculty with Doctoral Degree:	96%
Annual Research Funding:	–

KENT STATE UNIVERSITY, PhD IN BUSINESS ADMINISTRATION

UNIVERSITY AND LOCATION

Kent State University is a state-assisted comprehensive university dedicated to promoting academic excellence, advancing knowledge and providing public service. It offers more than 170 major career fields through the colleges of Arts and Science, Business Administration, Education, Fine and Professional Arts and the schools of Nursing and Technology. Kent also offers 13 degrees in 37 programs at the master's level and 20 areas of specialization study for the doctorate. Current enrollment is about 26,000, including close to 5,000 graduate students and approximately 500 international students from 70 countries.

Kent is fully accredited and has been granted maturity status for its graduate programs by the North-central Association of Colleges and Schools. Twenty-seven individual programs are accredited or approved by professional agencies and organizations and the university holds Research II status with the Carnegie Foundation.

The libraries at Kent make up the largest state-assisted library system in northeastern Ohio and their holdings include more than 1.8 million volumes, one million microforms and extensive collections of other media. Students are provided with free computer accounts with email and Internet access and residence halls are connected to the university's network.

Kent's housing program provides residence hall accommodation to 5,000 undergraduate and graduate students and apartment accommodations are available for students with spouses or children.

Situated on 824 acres of rolling, tree-covered land in Kent, Ohio, the university campus features 103 buildings.

The city of Kent has a population of approximately 30,000 people and lies within 50 miles of the northeastern Ohio cities of Cleveland, Youngstown, Akron and Canton. The Cleveland Orchestra, the Ohio Ballet, art galleries and museums are all within an hour's drive. Northeastern Ohio has 12 state parks and the Cuyahoga Valley National Recreation Area, which features hiking trails and nature preserves, and is the site of an annual traditional music festival. Other attractions include ski resorts and professional sports teams.

City Population:	30,000
Cost of Living:	medium
Climate Range:	18° to 82°F
Campus Setting:	suburban
Total Enrollment:	20,947
Graduate Enrollment:	4,633
Students in Residence:	5,000

FACULTY

- Acar, W. PhD, Pennsylvania
- Alam, P. PhD, Houston
- Albanese, P.J. PhD, Harvard
- Altieri, M. LLM, New York
- Baker, J.C. DBA, Indiana
- Bakes, C. PhD, Penn State
- Barniv, R. PhD, Ohio State
- Beier, L.Y. JD, Akron
- Booth, D.E. PhD, North Carolina
- Boyd, J.W. PhD, Arkansas
- Bridges, E. PhD, Northwestern
- Brown, J.R. PhD, MIT
- Brown, R.E. DPA, Harvard
- Casper, C.A. PhD, Case Western Reserve
- Curcio, R.J. PhD, Penn State
- DuBois, C.L. PhD, Minnesota
- Duncan, N. PhD, Texas A&M
- Ellis, M.A. PhD, Texas A&M
- Faley, R.H. PhD, Tennessee - Knoxville
- Fetyko, D.F. PhD, Michigan State
- Grimm, P. PhD, SUNY at Buffalo
- Healy, J.P. PhD, SUNY at Buffalo
- Howard, G. DBA, Kent State
- Hu, M.Y. PhD, Minnesota
- Jiang, C.X. PhD, Drexel
- Kent, R.J. PhD, Berkeley
- Kolbe, R.H. PhD, Cincinnati
- Krampf, R.F. PhD, Cincinnati
- Madey, G. PhD, Case Western Reserve
- Marks, L.J. PhD, Penn State
- Mayo, M.A. PhD, Kent State
- McKee, D.L. PhD, Notre Dame
- Mendelow, A.L. DBL, South Africa
- Mount, R.I. PhD, Purdue
- Offodile, O.F. PhD, Texas Tech
- Patuwo, B.E. PhD, Virginia Tech
- Pearson, M.A. DBA, Kent State
- Qi, M. PhD, Ohio State
- Ryans, Jr., J.K. DBA, Indiana
- Schroath, F.W. PhD, South Carolina
- Severiens, J.T. PhD, Iowa
- Shanker, M.S. PhD, Minnesota
- Shanklin, W.L. DBA, Maryland College Park
- Smith, R.D. PhD, Penn State
- Steinberg, G.D. PhD, Temple
- Stevens, G.E. DBA, Kent State
- Thomas, G.N. PhD, Washington - Seattle
- Troutt, M.D. PhD, Illinois
- Upton, C.W. PhD, Carnegie Mellon
- Weinroth, G.J. PhD, Union - Ohio
- Williams, D.R. PhD, Northwestern College
- Wilson, K. PhD, Wisconsin - Madison
- Zucca, L.J. PhD, Case Western Reserve

THE OHIO STATE UNIVERSITY
FISHER COLLEGE OF BUSINESS

Program Highlights

- *Ranked 25 by the Gourman Report*
- *Home of the Journal of Location Science and the International Journal of Logistics Management*
- *A Center for International Business Education and Research*
- *New integrated business campus*

CONTACT INFORMATION
100 Gerlach Hall
2108 Neil Avenue
Columbus, Ohio USA 43210-1144
PH: 1-614-292-8511
FAX: 1-614-292-9006
EMAIL: cobgrd@cob.ohio-state.edu
INTERNET: http://www.cob.ohio-state.edu

THE OHIO STATE UNIVERSITY, FISHER COLLEGE OF BUSINESS

PROGRAM OVERVIEW

The Fisher College of Business (Fisher) at The Ohio State University (OSU) offers three doctoral study options in business administration, labor and human resources, and accounting and management information systems.

The greatest strength of the Fisher College PhD program is its top faculty and concomitant emphasis on research and teaching. In addition, the facilities and resources on the Ohio State campus enhance the doctoral experience. Another strength is the College's proximity to the corporate headquarters of a variety of businesses within the technology, service and manufacturing sectors. Fisher College's involvement with the business community in Columbus offers students extensive access to research sites and senior executives.

The Fisher College strategically manages the size of its PhD programs through a careful analysis of market and budgetary conditions and other factors. The college matches national demand for doctoral student graduates and commitment to program quality. Over the past few years the college has dedicated more faculty time and a greater share of resources to each doctoral student. The result is a small and efficient, high quality program.

Accounting & Management Information Systems

The accounting and management information systems (AMIS) program involves specialization in either accounting or management information systems. Students often elect minors in microeconomic theory and statistics or decision theory.

The first three years of the program consist of coursework and seminars which emphasize current research. Courses stress information economics, behavioral accounting and information systems.

Students participate in the accounting and management information systems research workshop which is offered weekly during autumn, winter and spring quarters. The workshop keeps students abreast of current developments in their field, provides a forum for discussion and introduces them to many of the nation's top scholars.

Business Administration

Doctoral students who choose the business administration program can select from a number of areas of emphasis. Management sciences comprises two overarching disciplines: decision sciences and operations management. The finance faculty also teaches in real estate and insurance, and the marketing faculty is responsible for the logistics program. The management and human resources faculty includes international business, organizational theory, and strategy.

Labor & Human Resources

The PhD program in labor and human resources approaches the study of the employment relationship and the design and impact of alternative managerial systems such as recruitment, training, and compensation of employees from a foundation of various social sciences. The program also emphasizes human resource policy issues at the societal/governmental level.

In recent years, the labor and human resources program has been redesigned into a series of integrated modules, including a macro cohort offered in even years in the areas of strategic management and international business, and a micro cohort offered in odd number years consisting of courses in human resources, industrial relations, and organizational behavior. The new single track of study provides students with a comprehensive understanding of all aspects of the employment relationship, while the modular design affords greater flexibility in meeting market demands.

SELECTED RESEARCH AREAS
- Accounting information systems
- Business climate and culture
- Business ethics
- Consumer learning
- Corporate finance
- Economics of cardiovascular surgery
- Emerging employment relationships
- Employee motivation
- Employment law
- Executive compensation
- Facility location decisions
- International finance
- Joint ventures and alliances
- Managerial behavior
- Marketing of the Health Care services
- Negotiations dynamics and processes
- New product development
- Non-profit marketing
- Planning and financial analysis of the wholesale distribution industry
- Production scheduling
- Promotion strategies
- Real estate law
- Reengineering technology
- Risk management
- Shareholder wealth
- Strategic management
- Supply chain management
- Taxation
- Temporary employees
- The audit services market
- Total quality management
- Transportation planning
- Workforce development

THE OHIO STATE UNIVERSITY, FISHER COLLEGE OF BUSINESS

ADMISSIONS CRITERIA & PROCEDURES

The PhD program is designed for full-time students. Autumn Quarter entry into the program is strongly recommended. The application deadline is January 15.

Applicants must submit a completed application form and non-refundable fee (US$30 domestic, US$40 international), plus an official sealed copy of transcripts, with English translations, from each postsecondary institution attended. In addition, the Fisher College requires a copy of official TOEFL and TSE scores from students whose native language is not English, even if the applicant received a degree from an English-speaking university. All applicants are required to submit three references written on the referee's letterhead, a resume, and an autobiographical statement highlighting academic and work experience, career objectives and motivation for pursuing a PhD.

EXPENSES & FINANCIAL ASSISTANCE

The Ohio State University directs funds specifically to doctoral students at the university and college level. Grants to students come in the form of dissertation grants, fellowships, foreign government support and military fellowships.

All doctoral students in the college who are not otherwise funded are employed as graduate associates. These positions may involve teaching, assisting faculty in research, and/or administrative activities. Graduate funding is available for four years.

INTERNATIONAL STUDENT SUPPORT

OSU's International Friendships, Inc. student organization offers airport pick-up for arriving students, temporary housing arrangements with American host families and field trips to introduce international students to the Columbus area and American culture.

ADMISSIONS AT A GLANCE

Minimum GMAT:	600
Minimum GPA:	no set minimum
Minimum TOEFL (paper):	600
Minimum TOEFL (computer):	–
Application Fee:	
US$30 (dom)	
US$40 (int'l)	
Application Deadline:	Jan 15

EXPENSES AT A GLANCE

Tuition per year:	
In State:	US$5,730
Out-of-State:	US$14,865
Int'l Students:	US$14,865
Books & Supplies:	US$1,500 per year
Health Insurance:	US$594 per year
Accommodation:	
University Residences:	US$6,540 per year
Family Housing:	–
Private:	–

PROGRAM FACTS

# of Full-time Students:	70
# of Part-time Students:	0
# of Applications per year:	300
# Accepted per year:	20-25
# Enrolled per year:	15
Average GMAT Score:	656
Average Age:	28
% Men/Women:	64%/36%
Work Experience (avg yrs):	6.8
# of Faculty:	111
% Faculty with Doctoral Degree:	98%
Annual Research Funding:	US$236.3 million

THE OHIO STATE UNIVERSITY, FISHER COLLEGE OF BUSINESS

UNIVERSITY AND LOCATION

The Ohio State University has 27 individual libraries with nearly five million print volumes and 4.2 million microforms, one of the largest academic library systems in North America. In addition to this collection there is the OhioLINK system which includes library collections at other universities in the state.

The Fisher College of Business is served by its own library which contains more than 180,000 volumes, specialized indexes, over 1,900 current serials and approximately 360,000 microforms including corporate reports, annual reports and materials on CD-ROM. It also maintains the Bloomberg financial markets online service.

The FCB complex consists of six buildings with 390,000 square feet of offices, classrooms, seminar rooms, the Bank One Graduate Lounge, the Batten Investment Laboratory, a communications lab, offices for graduate assistants, and student activity rooms. Classrooms are equipped with computer ports and all students are provided with email accounts and access to the World Wide Web.

The Business Resource Building houses a reference library, a decision-conferencing lab, a computing center, a research lab, and an information and reference center.

The city of Columbus has professional symphony, ballet and opera companies. Recreational opportunities include a zoo, golf courses and a metro park system.

City Population:	670,235
Cost of Living:	medium
Climate Range:	27° to 74°F
Campus Setting:	urban
Total Enrollment:	52,233
Graduate Enrollment:	10,047
Students in Residence:	9,400

FACULTY

- Allenby, G.M. PhD, Chicago
- Alutto, J.A. PhD, Cornell
- Anil, A. PhD, Iowa
- Ballam, D.A. PhD, Ohio State
- Barney, J.B. PhD, Yale
- Benapudi, V. PhD, Kansas
- Bendapudi, N.M. PhD, Kansas
- Benton, W.C. PhD, Indiana
- Bentz, W.F. PhD, Ohio State
- Berry, W.L. DBA, Harvard
- Blackburn, J.D. JD, Cincinnati
- Blackwell, R.D. PhD, Northwestern
- Boone, T. PhD, North Carolina
- Brunarski, K. PhD, Ohio State
- Bryant, L. PhD, Colorado
- Burnkrant, R.E. PhD, Illinois
- Buser, S.A. PhD, Boston College
- Butler, J. PhD, Texas
- Carr, A.S. PhD, Arizona State
- Chu, P.C. PhD, Texas
- Cole, D.W. DBA, Indiana
- Collier, D.A. PhD, Ohio State
- Cooper, M.C. PhD, Ohio State
- Croxton, K.L. PhD, MIT
- Current, J.R. PhD, John Hopkins
- Dix, J.F. BS, John Carroll
- Easton, P.D. PhD, Berkeley
- Ellington, J. PhD, Minnesota
- Fellingham, J.C. PhD, UCLA
- Fine, L.M. PhD, Tennessee
- Ford, J.D. PhD, Ohio State
- Ginter, J.L. PhD, Purdue
- Goldstein, R.S. PhD, Berkeley
- Greenberg, J. PhD, Wayne State
- Greenberger, D.B. PhD, Wisconsin
- Hall, N. PhD, Berkeley
- Harris, J. PhD, Ohio State
- Haugtvedt, C.P. PhD, Missouri
- Helwege, J. PhD, UCLA
- Hendershott, P.H. PhD, Purdue
- Heneman, R.L. PhD, Michigan State
- Hills, S.M. PhD, Wisconsin
- Hirshleifer, D. PhD, Chicago
- Jennings, E.H. PhD, Michigan
- Jensen, D.L. PhD, Ohio State
- Josephs, S.L. MA, Warwick
- Karolyi, G.A. PhD, Chicago
- Kim, J.S. PhD, Michigan State
- Kinard, J.C. PhD, Stanford
- Kiousis, P.K. PhD, UCLA
- Klayman, E.I. LLM, Harvard
- Klein, H.J. PhD, Michigan State
- Krasniewski, R.J. PhD, Purdue
- La Londe, B.J. PhD, Michigan State
- Lambert, D.M. PhD, Ohio State
- Leiblein, M. PhD, Purdue
- Leone, R.P. PhD, Purdue
- Leong, G.K. PhD, South Carolina
- Lewicki, R.J. PhD, Columbia
- Mangum, S.L. PhD, G. Washington
- Mathews, H.L. PhD, Ohio State
- Milligan, G.W. PhD, Ohio State
- Minton, B.A. PhD, Chicago
- Mitchell, V. PhD, Florida State
- Muhanna, W.A. PhD, Wisconsin
- Murdock, R.J. PhD, Cornell
- Nault, B. PhD, British Columbia
- Noe, R. PhD, Michigan State
- Nutt, P.C. PhD, Wisconsin
- Pao, J. PhD, British Columbia
- Paul, T.D. DA, Ohio State
- Pelfrey, K.R. MBA, Armed Forces Command & General Staff College
- Peng, M. PhD, Washington
- Persons, J.C. PhD, Chicago
- Philipich, K.L. DBA, Indiana
- Racster, R.L. PhD, Illinois
- Ramamurthy, R.S. MAS, Illinois
- Reichers, A.E. PhD, Michigan State
- Rhee, W.T. PhD, Kent State
- Ryan, C. PhD, Ohio State
- Sanders, A.B. PhD, Georgia
- Sandver, M.H. PhD, Wisconsin
- Schilling, D.A. PhD, John Hopkins
- Schroeder, D.A. PhD, Kansas
- Sen, J. PhD, Chicago
- Shenkar, O. PhD, Columbia
- Smith, M.L. PhD, Minnesota
- Spires, E.E. PhD, Illinois
- Stewart, A.C. PhD, North Carolina
- Stiving, M.. PhD, Berkeley
- Strickland, D.D.. PhD, N. Carolina
- Stulz, R.M. PhD, MIT
- Talarzyk, W.W. PhD, Purdue
- Teoh, S.H. PhD, Chicago
- Todor, W.D. PhD, California - Irvine
- Tomassini, L.A. PhD, UCLA
- Unnava, H.R. PhD, Ohio State
- Walkling, R.A. PhD, Maryland
- Wallin, D.E. PhD, Arizona
- Wanous, J.P. PhD, Yale
- Ward, P.T. DBA, Boston
- Weinstock, P. JD, Boston
- Werner, I.M. PhD, Rochester
- West, P.M. PhD, Chicago
- Williams, D.D. PhD, Penn State
- Williams-Stanton, S.D. PhD, Michigan
- Wruck, K. PhD, Rochester
- Young, R.A. PhD, Ohio State
- Ziegler, T.J. MBA, Ohio State
- Zinn, W. PhD, Michigan State
- Zvinakis, K. PhD, Texas

THE PENNSYLVANIA STATE UNIVERSITY
PHD IN BUSINESS ADMINISTRATION

Program Highlights

- *Penn State ranks eleventh among US universities in total research expenditures*
- *Many opportunities for interdisciplinary research*
- *Students have the opportunity to work as both research and teaching assistants*
- *Program offers students the choice of five primary fields of study*

CONTACT INFORMATION

Office of PhD and MS Programs

The Smeal College of Business Administration

110 Business Administration Building

University Park, Pennsylvania USA 16802-3000

PH: 1-814-865-1255

FAX: not available

EMAIL: phd-ms@psu.edu

INTERNET: http://www.smeal.psu.edu/phd_ms/

THE PENNSYLVANIA STATE UNIVERSITY, PhD IN BUSINESS ADMINISTRATION

PROGRAM OVERVIEW

The Smeal College of Business Administration (Smeal) at The Pennsylvania State University (Penn State) offers a PhD in business administration degree program which provides students with sound knowledge in business, a research program solidly based in scientific method, experience in teaching and the publication of original research. PhD students have a choice of five fields of study: accounting, finance/insurance and real estate, management and organization, management science/operations/logistics, or marketing and distribution.

Students complete a minimum of four courses in a major field of study, three courses in research methods and one course in teaching methods. Other degree requirements include a candidacy examination, preparation and presentation of a working paper, written and oral comprehensive examinations, a doctoral dissertation and an oral defense.

Accounting

Students who choose accounting as their primary field of study take several research seminars designed to provide a framework for research in financial and managerial accounting, auditing and taxation. Students learn the best research methods to address certain issues, as well as the strengths and weaknesses of each method. Accounting students complete seminars in economics, finance and other supporting disciplines. The department also organizes a weekly colloquium where researchers from top universities present their research.

Finance/Insurance and Real Estate

Close interaction between faculty and students is one of the strengths of the finance/insurance and real estate program. Most students work on joint research projects with one or more of their professors. Assignments as research and teaching assistants expose students to different areas in the field and provide them with the opportunity to teach a range of courses.

Management and Organization

The faculty's diversity and range of expertise is one of the main reasons students choose a PhD in the field of management and organization. Cross-functional research is enhanced by associations with the Center for the Management of Technological and Organizational Change, which focuses on the impact the introduction of new technology has on organizations, and with the centers for Research in Conflict and Negotiation and for the Study of Business and Public Issues, which examine ways for organizations to effectively manage their relationships with external constituencies.

Management Science, Operations & Logistics

The concentration of research and teaching in this area include business statistics, decision analysis and game theory, mathematical programming, business logistics/operations management, and transportation. The methodologies have a broad application to manufacturing and logistics and are used extensively in the fields of marketing, finance and accounting. Students have a great deal of flexibility in developing a program to meet career goals.

Marketing and Distribution

Doctoral students in marketing and distribution can specialize in psychology, organizational theory, anthropology and sociology, or marketing models and econometrics, or in distribution with an emphasis on logistics. First-year students take core courses in marketing thought and theory, consumer behavior, mathematics for modeling and measurement methods. This establishes a common background of marketing knowledge and introduces students to the five areas of emphasis in the field. With the approval of their advisers, students in this field may combine more than one area of emphasis.

SELECTED RESEARCH AREAS
- Accounting theory and ethics
- Actuarial science
- Adverstising effects on children
- Asset pricing
- Auditor decision making
- Bargaining and dispute resolution
- Behavioral issues in salesperson performance
- Business ethics
- Capital budgeting
- Consumer behavior
- Consumer decision processes and models
- Corporate and securities law
- Corporate takeover decisions
- Customer service and channels of distribtuion
- Design of production systems
- Economic effects of accounting
- Employee turnover
- Expanding boundaries of the audit function
- Financial risk management
- Global economic assessment
- Human resources management
- Initial public offerings
- International insurance markets
- International logistics system design
- International trade and competitive strategies
- Management communications
- Management of renewable natural resources
- Managerial and international accounting
- Managerial stock ownership
- Marketing science and econometrics
- Microeconomic theory
- Monetary theory and policy
- Negotiations and shopping in electronic markets
- Operations strategy and decision-making
- Optimization models for manufacturing
- Organization of joint ventures
- Social issues management

THE PENNSYLVANIA STATE UNIVERSITY, PhD IN BUSINESS ADMINISTRATION

ADMISSIONS CRITERIA & PROCEDURES

Admission to the PhD in business administration program is based on the applicants' potential for teaching and research and ability to excel in the program. Admission decisions are not made on GMAT scores and grades alone. The admissions committee also considers scholarly achievement, the previous employment record, letters of recommendation, and applicant's statement of career objectives, interests and plans. Essays are weighted heavily and applicants are encouraged to consider the questions carefully, taking time to define and articulate goals and demonstrate how they relate to the proposed field of study.

A bachelor's degree is the minimum academic credential for admission to the PhD in business administration, though most students complete some graduate work before entering the program. Applicants who demonstrate exceptional scholarly ability in their undergraduate study may be considered for admission.

All applicants must take the GMAT.

International applicants whose native language is not English must achieve a minimum score of 585 on the paper-based TOEFL (or 240 on the computer-based version) to be considered for admission, unless they have completed undergraduate or graduate work at an American university.

Applications are accepted for the fall and spring semesters and the summer session, but most students are admitted in the fall. The final application deadline for fall admission is February 1. Late applications will be considered but will have a reduced likelihood of acceptance as space is limited.

EXPENSES & FINANCIAL ASSISTANCE

Pennsylvania residents enrolled in 12 or more credits pay tuition fees of US$3,267 per semester and students from out-of-state pay US$6,730 per semester. In-state students taking 11 credits or less pay US$276 per credit and those from out-of-state pay US$561 per credit.

PhD students are eligible for financial assistance in the form of teaching and research assistantships. The normal assignment is a half-time assistantship, which requires an average of 20 hours per week and allows students to enroll in three courses per semester.

Most doctoral students receive research assistantships before moving on to teaching assistantships. Research assistants involve library research and writing papers for publication, which means many students will have submitted a paper for publication before graduating. After the second year, PhD students usually move into a teaching assistantship, with duties ranging from assisting in a large lecture hall to designing and presenting a curriculum to a smaller class of students.

INTERNATIONAL STUDENT SUPPORT

The office for International Students and Scholars (ISS) helps international students comply with US government regulations, acts as a liaison with agencies responsible for sponsoring students, and provides academic and personal counseling and assistance with administrative and legal matters involving admission, visa extensions, passport renewal, internships and employment. ISS also serves as an advocate for international students, sponsors an annual International Festival and assists with the activities of the International Student Council (ISC) and over two dozen nationality clubs.

ADMISSIONS AT A GLANCE

Minimum GMAT: no set minimum
Minimum GPA: 3.3
Minimum TOEFL (paper): 585
Minimum TOEFL (computer): 240
Application Fee: US$40
Application Deadline: Feb 1

EXPENSES AT A GLANCE

Tuition:
 In State: US$3,267 per semester
 Out-of-State: US$6,730 per semester
 Int'l Students: –
Books & Supplies: –
Health Insurance: –
Accommodation:
 University Residences: US$600 per month
 Family Housing: –
 Private: US$525 per month

PROGRAM FACTS

of Full-time Students: 70 (f/t and p/t)
# of Part-time Students: incl above
# of Applications per year: 255
Accepted per year: 31
Enrolled per year: 16
Average GMAT Score: 690
Average Age: 29
% Men/Women: 67%/33%
Work Experience (avg yrs): 6
# of Faculty: 149
% Faculty with Doctoral Degree: 90%
Annual Research Funding: US$4,000,000

THE PENNSYLVANIA STATE UNIVERSITY, PHD IN BUSINESS ADMINISTRATION

UNIVERSITY AND LOCATION

Founded in 1885, The Pennsylvania State University system enrolls 80,000 students on 24 campuses located throughout the state, making it one of the 10 largest universities in the US. It comprises 10 academic colleges: Agricultural Sciences, Arts and Architecture, Earth and Mineral Sciences, the Eberly College of Science, Education, Engineering, Health and Human Development, Liberal Arts and the Smeal College of Business Administration.

Penn State's administrative facilities are located at the main campus at University Park. Leisure and recreation facilities at the main campus include the Palmer Museum of Art, the Center for the Performing Arts, racquetball and squash courts, a swimming pool complex and two 18-hole golf courses.

The University Park campus is located near the geographic center of Pennsylvania in State College, a town of 72,000 surrounded by fields, forests and waterways stocked with trout and bass. Popular activities in the region include the Central Pennsylvania Festival of the Arts, Bellefonte's Victorian Christmas, Aaronsburg's Dutch-style fall festival and Center Hall's Grange Fair.

FACULTY
- Angell, L.C. PhD, Boston
- Bagby, J.W. JD, Tulsa
- Balakrishnan, A. PhD, Massachusetts
- Barron, O.E. PhD, Oregon
- Baumgartner, J. PhD, Stanford
- Beatty, A. PhD, MIT
- Bergh, D. PhD, Colorado
- Bither, S.W. PhD, Washington
- Bolton, G.E. PhD, Carnegie Mellon
- Brass, D.J. PhD, Illinois
- Cao, Q. PhD, Chicago
- Cavinato, J.L. PhD, Penn State
- Chang, J. PhD, Northwestern
- Chatterjee, K. DBA, Harvard
- Christy, D.P. PhD, Georgia
- Cochran, P.L. PhD, Washington
- Coyle, Jr., J.J. DBA, Indiana
- Crum, R.P. DBA, Kentucky

- Dasgupta, A. PhD, Princeton
- Degeratu, A. PhD, Iowa
- DeSarbo, W. PhD, Pennsylvania
- DeWitt, R. PhD, Columbia
- Dirsmith, M.W. PhD, Northwestern
- Domowitz, I. PhD, California, San Diego
- Enis, C.R. DBA, Maryland
- Erickson, R. PhD, Washington
- Everett, P. PhD, North Carolina
- Ezzell, J.R. PhD, Penn State
- Field, L. PhD, California, Los Angleles
- Fong, D. PhD, Purdue
- Ghadar, F. DBA, Harvard
- Gioia, D.A. PhD, Florida State
- Goldberg, M. PhD, McGill
- Gray, B.L. PhD, Case Western Reserve
- Hammond, J.D. PhD, Pennsylvania
- Hanka, G. PhD, Chicago
- Hansen, G.A. PhD, Rochester
- Harris, D.G. PhD, Michigan
- Harris, M.S. PhD, Michigan
- Harrison, T.P. PhD, Tennessee
- Hatheway, F.M. PhD, Princeton
- Henszey, B.N. MLT, Georgetown
- Hollman, F. PhD, Florida
- Hottenstein, M.P. DBA, Indiana
- Huang, J. PhD, Northwestern
- Jablonsky, S.F. PhD, Illinois
- Jaffe, A.J. PhD, Illinois
- Kacker, M. PhD, Northwestern
- Ketz, J.E. PhD, Virginia Polytechnic
- Kilduff, M. PhD, Cornell
- Koehler, R.W. PhD, Michigan State
- Koot, R.S. PhD, Oregon
- Kracaw, W. PhD, Utah
- Lewis, H.S. PhD, South Carolina
- Lilien, G.L. DES, Columbia
- Lin, D.K.J. PhD, Wisconsin
- Lusht, K.M. PhD, Georgia State
- McDonnell, N. PhD, Penn State
- McKeown, J. PhD, Michigan State
- Melander, E.R. PhD, Minnesota
- Miles, J.A. PhD, Penn State

- Miller, J.H. PhD, Penn State
- Mulherin, J.H. PhD, California
- Muller III, K.A. PhD, Illinois
- Muscarella, C.J. PhD, Purdue
- Mutchler, J.F. PhD, Illinois
- Novack, R.A. PhD, Tennessee
- Nti, K.O. PhD, Yale
- Olson, J.C. PhD, Purdue
- Ord, J.K. PhD, London
- Pangburn, M. PhD, Rochester
- Posey, L.L. PhD, Pennsylvania
- Ramesh, K. PhD, Michigan State
- Rangaswamy, A. PhD, Northwestern
- Reutzel, E.T. PhD, Penn State
- Shapiro, A.F. PhD, Pennsylvania
- Sharp, J.M. PhD, Oklahoma
- Sheehan, D.P. PhD, California
- Smith, C.H. PhD, Penn State
- Snell, S.A. PhD, Michigan
- Snow, C.C. PhD, California
- Spychalski, J.C. DBA, Indiana
- Stavrulaki, E. PhD, Rochester
- Steensma, H.K. PhD, Indiana
- Stenger, A.J. PhD, Minnesota
- Stevens, J. PhD, SUNY
- Sujan, H. PhD, UCLA
- Sujan, M. PhD, UCLA
- Sundaresan, S. PhD, Rochester
- Susman, G.I. PhD, UCLA
- Thomas, J.B. PhD, Texas
- Thomchick, E.A. PhD, Clemson
- Trevino, L.K. PhD, Texas A&M
- Trevor, C. PhD, Cornell
- Twark, R. PhD, Penn State
- Tyworth, J.E. PhD, Oregon
- Verstraete, A. PhD, Penn State
- Vitolo, T. PhD, Pittsburgh
- Williams, J. PhD, Colorado
- Williams, L.R. PhD, Ohio State
- Wilson, D.T. PhD, Western Ontario
- Woolridge, J.R. PhD, Iowa
- Xu, S.H. PhD, Rensselaer
- Yavas, A. PhD, Iowa

City Population:	72,000
Cost of Living:	medium
Climate Range:	16° to 82°F
Campus Setting:	suburban
Total Enrollment:	41,050
Graduate Enrollment:	6,163
Students in Residence:	13,000

PURDUE UNIVERSITY
KRANNERT GRADUATE SCHOOL OF MANAGEMENT

Program Highlights

- *Doctoral programs in economics, management, and organizational behavior & human resource management*
- *Management PhD program with seven areas of concentration*
- *Tailored programs support individual interests*

CONTACT INFORMATION
PhD Admissions
Krannert Graduate School of Management
1310 Krannert Building, Room 719
West Lafayette, Indiana USA 47907-1310
PH: 1-765-494-4375
FAX: 1-765-494-1526
EMAIL: phd_admissions@mgmt.purdue.edu
INTERNET: http://www3.mgmt.purdue.edu/

PURDUE UNIVERSITY, KRANNERT GRADUATE SCHOOL OF MANAGEMENT

PROGRAM OVERVIEW

Purdue University's (Purdue) Krannert Graduate School of Management (KGSM) offers Doctor of Philosophy (PhD) degree programs in management, economics and organizational behavior and human resources management.

Management

The PhD program in management offers concentrations in accounting, finance, management information systems, marketing, operations management, quantitative methods and strategic management. To ensure the development of problem identification and analysis skills critical to administrative decision making, students are required to complete coursework in the core area of general managerial skills, research methods, in their concentration area, and in a related minor.

To satisfy requirements in general managerial skills, students complete courses in accounting, finance, marketing, operations management, strategic management and organizational behavior. The required research methods sequence includes courses and seminars in quantitative economics, statistics and/or optimization.

Students must complete a minimum of 12 credit hours in one of the seven concentration areas and a minimum of six credit hours of approved coursework in a related field in management, economics or organizational behavior and human resources management.

Upon completion of all coursework, students must pass a written preliminary examination in the area of concentration to demonstrate their mastery of the broad literature in the field and their knowledge of past and current research areas. Students must write and successfully defend a dissertation which demonstrates their ability to carry out a substantial research project.

Economics

The PhD in economics program has a strong quantitative and analytical component designed to provide a working knowledge of basic research skills and to broaden students' understanding of economic institutions.

This program requires completion of a minimum of 49 hours of study including six core courses in economic theory and three courses in quantitative economics. Students must develop proficiency in three fields of specialization, pass preliminary examinations covering core courses and specializations, and write and successfully defend a dissertation which demonstrates their ability to carry out a substantial research project.

Specializations include econometrics, economic development, economics of financial markets, industrial organization, international economics, labor economics, macro-monetary economics, mathematical economics, public finance, transportation and urban economics.

Organizational Behavior & Human Resources

The program in organizational behavior and human resource management integrates behavioral sciences with knowledge about organizational functions and management. Courses range from individual behavior in organizations to advanced labor economics and organizational theory.

The program emphasizes training in quantitative research methods and statistics. Students choose either organizational behavior or human resource management as their major, as well as a minor area to widen their knowledge base.

Upon completion of coursework, students write preliminary exams in research methods and their major area. The final stage of the program is the dissertation writing and defense.

SELECTED RESEARCH AREAS

- Accounting data
- Agency problems
- Analytical models of auditing
- Analyzing earning forecasts
- Arbitration
- Auditing expectation gaps
- Capital market variables
- Codetermination
- Computer database access
- Corporate diversification strategies
- Corporate governance
- Corporate ownership
- Data mining
- Discrimination
- Downsizing
- E-commerce
- Econometrics
- Economic education
- Economic history
- Economics of information
- Empirical financial accounting
- Environmental economics
- Experimental economics
- Financial accounting
- Financial engineering
- Industrial organization
- Information and competition
- Innovative product strategies
- International finance
- International marketing
- Job design
- Labor economics
- Labor hoarding
- Macro-monetary economics
- Market efficiency
- Marketing of high technology
- Mathematical economics
- Monetary economics
- Mortgage finance
- Motivation
- New product development
- Nonprofit accounting
- Operator theory
- Option markets
- Organizational psychology
- Product innovation
- Public economics
- Security returns
- Security risk
- Selection testing
- Sex discrimination
- Student motivation
- Temporary layoffs
- Trading strategies
- Transportation
- Unionism in professional sports
- Urban economics

PURDUE UNIVERSITY, KRANNERT GRADUATE SCHOOL OF MANAGEMENT

ADMISSIONS CRITERIA & PROCEDURES

Applicants must have completed at least six semester hours of college-level mathematics and statistics prior to enrollment.

Applicants to the economics program must have completed two semesters of calculus and one semester of linear algebra.

Admission to the program in organizational behavior and human resource management is based on demonstrated scholastic achievement and expressed commitment to research.

Applicants for the management program must submit GMAT scores and applicants for the economics program must submit GRE scores. Organizational behavior and human resource management applicants may submit either GMAT or GRE scores. Applicants should complete the tests no later than December or January to ensure results are available by the application deadline of February 15.

Applications must include official transcripts from all universities and colleges attended (along with official translations, if necessary), a certified copy of a diploma if transcripts do not state the awarding of a baccalaureate degree, and two letters of recommendation from former professors or supervisors. A written essay concerning the purpose for pursuing a PhD degree at Purdue, research interests and future professional plans are required.

TOEFL results are required from applicants whose native language is not English, even if they have studied English in their home countries or graduated from a US university. The minimum score required for admission is 575 on the paper-based test or 233 on the computer-based test.

EXPENSES & FINANCIAL ASSISTANCE

Most doctoral students receive a teaching or research assistantship to aid in development of their teaching skills and the application of research methodology. Students whose native language is not English must pass an oral evaluation before they are eligible for a teaching assistantship.

Assistantships require approximately 20 hours a week for which students receive a stipend to cover tuition and all students fees except for a graduate staff rate. Assistants are also enrolled in the students' health insurance plan.

Students may apply for fellowships based on academic merit. Fellowships provide a remission of tuition with a monthly stipend for the duration of their award.

Research grants for dissertations are available which incorporate remission of tuition and a stipend for research costs.

KGSM provides a travel allowance for students to travel to national meetings and make presentations or represent the school at doctoral consortiums.

Teaching awards are given each semester to students who have distinguished themselves in their performance as teaching assistants. Research awards are available as well.

INTERNATIONAL STUDENT SUPPORT

The International Students and Scholars Office (ISSO) provides an orientation program, advising on immigration, cultural issues as well as academic and career planning.

ADMISSIONS AT A GLANCE

Minimum GMAT:	80th percentile or above
Minimum GPA:	3.5
Minimum TOEFL (paper):	575
Minimum TOEFL (computer):	233
Application Fee:	US$30
Application Deadline:	Feb 15

EXPENSES AT A GLANCE

Tuition (with funding):
- In State: US$320 per semester
- Out-of-State: US$320 per semester
- Int'l Students: US$320 per semester

Books & Supplies: US$300 per year

Health Insurance: incl. with funding

Accommodation:
- University Residences: US$300–500 per month
- Family Housing: US$300–400 per month
- Private: US$250–600 per month

PROGRAM FACTS

# of Full-time Students:	112
# of Part-time Students:	n/a
# of Applications per year:	850
# Accepted per year:	–
# Enrolled per year:	30
Average GMAT Score:	690
Average Age:	28
% Men/Women:	75%/25%
Work Experience (avg yrs):	–
# of Faculty:	85
% Faculty with Doctoral Degree:	98%
Annual Research Funding:	–

PURDUE UNIVERSITY, KRANNERT GRADUATE SCHOOL OF MANAGEMENT

UNIVERSITY AND LOCATION

Established in 1869 by the Morrill Act, Purdue University is a public institution known for its agriculture and engineering programs. It also offers programs in consumer and family sciences, education, health sciences, liberal arts, management, nursing, pharmacy, technology, veterinary medicine and a range of sciences.

Purdue comprises five campuses in West Lafayette, Hammond, Fort Wayne, Westville and Indianapolis. West Lafayette is the main campus, with more than 37,000 students and 144 buildings on more than 600 acres of forested land along the banks of the Wabash River.

The university library collection contains 2.2 million volumes, more than two million microforms and 16,000 serial titles. The Management & Economics Library has 150,000 volumes, 5,000 annual corporate reports and a 7,500-volume collection of rare historical books.

There are many cultural and recreational facilities on campus, including the Elliot Hall of Music, four theatres, an art gallery and a fully equipped recreational gymnasium.

Purdue's West Lafayette campus is situated across the Wabash River from Lafayette, Indiana. Together, these two cities have a combined population of approximately 80,000 people and offer a safe, friendly living environment. The university is an hour's drive from the state capital of Indianapolis and two hours southeast of Chicago, the third-largest metropolitan area in the US.

City Population:	80,000
Cost of Living:	medium
Climate Range:	10° to 95°F
Campus Setting:	suburban
Total Enrollment:	37,762
Graduate Enrollment:	6,100
Students in Residence:	12,800

FACULTY

- Aliprantis, C. PhD, California Institute of Tech
- Altinkemer, K. PhD, Rochester
- Barron, J. PhD, Brown
- Berger, C. PhD, Wisconsin
- Blanchard, K. PhD, Purdue
- Bohlmann, J. PhD, MIT
- Brush, T. PhD, Michigan
- Camera, G. PhD, Iowa
- Campion, M. PhD, North Carolina State
- Carlson, J. PhD, Johns Hopkins
- Cason, T. PhD, Berkeley
- Chand, S. PhD, Indiana
- Chaturvedi, A. PhD, Wisconsin
- Cooper, A. DBA, Harvard
- Cooper, M. PhD, North Carolina at Chapel Hill
- Dada, M. PhD, MIT
- Denis, David. PhD, Michigan
- Denis, Diane. PhD, Michigan
- Duparcq, P. PhD, Purdue
- Dworkin, J. PhD, Minnesota
- Emrich, C. PhD, Rice
- Eskew, R. PhD, –
- Folta, T. PhD, Purdue
- Gjerde, T. PhD, Purdue
- Goodman, J. PhD, Georgia Institute of Technology
- Green, S. PhD, Washington
- Hatcher, J. MBA, Chicago
- Hueckel, G. PhD, Wisconsin
- Hundley, G. PhD, Minnesota
- Hussain, I. PhD, Missouri
- Iyer, A. PhD, Georgia Tech
- Jain, S. PhD, Arizona
- Kadiyala, R. PhD, Minnesota
- Kallapur, S. PhD, Harvard
- Kalwani, M. PhD, Columbia
- Kovenock, D. PhD, Wisconsin
- Kross, W. PhD, Iowa
- Lewellen, B. PhD, MIT
- Lynch, G. PhD, Kentucky
- McCarthy, P. PhD, Claremont
- McConnell, J. PhD, Purdue
- Miller, K. PhD, Minnesota
- Moore, J. PhD, Minnesota
- Moriarty, M. PhD, Purdue
- Mosakowski, E. PhD, Berkeley
- Moskowitz, H. PhD, UCLA
- Netz, J. PhD, Michigan
- Noussair, C. PhD, California Institute of Tech
- Novshek, W. PhD, Northwestern
- Papke, J. PhD, Cornell
- Penno, M. PhD, Northwestern
- Plante, B. PhD, Georgia
- Pomery, J. PhD, Rochester
- Popva, I. PhD, Case Western Reserve
- Rau, R. PhD, INSEAD
- Rees, J. PhD, Florida
- Ro, B. PhD, Michigan State
- Robinson, R. PhD, Michigan
- Schendel, D. PhD, Stanford
- Schoorman, D. PhD, Carnegie Mellon
- Schwarz, L. PhD, Chicago
- Smith, K. PhD, Purdue
- Sullivan, C. PhD, Purdue
- Tang, J. PhD, Bowling Green
- Thoman, L. PhD, Stanford
- Thursby, Jerry. PhD, North Carolina
- Thursby, Marie. PhD, North Carolina
- Umbeck, J. PhD, Washington
- Ward, J. PhD, Carnegie Mellon
- Watts, M. PhD, Louisiana State
- Watts, S. PhD, Iowa
- Weidnaar, D. PhD, Purdue

STANFORD UNIVERSITY
THE DOCTORAL PROGRAM IN BUSINESS

Program Highlights

- *Development of research skills through coursework, departmental colloquia and apprenticeships with Stanford professors*

- *Program majors incorporate interdisciplinary work utilizing resources available throughout the university*

- *Future Professors of Manufacturing Program for students with industry training*

CONTACT INFORMATION
Graduate School of Business
518 Memorial Way
Stanford, California USA 94305-5015
PH: 1-650-723-2831
FAX: 1-650-725-7462
EMAIL: PhD_Program_Inquiries@gsb.stanford.edu
INTERNET: http://www.gsb.stanford.edu

STANFORD UNIVERSITY, THE DOCTORAL PROGRAM IN BUSINESS

PROGRAM OVERVIEW

The Stanford Graduate School of Business (GSB) was created in 1924 when future US president Herbert Hoover recognized the need for a graduate school of business on the country's west coast. Together with 125 California business leaders, Hoover raised the necessary funds to create the GSB, which admitted its first students in 1925. Today, the Stanford GSB is a leader in the development of management theory, thinking, practice and performance.

The PhD Program

The rigorous doctoral program typically requires four to five years of full-time study. In the first and second years, students carry out general coursework requirements and complete field examinations, summer papers and research assistantships. In the third year, students move to directed readings and research projects, and advance to the status of doctoral candidate. An oral examination in defense of the candidate's research is carried out in the fourth year of studies prior to completion of the written dissertation.

Innovative Study Options

Students select a major field of study from accounting, economic analysis and policy, finance, marketing, operations, information and technology, organizational behavior, or political economics. Students frequently take courses from other university departments and schools, such as economics, industrial engineering, engineering management, political science, psychology, sociology and statistics.

The Importance of Research

Students receive intensive ongoing training in academic research. Through research apprenticeships with faculty members, students develop an appreciation for the importance of research to an academic career. For specific information about research assistantships, students can visit the university's website.

In addition to these apprenticeship positions, students receive research training through their participation in doctoral seminars and colloquia. These sessions provide students with the opportunity to share research ideas with colleagues and faculty members in an encouraging environment.

Success of PhD Graduates

The quality of the GSB doctoral program is evidenced by the successful placement of graduates. The following institutions employ the largest numbers of GSB graduates as business professors: Harvard University; INSEAD, France; Massachusetts Institute of Technology; New York University; Northwestern University; Stanford University; the Universities of California at Berkeley and Los Angeles; Chicago; North Carolina; Pennsylvania; Southern California; Texas, Austin; and Washington.

SELECTED RESEARCH AREAS

- Applications of management science and statistical procedures in business
- Applied microeconomics
- Building and maintaining positive cultures in rapidly growing, early-stage companies
- Choice models
- Corporate entrepreneurship
- Cost-effectiveness and cost-benefit analysis in health care
- Creative problem-solving strategies in business
- Decision making, trust, cooperation, leadership, creativity, and entrepreneurship in organizations
- Disclosure rules in financial markets
- Dynamic choice
- E-commerce
- Entrepreneurship
- Exchange rate and international interest rate determination
- FCC auctions of radio spectrum
- Global business ethics
- Improving management effectiveness
- Industrial organization economics
- International conflict and cooperation
- Leadership and the characteristics of high-performance teams at the executive level
- Management systems for start-up and entrepreneurial companies
- Models of gerrymandering
- Prospect theory and asset pricing
- Real estate development
- Social stereotyping and prejudice
- Stochastic models of processing systems
- Supply chain management
- The evolution of cooperation

STANFORD UNIVERSITY, THE DOCTORAL PROGRAM IN BUSINESS

ADMISSIONS CRITERIA & PROCEDURES

To be eligible for the Stanford GSB doctoral program, students must hold a bachelor's degree or its equivalent from a recognized institution. While a master's degree is not required, students should have a strong background in quantitative methods. In addition, particular fields of study have their own prerequisites. Applicants should familiarize themselves with both the admission policies of the GSB and the requirements of their desired field of study.

Admission officials take into account an applicant's academic performance, research potential, academic research experience, letters of recommendations, GRE or GMAT test scores and personal objectives. Because admission decisions are based on an entire application package, no minimum test scores are required.

To apply, students must send the following documents to the GSB by January 2, 2001: postsecondary academic transcripts, three letters of recommendation, GMAT or GRE scores (organizational behavioral applicants must submit GRE scores specifically), statement of purpose, and confidential financial statement.

Although TOEFL scores are not required from applicants whose native language is not English, students are expected to understand and participate in lectures and group discussions. At the time of application, language skills are assessed using the GRE or GMAT verbal score and the written materials submitted for admission purposes.

EXPENSES & FINANCIAL ASSISTANCE

The GSB is dedicated to helping students meet the financial challenges of intensive graduate-level studies. Through the provision of research and teaching assistantships, fellowships and loans, the GSB funds the majority of its doctoral students.

Typically, fellowship stipends and/or research or teaching assistantship positions cover the cost of tuition and at least 90 percent of estimated living expenses. Fellowship stipends for first-year students in the 1999-2000 year averaged US$18,434 for nine months of study, plus US$3,046 for a two-month summer research assistantship. Extra funding is also available for attending professional conferences.

INTERNATIONAL STUDENT SUPPORT

Since the school's inception in 1925, the Stanford GSB has maintained a tradition of and commitment to creating a vibrant and diverse community of business students. In the class entering the PhD program in 1999, approximately 43 percent were international students. The GSB offers its wide range of fellowships and loans to both domestic and international students.

For more general services, Stanford's Bechtel International Center provides counseling and other assistance. The Center works to bring together American and international students for a variety of social, cultural and educational activities. Admitted students should address correspondence about immigration and other challenges to the Bechtel International Center.

ADMISSIONS AT A GLANCE

Minimum GMAT:	no set minimum
Minimum GPA:	no set minimum
Minimum TOEFL (paper):	n/a
Minimum TOEFL (computer):	n/a
Application Fee:	US$55
Application Deadline:	January 2, 2001

EXPENSES AT A GLANCE

Tuition per year:	
In State:	US$27,243
Out-of-State:	US$27,243
Int'l Students:	US$27,243
Books & Supplies:	US$1,920 per year
Health Insurance:	US$633 per year
Accommodation:	
University Residences:	US$12,006 per year
Family Housing:	US$863–1,420 per month
Private:	US$600–900 per month

PROGRAM FACTS (1999-2000)

# of Full-time Students:	99
# of Part-time Students:	n/a
# of Applications:	630
# Accepted:	44
# Enrolled:	23
Average GMAT Score:	not tracked
Average Age:	22-37 (range)
% Men/Women:	57%/43%
Work Experience (avg yrs):	n/a
# of Faculty:	88
% Faculty with Doctoral Degree:	100%
Annual Research Funding:	–

STANFORD UNIVERSITY, THE DOCTORAL PROGRAM IN BUSINESS

UNIVERSITY AND LOCATION

Established in 1891, Stanford University has over 70 departments offering undergraduate and graduate programs through the Schools of Earth Science and Humanities & Science, as well as graduate programs through the Schools of Education, Business, Law and Medicine.

Over 14,000 students from all 50 states and 60 foreign countries are currently enrolled at Stanford. The university operates on a four-quarter system (fall, winter, spring and summer).

The university is committed to quality in teaching and to individual attention for students. The student-to-faculty ratio is kept low to ensure that all students are able to actively participate in class. The university employs 1,500 full-time faculty members, 99 percent of whom hold doctorate degrees in their area of instruction. Among the faculty are 14 Nobel Prize laureates and five Pulitzer Prize winners.

Stanford University stretches from the foothills of the Santa Cruz mountains to the edge of Palo Alto in the heart of the "Silicon Valley." At the center of the San Francisco Bay area, Stanford is 40 minutes south of the metropolitan city of San Francisco with its collection of some of the world's best art galleries, museums, sports teams and historical landmarks.

Stanford is within an hour from the beaches on the Pacific Ocean and a few hours from the ski slopes of the Sierras. California's mild weather ensures opportunities for year-round recreation such as hiking, cycling and boating.

City Population: (Palo Alto)	56,000
Cost of Living:	–
Climate Range:	45° to 73°F
Campus Setting:	suburban
Total Enrollment:	14,084
Graduate Enrollment:	7,553
Students in Residence:	9,500

FACULTY

- Aaker, J.L. PhD, Stanford
- Admati, A.R. PhD, Yale
- Bagley, C.E. JD, Harvard
- Barnett, W. PhD, UC Berkeley
- Baron, D.P. DBA, Indiana
- Baron, J.N. PhD, UC Santa Barbara
- Barth, M.E. PhD, Stanford
- Beaver, W.H. PhD, Chicago
- Bekaert, G. PhD, Northwestern
- Bendor, J. PhD, UC Berkeley
- Benkard, C.L. PhD, Yale
- Bonini, C.C. PhD, Carnegie Mellon
- Brady, D.W. PhD, Iowa
- Bulow, J.I. PhD, MIT
- Burgelman, R. PhD, Columbia
- Davila, A. DBA, Harvard
- Duffie, J.D. PhD, Stanford
- Enthoven, A.C. PhD, MIT
- Feinberg, Y. PhD, Hebrew Univ
- Fernandez, R.M. PhD, Chicago
- Flanagan, R.J. PhD, UC Berkeley
- Foster, G. PhD, Stanford
- Grenadier, S.R. PhD, Harvard
- Grier, S.A. PhD, Northwestern
- Groseclose, T.J. PhD, Stanford
- Hannan, M.T. PhD, North Carolina, Chapel Hill
- Harrison, J.M. PhD, Stanford
- Haunschild, P.R. PhD, Carnegie Mellon
- Hellman, T.F. PhD, Stanford
- Holloway, C.A. PhD, UCLA
- Joss, R.L. PhD, Stanford
- Jost, J.T. PhD, Yale
- Kasznik, R. PhD, UC Berkeley
- Kessler, D.P. PhD, MIT
- Kramer, R.M. PhD, UCLA
- Krehbiel, K. PhD, Rochester
- Kreps, D.M. PhD, Stanford
- Kumar, S. PhD, Illinois, C-U
- Lattin, J.M. PhD, MIT
- Lazear, E.P. PhD, Harvard
- Lee, H.L. PhD, Pennsylvania
- Martin, J. PhD, Harvard
- McDonald, J.G. PhD, Stanford
- McMillan, J. PhD, New South Wales
- McNichols, M.F. PhD, UCLA
- Mendelson, H. PhD, Tel Aviv
- Morris, M.W. PhD, Michigan
- Neale, M.A. PhD, Texas, Austin
- Nelson, K.K. PhD, Michigan
- O'Reilly, C.A. PhD, UC Berkeley
- Parker, G.C. PhD, Stanford
- Patell, J.M. PhD, Carnegie Mellon
- Pfeffer, J. PhD, Stanford
- Pfleiderer, P.C. PhD, Yale
- Podolny, J.M. PhD, Harvard
- Porras, J.I. PhD, UCLA
- Porteus, E.L. PhD, Case Institute
- Puri, M. PhD, New York
- Rady, S. PhD, LSE
- Ray, M.L. PhD, Northwestern
- Reiss, P.C. PhD, Yale
- Roberts, D.J. PhD, Minnesota
- Romer, P.W. PhD, U of Chicago
- Saloner, G. PhD, Stanford
- Sharpe, W.F. PhD, UCLA
- Shepard, A. PhD, Yale
- Simonson, I. PhD, Duke
- Singleton, K.J. PhD, Wisconsin, Madison
- Spence, A.M. PhD, Harvard
- Srinivasan, V. PhD, Carnegie Mellon
- Thomas, J.S. PhD, Northwestern
- Tiedens, L.Z. PhD, Michigan
- Van Horne, J.G. PhD, Northwestern
- Venkatachalam, M. PhD, Iowa
- Wacziarg, R. PhD, Harvard
- Whang, S. PhD, Rochester
- White, M.W. PhD, Berkeley
- Wilson, R.B. DBA, Harvard
- Wolfson, M.A. PhD, Texas, Austin
- Wood, S.C. PhD, Stanford
- Zenios, S. PhD, MIT
- Zuckerman Sivan, E.W. PhD, Chicago
- Zwiebel, J.H. PhD, MIT

SYRACUSE UNIVERSITY
SCHOOL OF MANAGEMENT

Program Highlights
- *More than three decades of excellence*
- *Opportunities for interdisciplinary programs*
- *A proving ground for researchers and teachers*
- *Accredited by AACSB*

CONTACT INFORMATION
Director, PhD Program
School of Management, Suite 200
Syracuse, New York USA 13244-2130
PH: 1-315-443-1001
FAX: 1-315-443-5389
EMAIL: phd@som.syr.edu
INTERNET: http://www.som.syr.edu/

SYRACUSE UNIVERSITY, SCHOOL OF MANAGEMENT

PROGRAM OVERVIEW

For more than three decades, the School of Management at Syracuse University (SU) has offered a rigorous and rewarding doctoral program in business administration. Its goal is to train students to become productive researchers and effective teachers. Students are encouraged to publish and have abundant opportunities to gain teaching experience. The school's research centers and ongoing research programs offer rich opportunities to work with members of the faculty on projects of mutual interest.

PhD candidates choose a major field of concentration and a supporting field. Areas of specialization include accounting, finance, marketing, quantitative methods (covering the fields of management information systems, managerial statistics and operations management), and strategy and human resources management. In addition, students with diverse academic interests may pursue an interdisciplinary study option with the consent of the faculty advisor. Courses in research methods are also required.

Because of the rigorous nature of doctoral studies, the school requires PhD candidates to register on a full-time basis. Year-round residency is mandatory for students until they reach the dissertation stage.

Research Experience

Doctoral students are required to carry out a six-credit summer research project, beginning during the first summer of studies and lasting until the end of second year. Throughout this project, students work closely with a faculty member of their choice. The resulting paper is evaluated by the advisor and another instructor in the same field of study. The goal of this project is to encourage PhD candidates to produce a paper of publishable quality that can be presented either at a conference or during a departmental colloquium.

Research Centers

Seven research centers within the School of Management offer students and faculty rich opportunities for intensive study and collaboration. These centers focus on studies in accounting research, operations management, entrepreneurship, transportation and distribution, international business studies and innovation management.

The schools research centers, institutes, and ongoing projects enrich the study of management at SU by coordinating visits with internationally renowned academics and business professionals, sponsoring conferences and seminars, and funding student research.

Teaching Experience

Students in the PhD program can take advantage of SU's dynamic Future Professoriate Program (FPP) to gain the pedagogical skills required of doctoral graduates.

As an offshoot of the university's Teaching Assistant program, the FPP offers students resources designed to enhance their potential for successful academic careers. Students who show exceptional promise as instructors are assigned an advanced teaching position, which typically entails responsibility for an undergraduate course under the supervision of a faculty mentor.

Students who pursue an intensive program of professional development in teaching in conjunction with their doctoral studies will be eligible for a Certificate in University Teaching. These students will be required to create a teaching portfolio documenting their progress as teaching associates at the university.

SELECTED RESEARCH AREAS

- Agency theory
- Auditor decision-making
- Capital assets pricing
- Corporate risk management
- Corporate venturing
- Decision support
- Derivative securities
- Design of distribution networks
- Electronic commerce
- Emerging markets
- Employment discrimination
- Employment testing
- Entrepreneurship
- Environmental policy
- Executive stock option
- Experimental economics
- Finanicial disclosure
- Governmental auditing
- Incentive issues
- Innovation management
- Intelligent reasoning architectures
- International finance
- International financial markets
- International liability
- Job shop scheduling
- Knowledge systems
- Management control systems
- Managing teams
- Market microstructure
- Marketing models
- Marketing strategy
- Mergers and acquisitions
- Neural network
- New product development
- Options and futures
- Organization design
- Organizational control
- Pricing strategies
- Privatization
- Product liability
- Service organizations
- Strategic cost management
- Strategic HR management
- Supply chain management
- Time series modeling
- Top management teams
- Transition economics
- Valuation
- Whistle-blowing

SYRACUSE UNIVERSITY, SCHOOL OF MANAGEMENT

ADMISSIONS CRITERIA & PROCEDURES

Successful applicants to the school's PhD program must display the drive, curiosity, knowledge and skills necessary to acquire a thorough understanding of current theory and methodology in their chosen field of management studies. Moreover, individuals must be able to apply and communicate what they know through independent research projects.

Applicants to the PhD program typically possess a bachelor's degree and, in most instances, a master's degree. An individual may be offered admission to the PhD program on the basis of an outstanding undergraduate record and exemplary GMAT scores alone. While a master's degree in business is not required for entry into the program, students who hold this degree will be eligible for transfer credit. The minimum GMAT score required of PhD applicants is 600, however, average scores of 660 are common among successful program applicants. A minimum GPA of 3.5 is also required for admission to the PhD program.

Requests for application forms can be made online at the school's website. Completed application forms must be returned with a US$50 nonrefundable application fee, letters of recommendation from three professors, GMAT scores, academic transcripts and evidence of English language proficiency (for students whose first language is not English). A minimum paper-based TOEFL score of 600 is required for admission. While applications are due February 15 for first consideration, students who wish to be considered for university fellowships must have their completed application package to the university by January 10.

EXPENSES & FINANCIAL ASSISTANCE

Domestic and international PhD students pay US$14,000 in tuition per year. Housing ranges from US$2,000 to $3,650 per semester graduate student residences, while family housing costs US$585 per month for one bedroom or US$670 per month for two bedrooms. Meal plan options range from US$790 per semester for packages of five meals per week, to US$1,985 per semester for a deluxe meal plan offering 19 meals per week and 15 guest passes per semester.

The Graduate School offers a limited number of fellowships and the School of Management provides funding through teaching and research assistantships. Students who show satisfactory progress receive funding for four years. Students may also receive financial assistance from SU's research centers or through summer appointments as research assistants or instructors.

ADMISSIONS AT A GLANCE

Minimum GMAT:	600
Minimum GPA:	3.5
Minimum TOEFL (paper):	600
Minimum TOEFL (computer):	–
Application Fee:	US$50
Application Deadline:	Feb 15 (fall semester)

EXPENSES AT A GLANCE

Tuition per year:	
In State:	US$14,000
Out-of-State:	US$14,000
Int'l Students:	US$14,000
Books & Supplies:	US$1,000 per year
Health Insurance:	US$455 per year
Accommodation:	
University Residences:	US$2,000–3,650 per semester
Family Housing:	US$585–670 per month
Private:	US$450–800 per month

PROGRAM FACTS

# of Full-time Students:	32
# of Part-time Students:	n/a
# of Applications per year:	–
# Accepted per year:	–
# Enrolled per year:	–
Average GMAT Score:	660
Average Age:	–
% Men/Women:	73%/27%
Work Experience (avg yrs):	–
# of Faculty:	55
% Faculty with Doctoral Degree:	100%
Annual Research Funding:	–

SYRACUSE UNIVERSITY, SCHOOL OF MANAGEMENT

UNIVERSITY AND LOCATION

Founded in 1870, Syracuse University is a private, nonsectarian research institution consisting of 12 colleges offering over 250 programs of study. With its range of academic choices, SU is recognized as a leading research university. One of the oldest schools in the state of New York, SU is also one of only 62 research universities in the US to be elected to the prestigious Association of American Universities (AAU).

The university's total student enrollment is 13,903, including 4,500 graduate students. In a typical year, three-quarters of these graduate students are registered in master's programs and one-quarter are pursuing doctoral studies. Every school and college at SU offers a graduate program. The importance of teaching and small class sizes is emphasized by the 12:1 student-to-faculty ratio.

The 220-acre campus overlooks the city of Syracuse, providing an ideal blend of urban and rural environments. SU consists of 170 buildings surrounding a historic, central quadrangle. Over 70 percent of SU's students live in 13 residence halls on campus that offer undergraduate, graduate and family housing options. An variety of meal plan options are available, designed to meet the diverse needs of full- and part-time students.

SU is a 20-minute walk from downtown Syracuse, a medium-sized city offering many recreational and cultural activities. These include the Thornden Rose Festival, held at one of the oldest gardens in America, and the Syracuse Jazzfest, an annual event that attracts more than 50,000 individuals from across Canada and the US. Located in the geographical center of New York state, Syracuse enjoys four distinct seasons and is only 300 miles from New York City.

INTERNATIONAL STUDENT SUPPORT

International students comprise more than 30 percent of the student body at the School of Management and approximately 25 percent of the graduate student population. These

City Population:	500,000
Cost of Living:	medium
Climate Range:	16° to 83°F
Campus Setting:	suburban
Total Enrollment:	13,903
Graduate Enrollment:	4,500
Students in Residence:	7,280

individuals hail from over 100 countries.

The school is dedicated to celebrating diversity on campus and to this end, it partly funds SU's International Day, a celebration of food, music, dancing and arts from countries around the globe.

International students at SU may use the resources of the Office of International Students (OIS), a university department designed to help with the transition to life at SU and the larger Syracuse community. Through the OIS, international students have access to services ranging from advice on immigration to personal matters. Programs designed to increase the positive interaction between visiting students and US citizens are also available, including orientation, American home hospitality, an international wives organization, seminars, and workshops for campus and community organizations.

OIS is housed in its own building and provides a comfortable place for all students to visit, relax and talk with staff. The office organizes many social and cultural events to promote on-campus diversity.

FACULTY 1999-2000

- Ahmed, A.S. PhD, Rochester
- Anderson, J.C. PhD, Syracuse
- Basu, A.K. PhD, Stanford
- Benaroch, M. PhD, New York
- Bobko, P. PhD, Cornell
- Bobrowski, P. PhD, Indiana
- Callahan, E.S. JD, Syracuse
- Chen, C. PhD, Wisconsin
- Chesser, R.J. PhD, Michigan State
- Cihon, P. LLM, Yale
- Collins, J. JD, Harvard
- Dharwadkar, R. PhD, Cincinnati
- Diz, F. PhD, Cornell
- Doty, D.H. PhD, Texas at Austin
- Easton, F. PhD, Washington
- Elder, R. PhD, Michigan State
- Fenzi, R. PhD, California at Davis
- Finucane, T.J. PhD, Cornell
- Fredrikson, E.B. PhD, Columbia
- George, G. PhD, Virginia Commonwealth
- Gillen, D.J. PhD, Maryland
- Grabner, J. DBA, Indiana
- Hanouille, L. PhD, Syracuse
- Harris, D. PhD, Michigan
- Harris, M. PhD, Michigan
- Hurd, S. JD, Syracuse
- Ismail, B. PhD, Illinois
- Karp, J.P. JD, Villanova
- Kim, M. PhD, Illinois, Urbana-Champaign
- Koveos, P. PhD, Penn State
- Lele-Pingle, S. PhD, Purdue
- Lobo, G. PhD, Michigan
- Long, S.B. PhD, Washington
- Madden, G. PhD, Penn State
- Man, K. PhD, Chicago
- Mathiyalakan, S. PhD, Kentucky
- Mazumdar, T. PhD, Virginia Polytechnic
- Onsi, M. PhD, Illinois
- Raj, S.P. PhD, Carnegie Mellon
- Roberge, L. PhD, Syracuse
- Shukla, R. PhD, SUNY, Buffalo
- Smith, K.A. PhD, Maryland
- Stevens, D. PhD, Indiana
- Tankersley, C.B. PhD, Cincinnati
- Thevaranjan, A. PhD, Minnesota
- Thieme, J. PhD, Michigan
- Tucker, F.G. PhD, Ohio State
- Velu, R. PhD, Wisconsin
- vonDran, G. DPA, Arizona
- Walker, J. PhD, Cornell
- Wallin, T.O. PhD, Cornell
- Webster, S. PhD, Indiana
- Wesman, E. PhD, Cornell
- Wilemon, D. PhD, Michigan State
- Wu, C. PhD, Illinois, Urbana-Champaign
- Young, A. PhD, Columbia
- Zinsser, P. PhD, Ohio State
- Zollers, F. JD, Syracuse

TEMPLE UNIVERSITY
PhD PROGRAMS

Program Highlights

- *Seven areas of specialization in business administration*
- *Separate programs in statistics and economics*
- *Research opportunities under the guidance of internationally renowned faculty*
- *Future Faculty Fellowship Program offering financial aid for individuals from groups historically excluded from higher education*
- *Accredited by AACSB*

CONTACT INFORMATION
1810 North 13th Street
111 Speakman Hall (006-00)
Philadelphia, Pennsylvania USA
   19122-6083
PH: 1-215-204-8465
FAX: 1-215-204-5698
EMAIL: rossw@sbm.temple.edu
INTERNET: http://www.sbm.temple.edu/
   programs/phdba.htm

TEMPLE UNIVERSITY, PhD IN BUSINESS ADMINISTRATION PROGRAM

PROGRAM OVERVIEW

Since 1918, The Fox School of Business and Management (Fox School) at Temple University (TU) has offered high caliber business study opportunities. Today, it is the largest business school in the Greater Philadelphia region and one of the largest in the world.

Graduate-level business programs, initiated in 1942, currently enroll about one quarter of the Fox School student population. Students in the PhD program are committed to research and understand the importance of disciplinary and interdisciplinary approaches to the study of business. Programs emphasize pedagogy to prepare students for careers as academics. All students teach at least one semester-long undergraduate course supervised by a faculty member. Graduates find positions at prestigious universities worldwide, including Indiana University and the Universities of Pittsburgh, Virginia and Miami.

The Fox School offers three PhD programs: business administration, economics and statistics. All Fox School programs are fully accredited by AACSB - The International Association for Management Education.

PhD in Business Administration

The PhD Program in business administration, the largest of the three Fox School PhD programs, offers seven areas of specialization: accounting, finance, international business, marketing, organizational management and human resources, policy and strategy, and risk, insurance and healthcare management (RIHM).

Students in the accounting program take seminars in interdisciplinary accounting, financial accounting theory and managerial accounting theory. Individuals pursuing the finance option take courses in financial theory, international finance and the theory of financial markets and institutions.

Students in international business take courses in international business theory and research along with courses in functional areas such as finance, marketing, or strategy and policy. Marketing majors enroll in marketing research, marketing theory development, behavioral research in marketing and quantitative research in marketing. Coursework in the organizational management and human resources program covers organization behavior and theory, human resource management, and industrial relations. Policy and strategy specialists take seminars in strategy formulation and environmental analysis, the administration of strategic decisions, global strategic management, and management control. RIHM majors take courses in risk theory, benefits, and healthcare management.

Statistics & Economics PhD Programs

In addition to the PhD in business administration, the Fox School offers separate doctoral programs in statistics and economics. The statistics option is designed for individuals pursuing professional roles in research and applications of statistics, operations research or biostatistics. The economics program is for students who wish to become university-level researchers and teachers, or who intend to work in applied fields of economics.

Requirements for Degree

In addition to the required units of coursework, doctoral students in business administration must write a statistics competency exam, as well as a comprehensive exam in their field of specialization. All PhD candidates must complete and successfully defend a dissertation. Given the rigorous nature of PhD studies, full-time status is required of all studentss. Most participants complete the program in four to five years.

SELECTED RESEARCH AREAS

- Analysis of health maintenance organizations
- Applications of statistics in business & economics
- Capital markets
- Communicating in organizations
- Consumer behavior
- Corporate finance
- Economics of multinational business
- Economics of state & local government
- Entrepreneurship
- Experimental designs
- Gender differences & public interest accounting
- Government policy
- Healthcare management
- Human capital & labor markets
- Insurer profitability & solvency
- International finance
- International marketing
- International trade theory
- Investment analysis & portfolio selection
- Land policy studies
- Management manufacturing & technology
- Management of financial institutions
- Marketing management
- Mathematical economics
- Multivariate analysis
- No-fault automobile insurance legislation
- Organization & environment
- Power, influence & conflict management
- Probability theory
- Productivity & efficiency in the insurance industry
- Risk management & insurance
- Survey sampling
- Target estimation
- The costs of semi-public goods among users
- The history & method of economic theory
- Time series analysis
- Vendor selection in purchasing

TEMPLE UNIVERSITY, PhD IN BUSINESS ADMINISTRATION PROGRAM

ADMISSIONS CRITERIA & PROCEDURES

The PhD Program at the Fox School is designed for individuals who possess a graduate degree or equivalent from a recognized college or university. Successful applicants whose graduate degree is not in a business-related field must demonstrate competency in core business disciplines. Individuals should have a minimum GPA of 3.5 in their undergraduate and graduate work to be eligible for PhD studies.

Applicants must submit GMAT scores or, in certain instances, GRE results. Average GMAT scores of PhD applicants are generally within the 80 to 99 percentile range (with 70 to 99 on the verbal test and 70 to 99 on the quantitative portion of the exam). For students whose first language is not English, a minimum paper-based TOEFL score of 600 is also required. Individuals who have a TOEFL score of 620 or higher may use this to supplement a marginal verbal score on the GMAT or GRE.

Applicants must also submit a statement of goals and two letters of recommendation from individuals familiar with the candidate's academic potential and abilities. The statement of goals should detail the applicant's reasons for pursuing a career in teaching and research.

Students should note that admission is competitive and possession of the minimum requirements does not ensure entry into the program. Admission officials at Fox take into account test results, past academic performance, future academic potential and the ability to research effectively, as evidenced by research publications. All applications must be received by March 15. International applicants and those seeking university fellowships should apply by February 1. Admission is for the fall semester only.

EXPENSES & FINANCIAL ASSISTANCE

Because Temple is a member of the Commonwealth of Pennsylvania System of Higher Education, tuition rates are reasonable. Pennsylvania residents pay US$348 per credit hour for graduate-level study, while out-of-state residents pay US$488.

Types of financial assistance in the Fox School include graduate assistantships (tuition remission and stipend worth US$10,500 per year), tuition scholarships, project completion grants and fellowships. The Future Faculty Fellowship Program provides additional financial assistance to individuals from groups historically excluded from higher education.

INTERNATIONAL STUDENT SUPPORT

Temple's Office of International Services (OIS) provides international students from more than 120 countries with services in cultural adjustment, budgeting, academic decisions and immigration status.

Student groups include the International Business Association (IBA), an organization that offers both domestic and international students the opportunity to learn about foreign business practices and customs. In addition, the IBA works with other international student organizations on campus and sponsors excursions to national points of interest, such as the New York Stock Exchange and the World Bank.

ADMISSIONS AT A GLANCE

Minimum GMAT:	600
Minimum GPA:	3.5
Minimum TOEFL (paper):	600
Minimum TOEFL (computer):	–
Application Fee:	US$40
Application Deadline:	
Mar 15 (fall semester)	

EXPENSES AT A GLANCE

Tuition per credit hour:	
In State:	US$348
Out-of-State:	US$488
Int'l Students:	US$488
Books & Supplies:	US$600 per year
Health Insurance:	US$700 per year
Accommodation:	
University Residences:	US$321–61 per month
Family Housing:	US$641 per month
Private:	US$450–700 per month

PROGRAM FACTS

# of Full-time Students:	50–60
# of Part-time Students:	n/a
# of Applications per year:	120–150
# Accepted per year:	20–30
# Enrolled per year:	10–20
Average GMAT Score:	–
Average Age:	–
% Men/Women:	–
Work Experience (avg yrs):	–
# of Faculty:	125
% Faculty with Doctoral Degree:	98
Annual Research Funding:	–

TEMPLE UNIVERSITY, PhD IN BUSINESS ADMINISTRATION PROGRAM

UNIVERSITY AND LOCATION

Established in 1884, Temple University has 16 schools and colleges that offer undergraduate and masters degrees in over 120 fields and over 60 doctoral degrees. Temple has four campuses in the Greater Philadelphia region, and offers programs in Rome, Tokyo, China, Israel, Greece, Britain, France and other countries.

Temple provides excellent research and recreational facilities. The main campus is the central location for Temple's Paley Library System and Computer Center. Athletic facilities include two Olympic-size pools, fully equipped gyms, weight rooms, racquetball courts and an outdoor recreation and sports complex with a 10,200-seat arena. The university has two theaters, two music recital halls, a dance theater, cinema and art gallery.

The 94-acre main campus is located one mile north of center city. Philadelphia, the fifth largest city in the US, is an important financial, cultural and intellectual center. One of America's most historically significant cities, Philadelphia is home to the famous Liberty Bell and was the site for the signing of the Declaration of Independence.

City Population:	4,500,000
Cost of Living:	medium
Climate Range:	23° to 86°F
Campus Setting:	urban
Total Enrollment:	28,337
Graduate Enrollment:	8,511
Students in Residence:	3,427

FACULTY

- Aaronson, W.E. PhD, Temple
- Andrisani, P.J. PhD, Ohio State
- Asabere, P.K. PhD, Illinois
- Asthana, S. PhD, Texas
- Aulakh, P. PhD, Texas
- Balsam, S. PhD, CUNY-Baruch
- Bandera, V.N. PhD, Berkeley
- Bernstein, R.E. PhD, Brown
- Blackstone, E.A. PhD, Michigan
- Blau, G.J. PhD, Cincinnati
- Bognanno, M. PhD, Cornell
- Bongiovanni III, J. JD, Temple
- Bowman, G.W. PhD, Carnegie Mellon
- Buck, A. PhD, Illinois
- Chaganti, R. PhD, SUNY at Buffalo
- Chandran, R. PhD, Syracuse
- Choi, J.J. PhD, New York
- Cottrell, J. PhD, Pennsylvania
- Daymont, T. PhD, Wisconsin
- Deckop, J.R. PhD, Minnesota
- Diamantaras, D.I. PhD, Rochester
- DiBenedetto, C.A. PhD, McGill
- Drennan Jr, R.B. PhD, Pennsylvania
- Dunkelberg, W.C. PhD, Michigan
- Elyasiani, E. PhD, Michigan State
- Fardmanesh, M. PhD, Yale
- Felt, H.M. DBA, USC
- Fernholz, L.T. PhD, Rutgers
- Fogg, S.L. PhD, New York
- Friedman, J. PhD, Berkeley
- Gaffney, M.A. PhD, Maryland
- Geddes, D. PhD, Purdue
- Gershon, M.E. PhD, Arizona
- Getzen, T. PhD, Washington
- Goetz, M. PhD, Minnesota
- Gupta, M.C. PhD, UCLA
- Hakim, S. PhD, Pennsylvania
- Halbert, T.A. JD, Rutgers
- Hall Jr, C.P. PhD, Pennsylvania
- Hamilton, R. PhD, Northwestern
- Heiberger, R.M. PhD, Harvard
- Hochner, A. PhD, Harvard
- Hodge Jr, S.D. JD, Temple
- Holland, B.S. PhD, NC State
- Holmes, W.L. PhD, Illinois
- Hopkins, H.D. PhD, Penn State
- Hsuan, F. PhD, Cornell
- Huffman, F. PhD, South Carolina
- Hunt, J. PhD, Cincinnati
- Iglewicz, B. PhD, Virginia Polytechnic
- Izenman, A. PhD, Berkeley
- Johannesson, R.E. PhD, Bowling Green
- Katrishen, F.A. PhD, South Carolina
- Klein, H.E. PhD, Columbia
- Klotz, B.P. PhD, Minnesota
- Konrad, A.M. PhD, Claremont
- Kopecky, K.J. PhD, Brown
- Kotabe, M. PhD, Michigan State
- Koziara, K.S. PhD, Wisconsin
- Krishnan, J. PhD, Ohio State
- Kushnirsky, F. PhD, NEI
- Lady, G. PhD, Johns Hopkins
- Lancioni, R.A. PhD, Ohio State
- Lawrence, V. JD, Pennsylvania
- Leeds, M.A. PhD, Princeton
- Lipka, R. PhD, Rutgers
- Mangel, R. PhD, Pennsylvania
- McClendon, J.A. PhD, South Carolina
- Milutinovich, J. PhD, NYU
- Moore, D.F. PhD, Washington
- Murphy, F.H. PhD, Yale
- Oliva, T.A. PhD, Alabama
- Parnes, M.N. PhD, Wayne State
- Phatak, A. PhD, UCLA
- Phelps, C.D. PhD, Yale
- Phillips, H.E. PhD, Washington
- Porat, M.M. PhD, Temple
- Portwood, J.D. PhD, Michigan
- Powers, M.R. PhD, Harvard
- Press, E.G. PhD, Oregon
- Rajhavarao, D. PhD, Bombay
- Raphaelson, A.H. PhD, Clark
- Rappoport, P.N. PhD, Ohio State
- Regan, L. PhD, Pennsylvania
- Rima, I.H. PhD, Pennsylvania
- Ritchie Jr, J.C. PhD, Pennsylvania
- Rosenthal, E.C. PhD, Northwestern
- Ross, W. PhD, Duke
- Ryan, D. PhD, Berkeley
- Ryan, D.H. PhD, South Carolina
- Sami, H. PhD, Louisiana State
- Sarkar, S.K. PhD, Calcutta
- Schmidt, S.M. PhD, Wisconsin
- Scott, J. PhD, Purdue
- Seidenstat, P. PhD, Northwestern
- Sen, S. PhD, Pennsylvania
- Singh, J. PhD, Florida State
- Sinha, I. PhD, Michigan
- Sklar, S.J. JD, Temple
- Smith, D.B. PhD, Michigan
- Smith, M. DBA, Indiana
- Smith, W. PhD, Johns Hopkins
- Sobel, M.J. PhD, Berkeley
- Sorrentino Jr, J.A. PhD, Purdue
- Stull, W.J. PhD, MIT
- Swanson, C. PhD, Minnesota
- Titus, G.J. PhD, Pennsylvania
- Valenza, M. JD, Temple
- Van Derhei, J.L. PhD, Pennsylvania
- Wei, W.W.S. PhD, Wisconsin
- Weiss, H.J. PhD, Northwestern
- Weiss, M.A. PhD, Pennsylvania
- Weiss, M.Y. PhD, Columbia
- Zeitz, G. PhD, Wisconsin-Madison
- Zinn, J. PhD, Pennsylvania
- Zissu, A. PhD, CUNY

TEXAS A&M UNIVERSITY
MAYS GRADUATE SCHOOL OF BUSINESS

Program Highlights

- *Major fields of study in accounting, finance, information and operations management, management, and marketing*
- *Program open to students with bachelor's or master's degrees*
- *Accredited by AACSB*

CONTACT INFORMATION

Lowry Mays College Graduate School of Business

413 Wehner Building

College Station, Texas USA 77843-4113

PH: 1-979-845-4711

FAX: 1-979-845-6639

EMAIL: PhDProgram@cgsb.tamu.edu

INTERNET: http://business.tamu.edu

TEXAS A&M UNIVERSITY, MAYS GRADUATE SCHOOL OF BUSINESS

PROGRAM OVERVIEW

The Mays Graduate School of Business (Mays) at Texas A&M University (TAMU) offers a PhD in business program with major fields of study in accounting, finance, information and operations management, management, and marketing.

The objectives of the PhD program are to provide comprehensive knowledge of the concepts and practices in functional business areas, to develop advanced competencies for conducting quality research, directing the research of others, and communicating research findings through teaching and writing. The program prepares candidates for the varied responsibilities of academic careers or other positions requiring research and analytical skills.

The PhD program normally consists of major and minor fields of study, plus supporting coursework. A minimum of 64 credit hours beyond the master's degree or 96 credit hours beyond the bachelor's degree are required. A typical PhD program includes 24 credit hours in the major field, 24 credit hours of dissertation research and six to 12 hours in both the minor and supporting fields.

An examination at the completion of coursework is required before formal dissertation research begins. The exam consists of oral and written sections covering the major and minor fields of study.

A written dissertation exhibiting knowledge of the specialty area and the results of research must be submitted and defended before an advisory committee, invited faculty and other doctoral students before the PhD degree is conferred.

Accounting

The primary objective of the doctoral program in accounting is to provide students with comprehensive knowledge of accounting concepts and practices in functional business areas to support teaching and research interests.

Finance

The doctoral program in finance brings PhD students to the leading edge of knowledge in corporate investment institutions and international finance. Rigorous coursework and research provide the student with an in-depth understanding of the theoretical and conceptual foundation of finance.

Information and Operations Management

The doctoral program in information and operations management is research-based and utilizes a systems approach that stresses the interrelations of the functional business areas and the importance of effective decision-making. The goal of the program is to develop professionals with a solid grounding in the underlying theory of their disciplines and refined problem-solving capabilities. The program offers specialized tracks in management information systems, production and operations management, and management science.

Management

The PhD in management offers specializations in strategic management, human resources, organizational behavior and theory, and business and public policy. Specialization is optional and students may choose to pursue a more general track.

Marketing

The doctoral program in marketing offers rigorous course and research activities that provide an in-depth understanding of the theoretical, conceptual and managerial foundations of marketing, and the research methods and analytical procedures necessary for a successful academic research career.

SELECTED RESEARCH AREAS

- Appraisal methods used to estimate real estate values
- Banking and financial markets
- Commercial feasibility studies of new products
- Compensation and employees benefit plans taxation
- Consumer judgment formation
- Corporate finance
- Database management
- Discrimination law
- Distribution strategy
- Emerging information technologies
- Executives and strategies
- Federal taxation
- Financial accoutning
- Forecasting
- Group processes and work group effectiveness
- Human resource management
- Income tax incentives
- Information engineering analysis and design
- International business
- International trade regulations
- Law and economics
- Management information systems
- Mathematical and multiple objective programming
- Organizational adaptation to institutional competitive pressures
- Planning for mergers and acquisitions
- Pricing strategy
- Real estate investment
- Regional trading blocks
- Reporting forecasted information
- Role of costly information in security markets
- Serice and marketing quality
- Statistics
- Systems analysis
- Use of computer models to analyze the impact of tax laws
- Vectorization of algorithms and parallel processing of computational technologies

TEXAS A&M UNIVERSITY, MAYS GRADUATE SCHOOL OF BUSINESS

ADMISSIONS CRITERIA & PROCEDURES

Mays Graduate School of Business has set high standards for admission to its PhD in business program. Each department considers multiple criteria when choosing candidates for admission, including performance in previous degree programs, GMAT or GRE scores, letters of recommendation, business and teaching experience, evidence of research and writing accomplishments, and personal interviews.

Admission prerequisites include a bachelor's degree in a field related to the area of doctoral study, competency in mathematics (at least through differential and integral calculus), knowledge of computers and competency in a computer language, and courses or equivalents to satisfy the AACSB's common body of knowledge.

Additional prerequisites specific to the doctoral program in accounting include an undergraduate major in accounting and graduate coursework in micro- and macro-economic theory, financial management and statistics. Other majors may have additional prerequisites.

All applicants must submit an application fee (US$35 for US applicants and US$75 for international applicants) along with a completed application, official test scores, official transcripts, a resume and three letters of recommendation.

EXPENSES & FINANCIAL ASSISTANCE

Texas residents pay US$72 per semester credit hour for graduate study. Out-of-state and international graduate students pay US$285 per semester credit hour. Educational expenses for nine months of study vary according to personal needs and the program of study. The Financial Aid Office's estimated annual cost for new resident graduate students including tuition and fees, books, supplies, transportation, room and board and incidental and living expenses is US$13,256 per year. The estimated cost for new nonresident and international students is US$17,516 per year. Total expenses for returning students during an academic year should be slightly less than those for new students.

Financial aid is available in the form of teaching and research assistantships, which also waive out-of-state tuition for non-Texas residents. Assistantships are usually awarded for the full academic year and are subject to the availability of funds. A limited number of fellowships are available for exceptionally well-qualified applicants.

INTERNATIONAL STUDENT SUPPORT

The International Student Association (ISA) promotes cultural exchange between international US students who attend TAMU. The ISA prides itself in bringing cultural diversity and global awareness to both the TAMU and Bryan-College Station communities.

ADMISSIONS AT A GLANCE

Minimum GMAT: 570
Minimum GPA:
  3.25 (master's)
  3.0 (bachelor's)
Minimum TOEFL (paper): 600
Minimum TOEFL (computer): –
Application Fee:
  US$35 (US)
  US$75 (int'l)
Application Deadline:
  US: Mar 15 (fall), Oct 15 (spring), Nov 1 (summer)
  Int'l: Mar 1 (fall), Aug 1 (spring), Nov 1 (summer)

EXPENSES AT A GLANCE

Tuition:
  In State: US$72 per credit hour
  Out-of-State: US$285 per credit hour
  Int'l Students: US$285 per credit hour
Books & Supplies: –
Health Insurance: –
Accommodation
  University Residences: –
  Family Housing: –
  Private: –

PROGRAM FACTS

of Full-time Students: 81
# of Part-time Students: n/a
# of Applications per year: 152
Accepted per year: 32
Enrolled per year: 19
Average GMAT Score: 658
Average Age: –
% Men/Women: 60%/40%
Work Experience (avg yrs): 8
# of Faculty: 146
% Faculty with Doctoral Degree: 84%
Annual Research Funding: US$1,081,432

TEXAS A&M UNIVERSITY, MAYS GRADUATE SCHOOL OF BUSINESS

UNIVERSITY AND LOCATION

The state's first public institution of higher education, founded in 1876, Texas A&M University is a land-grant, sea-grant and space-grant institution. The university has an enrollment of approximately 43,000 students who are working toward degrees in 10 academic colleges including agriculture, engineering, architecture, business, education, geosciences, liberal arts, medicine, science and veterinary medicine.

The university's 5,200-acre campus features a 434-acre research park and more than 100 buildings, including 41 residence halls that accommodate almost 11,000 students.

Seven open-access computer labs and one printing center provide students with email accounts, Internet access and a variety of software. Equipment varies from lab to lab, but most include Pentium-based PCs, Apple Macintosh systems, Sun SPARC stations and SGI workstations, which provide access to the campus supercomputers.

The Sterling C. Evans Library is the general academic library and includes the Cushing Memorial Library, housing rare books, special collections, manuscripts, and archives, and the West Campus Library, which serves the Lowry Mays College and Graduate School of Business, as well as departments within the College of Agriculture and Life Sciences. TAMU also has a Medical Sciences Library. Current library holdings include more than 2.4 million volumes, 4.7 million microform units, 20,000 serial titles and approximately 150,000 maps. Through the Online Computer Library Center national database, library users have access to more than 34 million bibliographic records in more than 22,000 libraries in over 63 countries.

The twin cities of Bryan and College Station are situated in the Brazos Valley, conveniently located at the heart of the Dallas/Fort Worth, Houston and Austin/San Antonio triangle and easily accessible from all areas of Texas. In its East Side Historical District and its revitalized downtown area, Bryan has an impressive collection of homes and business sites with historical and architectural significance, as well as fine restaurants and community theaters. College Station is an energetic and progressive city with 924 acres of parks and a statewide reputation for quality athletic events.

City Population:	93,750
Cost of Living:	medium
Climate Range:	39° to 95°F
Campus Setting:	suburban
Total Enrollment:	43,389
Graduate Enrollment:	7,500
Students in Residence:	11,000

FACULTY

- Barsness, Z. PhD, Northwestern
- Benjamin, J.J. DBA, Indiana
- Berry, L. PhD, Arizona State
- Bierman, L. JD, Pennsylvania
- Bravenec, L.L. LLM, NYU
- Buffa, F.P. PhD, Louisiana State
- Busch, P.S. PhD, Pennsylvania State
- Cannella, Jr., A.A. PhD, Columbia
- Choobineh, J. PhD, Arizona
- Cocanougher, A.B. PhD, Texas at Austin
- Conant, J.S. PhD, Arizona State
- Cooper, S.K. PhD, Texas at Austin
- Courtney, Jr., J.F. PhD, Texas at Austin
- Dacin, P.A. PhD, Toronto
- Daily, A. PhD, North Carolina at Chapel Hill
- Davis, R.A. PhD, South Carolina
- Dinkel, J.J. PhD, Northwestern
- Eden, L. PhD, Dalhousie
- El-Shinnaway, M. PhD, UCLA
- Etter, W.E. PhD, Texas at Austin
- Fields, P. PhD, South Carolina
- Flagg, J.C. PhD, Texas A&M
- Flores, B.E. PhD, Houston
- Fraser, D.R. PhD, Arizona
- Fuerst, W.L. PhD, Texas Tech
- Futrell, C.M. PhD, Arkansas
- Gimeno, J. PhD, Purdue
- Giroux, G.A. DBA, Texas Tech
- Griffin, R.W. PhD, Houston
- Groth, J.C. PhD, Purdue
- Haney, Jr., R.L. DBA, Indiana
- Hellriegel, D. PhD, Washington - Seattle
- Hise, R.T. DBA, Maryland
- Hitt, M.A. PhD, Colorado
- Holmes, S.A. PhD, North Texas
- Jones, G.R. PhD, Lancaster
- Kerr, D.S. PhD, Michigan State
- Kinney, M.R. PhD, Arizona
- Kolari, J.W. DBA, Arizona State
- Lassila, D.R. PhD, Minnesota
- Lee, D.S. PhD, Oregon
- Leigh, J.H. PhD, Michigan
- Loree, D. PhD, Texas at Dallas
- Loudder, M.L. PhD, Arizona State
- Mahajan, A. PhD, Georgia State
- McDaniel, S.W. PhD, Arkansas
- Murthy, U.S. PhD, Indiana
- Nixon, C.J. PhD, Texas A&M
- Olson, D.L. PhD, Nebraska
- Paetzold, R.L. JD, Nebraska
- Paradice, D.B. PhD, Texas Tech
- Pride, W.M. PhD, Louisiana State
- Pustay, M.W. PhD, Yale
- Richards, R.M. PhD, Michigan
- Robinson, Jr., E.P. PhD, Texas at Austin
- Rose, P.S. PhD, Arizona
- Ross, A. PhD, Indiana
- Sen, A. PhD, Pennsylvania State
- Shabana, A. PhD, California - Los Angeles
- Shearon, W. DBA, Virginia
- Shetty, B. PhD, Southern Methodist
- Smith, L.M. DBA, Louisiana Tech
- Stein, W.E. PhD, North Carolina
- Strawser, R.H. DBA, Maryland
- Swanson, E.P. PhD, Wisconsin
- Szymanski, D.M. PhD, Wisconsin - Madison
- Tretter, M.J. PhD, Wisconsin
- Varadarajan, R.R. PhD, Massachusetts
- Wichern, D.W. PhD, Wisconsin
- Wolfe, C.J. DBA, Kent State
- Woodman, R.W. PhD, Purdue
- Yadav, M. PhD, Virginia Tech
- Zardkoohi, A. PhD, Virginia Tech
- Zhou, Z. PhD, Illinois

UNIVERSITY OF ARKANSAS
PHD IN ECONOMICS

Program Highlights

- *Business administration and economics programs*
- *Five specialization areas in business administration and four in economics*
- *Graduate assistants receive a minimum of three years of tuition waivers and stipends*
- *Accredited by AACSB*

CONTACT INFORMATION

Sam M. Walton College of Business
   Administration

475 Business Administration Building

Fayetteville, Arkansas USA 72701

PH: 1-501-575-2851

FAX: 1-501-575-8721

EMAIL: gsb@walton.uark.edu

INTERNET: http://www.uark.edu/depts/
   badminfo/academic/phdprogs.html

UNIVERSITY OF ARKANSAS, PHD IN ECONOMICS

PROGRAM OVERVIEW

The Sam M. Walton College of Business Administration (WCBA) at the University of Arkansas (UA) offers a Doctor of Philosophy (PhD) degree in business administration or economics.

Business Administration

General requirements include completion of coursework, a comprehensive examination in an area of emphasis and the submission and oral defense of an original dissertation. Areas of emphasis are accounting, computer information systems and quantitative analysis, finance, management, and marketing.

Accounting coursework has three distinct components. Students complete four accounting seminars, a minimum of five tool courses and a minimum of three courses in a supporting field, along with an elective in the tool or supporting area for a total of 13 courses. The seminars are in research methods and design, managerial accounting, capital markets and financial reporting, positive accounting, behavioral accounting, auditing, tax, international accounting and accounting education. The tool component consists of three required statistics courses plus two elective courses in statistics, econometrics or other research tools. Courses in the supporting area may be from inside or outside the business school.

The program emphasis in computer information systems and quantitative analysis includes 24 semester hours of computer information systems major courses, nine semester hours of research tools courses and nine semester hours of supporting field courses.

The area of emphasis in finance stresses scholarly development in the related domains of corporate finance, investment analysis and portfolio management and financial institutions. It is composed of 39 credit hours of coursework including 15 credit hours in finance, 15 credit hours in economics and nine credit hours in research tools.

All students pursuing a management emphasis must complete 12 credit hours of management seminars, which cover the broad topics of organizational behavior, organizational theory, strategy research and human resource management. In addition, 18 credit hours of supporting field courses are required and 18 credit hours of research tools courses, which should provide the student with a knowledge of advanced descriptive and inferential statistics, research design and research methods.

The marketing emphasis allows students to concentrate within channels (retail, logistics, transportation), management (strategy, international) or communication (consumer behavior, promotion). Generally, the program consists of 42 credit hours of coursework, including 15 hours of marketing tools, nine credit hours in marketing theory, buyer behavior and strategic marketing management and 18 credit hours of supporting field courses.

Economics

To earn the economics degree, students must complete 27 hours of core courses, courses in two fields of specialization, electives and the dissertation. Core courses include economic theory, history of economic thought, econometrics and statistics and the graduate seminar in economics.

Specializations within economics are labor economics, international economics, economic growth and development and industrial organization and public policy. Students must select two fields of specialization, one of which may be complementary to economics, such as finance or statistics. Field requirements are satisfied by successfully completing six to nine hours of coursework and passing the comprehensive examination.

The dissertation demonstrates ability to select, define, organize and complete a major research project. Students must defend a dissertation proposal, complete the dissertation and successfully defend it.

SELECTED RESEARCH AREAS
- Aggressive work behavior
- Applications of psychology and sociology of science to consumer research
- Applied microeconomics
- Channels of distribution
- Communication networks
- Consumer behavior
- Consumer behavior in retailing and promotional contexts
- Corporate governance
- Dissemination, interpretation and filtering of information by management both internal and external to the organization
- Effects of logistical service on costs and revenues
- Employee withdrawal behavior
- Experimental economics
- Health care marketing
- Inbound transportation strategy in global purchasing
- International management accounting
- Legal constraints on business and marketing acitvities
- Marketing research
- Organization theory and behavior
- Principles of investments
- Quantitative modeling
- Real estate loan compliance
- Relationship of regional subcultures and management practices
- Sales management
- Small business mangement
- Strategic human resource management
- Strategy implemantation
- The design of a management accounting system on managers' judgment and decision making behaviors
- Total quality management
- Worker health and well-being and occupational stress

UNIVERSITY OF ARKANSAS, PHD IN ECONOMICS

ADMISSIONS CRITERIA & PROCEDURES

A Master of Business Administration (MBA) degree or other appropriate master's degree is generally required. Admission is based on previous academic work, GMAT scores, recommendations and professional experience.

All applicants should submit a completed Graduate School application, two official transcripts from each college or university attended and a US$40 application fee. An official copy of the GMAT score, or GRE for economics applicants, three recommendation forms and a statement of objectives that describes the influence of past academic and work experiences, personal strengths and weaknesses and the benefits anticipated from a doctoral education should be submitted. All materials should be sent to the WCBA. The application for assistantship should also be submitted to the WCBA. All materials should be received by March 1 for fall admission

International applicants pay an application fee of US$50 and must provide TOEFL and TSE scores, if their native language is other than English, along with the materials requested on the supplemental information form for foreign applicants. The minimum acceptable TOEFL score is 550 on the paper-based test or 213 on the computer-based version. Materials should be received by February 1 to ensure consideration for admission and financial aid in the fall.

EXPENSES & FINANCIAL ASSISTANCE

Financial aid is granted to outstanding students in the form of assistantships. All assistantships are awarded on a competitive basis in consultation with the graduate advisory committee and the faculty in the area of emphasis.

Assistantships pay US$9,800 per academic year in exchange for 20 hours of service per week teaching courses and fulfilling departmental research assignments. Assistants must possess the academic preparation and communication skills — including TOEFL and TSE scores, if necessary — required for teaching duties. Tuition is paid for the semesters on appointment and assistantships are usually renewable for six semesters.

Incoming doctoral students who meet departmental criteria may also be recommended for US$3,000 fellowships.

INTERNATIONAL STUDENT SUPPORT

There are 782 international students from 98 countries currently attending UA.

UA's International Programs Office (IPO) prepares international students for their transition to life in the area by providing pre-arrival information, transportation to the campus from the airport and temporary housing. The pre-enrollment orientation introduces international students to the library and the health center, and provides information about banking, housing, shopping and US Immigration and Naturalization Service regulations and requirements.

New international students are partnered with American families through the Friendship Family program. The speaker's bureau encourages students to talk about different cultures to public schools and community organizations. Other programs coordinated by the IPO include pre-departure orientation workshops, programs for families of students, tax workshops and the Language Partners program.

There are 18 student organizations with an international focus at UA, including the International, Malaysian, African, Bangladeshi and Turkish student organizations.

ADMISSIONS AT A GLANCE

Minimum GMAT:	no set minimum
Minimum GPA:	no set minimum
Minimum TOEFL (paper):	550
Minimum TOEFL (computer):	213
Application Fee:	US$40
Application Deadline:	US: Mar 1; Int'l: Feb 1

EXPENSES AT A GLANCE

Tuition per year:	
In State:	US$3,717
Out-of-State:	US$8,820
Int'l Students:	US$8,820
Books & Supplies:	US$1,000-1,400 per year
Health Insurance:	US$547 per year
Accommodation:	
University Residences:	US$378 per month
Family Housing:	US$320 per month
Private:	US$450 per month

PROGRAM FACTS

# of Full-time Students:	45
# of Part-time Students:	–
# of Applications per year:	28
# Accepted per year:	13
# Enrolled per year:	9
Average GMAT Score:	619
Average Age:	37
% Men/Women:	75%/25%
Work Experience (avg yrs):	13
# of Faculty:	91
% Faculty with Doctoral Degree:	73%
Annual Research Funding:	US$880,049

UNIVERSITY OF ARKANSAS, PhD IN ECONOMICS

UNIVERSITY AND LOCATION

The University of Arkansas was established in 1871 as a land-grant university for the state of Arkansas and its first classes were held in 1872. It has an annual enrollment of 15,000 students in eight colleges and schools, offering 230 undergraduate and graduate degrees in more than 150 fields of study in agriculture, food and life sciences, arts and sciences, business, education, engineering, architecture and law. It is the only comprehensive doctoral degree-granting university in Arkansas and is classified as a Carnegie II research institution.

There are 167 buildings on UA's 420-acre campus, including Old Main, one of the oldest buildings in the state and the symbol of higher education in Arkansas. The Mullins Library, which was recently expanded by 75,000 square feet, houses almost 1.5 million volumes, 16,224 subscriptions to periodicals, 2.8 million titles on microform, almost 8,000 feet of manuscripts and provides access to hundreds of databases through several online bibliographic services.

The Health, Physical Education and Recreation (HPER) building is the center of recreational activities on campus, with dance floors, gyms, an indoor jogging track, racquetball courts, a fitness center and an Olympic-sized swimming pool. UA's Outdoor Recreation Center provides students with outdoor recreation equipment and information.

Fayetteville is located in the Ozark Mountain Range in northwest Arkansas, where seasons are distinct and beautiful. The city conveys the atmosphere of a small town yet offers the advantages of larger cities. There are numerous historical sites in the region related to early explorers, the Civil War and Native American history. Nearby Buffalo National River, the Ozark National Forest and numerous lakes and state parks offer canoeing, backpacking, hiking, fishing, camping, boating and water-skiing.

City Population:	52,000
Cost of Living:	medium
Climate Range:	32° to 97°F
Campus Setting:	urban
Total Enrollment:	15,060
Graduate Enrollment:	2,751
Students in Residence:	–

FACULTY

- Ashton, D. PhD, Georgia
- Barnett, R.C. PhD, Minnesota
- Bouwman, M.J. PhD, Carnegie Mellon
- Britton, C.R. PhD, Iowa
- Burton, S. PhD, Houston
- Cheng, C.S. PhD, Illinois
- Cook, D.M. PhD, Texas
- Creyer, E.H. PhD, Duke
- Cronan, T.P. DBA, Louisiana Tech
- Curington, W.P. PhD, Syracuse
- Davis, F. PhD, Michigan
- Delery, J.E. PhD, Texas A&M
- Douglas, D.E. PhD, Arkansas
- Farmer, A. PhD, Duke
- Ferrier, G.D. PhD, North Carolina
- Ganster, D.C. PhD, Purdue
- Gay, D.E.R. PhD, Texas A&M
- Glezen, G.W. PhD, Arkansas
- Glorfeld, L. PhD, North Colorado
- Gupta, N. PhD, Michigan
- Hardgrave, B.C. PhD, Oklahoma State
- Hardin, W. PhD, North Carolina
- Hearth, D. PhD, Iowa
- Horowitz, A.W. PhD, Wisconsin-Madison
- Jensen, T.D. PhD, Arkansas
- Johnson, J. PhD, Indiana
- Jones, T.W. PhD, Virginia Polytechnic
- Kennedy, R. PhD, Texas
- Kurtz, D.L. PhD, Arkansas
- Lee, W. PhD, California
- Liu, P. PhD, Indiana
- Lynch, G. PhD, Texas
- McKinnon, T.R. PhD, Mississippi
- Millar, J.A. PhD, Oklahoma
- Murray, J. PhD, Virginia Polytechnic
- Murray, T. PhD, Michigan State
- O'Leary-Kelly, A.M. PhD, Michigan State
- O'Leary-Kelly, S. PhD, Texas A&M
- Ozment, J. PhD, Minnesota
- Perry, L. DBA, Louisiana Tech
- Pincus, K.V. PhD, Maryland
- Reeves, C.A. PhD, Georgia
- Rimbey, J. PhD, Kentucky
- Schulman, C. PhD, Texas A&M
- Sellers, K.F. DBA, Memphis
- Stassen, R.E. PhD, Nebraska
- Taylor, P.H. PhD, Arkansas
- Thomas, D.W. MSA, Arkansas
- Todd, J. DBA, Harvard
- White, D. PhD, Nebraska
- Williams, D.Z. PhD, Louisiana State
- Williams, L. PhD, Ohio State
- Ziegler, J.A. PhD, Notre Dame

UNIVERSITY OF CALIFORNIA, IRVINE
GRADUATE SCHOOL OF MANAGEMENT

Program Highlights

- *Six specializations*
- *Small size of program with individualized format*
- *Research and teaching assistantships and fellowships*

CONTACT INFORMATION

PhD Program Coordinator

Graduate School of Management

Room 418

Irvine, California USA 92697-3125

PH: 1-949-824-8318

FAX: 1-949-824-8469

EMAIL: gsm-phd@uci.edu

INTERNET: http://www.gsm.uci.edu

UNIVERSITY OF CALIFORNIA, IRVINE, GRADUATE SCHOOL OF MANAGEMENT

PROGRAM OVERVIEW

Th Graduate School of Management (GSM) at the University of California - Irvine (UCI) offers a full-time Doctor of Philosophy (PhD) degree program with specializations in accounting, finance, information systems, marketing, operations and decision technologies and organization and strategy.

The doctoral program, designed to prepare students for teaching and research positions in academic institutions, offers a broad and cross-functional knowledge base. The program is small, allowing students to pursue their personal interests and develop interdisciplinary research topics.

There are two phases to the PhD program. During the qualification phase, students learn to conduct original research and scholarship in their selected area of business management. Required coursework is followed by a written preliminary examination and a formal oral qualifying examination.

The dissertation phase requires the completion of significant original research and a dissertation demonstrating the candidate's creativity and ability to launch and sustain a career in research. This phase generally takes 12 to 18 months to complete and concludes with an oral defense.

Doctoral students are expected to complete the program in four years.

Accounting

The accounting specialization focuses on accounting methods and their impact on organizational issues such as management, earnings and firm performance. Students examine principal theories and methodologies. The accounting program is flexible to allow students to pursue their own areas of interest.

Finance

Research topics in the finance program include corporate finance, international finance, derivatives, financial risk, management, executive compensation and capital markets.

Information Systems

The information systems program examines the field of information technology and its impact on modern organizations, markets and society.

The Center for Research on Information Technology and Organizations (CRITO) within the GSM conducts research projects and provides access to the latest developments in information technology.

Marketing

Students in the marketing program study the background and recent advances in marketing theory in the context of the modern business environment. Faculty and student research topics include the emerging role of electronic commerce, the impact of advertising on social issues, the econometric modeling of consumer decisions, high-tech distribution systems, advertising's effect on employees, and marketing in ethnic communities and the global marketplace.

Operations and Decision Technologies

Students of operations and decision technologies study the scientific foundations of management science and operations management. Research areas include mathematical programming, decision and risk analysis, network design and analysis, stochastic processes, queuing systems, inventory control, automated manufacturing systems, quality management and supply-chain management.

Organization and Strategy

The concentration organization and strategy examines topics in work motivation, organizational commitment and leadership, organizational design and industry structure, strategic alliances, inter-organizational relationships, the role of upper management, corporate restructuring, and global strategy.

SELECTED RESEARCH AREAS
- Advertising's impact on employees and social issues
- Application of economic value-added concepts
- Behavioral decision making in accounting and auditing
- Capital markets
- Compensation
- Consumer decision making
- Corporate finance
- Corporate governance and disclosure
- Corporate restructuring
- Decision analysis
- Derivatives
- Earnings management
- Economic impacts of information systems
- Electronic commerce marketing
- Electronic commerce strategies
- Executive compensation
- Finance risk management
- Financial aspects of executive compensation
- Firm performance
- First mover positioning strategies
- Global business strategies
- Information systems and business performance
- Information technology industry
- Inter-organizational relationships
- Knowledge based expert systems
- Management of information systems
- Managerial performance measurements
- Manufacturing and service operations
- Marketing in multi-ethnic communities
- Optimization theory and applications
- Organizational design and leadership
- Production and inventory planning
- Risk management
- Role of upper management
- Social impact of information systems
- Strategic alliances
- Supply chain management
- Work motivation

UNIVERSITY OF CALIFORNIA, IRVINE, GRADUATE SCHOOL OF MANAGEMENT

ADMISSIONS CRITERIA & PROCEDURES

The GSM considers the applicant's transcripts of previous academic work, GMAT or GRE results, letters of recommendation from current or former professors and a personal statement outlining reasons for pursuing doctoral study and the proposed area of concentration. Applicants may also choose to submit a previously prepared research report, essay, master's thesis or case study indicative of their interests and capabilities.

Applicants must have a minimum GPA of 3.0 in previous academic work. There are no set minimum scores for standardized tests but a 680 on the GMAT or a combined 1300 on the GRE are considered competitive.

International applicants whose native language is not English must provide proof of English language proficiency by achieving a minimum score of 600 on the paper-based TOEFL.

Applications must be accompanied by a US$40 application fee. PhD students are admitted in the fall quarter only and the application deadline is January 15.

EXPENSES & FINANCIAL ASSISTANCE

Fees for the PhD program are US$5,178 per academic year for legal residents of California. International and out-of-state students pay US$5,368 per year and an additional tuition fee of US$9,804 per year for a total cost of approximately US$15,200.

Several types of financial assistance, including fellowships, teaching and research assistantships, grants-in-aid and student loans are available. The GSM offers teaching assistantships requiring approximately 20 hours of service per week, to outstanding PhD students. Research assistantships are also available.

Regents' Fellowships and UCI Chancellor's Fellowships are awarded to outstanding students entering UCI for doctoral study and include a 12-month stipend, all required student fees and nonresident tuition, if applicable.

Through the Graduate and Professional Opportunity Program (GPOP), some fellowships are awarded to graduate students of underrepresented groups on the basis of need or academic promise.

INTERNATIONAL STUDENT SUPPORT

The International Center (IC) at UCI provides international students with assistance on immigration, employment and adjusting to life at UCI.

A seven-day orientation occurs the week before classes begin in the fall quarter. Events are designed to familiarize students with the UCI campus and introduce them to other students. IC staff are able to advise on issues such as banking services and driver's license regulations to assist in the resolution of minor details.

Each quarter, the Friends Club International arranges social activities for students, faculty and staff.

ADMISSIONS AT A GLANCE

Minimum GMAT:	no set minimum
Minimum GPA:	no set minimum
Minimum TOEFL (paper):	600
Minimum TOEFL (computer):	250
Application Fee:	US$40
Application Deadline:	Jan 15

EXPENSES AT A GLANCE

Tuition & Fees:
- In State: US$5,178 per year
- Out-of-State: US$15,200 (1st yr)
- Int'l Students: US$15,200 per year

Books & Supplies: varies
Health Insurance: covered
Accommodation:
- University Residences: US$675–875 per month
- Family Housing: n/a
- Private: US$1,000 per month

PROGRAM FACTS

# of Full-time Students:	31
# of Part-time Students:	0
# of Applications per year:	120 (approx)
# Accepted per year:	15–20
# Enrolled per year:	6–10
Average GMAT Score:	680 (approx)
Average Age:	34
% Men/Women:	75%/25%
Work Experience (avg yrs):	5–10
# of Faculty:	42
% Faculty with Doctoral Degree:	100%
Annual Research Funding:	–

UNIVERSITY OF CALIFORNIA, IRVINE, GRADUATE SCHOOL OF MANAGEMENT

UNIVERSITY AND LOCATION

One of nine campuses in the University of California system, UCI was founded in 1965 and sits on what was originally a 172,000-acre ranch owned by the Irvine family. Two of its founding professors have been awarded Nobel Prizes. UCI is consistently ranked among the top 10 public universities in the US. UCI is a member of the American Association of Universities (AAU), a group of 60 of the most distinguished research institutions in the nation.

UCI's 1200-acre campus, designed in the early 1960s by architect William Periera, features many green spaces, including Aldrich Park and the San Joaquin Freshwater Marsh Reserve. It is considered to be the most successfully planned campus in the UC system.

The campus library system consists of the Main Library, which houses arts, humanities, education, social sciences, social ecology, and business and management materials. The library's multimedia resource center provides collections including videocassettes, laserdisks, 16mm films, sound recordings, interactive multimedia, slide sets, data files, a wide variety of CD-ROM titles and Internet access.

A residence complex is reserved especially for graduate students, including apartments designed for students with families. Half of UCI's graduate students live on campus.

Irvine is located in Orange County, one of the fastest-growing areas in the US. The surrounding region features a variety of landscapes, including spectacular mountains and stunning beaches, which enable students to take part in recreational activities such as waterskiing sailing, surfing, skiing and hiking. Halfway between Los Angeles and San Diego, Orange County supports countless cultural and entertainment resources such as theatre, museums, restaurants and nightlife.

City Population:	126,000
Cost of Living:	medium
Climate Range:	44° to 82°F
Campus Setting:	suburban
Total Enrollment:	18,210
Graduate Enrollment:	3,640
Students in Residence:	5,800

FACULTY
- Aigner, D. PhD, Berkeley
- Barron, L. PhD, UCLA
- Beckman, C. PhD, Stanford
- Blake, D. PhD, Rutgers
- Buchmueller, T. PhD, Wisconsin - Madison
- Chen, N. PhD, Berkeley, UCLA
- Chwelos, P. PhD, British Columbia
- Currim, I. PhD, Stanford
- Elvira, M. PhD, Berkeley
- Feldstein, P. PhD, Chicago
- Gilly, M. PhD, Houston
- Givoly, D. PhD, New York
- Graham, J. PhD, Berkeley
- Gurbaxani, V. PhD, Rochester
- Ho, J. PhD, Texas at Austin
- Jorion, P. PhD, Chicago
- Keller, R. PhD, UCLA
- Killaly, B. MPA, Princeton

- King, J. PhD, UC Irvine
- Kraemer, K. PhD, Southern California
- Lougee, B. PhD, Cornell
- Lukin, D. PhD, INSEAD
- McKenzie, R. PhD, Virginia Polytechnic Institute
- Navarro, P. PhD, Harvard
- Pearce, J. PhD, Yale
- Pechmann, C. PhD, Vanderbilt
- Porter, L. PhD, Yale
- Rosener, J. PhD, Claremont Graduate School
- Schoonhoven, C.B. PhD, Stanford
- Scott, C. Phd, New South Wales
- So, R. PhD, Stanford
- Song, J. PhD, Columbia
- Stoughton, N. PhD, Stanford
- Talmor, E. PhD, North Carolina at Chapel Hill
- Town, R. PhD, Wisconsin
- Tyagi, R. PhD, Pennsylvania
- Venkatesh, A. PhD, Syracuse
- Wallace, J. PhD, Washington
- Wiersema, M. PhD, Michigan at Ann Arbor
- Wright, W. PhD, Berkeley
- Yu, F. PhD, Cornell
- Zhu, K. PhD, Stanford

UNIVERSITY OF CENTRAL FLORIDA
PhD IN BUSINESS ADMINISTRATION

Program Highlights

- *Majors in accounting, finance, management and marketing*
- *Tuition waivers, graduate assistantships and fellowships*
- *Accredited by AACSB*

CONTACT INFORMATION

Judy Ryder, Director of Graduate Admissions, PO Box 161400

Orlando, Florida USA 32816-1400

PH: 1-407-823-2184 Option #4

FAX: 1-407-823-6206

EMAIL: judy.ryder@bus.ucf.edu

INTERNET: http://www.bus.ucf.edu

UNIVERSITY OF CENTRAL FLORIDA, PHD IN BUSINESS ADMINISTRATION

PROGRAM OVERVIEW

The College of Business Administration (CBA) at the University of Central Florida (UCF) offers a Doctor of Philosophy (PhD) degree with majors in accounting, finance, management and marketing.

Beginning students must demonstrate that they possess a foundation body of knowledge in the major area. All PhD students must complete a program of study that is approved by an advisory committee and includes 12 to 21 semester hours of coursework in the major area, six to nine semester hours of coursework in a minor or supporting area, 12 to 15 semester hours of research tools coursework, up to three semester hours of teaching coursework, a candidacy examination and 24 semester hours of dissertation research.

Accounting

The accounting foundation may be satisfied by the completion of a Master of Science in Accounting (MSA) degree, a Master of Science in Taxation (MST) degree, a master's degree from an accredited program plus a CPA degree or a 150-hour Florida CPA degree that includes accounting courses deemed essential by the accounting PhD program coordinator or the advisory committee.

The accounting major requires the completion of at least 16 semester hours of seminars, forums and directed research in accounting. Students must also complete nine semester hours of coursework in a supporting area such as computer science, economics, engineering, finance, management, mathematics, marketing, political science, psychology, sociology or statistics. The research tools requirement consists of 15 semester hours of coursework, including two courses in corporate finance theory, research methods in business or applied business statistics.

Finance

The foundation for finance includes a Master of Business Administration (MBA) or equivalent, six graduate semester hours in macro- and micro-economic theory and graduate courses in financial management, investments, financial institutions and international finance.

The finance concentration consists of 12 semester hours of courses and seminars and the minor includes three semester hours each in microeconomic and macroeconomic theory. The research tools component is made up of 12 semester hours of courses in econometrics, applied models and time series.

Management

In management, the foundation should include an MBA or its equivalent from an AACSB-accredited school.

The major in management requires the completion of 21 semester hours of courses in topics such as organizational behavior, organization theory, strategic management, management information systems and others. Six semester hours in areas such as accounting, communication, economics, finance, marketing, psychology, sociology or statistics make up the minor. The research tools component consists of six semester hours in applied models and an additional six hours approved by the advisory committee.

Marketing

The marketing foundation is satisfied by an MBA or its equivalent from an AACSB-accredited school.

The marketing concentration comprises 15 semester hours of seminars in consumer behavior, marketing theory, marketing models, and marketing strategy, plus a comprehensive research project. A minimum of nine hours of coursework is required in a minor/support area. This coursework, typically in a unified area, is intended to accommodate and support the student's individual research interests whenever possible.

In addition, doctoral students majoring in marketing are required to take a minimum of 12 hours of research tools.

SELECTED RESEARCH AREAS
- Assembly systems
- Business cycle theory and economic growth
- Development economics
- Economics and finance
- Effective organizations
- Energy economics
- Finance
- Forecasting
- Forecasting methods
- Futures and options markets
- Game theory
- Interest rate models
- International business
- International finance
- Inventory policy
- Investments
- Management science
- Mathematical programming and its application
- Models and techniques for options pricing
- Optimal control of queuing systems
- Production and operations management
- Production planning and control
- Productivity improvement
- Quality control
- Quality improvement
- Quantitative research models in finance
- Quantity discounts in inventory planning
- Queuing theory
- Risk management
- Statistical modeling and computer programming for manufacturing processes
- Statistics
- Strategic planning

UNIVERSITY OF CENTRAL FLORIDA, PhD IN BUSINESS ADMINISTRATION

ADMISSIONS CRITERIA & PROCEDURES

Admissions decisions for the PhD program in business administration are made on the recommendation of the faculty of the department to which the application is made.

Applicants must submit a completed application, US$20 application fee, a residency classification form, two official transcripts in sealed envelopes from each college or university attended and GMAT scores sent directly from the testing agency to the UCF graduate studies admissions department. Other required application materials include three letters of recommendation from former professors or employers, an essay, a statement of goals, a research statement and a personal statement.

International students must submit a minimum score of 577 on the paper-based TOEFL (233 on the computer-based version) and a minimum score of 240 on the TSE, unless they have graduated from an accredited college or university in the US.

Application documents must be received by May 15. Applicants who wish to be considered for financial assistance must submit applications by February 1.

Admissions occur only in the fall semester, every other year.

EXPENSES & FINANCIAL ASSISTANCE

Florida residents pay tuition fees at a rate of US$146 per semester hour and residents of other states and international students pay US$506.95 per semester hour. On-campus room and board ranges from US$480 to $640 per month and off-campus accommodation, including meals, is available for as little as US$550 per month.

Full time students enrolled in the doctoral program are eligible to receive tuition waivers, to be requested when they register for classes. UCF offers both in-state and out-of-state waivers.

Assistantships are available to teach, conduct research or perform other tasks for the department. Guidelines for the assistantship are established by the faculty and department. Assistantships must employ students at a minimum of 10 hours a week for at least minimum wage.

Individual programs also offer students fellowships. Students who were recruited by the program and are first time PhD students are nominated by the department.

INTERNATIONAL STUDENT SUPPORT

The Office of International Student Services (ISS) provides international students with arrival and pre–arrival assistance and information, information on immigration and visa regulations and advising on financial, academic, housing and employment issues. The ISS also provides an orientation picnic for incoming students and opportunities for students to participate in cross–cultural events.

ADMISSIONS AT A GLANCE

Minimum GMAT:	500
Minimum GPA:	3.0
Minimum TOEFL (paper):	577
Minimum TOEFL (computer):	233
Application Fee:	US$20
Application Deadline:	May 15; Feb 1 for consideration for fellowships or assistantships.

EXPENSES AT A GLANCE

Tuition per semester hour:
- In State: US$146
- Out-of-State: US$507
- Int'l Students: US$507

Books & Supplies: US$1,500 per year
Health Insurance: US$444 per year
Accommodation:
- University Residences: US$480–640 per month
- Family Housing: –
- Private: US$550–650 per month

PROGRAM FACTS

# of Full-time Students:	9
# of Part-time Students:	–
# of Applications per year:	67
# Accepted per year:	12 (2 years)
# Enrolled per year:	9
Average GMAT Score:	605
Average Age:	43
% Men/Women:	45%/55%
Work Experience (avg yrs):	15
# of Faculty:	101
% Faculty with Doctoral Degree:	100%
Annual Research Funding:	–

UNIVERSITY OF CENTRAL FLORIDA, PHD IN BUSINESS ADMINISTRATION

UNIVERSITY AND LOCATION

Founded in 1963, the University of Central Florida is a member of the 10-campus state university system of Florida and offers 73 bachelor's degree programs, 51 master's, 3 advanced master's and specialist programs and 15 doctorates. UCF comprises the colleges of arts and sciences, business administration, health and public affairs, education and engineering and has a total enrollment of just over 30,000 students.

UCF's main campus consists of 79 buildings situated on over 1,400 acres. There are also four satellite campuses in Brevard, Daytona Beach, South Orlando and one in the downtown core of Orlando.

Students have access to the main library collection which includes 1.2 million bound volumes, serials and government documents, more than 6,400 current periodical subscriptions, over two million microfilms and microfiche and 30,000 non-print items.

Recreational facilities include lighted outdoor tennis and basketball courts, an outdoor swimming pool, a golf driving range, a frisbee golf course, volleyball and basketball courts and multipurpose playing fields.

Th university is located in east-central Florida, which is one of the fastest-growing regions in the US and has a population of about two million. Area attractions include the beautiful beaches on the Atlantic, located about an hour's drive from campus, Walt Disney World and professional sports teams such as the NBA's Orlando Magic basketball team.

City Population:	1,400,000
Cost of Living:	medium
Climate Range:	48° to 90°F
Campus Setting:	urban
Total Enrollment:	30,100
Graduate Enrollment:	4,900
Students in Residence:	–

FACULTY

- Allen, J.W. PhD, Kentucky
- Ambrose, M.K. PhD, Illinois
- Bailey, C.D. PhD, Georgia State
- Bandy, D.D. PhD, Texas at Austin
- Bobek, D. PhD, Florida
- Bogumil, W.A. PhD, Georgia
- Borde, S.F. PhD, Florida Atlantic
- Braun, B.M. PhD, Tulane
- Callarman, W.G. PhD, Arizona State
- Cheney, J.M. DBA, Tennessee
- Cheney, P. PhD, Minnesota
- Cherry, T.L. PhD, Wyoming
- Davis, D. DBA, Kentucky
- Day, A.E. PhD, Purdue
- D'Cruz, C. –
- DeGeorge, L. –
- Desiraju, R. –
- Dwyer, P.D. PhD, Missouri-Columbia
- Ellis, T. PhD, Texas A&M
- Escarraz, D. –
- Evans, T.G. PhD, Michigan State
- Fernald, L.W. DBA, George Washington
- Ford, C.M. PhD, Pennsylvania State
- Ford, R.C. PhD, Arizona State
- Frye, M.B. PhD, Georgia Inst of Tech
- Fuller, D.A. PhD, Georgia State
- Gibbs, E. PhD, Rutgers
- Gillet, P.L. PhD, Michigan State
- Goldwater, P.M. PhD, Louisiana State
- Goodman, S.H. PhD, Pennsylvania State
- Gowan, M.A. PhD, Georgia
- Harrison, J.S. PhD, Utah
- Hess, T.J. PhD, Virginia Polytechnic
- Hightower, R. PhD, Georgia State
- Hofler, R.A. PhD, North Carolina
- Huseman, R.C. PhD, Illinois
- Johnson, W. PhD, Texas at Austin
- Jones, F.F. PhD, Georgia
- Judd, A.J. PhD, Florida
- Kelliher, C.F. PhD, Texas A&M
- Keon, T.L. PhD, Michigan State
- Lee, J. PhD, Michigan State
- Leigh, W.E. PhD, Cincinnati
- List, J.A. PhD, Wyoming
- Mahoney, L. PhD, Central Florida
- Martin, T.L. PhD, Rice
- McHone, W. PhD, Pennsylvania
- McQuillen, C. PhD, Florida
- Michaels, R.E. PhD, Indiana
- Michelson, S.E. PhD, Kansas
- Modani, N.K. PhD, South Carolina
- Park, H. PhD, Georgia State
- Pennington, R.L. PhD, Texas A&M
- Potts, J.H. PhD, Alabama
- Ramanlal, P. PhD, Michigan
- Roberts, R.W. PhD, Arkansas
- Roberts, T. PhD, Auburn
- Rodriguez, M. –
- Roush, P.Y. PhD, Georgia State
- Rubin, R.S. PhD, Massachusetts
- Rungeling, B.S. PhD, Kentucky
- Salter, J.H. PhD, Louisiana State
- Sarker, M. PhD, Michigan State
- Savage, L.J. PhD, Florida
- Schminke, M.J. PhD, Carnegie Mellon
- Scott, D.F. PhD, Florida
- Smith, S.D. PhD, Arizona State
- Soskin, M.D. PhD, Pennsylvania State
- Stone, D.L. PhD, Purdue
- Sweeney, P.D. PhD, Pittsburgh
- Uhl-Bien, M. PhD, Cincinnati
- Weaver, W.C. PhD, Georgia State
- Welch, J.K. PhD, Florida State
- West, L. PhD, Texas A&M
- White, K.R. PhD, Oklahoma
- Whyte, A.M. PhD, Florida Atlantic
- Winters, D.B. PhD, Georgia
- Wolpert, E. PhD, Florida State
- Xander, J.A. PhD, Georgia

UNIVERSITY OF CHICAGO
PHD PROGRAM IN BUSINESS

Program Highlights

- *Nobel Prize won by three current and two past faculty from the Graduate School of Business*
- *Tuition and tuition-plus-fellowship stipend awards provide funding for up to five years*
- *Nine areas of specialization*
- *Accredited by AACSB*

CONTACT INFORMATION
Graduate School of Business
1101 East 58th Street
Chicago, Illinois USA 60637
PH: 1-773-702-7298
FAX: 1-773-702-5257
EMAIL: gsbphd@uchicago.edu
INTERNET:
http://www.gsb.uchicago.edu/programs/phd

UNIVERSITY OF CHICAGO, PHD PROGRAM IN BUSINESS

PROGRAM OVERVIEW

Established in 1920, the University of Chicago's (UC) Graduate School of Business (GSB) has the oldest doctoral program in business in the US. It awarded the first business PhD in 1922. The GSB offers dissertation areas in accounting, econometrics and statistics, economics, finance, marketing, management science, managerial and organizational behavior, organizations and markets and production.

Degree requirements include the completion of a general examination in both the dissertation area and a supporting discipline, completion of a three-course sequence in an area other than the dissertation or support area and of any four GSB courses that are not in the dissertation, support or coordination sequence areas. Participation in a total of six quarters of workshops in the dissertation area is also mandatory, as is the completion of an original research paper during the third year and the completion and successful defense of an original dissertation. Students generally take four to five years of full-time study to complete the PhD program.

Dissertation Areas

Topics considered within the accounting area range broadly from capital markets research to agency models to taxation and auditing research. Courses offered by the GSB can be supplemented by courses in the departments of behavioral sciences, economics, mathematics and statistics.

Study in the area of econometrics and statistics combines courses in specific areas of business such as economics, finance, accounting, marketing or international business with advanced courses in statistical methods.

Students in economics have a wide range of course offerings in the GSB and the Department of Economics and generally write dissertations in industrial organization, labor economics, macroeconomics, microeconomics or related areas.

The finance program is concerned with the behavior of security prices, portfolio management, the management of corporate and public funds, and the management and regulation of financial institutions.

Management science is concerned with the application of mathematics and computer methods to management problems, primarily mathematical programming, queuing theory and inventory theory.

The managerial and organizational behavior option applies theory and research from cognitive and social psychology, economics and other related fields to the study of human behavior relevant to a range of managerial contexts. Research topics may include cognitive processes of judgment and decision-making, psychological aspects of economic behavior, power and influence, teamwork and group processes and organizational decision-making.

Advanced research in marketing issues uses skills acquired in consumer behavior, economics, or econometrics and statistics. Students take courses in the GSB and in the psychology, sociology, and econometrics and statistics departments. Research includes the study of consumer decision-making, analysis of the effect of consumer and trade promotions and cross-category analysis of marketing effects on brand choice behavior.

The organizations and markets program offers training in economic sociology and explores how social networks and institutions affect competition. It provides conceptual grounding in the operation and interaction of organizations and the people functioning within them.

The production dissertation area focuses on concepts, models and data which contribute to systems and operations development. This program includes reading courses in production and distribution research and courses in linear and integer programming and stochastic and combinatorial optimization.

SELECTED RESEARCH AREAS

- Accounting information
- Acquisition and transmission of knowledge
- Analysis of household purchase behavior
- Asset allocation
- Asset pricing
- Categorial data analysis
- Consumer and retail sales promotion
- Consumer behavior
- Corporate finance
- Cross-cultural psychology
- Econometric theory
- Economic geography
- Economic growth
- Economics of contracts
- Economics of information
- Education and training of the workforce
- Entrepreneurship
- Exchange rate issues
- Executive compensation
- Financial contracting
- Financial markets with imperfect information
- Financial risk management and measurement
- Graphical methods
- International finance
- Investment behavior of financially constrained firms
- Judgement under uncertainty
- Logistics of production and inventory systems
- Macroeconomics
- Management science in marketing
- Negotiation and decision making
- Panel data models
- Personal economics
- Portfolio allocation
- Price formation in capital markets
- Pricing and promotion policies
- Productivity
- Program evaluation
- Real estate
- Social cognition and interpersonal perception
- Taxes and corporate restructuring
- Technology and business startegy
- Transaction costs
- Voluntary disclosure

UNIVERSITY OF CHICAGO, PHD PROGRAM IN BUSINESS

ADMISSIONS CRITERIA & PROCEDURES

Prospective PhD students must indicate the area in which they intend to develop expertise and write a dissertation. Applicants planning to specialize in business economics must submit the GRE, including the writing assessment. For those planning to study finance, the GRE, including the writing assessment, is preferred, but the GMAT is acceptable. Those intending to specialize in all other areas may submit either the GRE or the GMAT. Students admitted to the program usually score above the 90th percentile in these tests.

International applicants should submit both original language records and certified, literal translations. Those whose native language is not English must achieve minimum scores of 600 or 60, respectively, on the paper-based TOEFL and TSE or 250 and 25 on the computer-based tests.

A complete application packet must contain an application for admission, a resume, official transcripts from all postsecondary institutions attended, two letters of reference, the application fee and official test scores.

Admission takes place in the autumn quarter only. The application deadline is January 15. International applicants are urged to submit applications by January 1.

EXPENSES & FINANCIAL ASSISTANCE

All students who are admitted to the PhD program are automatically considered for financial aid consisting of tuition for five years and a stipend for four years.

As students progress they have the opportunity to apply for supplemental merit-based financial support such as summer research grants and a variety of fellowship awards.

Students who wish to be considered for additional need-based financial aid such as loans should contact the GSB's Office of Financial Aid.

INTERNATIONAL STUDENT SUPPORT

The Office of International Affairs (OIA) advises international students about their applications for admission to the university and provides information about US government regulations and UC rules and policies. OIA staff assist international students with personal problems and concerns arising from study in a foreign country and also act as a liaison with international groups and activities on and around campus.

ADMISSIONS AT A GLANCE

Minimum GMAT:	630
Minimum GPA:	3.5
Minimum TOEFL (paper):	600
Minimum TOEFL (computer):	250
Application Fee:	US$65
Application Deadline:	Jan 15 (Jan 1 preferred for international students)

EXPENSES AT A GLANCE

Tuition:
- In State: waived with admission
- Out-of-State: waived with admission
- Int'l Students: waived with admission

Books & Supplies: –
Health Insurance: –
Accommodation:
- University Residences: US$6,315–7,660 per year
- Family Housing: n/a
- Private: US$500–1,000 per month

PROGRAM FACTS

# of Full-time Students:	96
# of Part-time Students:	0
# of Applications per year:	300
# Accepted per year:	35
# Enrolled per year:	20
Average GMAT Score:	693
Average Age:	26
% Men/Women:	80%/20%
Work Experience (avg yrs):	–
# of Faculty:	132
% Faculty with Doctoral Degree:	100%
Annual Research Funding:	–

UNIVERSITY OF CHICAGO, PhD PROGRAM IN BUSINESS

UNIVERSITY AND LOCATION

The University of Chicago has a total enrollment of approximately 12,500 students including 8,600 graduate students and employs close to 2,000 full-time faculty members. UC comprises the undergraduate college, four graduate divisions, six graduate professional schools, the Graham School of General Studies and the University of Chicago Press, the largest university press in the US.

The university's 203-acre campus stretches along both sides of the Midway Plaisance, designed for the World's Columbian Exposition of 1893. It features tree-shaded quadrangles, gray limestone buildings with gargoyles, and contemporary buildings such as Frank Lloyd Wright's Robie House, a national historic landmark. The UC's eight libraries hold over six million volumes and 21,000 linear feet of manuscripts and archival materials. The university is home to cultural resources such as the Oriental Institute Museum, Court Theatre and the Renaissance Society.

The university is located in Hyde Park-South Kenwood, a residential community15 minutes south of the Chicago Loop on Lake Michigan. Two-thirds of the faculty and most students live in this area, which offers a selection of markets, specialty shops and professional and recreational services. Chicago's Museum of Science and Industry and the DuSable Museum of African-American History are located here.

City Population:	2,700,000
Cost of Living:	medium
Climate Range:	16° to 82°F
Campus Setting:	urban
Total Enrollment:	12,441
Graduate Enrollment:	8,125
Students in Residence:	–

FACULTY
- Abrevara, J. PhD, Harvard
- Adelman, D. PhD, Georgia Tech
- Aguiar, M. PhD, MIT
- Aliber, R.Z. PhD, Yale
- Anderson, E. PhD, MIT
- Barberis, N. PhD, Harvard
- B-Shuster, D. PhD, Northwestern
- Blout-Lyon, S. PhD, Northwestern
- Burt, R.S. PhD, Chicago
- Carlton, D.W. PhD, MIT
- Caselli, F. PhD, Harvard
- Chevalier, J. PhD, MIT
- Chintagunta, P.K. PhD, Northwestern
- Cochrane, J.H. PhD, Berkeley
- Constantinides, G.M. DBA, Indiana
- Davis, H.L. PhD, Northwestern
- Davis, S.J. PhD, Brown
- Dhar, S.K. PhD, California
- Diamond, D.W. PhD, Yale
- Eisenstien, D.D. PhD, Georgia Institute of Technology
- Engel, E. PhD, Stanford
- Eppen, G.D. PhD, Cornell
- Erikson, M. PhD, Arizona
- Fama, E.F. PhD, Chicago
- Fogel, R.W. AM, Columbia
- Frenzen, J.K. PhD, Chicago
- Garicano, L. PhD, Chicago
- Garmaise, M. PhD, Stanford
- Gaspar, J. PhD, Stanford
- Gertner, R.H. PhD, MIT
- Ginzel, L.E. PhD, Princeton
- Goolsbee, A. PhD, MIT
- Gordon, E.A. PhD, Columbia
- Gross, D.B. PhD, MIT
- Gould, J.P. PhD, Chicago
- Hamada, R.S. PhD, MIT
- Hanna, J.D. PhD, Cornell
- Harris, M. PhD, Chicago
- Hemmer, T. PhD, Odense
- Hogarth, R.M. PhD, Chicago
- Hsee, C.K. PhD, Yale
- Hubbard, T. PhD, Stanford
- Huizinga, J. PhD, MIT
- Hummels, D. PhD, Michigan
- Hurst, E. PhD, Michigan
- Jenner, M. MBA, Harvard
- Jeuland, A.P. PhD, Purdue
- Kaplan, S.N. PhD, Harvard
- Kashyap, A. PhD, MIT
- Klayman, J. PhD, Minnesota
- Klenow, P.J. PhD, Stanford
- Knez, M. PhD, Pennsylvania
- Kroszner, R.S. PhD, Harvard
- Lamont, O. PhD, MIT
- Larrick, R. PhD, Michigan
- Leclerc, F. PhD, Cornell
- Leftwich, R. PhD, Rochester
- Madansky, A. PhD, Chicago
- Madrian, B.C. PhD, MIT
- Manchanda, P. PhD, Columbia
- Martin, R.K. PhD, Cincinnati
- McCulloch, R.E. PhD, Minnesota
- McGill, A.L. PhD, Chicago
- Menon, S. PhD, Pennsylvania
- Miller, M.H. PhD, John Hopkins
- Monahan, S. PhD, North Carolina
- Moskowitz, T. PhD, UCLA
- Murphy, K.M. PhD, Chicago
- Myers, M. PhD, North Carolina
- Northcut, W. PhD, S.California
- Parzen, M.I. DSc, Harvard
- Pashigian, B.P. PhD, MIT
- Pastor, L. PhD, Pennsylvania
- Peltzman, S. PhD, Chicago
- Petrin, A. PhD, Michigan
- Phillips, D. PhD, Stanford
- Piotroski, J. PhD, Michigan
- Polson, N. PhD, Nottingham
- Prendergast, C. PhD, Yale
- Raith, M. PhD, LSE
- Rajan, R. PhD, MIT
- Rajiv, S. PhD, Carnegie Mellon
- Rossi, P.E. PhD, Chicago
- Rottenstreich, Y. PhD, Stanford
- Rudnick, E.A. MBA, Chicago
- Russell, J. PhD, California-San Diego
- Santos, J. PhD, Chicago
- Schipper, K. PhD, Chicago
- Schrage, L.E. PhD, Cornell
- Schrager, J.E. PhD, Chicago
- Serrat, A. PhD, MIT
- Shibano, T. PhD, Stanford
- Smith, A.J. PhD, Cornell
- Sorenson, J. PhD, Stanford
- Stole, L. PhD, MIT
- Stromberg, P. PhD, Carnegie Mellon
- Stuart, T.E. PhD, Stanford
- Surdam, D. PhD, Chicago
- Thaler, R.H. PhD, Rochester
- Tiao, G.C. PhD, Wisonsin
- Topel, R.H. PhD, California
- Tsay, R.S. PhD, Wisconsin
- van Osselaer, S. PhD, Florida
- Veronesi, P. PhD, Harvard
- Vilcassim, N. PhD, Cornell
- Vishny, R.W. PhD, MIT
- Weil, R.L. PhD, Carnegie Mellon
- Wildman, W.A. AM, Chicago
- Wittenbrink, B. PhD, Michigan
- Wu, G. PhD, Harvard
- Yang, D.L. PhD, Princeton
- Young, A. PhD, Columbia
- Zangwill, W.I. PhD, Stanford
- Zingales, L. PhD, MIT
- Zmijewski, M.E. PhD, SUNY
- Zonis, M. PhD, MIT

UNIVERSITY OF CINCINNATI
PhD IN BUSINESS ADMINISTRATION

Program Highlights

- *Five areas of concentration*
- *Limited enrollment ensures close interaction with faculty members*
- *Graduate scholarships and research and teaching assistantships with full-tuition waivers*
- *GE Faculty for the Future Fellowships*

CONTACT INFORMATION
PhD Program
103 Carl H. Lindner Hall
Cincinnati, Ohio USA 45221-0020
PH: 1-513-556-7020
FAX: 1-513-556-4891
EMAIL: Katerbrj@UC.edu
INTERNET: http://www.cba.uc.edu/

UNIVERSITY OF CINCINNATI, PHD IN BUSINESS ADMINISTRATION

PROGRAM OVERVIEW

The University of Cincinnati's (UC) College of Business Administration (CBA) offers a Doctor of Philosophy (PhD) degree program in business administration with five concentrations in finance, management, marketing, operations management and quantitative analysis. The program provides the knowledge and skills required to perform original, independent research and to prepare students for careers in business administration teaching and research.

The degree requires the completion of 135 graduate credits, the equivalent of three years of full-time study, including 90 credits of coursework and 45 credits of dissertation research.

Seminars

All students must complete a three-credit introductory doctoral seminar. This seminar focuses on key issues and topics in business administration education, and the role of writing in research and publishing. It introduces students to the range of research conducted in the CBA and to the resources available.

A three-credit philosophy of science seminar must be completed in the first summer quarter or in the fall quarter of the second year of study.

Statistics & Business Cores

Students must fulfill the statistics requirement by completing three-credit courses in statistical methodology and regression analysis.

The core requirement consists of 21 business credits selected from microeconomics, macroeconomics, managerial communication, competitive analysis, strategic management, financial accounting, managerial accounting, legal and regulatory environment, operations management, financial analysis, financial management, organizations, marketing management, decisions models/optimization and information systems for managers. It fosters a thorough understanding of the functional areas of business in a global context. In most cases, students who hold Master of Business Administration (MBA) degrees will already have satisfied this requirement.

Area of Concentration

The area of concentration is the focal point of the PhD program and coursework in this area provides students with the specialized knowledge required to undertake substantive research. Most students select a concentration from among the five areas offered by the CBA but it is also possible to develop an area of interest that overlaps the college's traditional departments.

A minimum of 24 credit hours of graduate-level coursework must be taken in the area of concentration, including specific courses determined by students' program committees.

A further 15 credits must be taken in area related to, but separate from, the concentration, including any discipline or combination of disciplines within the university with the approval of the program committee.

Comprehensive Exams & Dissertation

Each PhD student must pass written and oral comprehensive examinations in the area of concentration when all prescribed coursework has been completed.

The doctoral dissertation is the culmination of the PhD student's research training and it must be a significant and original contribution to the literature of the field. A total of 45 credit hours is granted for the successful completion of the dissertation, which must be defended orally in front of a committee of faculty members before the PhD degree is awarded.

SELECTED RESEARCH AREAS

- Accounting systems
- Banking
- Capital markets
- Corporate finance
- Customer focus
- Database design
- Diffusion of innovation
- Direct marketing
- Distributions system design
- E-Commerce
- Econometric applications
- Experimental finance
- Facilities location
- Financial accounting
- Forecasting
- Geodemographic systems
- Incentives
- International accounting
- Interpersonal relationships
- Intersectional and procedural justice in organizations
- Investments
- Leasing
- Logistics
- Management information systems
- Management of innovation
- Multi-level inventory analysis
- Organizational effectiveness
- Organizational learning
- Persuasion
- Portfolio management
- Prediction analysis
- Product cost systems
- Real Estate
- Services marketing
- Speculative markets
- Strategic decision making
- Supplier management in global competition
- Supply chain modeling
- Taxation
- Telecommunications
- Vendor selection
- Working capital management

UNIVERSITY OF CINCINNATI, PHD IN BUSINESS ADMINISTRATION

ADMISSIONS CRITERIA & PROCEDURES

The CBA's PhD programs are highly selective and successful applicants must display strong intellectual abilities and a commitment to research. A bachelor's degree from an accredited college or university is required. Applicants should have a minimum B average or equivalent in relevant undergraduate coursework or otherwise give evidence of promise satisfactory to the admitting department. Students deficient in undergraduate preparation may be required to enroll in appropriate undergraduate courses.

Completed applications should include the university dean's application form, application fee, statement of purpose identifying areas of research interest, three letters of recommendation from faculty members or professional colleagues, official GMAT scores, official transcripts of all previous graduate and undergraduate work and a resume outlining educational and work experience. International students whose native language is not English must include official results of the TOEFL with their application. The minimum acceptable TOEFL score for graduate work in the CBA is 600 on the paper-based test or 250 on the computer-based test. This requirement may be waived for international students who hold a degree from an accredited US university or college and who studied oral and written English while they were attending that institution.

Both US students and international applicants are admitted for the fall quarter only and the application deadline is February 15.

Accepted international students must provide an official certification of sources of support and amounts before an I-20 can be issued by the Office of International Student Services.

EXPENSES & FINANCIAL ASSISTANCE

University Graduate Scholarships cover full tuition excluding general fees and other expenses. Under the auspices of the GE Faculty for the Future Program, minority students in the doctoral program may be eligible for additional financial assistance.

Students with full course loads may be awarded assistantships including a full tuition waiver, general fees and a stipend of US$11,000 for a 10-month period. Summer assistantships are also available. Assistantships are usually up to 20 hours a week of departmental research or teaching aid.

INTERNATIONAL STUDENT SUPPORT

The International Student Services Office (ISSO) at UC advises students on immigration issues, cross-cultural differences, financial matters and any other concerns which may arise during transitions into a new culture. A quarterly international student newsletter keeps students updated on educational, social and cultural activities.

ISSO provides assistance with extending stays in the US, regulations concerning school transfers and the entry of family members, applying to new programs of study and re-entering the US.

All new students must attend an orientation organized by ISSO prior to the beginning of classes. ISSO facilitates the invitation of international students to the homes of local community families for meals, holiday celebrations and cultural exchange.

ADMISSIONS AT A GLANCE

Minimum GMAT:	600
Minimum GPA:	3.0
Minimum TOEFL (paper):	600
Minimum TOEFL (computer):	250
Application Fee:	US$30
Application Deadline:	Feb 15

EXPENSES AT A GLANCE

Tuition per year:	
In State:	US$8,000
Out-of-State:	US$14,800
Int'l Students:	US$14,800
Books & Supplies:	US$400–450
Health Insurance:	US$207
Accommodation:	
University Residences:	US$600 per month
Family Housing:	–
Private:	US$700 per month

PROGRAM FACTS

# of Full-time Students:	35
# of Part-time Students:	0
# of Applications per year:	85
# Accepted per year:	14
# Enrolled per year:	9
Average GMAT Score:	650
Average Age:	33
% Men/Women:	50%/50%
Work Experience (avg yrs):	2.5
# of Faculty:	70
% Faculty with Doctoral Degree:	100%
Annual Research Funding:	US$0.3m

UNIVERSITY OF CINCINNATI, PhD IN BUSINESS ADMINISTRATION

UNIVERSITY AND LOCATION

Established by the City of Cincinnati in 1870, the University of Cincinnati became the first municipally sponsored, state-affiliated university in 1968 and was designated a state university in 1977. UC comprises colleges of applied science, arts and sciences, architecture and planning, business administration, education, engineering, continuing education, law, medicine, nursing and health and pharmacy, divisions of research and advanced studies and professional practice, the School of Social Work, Allied Health Services, Clermont College, Raymond Walters College, University College and the College-Conservatory of Music. The university is accredited by the North Central Association of Colleges and Schools.

UC has a total enrollment of 35,000 students, including over 6,000 full- and part-time graduate students, who attend classes on five campuses located on 390 acres of land contained by Burnet Woods and easily accessible by foot.

The university is the home of the first cooperative education program offered in the US, established in 1906, which now places 1,100 student with more than 400 organizations in the Cincinnati metropolitan area alone.

UC's supports 18 libraries, including medical, law, departmental and branch campus libraries and an extensive general library, housing over 2.1 million bound volumes, three million microfilms and 19,500 serial subscriptions and access to more than 120 electronic databases.

The city of Cincinnati, situated on the Ohio River, has a total metropolitan population of 1.5 million people and is the home of 15 Fortune 500 corporate headquarters and over 300 offices of other Fortune 500 companies. Cincinnati is home to several museums, art galleries, theatres and symphonies and offers a variety of outdoor activities in the nearby lakes, rivers and hills. Fountain Square and its surrounding park serve as a central meeting place. Sports fans can attend Cincinnati Reds major-league baseball games and Bengals NFL football games.

City Population:	1,500,000
Cost of Living:	medium
Climate Range:	21° to 86°F
Campus Setting:	urban
Total Enrollment:	35,500
Graduate Enrollment:	6,210
Students in Residence:	4,000

FACULTY

- Adams, P.D. PhD, Ohio State
- Allen, C.T. PhD, Ohio State
- Anderson, D.R. PhD, Purdue
- Angle, H.L. PhD, California, Irvine
- Baker, N.R. PhD, Northwestern
- Bigley, G.A.. PhD, California,Irvine
- Boyer, C.K. PhD, Case Western Reserve
- Bruvold, N.T. PhD, Purdue
- Byard, D.A.. PhD, Maryland
- Camm, J.D. PhD, Clemson
- Chandrashekaran, M. PhD, Arizona State
- Chiang, R.H.L. PhD, Rochester
- Clayton, J. PhD, UBC
- Comer, J.M. PhD, Northwestern
- Curry, D.J.. PhD, Berkeley
- Dean, M. PhD, Ohio State
- Dixon, A.L.. PhD, Indiana
- Drake, A. PhD, Michigan State
- Dwyer, F.R. PhD, Minnesota
- Evans, J.R. PhD, Georgia Institute of Tech
- Ferguson, M. PhD, Indiana
- Gales, L.M. PhD, North Carolina at Chapel Hill
- Ganeshan, R. PhD, Penn State
- Geltner, D.M. PhD, MIT
- Hatch, B.C.. PhD, Indiana
- Henderson, G.V. DBA, Florida State
- Jain, N. PhD, Texas at Austin
- Johnson, S.A. PhD, Louisiana State
- Kamath, R.R. PhD, Michigan
- Kang, D. PhD, Southern California
- Kardes, F.R. PhD, Indiana
- Katerberg, R. PhD, Illinois
- Kellaris, J.J. PhD, Georgia State
- Kelton, W.D. PhD, Wisconsin
- Kim, K.K.. PhD, Utah
- Kim, Y.H. PhD, Penn State
- Kluger, B.D. PhD, Tulane
- Levy, M.L. PhD, Kansas State
- Lewis, M.W.. PhD, Kentucky
- Machleit, K.A. PhD, Michigan State
- Macklin, M.C. PhD, Ohio State
- Magazine, M.J. PhD, Florida
- Masterson, S.S.. PhD, Maryland
- Matthews, C.H. PhD, Cincinnati
- Mehra, A. PhD, Penn State
- Mehta, R.B. PhD, Utah
- Miller, N.G. PhD, Ohio State
- Prabhakar, B. DBA, Mississippi State
- Raturi, A.S. PhD, Minnesota
- Reed, M.P.. PhD, Kansas
- Rogers, D.F. PhD, Purdue
- Sachs, K.D.. PhD, SUNY-Buffalo
- Sale, J.T. PhD, Cincinnati
- Salter, S.B. PhD, South Carolina
- Siff, F. PhD, New York
- Sundaramurthy, C. PhD, Illinois at Urbana-Champaign
- Swanson, P.J. PhD, Illinois
- Sweeney, D.J. DBA, Indiana
- Umanath, N.S. PhD, Houston
- Walker, M.C. PhD, Houston
- Welsh, M.A. PhD, Missouri
- Willems, S. PhD, MIT
- Wong, J.A.. PhD, Oregon
- Wyatt, S.B. PhD, Texas
- Zirger, B.J. PhD, Stanford

UNIVERSITY OF CONNECTICUT
SCHOOL OF BUSINESS ADMINISTRATION

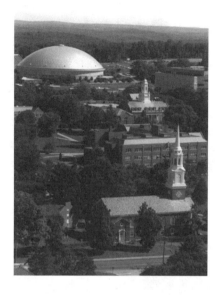

Program Highlights

- *Program's small size ensures students have the opportunity to work closely with faculty members who share similar research interests*
- *Students design and conduct research during the first year of the program*
- *Graduate faculty recognized worldwide for their research expertise*
- *Students gain teaching experience as part of their professional development*
- *Five areas of concentration offered*

CONTACT INFORMATION

PhD Program

368 Fairfield Road, U-41 P

Storrs, Connecticut USA 06269-1006

PH: 1-860-486-5822

FAX: 1-860-486-0270

EMAIL: phdmail@sba.uconn.edu

INTERNET:

http://www.sba.uconn.edu/phd/index.htm

UNIVERSITY OF CONNECTICUT, SCHOOL OF BUSINESS ADMINISTRATION

PROGRAM OVERVIEW

The University of Connecticut (UConn) School of Business Administration (SBA) offers a Doctor of Philosophy (PhD) in business administration with concentrations in accounting, finance, management, marketing and operations and information management.

All areas of concentration have the same general requirements, including a qualifying research paper, a comprehensive general examination and a dissertation. Students in the accounting program take a minimum of 49 credits of coursework, those in marketing a minimum of 40 credits, and the other concentrations require 37 credits.

Accounting

The concentration in accounting is designed to give students a broad understanding of the multidisciplinary nature of the accounting literature and develop the knowledge and skills necessary to conduct original research on accounting problems. Students select a specialization in accounting and cognitive psychology, accounting and social psychology or accounting and economics.

Accounting students work with faculty on collaborative research projects and develop lecturing skills by assisting with undergraduate courses. Students also participate in an accounting research workshop in which students, faculty and scholars from around the country present research papers.

Finance

The PhD with a concentration in finance involves the study of financial management, investments, financial markets, corporate finance, banking, insurance, real estate, and urban economics and international finance. It builds on preparatory work in economics, mathematics, statistics and MBA-core courses including accounting. Finance students generally major in one of these areas. The finance faculty have diverse interests and students will find a faculty member to work with them in almost any area they choose to pursue.

Management

Management research is divided into the two broad categories: organizational behavior and strategic management. Organizational behavior is primarily based on theories and methodologies used in psychology and sociology, and strategic management focuses on economics and marketing. Students in the PhD in management program are exposed to both areas but concentrate their studies in one. The curriculum prepares students to conduct original research to explain phenomena previously not well understood and to test proposed explanations empirically.

Marketing

The PhD in marketing program helps students acquire the research skills to make significant contributions to the marketing discipline. Students are required to complete a minimum of 40 credits of coursework, including five advanced courses in marketing, but are given the flexibility to select the research methods and supporting courses that best suit their needs, talents and interest areas. Marketing faculty have a wide range of interests and strengths in areas such as advertising, consumer behavior, international marketing, marketing research, marketing strategy, pricing and retailing.

Operations & Information Management

Students pursuing a PhD concentration in operations and information management can specialize in operations management, management information systems or in a combination of the two.

SELECTED RESEARCH AREAS
- Accounting for financial derivatives
- Advertising
- Auditor expertise
- Bankruptcy/Going concern decisions
- Capital markets research
- Consumer behavior
- Corporate control
- Corporate financial reporting
- Cultural transfer of accounting
- Database design and security
- Economic effects of taxation
- Economics of auditing
- Effect of accounting/auditing standards on capital markets
- Electronic markets and e-commerce
- Entrepreneurship
- Expert system modeling of microeconomic markets
- Fairness in the workplace
- Financial accounting
- Financial futures
- Human resources management
- Information economics
- Info tech performance evaluation
- Initial public offerings
- Interactive marketing
- International capital markets
- International financial management
- International marketing
- Lab experimentation of info values
- Linear and nonlinear programming algorithms
- Management of innovation
- Manufacturing planning and control
- Manufacturing technology
- Market adjustment
- Market microstructure
- Marketing on the Internet
- Marketing strategy
- Mathematical modeling and simulation
- Mortgage markets
- Negotiations
- Online auctions
- Organizational behavior
- Product and brand management
- Rate regulation
- Real estate and urban economics
- Relationship marketing
- Retail management
- Risk management
- Signaling theory
- Software project management
- Strategic management
- Tax policy
- Valuation of corporate obligations
- Value of information
- Women and men in management
- Workflow systems
- Workplace diversity

UNIVERSITY OF CONNECTICUT, SCHOOL OF BUSINESS ADMINISTRATION

ADMISSIONS CRITERIA & PROCEDURES

Applicants to the PhD in business administration program must apply and be admitted to both the Graduate School and the SBA. The Graduate School requires a bachelor's degree from an accredited college or university with a minimum GPA of 3.0 for admission to any doctoral program at UConn. Within the SBA, admissions decisions are made by faculty in the applicant's area of concentration and a school-wide PhD admissions committee. An applicant's ability to perform original research at the doctoral level is the primary basis for admission to the program, but decisions are also influenced by the applicant's overall standing and the availability of positions in the applicant's area of concentration.

Applicants should submit official transcripts from all colleges and universities previously attended, official GMAT scores and letters of recommendation from academic faculty in a position to comment on the applicant's potential for intensive study, scholarly research and teaching.

Students whose native language is not English must submit results of the TOEFL and the TSE. The minimum acceptable TOEFL score is 550 on the paper-based test.

Students are normally admitted to the PhD program in the fall semester only and completed applications should be submitted to both the Graduate School and the SBA no later than February 1.

EXPENSES & FINANCIAL ASSISTANCE

Most doctoral students entering the program at UConn receive a full assistantship with a stipend of US$14,000 for a nine-month period, a full tuition waiver and health insurance benefits. The assistantship is guaranteed for at least three years as long as students remain in good academic standing.

UConn offers predoctoral fellowships, summer fellowships, dissertation fellowships, minority fellowships and outstanding scholar fellowships. Funding is also available to help cover travel costs incurred by students making presentations at professional conferences.

INTERNATIONAL STUDENT SUPPORT

The Department of International Services and Programs (DISP) offers a week-long fall orientation for new international students. Activities during this week include information sessions on registration, health insurance and US immigration regulations and there is a period set aside for students to questions about issues such as local banking, arranging for telephone service and getting student ID cards. Students are given a tour of the campus, university library and local community and encouraged to attend orientation social activities.

Throughout the year, DISP provides academic, personal and career advising as well as English language training at the American English Language Institute. To satisfy US immigration requirements, international students arriving at the school must report to the DISP before they register for classes.

International House organizes programs for international students. The facility is open every day for individual and group use by all students.

ADMISSIONS AT A GLANCE

Minimum GMAT:	no set minimum
Minimum GPA:	3.0
Minimum TOEFL (paper):	550
Minimum TOEFL (computer):	–
Application Fee:	
US$40 (dom)	
US$45 (int'l)	
Application Deadline:	Feb 1

EXPENSES AT A GLANCE

Tuition per year:	
In State:	US$5,272
Out-of-State:	US$13,696
Int'l Students:	US$13,696
Books & Supplies:	US$1,200 per year
Health Insurance:	–
Accommodation:	
University Residences:	US$1,605 per semester
Family Housing:	–
Private:	US$400-1,000 per month

PROGRAM FACTS

# of Full-time Students:	40
# of Part-time Students:	0
# of Applications per year:	75
# Accepted per year:	15
# Enrolled per year:	12
Average GMAT Score:	640
Average Age:	35
% Men/Women:	70%/30%
Work Experience (avg yrs):	–
# of Faculty:	50
% Faculty with Doctoral Degree:	100%
Annual Research Funding:	–

UNIVERSITY OF CONNECTICUT, SCHOOL OF BUSINESS ADMINISTRATION

UNIVERSITY AND LOCATION

The University of Connecticut was originally the Storrs Agricultural School, founded in 1881. Since that time it has grown into a comprehensive postsecondary institution with 24,000 students and over 1,200 faculty members. Seventeen schools and colleges offer undergraduate and graduate degrees. UConn is currently the only PhD-granting public university in the state and one of only two research I public universities in New England.

UConn operates six regional campuses across the state. The main campus has more than 120 buildings on approximately 3,000 acres, located 35 miles east of Hartford midway between New York City and Boston.

The University Computing Center in the Math and Science building has three main servers which provide access to 5,000 workstations throughout the university. There is a Macintosh lab, Micro lab, PC homework lab, and 24 hour input/output terminal room. A faculty resource lab has been created to assist instructors and their assistants with preparing presentations.

The Homer Babbidge Library holdings include 2.1 million volumes of the university's 2.8 million volume collection. The university subscribes to 19,300 serials, of which 8,250 are housed in the Babbidge Library. Many of UConn's library collections are available through electronic resources.

The Graduate Residences consist of a complex of three coeducational buildings that contain 440 single rooms. Open year-round, including recess periods, the complex is located in the center of campus, providing residents with easy access to the Graduate Center, the library and other academic facilities.

Storrs is located in northeastern Connecticut, a rural area of woodlands and rolling hills. The quiet, safe setting is ideal for studying, and the friendly town of Storrs offers many amenities and activities for students. Storrs is located 30 minutes from Hartford and two hours from Boston.

City Population:	12,200
Cost of Living:	medium
Climate Range:	17° to 84°F
Campus Setting:	suburban
Total Enrollment:	24,000
Graduate Enrollment:	8,000
Students in Residence:	–

FACULTY

- Albert, T. PhD, Southern California
- Beliveau, B. PhD, Yale
- Bhattacharjee, S. PhD, SUNY
- Biggs, S.F. PhD, Minnesota
- Born, P. PhD, Duke
- Buzby, B. PhD, Indiana
- Campbell, G.M. PhD, Indiana
- Cann, W. JD, Connecticut
- Carrafiello, V. PhD, JD, Connecticut
- Chiang, I. PhD, Washington
- Clapp, J.M. PhD, Columbia
- Clifford, P. PhD, Case Western
- Coulter, R.H. PhD, Pittsburgh
- Dechant, K. EdD, Columbia
- Diaby, M. PhD, SUNY
- Dino, R. PhD, SUNY
- Dolde, W.C. PhD, Yale
- Dunbar, A. PhD, Texas
- Earley, C. PhD, Pittsburgh
- Fields, J.A. PhD, Pennsylvania State
- File, K. PhD, Temple
- Floyd, S.W. PhD, Colorado
- Fox, K. JD, Duke
- Garfinkel, R. PhD, John Hopkins
- Ghosh, C. PhD, Pennsylvania State
- Giaccotto, C. PhD, Kentucky
- Goes, P. PhD, Rochester
- Gopal, R. PhD, SUNY
- Gramling, L. PhD, Maryland
- Gupta, A. PhD, Texas at Austin
- Gutteridge, T. PhD, Purdue
- Harding, J. PhD, Berkeley
- Harris, W. PhD, Oklahoma
- Hegde, S. PhD, Massachusetts
- Hewett, K. PhD, South Carolina
- Hoskin, R.E. PhD, Cornell
- Hurley, R. PhD, Connecticut
- Hussein, M.E. PhD, Pittsburgh
- Jain, S.C. PhD, Oregon
- Johnson, R. PhD, Rochester
- Kidder, D. PhD, Minnesota
- Klein, L.S. PhD, Florida State
- Kochanek, R.F. PhD, Missouri
- Kramer, J. PhD, Connecticut
- Kung, S. PhD, Kentucky
- LaPlaca, P.J. PhD, Rensselaer
- Lelas, V. PhD, Texas
- Lubatkin, M.L. DBA, Tennessee
- Marsden, J.R. PhD, Purdue
- Martins, L. PhD, NYU
- Mathieu, J. PhD, Old Dominion
- Moore, N. PhD, Florida State
- Nair, S.K. PhD, Northwestern
- Nelson, C. DBA, Illinois
- Nunn, K.P. PhD, Massachusetts
- O'Brien, T.J. PhD, Florida
- Palmer, D.D. PhD, SUNY
- Pancek, K. JD, Boston College
- Phillips, J. PhD, Iowa
- Powell, G.N. PhD, Massachusetts
- Punj, G.N. PhD, Carnegie Mellon
- Ratneshwar, S. PhD, Vanderbilt
- Rich, J. PhD, Illinois
- Rosman, A.J. PhD, North Carolina
- Rummel, J.L. PhD, Rochester
- Samuel, S. PhD, Penn State
- Schrager, S. JD, Miami
- Scott, G. PhD, Washington
- Seow, G.S. PhD, Oregon
- Sewall, M.A. PhD, Washington
- Sirmans, C.F. PhD, Georgia
- Sottile, G. MBA, Connecticut
- Spiggle, S. PhD, Connecticut
- Srinivasan, N. PhD, SUNY
- Subramaniam, M. DBA, Boston
- Thakur, L.S. EngScD, Columbia
- Tubbs, R, PhD, Florida
- Tucker, E, SJD, New York Law School
- Veiga, J.F. DBA, Kent State
- Vertefeuille, M. BA, CCSU
- Walter, Z. PhD, Rochester
- Willenborg, M. PhD, Penn State

UNIVERSITY OF FLORIDA
WARRINGTON COLLEGE OF BUSINESS ADMINISTRATION

Program Highlights

- *Six areas of specialization*
- *Assistantships and fellowships for up to four years*
- *Program's small size ensures close interaction with faculty*

CONTACT INFORMATION

Warrington College of Business Administration

PO Box 117150

Gainesville, Florida USA 32611 - 7150

PH: 1-352-392-1210

FAX: 1-352-392-2086

EMAIL: ufwcba@dale.cba.ufl.edu

INTERNET: http://www.cba.ufl.edu/

UNIVERSITY OF FLORIDA, WARRINGTON COLLEGE OF BUSINESS ADMINISTRATION

PROGRAM OVERVIEW
The Warrington College of Business Administration (WCBA) at the University of Florida (UF) offers a Doctor of Philosophy (PhD) degree program with major areas of specialization in accounting, decision and information sciences, economics, finance, insurance and real estate, management, and marketing.

Candidates for the PhD in business administration must satisfy the WCBA's breadth and research foundations requirements. Students with prior business-related graduate or undergraduate level coursework generally meet breadth requirements upon admission. Those without prior coursework must take a minimum of three graduate courses in at least two fields other than the chosen area of concentration. A required six-course research skills sequence prepares students for scholarly research.

Other requirements include completion of graduate coursework in the major field of concentration and one or two supporting fields to add depth to the student's research training.

Accounting
The accounting concentration is designed to be completed in four to five years. In the second year, individual course work is tailored by students in consultation with supervisory committees and the accounting graduate coordinator. Other than the accounting seminars, there are no specific required courses after the first year of the program. Students must participate in the Accounting Research Colloquium, a forum for faculty, students and visiting scholars.

Decision and Information Sciences
The PhD curriculum in decision and information sciences is structured around students' academic background and interests, beginning with a required set of methods/skills courses and major-area specific courses. Specializations offered by the department are information systems and technology and operations management. PhD students are required to attend information systems and technology and operations management seminars offered within the department, as well as decision information sciences research workshops.

Economics
Students in economics take five required courses and six half-semester modules. Topics include mathematical methods and applications to economics, statistical methods in economics, microeconomic and macroeconomic theory, econometric models and methods, game theory, dynamic economics, equilibrium, and welfare economics, information economics and growth.

Students undertake coursework in at least three fields of specialization during the first two years of study. Specializations include industrial organization, international economics, econometrics, public economics and economic theory. Qualifying exams are written at the end of the second year.

Finance, Insurance and Real Estate
Students in finance, insurance and real estate take at least 16 credit hours of graduate coursework in finance or real estate and may elect to complete one or two minors including courses from several departments.

Management
The management program is designed to help students develop strong competence in the base discipline crucial to the study of organizations and their processes while completing a specialization in organizational behavior, organizational theory, human resource management or strategic studies.

Marketing
The marketing program consists of coursework in the breadth requirement, research foundations, the major field and electives. Major field coursework comprises five required marketing seminars completed during the first two years. Electives are selected from marketing and other related disciplines.

SELECTED RESEARCH AREAS
- Accounting theory
- Advertising response
- Agency theory
- Attestation
- Auditing
- Choice behavior
- Consumer behavior
- Corporate taxation
- Data mining
- Decision theory
- Economic development
- Electronic commerce
- Financial reporting
- Franchise law
- Game theory
- Global optimization
- Government regulation
- Hyperinflation
- Imperfect competition
- Industrial organization
- Information economics
- Interactive shopping
- International marketing
- Litigation
- Machine learning
- Managerial accounting
- Market organization
- Measurment theory
- Mergers
- Negotiation and conflict
- Pricing systems
- Real estate
- Securities pricing
- Tort liability

UNIVERSITY OF FLORIDA, WARRINGTON COLLEGE OF BUSINESS ADMINISTRATION

ADMISSIONS CRITERIA & PROCEDURES

The WCBA PhD program is highly selective. Entering classes annually range from 10 to 15 students chosen from over 200 applications.

WCBA's departments consider the qualifications of applicants, the size of the applicant pool in the particular program of study, the availability of faculty supervision and the availability of appropriate course content.

The required minimum GPA is 3.0 for the last two years of undergraduate work, though successful applicants have significantly higher GPAs. The college does not require applicants to hold a master's degree, but a graduate degree in a core social science discipline such as economics, engineering, mathematics, operations research or psychology is beneficial. A minimum score of 600 on the GMAT or a combined score of 1250 on the verbal and quantitative sections of the GRE is required.

Applicants must submit letters of recommendation from three professors or others familiar with their academic potential, and a personal statement indicating how the program of study satisfies the student's interests and how the student would contribute to the program.

International students must submit a minimum TOEFL score of 550 and a Certification of Financial Responsibility form.

Applications must be received by February 1. Admission takes place in the fall semester only.

EXPENSES & FINANCIAL ASSISTANCE

Financial support for PhD students includes graduate assistantships and fellowships. Assistantships are salaried positions that require students to support faculty members in research and/or teaching, 10 to 13.5 hours per week. Fellowships are salaried positions without work requirements that allow students to devote more time to research activities.

Most assistantships and fellowships are extended for a duration of four years. Students holding at least quarter-time graduate assistantships or fellowships paying at least US$3,150 per semester are eligible for in-state or out-of-state tuition waivers up to the minimum credits required for full-time enrollment. Tuition waivers for each semester will be granted to qualifying assistants and fellows, provided they maintain a 3.0 GPA and are employed on or before the first day of classes through the end of final exams. Tuition waivers do not cover fees associated with registration (approximately $400 per semester).

Applications for graduate assistantships and fellowships are made by submitting the Fellowship / Assistantship Application to the appropriate department by February 1.

INTERNATIONAL STUDENT SUPPORT

International Student and Scholar Services (ISSS) delivers administrative and support services to international students, exchange students, scholars and their families. In cooperation with government and university agencies, ISSS evaluates international student financial statements, issues IAP-66s and I-20s, counsels international students on academic, financial, cultural and personal matters, runs international student orientation programs and organizes cross-cultural workshops. ISSS also acts as a liaison with foreign and domestic embassies, consulates, foundations and US government agencies.

ADMISSIONS AT A GLANCE
Minimum GMAT:	550-600
Minimum GPA:	3.0
Minimum TOEFL (paper):	550-600
Minimum TOEFL (computer):	213
Application Fee:	US$20
Application Deadline:	Feb 1

EXPENSES AT A GLANCE
Tuition per semester:
In State:	US$1,729
Out-of-State:	US$6,060
Int'l Students:	US$6,060

Books & Supplies:
    US$735 per year
Health Insurance:
    US$707 per year & up
Accommodation:
  University Residences:
    US$271 per month & up
  Family Housing:
    US$300 per month & up
  Private:
    US$315–750 per month

PROGRAM FACTS
# of Full-time Students:	80
# of Part-time Students:	0
# of Applications per year:	296
# Accepted per year:	64
# Enrolled per year:	38
Average GMAT Score:	665
Average Age:	31
% Men/Women:	68%/32%
Work Experience (avg yrs):	n/a
# of Faculty:	97
% Faculty with Doctoral Degree:	100%
Annual Research Funding:	US$1,291,094

 UNIVERSITY OF FLORIDA, WARRINGTON COLLEGE OF BUSINESS ADMINISTRATION

UNIVERSITY AND LOCATION

Established in 1853, the University of Florida is the state's oldest and largest university. UF is a comprehensive university with internationally known training and research programs in all fields, including engineering, business, law and medicine. It attracts students from all 50 states and over 100 countries. There are currently 43,000 students and 4,000 faculty members at the university and more than 500 student organizations on campus.

Located on a 2,000-acre campus in the city of Gainesville, UF has three Olympic-size pools, two gyms, four art galleries, 34 residence halls and several restaurants and cafeterias. It is home to the Florida Museum of Natural History, and is the world's largest citrus research center. The campus has an 81-acre wildlife sanctuary displaying Florida's unique ecosystem.

UF employs the latest in technological equipment and resources. It operates the second largest academic computing center in the southern US and its nine libraries form the largest information resource system in Florida. Altogether, UF's libraries contain over three million volumes and over five million microforms.

The Gainesville area in north-central Florida is home to more than 100,000 people. It provides all of the amenities of a modern city while preserving a friendly, small-town atmosphere. Residents can enjoy the city's five golf courses and miles of bicycle paths. The moderate climate and the area's many parks and lakes provide opportunities for year-round recreational pursuits. Gainesville is a two-hour drive from Orlando, Tampa and Jacksonville, close enough for one-day excursions and weekend trips to Disney World, the Epcot Center, Busch Gardens and the beaches of the Gulf of Mexico and the Atlantic Ocean.

FACULTY/THESIS ADVISORS
- Abdel-Khalik, R. PhD, Illinois at Urbana-Champaign
- Ai, C. PhD, MIT
- Ajinkya, B. PhD, Minnesota
- Alba, J.W. PhD, Temple
- Asare, S. PhD, Arizona
- Benson, H.P. PhD, Northwestern
- Berg, A.V. PhD, Yale
- Bomberger, W.A. PhD, Brown
- Bose, I. PhD, Purdue
- Brenner, L. PhD, Stanford
- Chen, H.K. PhD, Rochester
- Cohen, J.B. PhD, UCLA
- Conway, D.G. PhD, Indiana
- Cooke, A. PhD, Berkeley
- Demski, J. PhD, Chicago
- Denslow, D.A. PhD, Yale
- Dinopoulos, E. PhD, Columbia
- Elms, H. PhD, UCLA
- Elnicki, R.E. DBA, Harvard
- Emerson, R.W. PhD, Harvard
- Erenguc, S.S. DBA, Indiana
- Erez, A. PhD, Cornell
- Figlio, D.N. PhD, Wisconsin-Madison
- Flannery, M. PhD, Yale
- Hackenbrack, K. PhD, Ohio State
- Hamilton, J.H. PhD, MIT
- Hargadon, A.B. PhD, Stanford
- Horowitz, I. PhD, MIT
- Houston, J. PhD, Pennsylvania
- Jamison, D.J. PhD, Florida
- Janiszewski, C.A. PhD, Northwestern
- Kenny, L.W. PhD, Chicago
- Knechel, R. PhD, North Carolina
- Koehler, G.J. PhD, Purdue
- Kramer, J. PhD, Michigan
- Kramer, S. PhD, Texas at Austin
- LePine, J.A. PhD, Michigan State
- Lewis, T.R. PhD, California
- Lutz, R.J. PhD, Illinois
- Mahajan, J. PhD, Wisconsin, Madison
- Mantrala, M.K. PhD, Northwestern
- Maurer, V.G. JD, Stanford
- McGill, G. PhD, Texas Tech
- Motowidlo, S.J. PhD, Minnesota
- Nimalendran, M. PhD, Michigan
- Piramuthu, S. PhD, Illinois at Urbana-Champaign
- Ritter, J. PhD, Chicago
- Romano, R.E. PhD, Pittsburgh
- Rush, M. PhD, Rochester
- Ryngaert, M. PhD, Chicago
- Sappington, D. PhD, Princeton
- Sawyer, A.G. PhD, Stanford
- Scully, J.A. PhD, Maryland
- Shugan, S.M. PhD, Northwestern
- Slutsky, S.M. PhD, Yale
- Snowball, D. PhD, Washington
- Thomas, R.E. PhD, Stanford
- Tosi, H.L. PhD, Ohio State
- Vakharia, A.J. PhD, Wisconsin
- Waldo, D.G. PhD, North Carolina
- Weitz, B.A. PhD, Stanford
- Werner, M.J. PhD, UC San Diego
- West, C. PhD, Michigan
- Xie, J. PhD, Carnegie Mellon
- Xu, Bin. PhD, Columbia

City Population:	100,030
Cost of Living:	medium
Climate Range:	43° to 90°F
Campus Setting:	urban
Total Enrollment:	43,108
Graduate Enrollment:	10,350
Students in Residence:	10,944

UNIVERSITY OF GEORGIA
PhD in Business Administration & Economics

Program Highlights

- *Seven major fields in business administration*
- *Limited enrollment optimizes student-faculty interaction*
- *Production of publishable-quality research papers from first year*
- *Accredited by AACSB*

CONTACT INFORMATION
PhD Admissions
Terry College of Business, Brooks Hall
Athens, Georgia USA 30602
PH: 1-706-542-8100
FAX: 1-706-542-3835 (specify on fax
   ATTN: PhD Admissions)
EMAIL: PhD@terry.uga.edu
INTERNET: http://www.terry.uga.edu

UNIVERSITY OF GEORGIA, PHD IN BUSINESS ADMINISTRATION & ECONOMICS

PROGRAM OVERVIEW

The University of Georgia's (UGA) Terry College of Business (TCB) offers Doctor of Philosophy (PhD) degrees in business administration and economics. Students pursuing a PhD in business administration choose a major field in accounting, finance, management, management information systems, marketing, real estate and risk management and insurance.

Programs emphasize the development of research and teaching skills. The small size of the program optimizes close, long-term interaction between students and faculty. The curriculum consists of a minimum of 30 hours of coursework and a minimum of 10 hours of dissertation work for individuals with an appropriate master's degree. Students entering with a bachelor's degree will need a minimum of 57 credit hours of graduate coursework while those beginning without a business background may need an additional 12 to 18 hours of business administration and mathematics.

Minor fields and research methodology courses may be chosen from inside or outside the TCB. The research apprenticeship, consisting of three hours of coursework, is done under faculty guidance and involves research-oriented activities that help build the skills needed to undertake a dissertation.

Comprehensive written and oral preliminary exams follow the completion of all coursework. A dissertation completes the program.

Major Fields

Students in the PhD program in accounting may concentrate in one or more specialties such as financial accounting, managerial accounting, systems, auditing and taxation. Extensive study in research methodology, related fields and supporting disciplines is required for the degree.

The economics program comprises a focus on research through sequences in microeconomic and macroeconomic theory, analytical methods and econometrics and involvement in faculty research projects. To build further on the analytical and quantitative skills developed in the core, three research areas must be chosen for special emphasis.

The finance program consists of a foundation in financial and economic theory, advanced seminars in corporate finance, investments, financial institutions and markets and a research methodology course in statistics and econometrics.

Within the management program, students specialize in human resources management production, operations management or strategic management. Students are actively involved with faculty mentors in teaching and conducting research leading to professional presentations and publications.

The focus of the management information systems program is on behavioral and applied research that blends information technology with management, decision support and applied psychology. Students become involved with research projects leading to publication starting in the first year.

Marketing students complete a series of marketing seminars and additional marketing courses based upon their background and interests. Each student also selects courses outside of marketing to improve research skills and knowledge in areas related to marketing.

The emphasis in the real estate program is on real estate investments, finance and appraisal while building on a strong foundation in economics, finance theory and research tools in statistics and econometrics

Risk management coursework includes theoretical and applied aspects of insurance, risk management and employee benefits. Students obtain a background in financial theory and develop research methodology skills. They participate in doctoral seminars which include individual projects, often leading to publication prior to graduation.

SELECTED RESEARCH AREAS

- Advertising law
- Applied microeconomics
- Bankruptcy
- Brand communities
- Capital structure and indutry organization
- Commercial banking
- Commercial transactions
- Computer-supported group work
- Corporate image
- Corporate social performance
- Data warehouse usage
- Derivative securities
- Earnings management
- Electronic commerce
- Employment law
- Executive information systems
- Financial accounting
- Financial markets and institutes
- Governmental accounting and auditing
- Group support systems
- Human resource recruitment
- Institutional investment in real estate
- Insurance regulation
- Insurer insolvency
- Investments
- Knowledge creation and management
- Lending discrimination
- Liability insurance issues
- Managerial ethics
- Marketing research
- Mortgage markets
- Personal selling
- Privatizations
- Public policy
- Public utility finance
- Real estate development
- Strategic management
- Theory of constraint
- Top management composition
- Underwriting cycle
- Urban economics
- Urban land economics
- White-collar crime

UNIVERSITY OF GEORGIA, PhD IN BUSINESS ADMINISTRATION & ECONOMICS

ADMISSIONS CRITERIA & PROCEDURES

Admission to the PhD programs in business administration and economics is highly selective. Students with four-year baccalaureate degrees from accredited institutions and an undergraduate GPA of 3.0 (on a scale of 4.0) are eligible. All applicants should have six credit hours of calculus.

Completed applications include the Graduate School application form, a nonrefundable US$30 application fee, a PhD supplemental application and essays, three letters of recommendation from former professors or professional employers, two official transcripts from all colleges or universities previously attended and GMAT or GRE scores. International students must submit official transcripts in the original language, accompanied by certified, literal English translations, if necessary.

Applicants whose primary language is not English must submit official TOEFL scores, unless they have received a degree from an accredited US institution or from a university in an English-speaking country.

The programs admit students at the beginning of each fall semester. Deadlines are January 14 for students requesting financial aid and March 1 for all others.

EXPENSES & FINANCIAL ASSISTANCE

University-wide graduate research assistantships include stipends which range from US$10,700 to U$12,350 and recipients are expected to devote 16 to 18 hours per week to their duties. TCOB graduate teaching or research assistantships of 16 hours of work per week are granted in the student's major field of study and include a US$11,000 stipend. International students receiving teaching assistantships must present their scores on the TSE to their department head.

The Alvin B. Biscoe fellowship is awarded annually to the top two entering PhD students in business or economics. Edward T. Comer fellowships are worth US$2,000 per year for three years and are awarded to incoming and first-year students. Each department also awards a one-year Comer fellowship of US$2,000. TCOB US$2,000 research awards are awarded annually and out-of-state fee waivers are available from UGA.

INTERNATIONAL STUDENT SUPPORT

The International Student Life office assists international students with cross-cultural adjustment, orientation and integration into the university and Athens. The International Education office helps international students in immigration or financial concerns, health insurance and administrative details.

ADMISSIONS AT A GLANCE

Minimum GMAT:	no set minimum
Minimum GPA:	3.0
Minimum TOEFL (paper):	–
Minimum TOEFL (computer):	–
Application Fee:	US$30
Application Deadline:	
Jan 14 for students requesting financial aid	
Mar 1 (fall admission)	

EXPENSES AT A GLANCE

Tuition per year:	
In State:	US$3,516
Out-of-State:	US$12,204
Int'l Students:	US$12,204
Books & Supplies:	US$600
Health Insurance:	–
Accommodation:	
University Residences:	US$775–1,000 per month
Family Housing:	–
Private:	–

PROGRAM FACTS

# of Full-time Students:	–
# of Part-time Students:	–
# of Applications per year:	–
# Accepted per year:	–
# Enrolled per year:	–
Average GMAT Score:	–
Average Age:	–
% Men/Women:	–
Work Experience (avg yrs):	–
# of Faculty:	102
% Faculty with Doctoral Degree:	–
Annual Research Funding:	–

UNIVERSITY OF GEORGIA, PhD IN BUSINESS ADMINISTRATION & ECONOMICS

UNIVERSITY AND LOCATION

Established in 1785, the University of Georgia is the state's largest, most comprehensive educational institution and the oldest chartered state university in the US.

UGA Libraries house over two million bound volumes, more than 16,000 journals and periodicals and serve as a regional depository for US and Canadian government documents.

The university's 425,000-square-foot Ramsey Student Physical Activities Center is a recreational and exercise facility for students and teams. The university provides dormitories for 6,500 undergraduate, graduate and married students.

Situated in the rolling, wooded hill country of northeast Georgia, Athens has an Old South charm that lives on in its architecture and gardens, balanced by events such as the Twilight Criterium bicycle race attended by many Olympic and international competitors. Athens's location allows students access to the metropolitan bustle of Atlanta, 70 miles southwest, the solitude of the Appalachian mountains and the recreational opportunities of the southeastern seacoast.

City Population:	45,734
Cost of Living:	medium
Climate Range:	52° to 77°F
Campus Setting:	urban
Total Enrollment:	30,000
Graduate Enrollment:	6,530
Students in Residence:	6,000

FACULTY

- Aarstol, M.P. PhD, Stanford
- Amason, A.C. PhD, South Carolina
- Aronson, J.E. PhD, Carnegie Mellon
- Atkinson, S.E. PhD, Colorado
- Ayers, B.C. PhD, Texas at Austin
- Bamber, E.M. PhD, Ohio State
- Barrack, J.B. PhD, Oklahoma State
- Bateman, F. PhD, Tulane
- Bennett-Alexander, D.D.
- Benson, P.G.
- Beresford, D.R.
- Blackstone, Jr., J.H. PhD, Texas A&M
- Boehmer, R.G.
- Bostrom, R.P. PhD, Minnesota
- Brohman, K. PhD, Western Ontario
- Buchholtz, A.K. PhD, New York
- Caroll, B.A. PhD, Indiana
- Carroll, A.B. PhD, Florida State
- Conchar, M. PhD, Georgia
- Copley, P.A. PhD, Alabama
- Cornwell, C.M. PhD, Michigan State
- Corwin, S.A. PhD, Ohio State
- Cox III, J.F. PhD, Clemson
- Crask, M. DBA, Indiana
- Davis, K.R.
- Dawkins, M.C. PhD, Florida State
- Day, E. PhD, Indiana
- DeLorme, Jr., C.D. PhD, Louisiana State
- Dennis, A.R. PhD, Arizona
- Downs, D. PhD, North Carolina at Chapel Hill
- Fox, R. PhD, Michigan State
- French, W. PhD, Penn State
- Friedmann, R. PhD, Kansas
- Gatewood, R.D. PhD, Purdue
- Gaver, J.J. PhD, Arizona
- Gaver, K.M. PhD, Carnegie Mellon
- Goodhue, D.L. PhD, MIT
- Grover, R. PhD, Massachusetts
- Gustavson, S.G. PhD, Illinois
- Henkel, J.W.
- Hilliard, J.E. Tennessee
- Hofer, C.W. DBA, Harvard
- Holman, J. PhD, Colorado
- Hoyt, R. PhD, Pennsylvania
- Huber, M. PhD, Georgia
- Kamerschen, D.R. PhD, Michigan State
- Kau, J.B. PhD, Washington
- Keenan, D. DSC, Washington University
- Kefalas, A.. PhD, Iowa
- Klein, P.G. PhD, Berkeley
- Lastrapes, W.D. PhD, North Carolina
- Ledvinka, J.D. PhD, Michigan
- Lee, D.R. PhD, California - San Diego
- Leigh, T.W. DBA, Indiana
- Lewis, W. PhD, Florida State
- Lipson, M.L.
- Lovell, C.A.K. PhD, Duke
- Marchand, P.H.
- Martin, R. PhD, Illinois at Urbana-Champaign
- May, G.S. PhD, Michigan State
- McKeown, P.G. PhD, North Carolina at Chapel Hill
- McNatt, B.
- Milne, S.
- Morehead, J.W.
- Munneke, H. PhD, Illinois at Urbana-Champaign
- Mustard, D. PhD, Chicago
- Napoleon, K.J.
- Netter, J.M. PhD, Ohio State
- Okleshen, C. PhD, Nebraska
- Peters, G. PhD, Oregon
- Petrie, K.
- Pottier, S.W. PhD, Texas at Austin
- Poulsen, A.B.
- Reddy, Srinivias. PhD, Columbia
- Reed, O.L.
- Riordan, C.M. PhD, Georgia State
- Ryan, L.J. PhD, Washington
- Seila, A.F.
- Selgin, G.A. PhD, New York
- Shedd, P.
- Shockley, R.A. PhD, North Carolina at Chapel Hill
- Sinkey, Jr., J.F.
- Smith, E.D. PhD, Ohio State
- Snow, A.A.
- Sommer, D.W. PhD, Pennsylvania
- Stam, A. PhD, Kansas
- Stephenson, F. PhD, Minnesota
- Steuer, R.E.
- Stewart, M.M.
- Stivers, C.
- Streer, P.J. PhD, Illinois
- Trandel, G. PhD, Princeton
- Trieschmann, G.A. DBA, Indiana
- Vandenberg, R.J. PhD, Georgia
- Verbrugge, J.A.
- Warren, C.S. PhD, Michigan State
- Warren, R.S. PhD, North Carolina at Chapel Hill
- Watson, H.J.
- Watson, R.T. PhD, Minnesota
- White, L.H. PhD, UCLA
- Zimmer, M. PhD, Texas at Austin
- Zinkhan, G. PhD, Michigan

UNIVERSITY OF ILLINOIS AT CHICAGO
COLLEGE OF BUSINESS ADMINISTRATION

Program Highlights

- *PhD programs in business administration, economics and management information systems*
- *Business administration specializations in business economics, finance, human resource management and marketing*
- *Programs accredited by AACSB*

CONTACT INFORMATION

601 South Morgan Street

Room 2231 UH

Chicago, Illinois USA 60607-7122

PH: 1-312-996-4751

FAX: 1-312-996-5492

EMAIL: gradbus@uic.edu

INTERNET: http://www.uic.edu/cba

UNIVERSITY OF ILLINOIS AT CHICAGO, COLLEGE OF BUSINESS ADMINISTRATION

PROGRAM OVERVIEW

The College of Business Administration (CBA) at the University of Illinois at Chicago (UIC) offers Doctor of Philosophy (PhD) degree programs in business administration, economics and management information systems. Students pursuing a PhD in business administration choose specializations from business economics, finance, human resource management and marketing.

The programs in business administration and management information systems require completion of a minimum of 96 graduate semester hours beyond the baccalaureate or a minimum of 64 graduate semester hours beyond the Master of Business Administration (MBA) degree, including at least 32 hours of dissertation research. The PhD in economics degree requires at least 104 hours beyond the bachelor's degree and 72 hours beyond the master's degree.

Business Administration

The PhD in business administration with a specialization in business economics is intended to provide advanced training in economics with an emphasis on business research. Students who plan to major in business economics must take two additional courses in economics to satisfy the MBA requirements for an economics specialization. One other field of concentration consisting of at least two courses must also be completed.

Students pursuing a specialization in finance study the theory and practice of finance, which can include financial management, valuation and financial analysis and planning. Proficiency in calculus and linear algebra is required for this specialization.

Human resource management is a research oriented program intended for students who wish to pursue careers in colleges and universities, research institutes, public agencies or industrial or business organizations. Emphasis is placed on the theoretical and conceptual foundations of knowledge as well as on statistical, quantitative and computer methods.

A marketing concentration support study of consumer behavior, entrepreneurship, new product development, choice models, information processing and international marketing. Students are encouraged to extend their research into other areas of business as well.

Economics

The economics program offers advanced study in economics, with an emphasis on applied fields. It prepares students for careers at colleges and universities or research positions in government, non-profit agencies and business. The program provides students with a solid grounding in economic theory and quantitative analysis through six core courses, two each in microeconomic theory, macroeconomic theory and econometrics. Students also receive in-depth training in at least two fields of economics. The final stage of the program, the dissertation, represents an original contribution to the state of economic knowledge.

Management Information Systems

The PhD program in management information systems examines how technology can affect an organization's behavior, structure and function and the effective use and control of information and computer systems by management. Students pursuing a PhD in management information systems must show proficiency in systems design and databases through previous coursework or by completing courses in business information systems analysis and design and administrative computer technology.

SELECTED RESEARCH AREAS
- Actuarial science
- Capital market microstructure
- Cluster analysis
- Consumer behavior
- Corporate finance
- Corporate strategy
- Cost analysis
- Culture of organizations
- Economic history
- Empirical analysis of accounting
- Executive leadership
- Experimental economics
- Futures
- Game theory
- Health economics
- Human resource management
- Immigration
- Industrial organization
- Information and capital market valuation
- International electronic commerce
- International marketing
- International trade
- Knowledge and data
- Labor relations
- Macroeconomics
- Managerial finance
- Mathematical programming
- Nonprofit accounting
- Operations research
- Performance measures
- Product management
- Public finance
- Public sector unionism
- Real estate finance
- Reliability and network algorithms
- Research methodology
- Risk analysis
- Security markets
- Social choice theory
- Statistical software development
- Stochastic process
- Strategic planning
- Time series analysis

UNIVERSITY OF ILLINOIS AT CHICAGO, COLLEGE OF BUSINESS ADMINISTRATION

ADMISSIONS CRITERIA & PROCEDURES

Applicants must be admitted to both the PhD program and the Graduate College. The minimum requirements for admission to the Graduate College include a baccalaureate or equivalent from an accredited college or university, a cumulative GPA of at least 3.75 (on a scale of five) for the final 60 hours of undergraduate study, official transcripts from all postsecondary institutions attended and a recommendation for admission by both the graduate program applied to and the dean of the Graduate College.

Admission to the PhD program in business administration is based on an acceptable GMAT or GRE score, the GPA achieved in the last two years of undergraduate study and in any graduate-level work, letters of recommendation from three people familiar with the applicant's mental aptitude and the applicant's statement of research interests and educational and career goals. Applicants whose native language is not English must achieve an acceptable score on the TOEFL unless they have completed at least two years of full-time study in a country where English is the native language and in a school where English is the language of instruction. The minimum required score is 600 on the paper-based test but successful applicants usually average above 600. International students must provide the university with proof of financial support.

Admission takes place in the fall term only and the deadline for receipt of all application materials is February 1. The application fee is US$40 for domestic students and US$50 for international students.

EXPENSES & FINANCIAL ASSISTANCE

The CBA and its academic departments make every effort within their budgetary constraints to offer financial support to full-time doctoral students. Support may include teaching, research or graduate assistantships, which include full tuition and service fee waivers and a stipend. The CBA offers fellowships in addition to departmental awards that make financial support competitive with other public institutions.

UIC also administers a number of fellowships that are available to graduate students, including University Fellowships, Abraham Lincoln Graduate Fellowships, the Martin Luther King, Jr. Scholarship and the Diversity Fellowship.

Some funds for students traveling to and presenting research at conferences are available from the PhD program, the Graduate College and from individual departments.

INTERNATIONAL STUDENT SUPPORT

The Office of International Services (OIS) provides international students at UIC with guidance and counseling as well as information on immigration regulations and cross-cultural activities and programs.

UIC offers English as a Second Language courses and a tutorial in intensive English for students who need to improve their language skills.

ADMISSIONS AT A GLANCE

Minimum GMAT:	no set minimum
Minimum GPA:	4.00
Minimum TOEFL (paper):	600
Minimum TOEFL (computer):	–
Application Fee:	
US$40 (dom)	
US $50 (int'l)	
Application Deadline:	Feb 1

EXPENSES AT A GLANCE

Tuition per semester (1999–2000):	
In State:	US$1,820
Out-of-State:	US$5,138
Int'l Students:	US$5,138
Books & Supplies:	US$700 per year
Health Insurance:	US$248
Accommodation:	
University Residences:	US$750–1,000 per month
Family Housing:	–
Private:	US$700–900

PROGRAM FACTS (1999)

# of Full-time Students:	24
# of Part-time Students:	22
# of Applications per year:	102
# Accepted per year:	16
# Enrolled per year:	10
Average GMAT Score:	640
Average Age:	32
% Men/Women:	63%/37%
Work Experience (avg yrs):	–
# of Faculty:	89
% Faculty with Doctoral Degree:	85%
Annual Research Funding:	US$362,733

UNIVERSITY OF ILLINOIS AT CHICAGO, COLLEGE OF BUSINESS ADMINISTRATION

UNIVERSITY AND LOCATION

Established in 1982 through the consolidation of the University of Illinois Medical Center and Chicago Circle campuses, the University of Illinois at Chicago is a comprehensive university with a total enrollment of about 25,000, including over 6,000 graduate students. It is one of three campuses in the University of Illinois system and the major public university of the Chicago metropolitan area. UIC offers 99 bachelor's, 90 master's and 53 doctoral degree programs. The university's faculty attract over US$95 million in research funding every year.

The Richard J. Daley Library collections include over 1.9 million volumes, 2.4 million microforms and 16,000 serial titles housed at eight sites. The library provides access to over 40 libraries via the Illinois Library computer systems. Business students have access to one of the largest library business collections in the US through UIC's sister campus at Urbana-Champaign.

UIC is a member of the Committee on Institutional Cooperation (CIC), an academic consortium of research universities including the University of Chicago and the University of Wisconsin at Milwaukee. The CIC operates a traveling scholar program, enabling doctoral students at member universities to take advantage of opportunities on other campuses.

The university is one of only 88 institutions in the US to be granted a Research I designation by the Carnegie Foundation for the Advancement of Teaching.

UIC is located just west of Chicago's Loop. The city hosts award-winning theatre and concert productions, neighborhood ethnic feasts and professional football, baseball, basketball and hockey teams. The location gives business administration students a glimpse of the city's financial markets and business community. Chicago features 15 miles of beaches and over 18 miles of bike paths along the shores of Lake Michigan.

City Population:	2,731,743
Cost of Living:	medium
Climate Range:	15° to 82°F
Campus Setting:	urban
Total Enrollment:	24,578
Graduate Enrollment:	6,013
Students in Residence:	–

FACULTY

- Abrams, R. PhD, Northwestern
- Acharya, S. PhD, Northwestern
- Albrecht, M. PhD, Emory
- Babad, Y. PhD, Cornell
- Barnum, D.T. PhD, Pennsylvania
- Bassett, G.W. PhD, Michigan
- Bauman, M. PhD, Wisconsin-Madison
- Bhattacharyya, S. PhD, Florida
- Binder, J.J. PhD, Chicago
- Bondarenko, O.P. PhD, CalTech
- Burack, E.H. PhD, Northwestern
- Camacho, A. PhD, Minnesota
- Chalos, P. PhD, Illinois, Urbana-Champaign
- Chaloupka, F. PhD, CUNY
- Chan, J.L. PhD, Illinois, Urbana-Champaign
- Chen, H. PhD, Illinois, Urbana-Champaign
- Chen, J.T. PhD, Illinois, Urbana Champaign
- Chen, R. PhD, Carnegie Mellon
- Cherian, J. PhD, Texas at Austin
- Chiswick, B.R. PhD, Columbia
- Chiswick, C.U. PhD, Columbia
- Cooke, R.A. PhD, Northwestern
- Das, S. PhD, Carnegie Mellon
- Gregory, O. PhD, Case Western
- Hagstrom, J. PhD, California, Berkeley
- Hills, G. DBA, Indiana
- Ho, J.K. PhD, Stanford
- Hoffman, E. PhD, Pennsylvania
- Ierulli, K. PhD, Chicago
- Karras, G. PhD, Ohio State
- Kim, B. PhD, Texas at Austin
- King, C. PhD, Harvard
- Kosobud, R.F. PhD, Pennsylvania
- Kurish, J.B. PhD, Yale
- Lee, B. PhD, Texas at Austin
- Lee, Y.S. PhD, Yale
- Lehrer, E. PhD, Northwestern
- Liden, R.C. PhD, Cincinnati
- Liu, L.M. PhD, Wisconsin at Madison
- Lumpkin, T. PhD, Texas at Arlington
- Mak, K.T. PhD, California at Berkeley
- Malaviya, P. PhD, Northwestern
- Manheim, M.B.W. PhD, Georgia Tech
- McDonald, J. PhD, Yale
- Nakata, C. PhD, Illinois at Chicago
- Narayana, C. PhD, Iowa
- Officer, L.H. PhD, Harvard
- Omer, T.C. PhD, Iowa
- Ouksel, M.A. PhD Northwestern
- Pagano, A.M. PhD, Pennsylvania State
- Page, A. PhD, Northwestern
- Park, Y. PhD, Pittsburgh
- Peck, R.M. PhD, Princeton
- Persky, J.J. PhD, Harvard
- Picur, R. PhD, Northwestern
- Pieper, P. PhD, Northwestern
- Pliska, S.R. PhD, Stanford
- Popwits, M. MSA, Illinois at Urbana-Champaign
- Potter, R. PhD, Arizona
- Ramakrishnan, R.T.S. PhD, Northwestern
- Riahi-Belkaoui, A. PhD, Syracuse
- Sage, J.A. PhD, Oklahoma State
- Sclove, S.L. PhD, Columbia
- Shelton, L.M. PhD, Harvard
- Shrader, R. PhD, Georgia State
- Sivakumar, K. PhD, Syracuse
- Stanford, W.G. PhD, Northwestern
- Stokes, H.H. PhD, Chicago
- Sung, J. PhD, Washington
- Suntrup, E.L. PhD, Minnesota
- Tam, M.Y. PhD, SUNY at Stony Brook
- Wayne, S.J. PhD, Texas A&M

UNIVERSITY OF ILLINOIS AT URBANA-CHAMPAIGN
PhD IN BUSINESS ADMINISTRATION

Program Highlights

- *Seven areas of concentration in business administration*
- *Assistantships for all admitted students*
- *Third largest academic library in the US*
- *Accredited by AACSB*

CONTACT INFORMATION

College of Commerce & Business Administration

350 Commerce West Building

1206 South Sixth Street

Champaign, Illinois USA 61820

PH: 1-217-333-4240

FAX: 1-217-244-7969

EMAIL: ba@cba.uiuc.edu

INTERNET: http://www.uiuc.edu/

UNIVERSITY OF ILLINOIS AT URBANA–CHAMPAIGN, PHD IN BUSINESS ADMINISTRATION

PROGRAM OVERVIEW

The College of Commerce and Business Administration (CCBA) at the University of Illinois at Urbana-Champaign (UIUC) offers Doctor of Philosophy (PhD) degree programs in business administration, finance and accountancy. The half-semester module structure of the program provides all students with a strong foundational core and the flexibility to customize individual programs to suit specific areas of research interest.

Business Administration

The doctoral program in business administration offers seven areas of concentration: management science, information systems, international business, marketing, process management, organizational behavior and strategic management.

Management science combines mathematical modeling and microeconomic reasoning in the pursuit of solutions to a wide variety of business problems.

In the information systems concentration, students develop the ability to solve business and industrial information problems through rigorous research.

Marketing students are introduced to the entire spectrum of marketing thought, enabling them to conduct research in any area of choice.

Students in process management investigate how organizations can design, improve and execute numerous business processes. Research may focus on tactical concerns or on strategic issues.

Organizational behavior students examine topics related to worker motivation and morale, reward systems, leadership, organizational structure and inter-organizational relationships, among others.

The concentration in strategic management explores the fundamentals of organizational intent, competitive and technological strategy, entrepreneurship and performance, and focuses on integration across the various business disciplines.

Finance

The finance study option permits students to specialize in one of five areas: banking, corporate finance, insurance, investment or real estate. Coursework required of all finance majors includes classes in econometric analysis, mathematical statistics and probability, and the theory of finance.

Students in the finance option must also take seminars economic theory and in two of the following areas: banking and financial institutions, corporate finance, insurance and risk management, investments and real estate, or urban economics. An elective is also required of all finance students; this may be in quantitative methods or a second area of financial concentration, or it may be picked from a field related to finance.

Accountancy

The PhD program in accountancy emphasizes the economics, finance and behavioral science roots of the accountancy discipline and provides institutional background and knowledge about research methods.

Accountancy coursework comprises core studies and the advanced application of a research paradigm to one or more functional areas within the discipline.

Accounting research encompasses a broad range of topics, including laboratory experiments in the use of accounting information, empirical tests of market reactions to publicly available accounting information, analytical models of conflict resolution, research related to taxation policy, artificial intelligence and expert systems in the auditing area, and the development of experimental markets.

SELECTED RESEARCH AREAS

- Agricultural finance
- Auditing
- Bond finance
- CEO compensation
- Contract theory
- Database marketing
- Developing economics
- Econometric models
- Economic effects of gambling
- Effects of paternalism on 19th century American agriculture
- Financial institutions
- Financial pricing models
- Financing emerging business
- Game theory
- Global competitive strategy
- Health care policy
- Human capital acquisition
- Human learning, judgement and decision making
- Impact fees
- Industrial organization
- Insurance and risk management
- Labor economics
- Logistics, scheduling and product/process design
- Long-term contracts
- Management incentives
- Mathematical economics
- Organization design for global operations
- Payment systems
- Portfolio management
- Privatization in Latin America
- Property taxation
- Public choice
- Public economics
- Real estate valuation
- Sales promotion
- Statistics
- Tax evasion
- Taxation
- Taxpayer compliance
- The application of financial theory to property-liability insurance
- Third-world urbanization

UNIVERSITY OF ILLINOIS AT URBANA–CHAMPAIGN, PHD IN BUSINESS ADMINISTRATION

ADMISSIONS CRITERIA & PROCEDURES

Students entering the PhD program must demonstrate a basic level of proficiency in statistics and some breadth in business-related disciplines such as microeconomics, behavioral sciences, accounting, finance, marketing and strategy. This proficiency requirement may be satisfied by prior coursework, relevant work experience or the completion of additional courses.

Admission is based on a variety of criteria including previous academic accomplishments, educational goals, letters of recommendation and demonstrated success in research.

The Graduate College of UIUC has established a minimum GPA of 3.0 (on a scale of four) for admission. An acceptable GMAT score is also required. Successful applicants usually score in the ninetieth percentile or better.

All international students are required to submit acceptable scores from the TOEFL if their native language is not English. Graduate applicants are exempt only if they have completed at least two years of full-time study at a university or college (within five years of the proposed date of enrollment at UIUC) where English is the language of instruction. For international students, financial assistance is contingent upon the student being certified to teach by passing either the TSE or the SPEAK test.

Applications are considered for fall semester admissions only. The application deadline is generally the first Monday in February for the business administration program, February 1 for the finance PhD and June 15 for the accountancy program. Applicants who wish to be considered for financial assistance should submit applications by mid-January.

EXPENSES & FINANCIAL ASSISTANCE

Tuition fees for Illinois residents are US$4,242 per year and US$11,752 per year for out-of-state and international students. Other expenses include an estimated US$714 for books and supplies and US$680 per year for health insurance. On-campus room and board is available at a cost of about US$670 per month. Private accommodation averages US$950 per month, including meals.

Assistantships, which include waivers of tuition and most service fees, are usually included with offers of admission. Some exceptional candidates may be offered additional awards. The letter of acceptance sent to admitted students specifies the nature of the assistantship and/or fellowship.

INTERNATIONAL STUDENT SUPPORT

The Office of International Student Affairs (OISA) provides international students with an orientation to the campus and community and advising services on academic issues, immigration law, income tax and English language programs. The office also provides cross cultural opportunities such as the cosmopolitan club and student organizations.

ADMISSIONS AT A GLANCE
Minimum GMAT:	no set minimum
Minimum GPA:	3.0
Minimum TOEFL (paper):	600
Minimum TOEFL (computer):	–
Application Fee:	US$40 (dom), $50 (int'l)
Application Deadline:	
Bus Admin: first Monday in Feb	
Finance: Feb 1	
Accountancy: June 15	

EXPENSES AT A GLANCE
Tuition per year:	
In State:	US$4,242
Out-of-State:	US$11,752
Int'l Students:	US$11,752
Books & Supplies:	US$714 per year
Health Insurance:	US$680 per year
Accommodation:	
University Residences:	US$670 per month
Family Housing:	–
Private:	–

PROGRAM FACTS*
# of Full-time Students:	43
# of Part-time Students:	0
# of Applications per year:	102
# Accepted per year:	24
# Enrolled per year:	11
Average GMAT Score:	660
Average Age:	29
% Men/Women:	73%/27%
Work Experience (avg yrs):	8
# of Faculty:	60
% Faculty with Doctoral Degree:	100%
Annual Research Funding:	US$1.6m

*Program facts are for the Business Adminstration program. Information on Finance and Accountancy programs is available throught the college.

UNIVERSITY OF ILLINOIS AT URBANA–CHAMPAIGN, PhD IN BUSINESS ADMINISTRATION

UNIVERSITY AND LOCATION

Located in east central Illinois in the twin cities of Urbana and Champaign, UIUC is the state's main public university, providing undergraduate and graduate education in more than 150 fields of study through the colleges of Agriculture, Consumer and Environmental Sciences, Applied Life Studies, Commerce and Business Administration, Communications, Education, Engineering, Fine and Applied Arts, Law, Liberal Arts and Sciences, Medicine and Veterinary Medicine, the institutes of Aviation and Labor and Industrial Relations, the School of Social Work, the Graduate School of Library and Information Sciences and the Graduate College.

The campus includes 200 major buildings on 1,470 acres. The university library is the third-largest academic library in the US and holds the personal papers of John Milton, Marcel Proust, H.G. Wells and Carl Sandburg in its collections.

Situated about 140 miles south of Chicago, the twin cities of Urbana and Champaign were recently profiled in a Newsweek article about the 10 hottest high-tech cities in the world. Allerton Park contains an outstanding collection of sculpture and statuary from Cambodia, Thailand and China. The city has theaters and art galleries, a performing arts center and six museums.

City Population:	100,000
Cost of Living:	medium
Climate Range:	18° to 85° F
Campus Setting:	urban
Total Enrollment:	36,000
Graduate Enrollment:	10,000
Students in Residence:	–

FACULTY

- Alston, L.J. PhD, Washington
- Arnould, R.J. PhD, Iowa State
- Arvan, L. PhD, Northwestern
- Baer, W. PhD, Harvard
- Bailey, A.D. PhD, Ohio State
- Beck, P.J. PhD, Texas - Austin
- Bera, A.K. PhD, Australian National
- Bernhardt, D. PhD, Carnegie Mellon
- Berry, M.H. PhD, Cal State - LA
- Blair, C.E. PhD, Carnegie Mellon
- Broschak, J. –
- Brown, C.E. PhD, Florida
- Brueckner, J.K. PhD, Stanford
- Cannaday, R.E. PhD, South Carolina
- Chan, L.K.C. PhD, Rochester
- Chandler, J.S. PhD, Ohio State
- Cheng, J.L. PhD, Michigan
- Chhajed, D. PhD, Purdue
- Cohen, S.I. PhD, Northwestern
- Colwell, P.F. PhD, Wayne State
- Conley, J.P. PhD, Rochester
- D'Arcy, S.P. PhD, Illinois
- Davis, J.S. PhD, Arizona
- DeBrock, L. PhD, Cornell
- Dietrich, J.R. PhD, Carnegie Mellon
- Engelbrecht-Wiggans, R. PhD, Cornell
- Esfahani, H.S. PhD, California
- Finnerty, J.E. PhD, Michigan
- Gahvari, F. PhD, UCLA
- Gardner, D.M. PhD, Minnesota
- Gentry, J.A. DBA, Indiana
- Giertz, J.F. PhD, Northwestern
- Gottheil, F.M. PhD, Duke
- Griffin, A. PhD, MIT
- Grinols, E.L. PhD, MIT
- Hendricks, W.E. PhD, Berkeley
- Hess, J.D. PhD, MIT
- Hill, R.M. PhD, Columbia
- Husby, R.D. PhD, Cornell
- Jegadeesh, N. PhD, Columbia
- Kahn, C.M. PhD, Harvard
- Kindt, J.W. SJD, Virginia
- Kleinmuntz, D.N. PhD, Chicago
- Koenker, R. PhD, Michigan
- Krasa, S. PhD, Vienna
- Kwon, Y.K. PhD, UCLA
- Lakonishok, J. PhD, Cornell
- Lansing, P. JD, Illinois
- Leblebici, H. PhD, Illinois
- Leuthold, J.H. PhD, Wisconsin
- Linke, C.M. DBA, Indiana
- Liu, B. PhD, SUNY-Buffalo
- Lynge, M.J. PhD, Michigan
- Mahoney, J.T. PhD, Pennsylvania
- McDonald, W.F. JD, Illinois
- Molloy, K.H. PhD, Virginia Polytechnic Institute
- Monahan, G.E. PhD, Northwestern
- Monroe, K.B. DBA, Illinois
- Nasr, N. –
- Neal, L.D. PhD, California
- Neumann, F.L. PhD, Chicago
- Northcraft, G.B. PhD, Stanford
- Oldham, G.R. PhD, Yale
- Orr, D. PhD, Princeton
- Park, H.Y. PhD, Ohio State
- Pearson, N.D. PhD, MIT
- Peecher, M. –
- Pennacchi, G.G. PhD, MIT
- Qualls, W.J. PhD, Indiana
- Rashid, S. PhD, Yale
- Resek, R.W. PhD, Harvard
- Ritz, Z. PhD, Northwestern
- Roberts, D.M. PhD, Stanford
- Roszkowski, M.E. JD, Illinois
- Schoenfeld, H.M.W. PhD, Braunschweig
- Schran, P. PhD, Berkeley
- Seth, A. PhD, Michigan
- Shafer, W.J. PhD, California - Santa Barbara
- Shaw, M.J. PhD, Purdue
- Shupp, F.R. PhD, Princeton
- Silhan, P.A. DBA, Tennessee
- Solomon, I. PhD, Texas - Austin
- Sougiannis, T. PhD, Berkeley
- Stone, D.N. PhD, Texas
- Sudharshan, D. PhD, Pittsburgh
- Sudman, S. PhD, Chicago
- Taira, K. PhD, Stanford
- Taub, B. PhD, Chicago
- Thomas, H. PhD, Edinburgh
- Vallamil, A.P. PhD, Minnesota
- Wansink, B. PhD, Stanford
- Whitford, D.T. PhD, Georgia State
- Williams, S.R. PhD, Northwestern
- Williamson, H.F. PhD, Yale
- Willis, E. PhD, Cincinnati
- Yannelis, N.C. PhD, Rochester
- Ziebart, D.A. PhD, Michigan State
- Ziegler, R.E. PhD, North Carolina

UNIVERSITY OF KANSAS
DOCTORAL PROGRAM IN BUSINESS

The University Of Kansas **School of Business**

Program Highlights

- *School of Business accredited by AACSB*
- *Attractive financial aid package available*
- *Limited enrollment ensures students receive substantial individual attention from faculty*
- *World-renowned research faculty*

CONTACT INFORMATION
School of Business
206 Summerfield Hall
Lawrence, Kansas USA 66045-2003
PH: 1-785-864-3841
FAX: 1-785-864-5328
EMAIL: grad@bschool.wpo.ukans.edu
INTERNET: http://www.bschool.ukans.edu

UNIVERSITY OF KANSAS, DOCTORAL PROGRAM IN BUSINESS

PROGRAM OVERVIEW

Established in 1924, the School of Business at the University of Kansas (KU) offers broad-based degrees that recognize the importance of liberal arts and related courses to a business-centered curriculum. The school is accredited by AACSB – The International Association for Management Education.

With instruction at the doctoral level dating back more than thirty years, the School of Business has extensive experience in the provision of business education at the PhD level. The program's mandate is to provide students with a comprehensive background in existing research in their field, instill an understanding of relevant research methodology and prepare them to conduct and direct research, and to effectively publish the results of their research.

The PhD program requires four to five years of full-time study. Coursework in major and minor areas of concentration, the completion of written and oral comprehensive exams, and the successful defense of a research dissertation. A second-year review of each PhD participant's progress ensures that degree requirements are met in a thorough and timely manner.

The doctoral program prepares students for careers in industry, government and institutions of higher learning. KU doctoral business graduates have gone on to fill teaching positions at many universities including Cornell, Duke, Michigan State and Simon Fraser.

First Year Foundation

Doctoral students in the first year of the PhD program receive a fundamental grounding in three key areas of business studies: behavioral sciences, economic theory, and probability and statistics. Courses include seminars in organizational behavior and theory, statistics and probability for business research, and micro- and macroeconomics.

By the end of the first year, students will be required to complete a curriculum and background sheet. This document is designed to assist students in organizing and charting the long-term progress of their PhD program.

Areas of Specialization

In the second year of the doctoral program, students specialize in one of seven majors: accounting, finance, human resources, marketing, management science, organizational behavior or strategic management. Five advanced courses in the area of specialization are required. Those interested in pursuing an interdisciplinary program may combine areas of specialization or focus on a particular topic involving subject areas outside of the field of business.

Coursework in supplementary areas is also required and students select either four advanced courses in one area, or two courses from each of two supporting areas, to complement their specialization.

The Importance of Teaching

To successfully fulfill PhD degree requirements, doctoral students must complete a graduate seminar in teaching. This course lasts for two semesters and must be taken within the first two years of the program. Before graduation, each PhD student completes a period of instruction equivalent to independently teaching two undergraduate courses in two different semesters.

Academic Facilities

There are a number of resources designed exclusively for business students at KU. The Richard S. Howey Reading Room, located in Summerfield Hall, contains a large study area, small print collection and access to many electronic databases for business and economics. Computing facilities for business students include the Wagnon Microcomputer Laboratory, with 40 workstations and 65 software programs, and the Harper Computing Classroom, designed for classes where instruction relies on the use of computers.

SELECTED RESEARCH AREAS

- Attorney-corporate client privilege
- Competitor analysis
- Consumer choice/decision making
- Current cost accounting
- Customer loyalty
- Dispute resolution
- Economics of the accounting profession
- Electric power markets
- Financing small business
- Gender-earning differentials
- Habitual domain theory
- Institutional ownership of corporate bonds, debt contracts and bankruptcy
- International auditing standards
- International finance
- Intraregional trade and investment issues
- Law and economics federalism health care policy
- Management issues in binational organizations
- Measurement and impact of compensation of satisfaction
- Mergers and acquisitions
- Personality and work outcomes
- Portfolio management
- Salesforce retention
- State-community economic development strategy
- Statistical analysis of simulation output
- Structured methods
- Taxation
- Total quality management
- Transforming and customizing organizations
- Uncertainty in artificial intelligence
- University-industry liaison and technology transfer
- Valuation of company stock and assets
- Virtual organizations
- Western European (EC) economic integration

UNIVERSITY OF KANSAS, DOCTORAL PROGRAM IN BUSINESS

ADMISSIONS CRITERIA & PROCEDURES

The doctoral program at KU admits, on average, six or seven new students each year. To be considered for this program, applicants must demonstrate their potential for success at projects requiring sustained planning and research. While a master's level degree in business or a related discipline is commonly held by program applicants, individuals with an exemplary academic record in an undergraduate business program will also be considered.

Minimum requirements for admission to the PhD program include a GMAT score of 500 and, for individuals whose first language is not English, a paper-based TOEFL score of 570. A minimum GPA requirement is not in effect since admissions officials at the School of Business consider prior academic experience in conjunction with other indicators of merit. In past years, the average GMAT score of students in the PhD program has been 670.

Completed application packages should include a US$50 nonrefundable application fee, three letters of recommendation, official transcripts from all undergraduate and graduate institutions attended, TOEFL scores (where applicable), GMAT scores, a completed supplemental data sheet and a completed Graduate School application form.

The PhD program accepts applicants in the fall semester only and the deadline for submission of the admissions package is January 15. Applicants are automatically considered for financial aid. Applications received after February 15 will only be considered for the following academic year.

EXPENSES & FINANCIAL ASSISTANCE

Tuition for PhD students in the School of Business is US$103 per credit hour for in-state residents and US$338 per credit hour for out-of-state and international students. In most instances, this works out to an average of US$927 per semester for in-state residents and US$3,042 per semester for out-of-state and international students.

Funding for doctoral business students is available through assistantships, fellowships, grants, loans and employment and most students in the program will receive one of these forms of financial assistance. Teaching assistantships, involving responsibilities roughly equal to 50 percent of full-time employment, entitle qualified students to a 100 percent tuition waiver. Non-native speakers of English who intend to work as a teaching assistant must first pass the Test of Spoken English (TSE) administered by KU's Applied English Center.

For students interested in applying for external forms of funding, such as American Accounting Association and the Richard D. Irwin Foundation awards, the School of Business offers assistance with preparing dossiers and other application material.

INTERNATIONAL STUDENT SUPPORT

At the present time, forty-eight percent of students enrolled in the doctoral business program at KU are international students. The university as a whole maintains a strong international student population, with more than 2,000 students and scholars from over 100 countries pursuing programs at both undergraduate and graduate levels of study.

University support services for non-domestic students are offered through the Office of International Programs (OIP). From orientation programs to cultural excursions, these initiatives are designed to help international students adjust to life in the US.

Working closely with the OIP, the Applied English Center also assists international students at KU by providing a full range of English language programs. Through specially-designed programs, graduate students intending to work as teaching assistants can develop English language fluency and pronunciation, and learn valuable information about American teaching methods and classroom styles.

ADMISSIONS AT A GLANCE
Minimum GMAT:	500
Minimum GPA:	n/a
Minimum TOEFL (paper):	570
Minimum TOEFL (computer):	–
Application Fee:	US$50
Application Deadline:	Jan 15

EXPENSES AT A GLANCE
Tuition:
- In State: US$103 per credit hour
- Out-of-State: US$338 per credit hour
- Int'l Students: US$338 per credit hour

Books & Supplies:	varies
Health Insurance:	–

Accommodation:
- University Residences: varies
- Family Housing: –
- Private: US$435–600 per month

PROGRAM FACTS
# of Full-time Students:	27
# of Part-time Students:	n/a
# of Applications per year:	60
# Accepted per year:	6–8
# Enrolled per year:	4–6
Average GMAT Score:	641
Average Age:	35
% Men/Women:	41%/59%
Work Experience (avg yrs):	not available
# of Faculty:	48
% Faculty with Doctoral Degree:	100%
Annual Research Funding:	US$530,000

UNIVERSITY OF KANSAS, DOCTORAL PROGRAM IN BUSINESS

UNIVERSITY AND LOCATION

Founded in 1864, the University of Kansas (KU) has become a premier academic institution serving more than 27,000 students. Over 40 independent research facilities complement the extensive departmental resources. The Carnegie Foundation ranks the university as a Research I institution and KU belongs to the American Association of Universities, an organization whose members are selected for their national significance in graduate studies and research.

Academic programs are offered through 14 schools and colleges: the College of Liberal Arts & Sciences, the Graduate School, and the Schools of Allied Health, Architecture & Urban Design, Business, Education, Engineering, Fine Arts, Journalism & Mass Communication, Law, Medicine, Nursing, Pharmacy, and Social Welfare. The university is known for its innovative programs, such as a master's level business option in city management-urban policy.

Facilities at KU provide diverse academic, social and cultural opportunities. The 2,020-seat Lied Center hosts many talented performers every year, while special exhibitions are on public display at the Spencer Museum of Art, the Museum of Anthropology and the Natural History Museum. Library resources include more than 3.5 million volumes, including microforms, manuscripts, maps and photographs.

KU is situated in Lawrence, a city of 75,000 in the eastern part of the state, approximately a 45 minute drive from Kansas City. Lawrence has excellent entertainment and recreational facilities, and is close to four lake resort areas.

City Population:	65,000
Cost of Living:	–
Climate Range:	19° to 91°F
Campus Setting:	urban
Total Enrollment:	28,000
Graduate Enrollment:	6,454
Students in Residence:	–

FACULTY
- Ahluwalia, R. PhD, Ohio State
- Ash, R.A. PhD, South Florida
- Beedles, W.L. PhD, Texas at Austin
- Birch, M.H. PhD, Illinois
- Bublitz, B. PhD, Illinois
- Butler, H.N. PhD, Virginia Polytechnic Inst
- Charnes, J.M. PhD, Minnesota
- Chauvin, K.W. PhD, Illinois
- Datta, D.K. PhD, Pittsburgh
- Ettredge, M. PhD, Texas at Austin
- Fitch, H.G. PhD, Purdue
- Ford, A. PhD, Arkansas
- Garland, J. DBA, Indiana
- Gergacz, J.W. JD, Indiana
- Guthrie, J.P. PhD, Maryland
- Heintz, J.A. DBA, Washington
- Hillmer, S.C. PhD, Wisconsin-Madison
- Hirschey, M. PhD, Wisconsin-Madison
- Houston, D.A. DBA, Indiana
- Joseph, K. PhD, Purdue
- Karney, D.F. PhD, Illinois
- Kleinberg, J. PhD, Michigan
- Koch, P.D. PhD, Michigan State
- Krider, C.E. PhD, Chicago
- Lessig, V.P. PhD, Kansas
- Levin, M.S. JD, Kansas
- Mackenzie, K.D. PhD, Berkeley
- Mai-Dalton, R. PhD, Washington-Seattle
- Mishra, S. PhD, Washington State
- Narayanan, V.K. PhD, Pittsburgh
- Reitz, H.J. PhD, MIT
- Richardson, V.J. PhD, Illinois at Urbana-Champaign
- Rosen, D.L. PhD, Minnesota
- Scholz, S.W. PhD, Southern California
- Schwoerer, C. PhD, North Carolina at Chapel Hill
- Shaftel, T.L. PhD, Carnegie Mellon
- Shenoy, P.P. PhD, Cornell
- Shulenburger, D.E. PhD, Illinois
- Singh, S. PhD, Wisconsin
- Spencer, D.G. PhD, Oregon
- Srivastava, R.P. PhD, Oklahoma
- Stoltenberg, C.D. JD, Harvard
- Waegelein, J.F. PhD, Penn State
- Welch, K.D. PhD, Chicago
- Whitman, D.F. JD, Missouri at Columbia
- Yu, P.L. PhD, Johns Hopkins

UNIVERSITY OF MARYLAND - COLLEGE PARK
THE ROBERT H. SMITH SCHOOL OF BUSINESS

Program Highlights

- *Eight areas of concentration offered to students in the PhD program*
- *Curriculum combines foundational knowledge with exposure to high-quality research and training in research methods*
- *University of Maryland - College Park is one of the 10 top-rated research institutions in the US*
- *Accredited by AACSB*

CONTACT INFORMATION
Doctoral Program Office
2410 F Van Munching Hall
College Park, Maryland USA 20742
PH: 1-301-405-2214
FAX: 1-301-314-9157
EMAIL: bphdgrad@deans.umd.edu
INTERNET: http://www.rhsmith.umd.edu

UNIVERSITY OF MARYLAND - COLLEGE PARK, THE ROBERT H. SMITH SCHOOL OF BUSINESS

PROGRAM OVERVIEW

A Doctor of Philosophy (PhD) degree with specializations in accounting, finance, human resource management, decision and information technologies, marketing, organizational behavior, strategic management and transportation and logistics is offered by the Robert H. Smith School of Business (Smith School) at the University of Maryland - College Park (UMCP).

The PhD program curriculum is designed to ensure students are exposed to high-quality current research and trained in research methods while acquiring necessary foundational knowledge. It is a full-time program and students generally take three courses each semester until all course requirements are complete. Coursework consists of six courses in the area of the student's major, four courses in research tools for the required first minor, and four courses for the second minor. Depending on the specialization, additional requirements may include two courses from the Master of Business Administration (MBA) core program (accounting, finance, marketing and organizational behavior), one or two graduate courses in economics, and one course in research methodology.

The Smith School PhD program also requires students to pass a written comprehensive examination in the area of concentration and a subsequent oral comprehensive examination, unless a pass or high pass is achieved on the first attempt on the written exam.

Additional requirements include the preparation and oral defense of both a dissertation proposal and the dissertation. Students are required to submit a satisfactory research working paper during their third year of doctoral studies. Finance students must pass a qualifying examination at the end of the first year.

The first minor area generally requires the completion of a set of courses determined by the department faculty.

Students in all specializations except finance have an open choice regarding the area of study for the second minor requirement. Finance students must take economics as the second minor. An international business concentration is available as a minor field in the doctoral program.

Research Centers

Business studies at the Smith School are supported by a number of campus research centers including the Center for Global Business (CGB), the Center for Knowledge and Information Management (CKIM) and the Supply Chain Management Center (SCMC).

The mission of the CGB is to integrate a global dimension into all the activities and programs of the Smith School, including undergraduate and graduate business education, faculty research, management education and training, and distance education.

Some of the current research areas at CKIM include e-commerce, virtual enterprises, data mining and analysis, telecommunications economics, knowledge management, strategic information technology management, valuation of knowledge assets and netcentricity. Research conducted at the SCMC identifies and investigates the best practices in managing the interdependent relationships among suppliers, manufacturers, carriers and customers. Research conducted at the center has been featured in a number of publications, including the Harvard Business Journal and the Journal of Commerce

SELECTED RESEARCH AREAS

- Accounting ethics
- Accounting regulations
- Applied probability
- Compensation
- Competitive advantage
- Consumer behavior
- Consumer loyalty
- Corporate advertising
- Corporate governance issues
- Corporate restructuring
- Cost allocations
- Cross-cultural management
- Distribution management
- Effiecient risk allocation in modern economies
- Electronic commerce
- Electronic commerce innovations
- Financial reporting
- Forecasting
- Forward oil markets
- Game theory
- International finance
- Job search and choice
- Joint ventures
- Linear programming
- Logistics systems
- Managerial decision making under uncertainty
- Mangerial accounting
- Market reforms
- Market signaling
- Mathematical programming
- Network optimization
- Organizational behavior
- Quality control
- Regulation and competition in international air markets
- Risk management decisions
- Simulation modeling and analysis
- Social responsibility of the management of the supply chain
- Strategic human resource management
- Strategic leadership and coordination
- Supply chain management
- Trading volume
- Transfer pricing
- Transportationn planning

UNIVERSITY OF MARYLAND - COLLEGE PARK, THE ROBERT H. SMITH SCHOOL OF BUSINESS

ADMISSIONS CRITERIA & PROCEDURES

Admission to the Smith School PhD program is determined on the basis of several factors including previous academic performance, GMAT or GRE scores, the applicant's statement of purpose and reference letters. Prospective PhD students should have two semesters of calculus before being admitted to the program. The admission decision is made by the faculty in the major area of concentration.

For admission to UMCP, the Graduate School generally requires a B average or a GPA of 3.0 on a scale of 4.0 in a bachelor's degree program. There are no minimum GMAT or GRE scores but successful applicants will have scores within the range of the average scores of previously admitted students. Applicants whose first language is other than English must achieve a minimum score of 575 on the paper-based TOEFL.

The admissions process requires submission of two application packages. The first package contains the yellow copy of the application, three letters of recommendation, a statement of purpose and experience, copies of official transcripts and copies of GMAT or GRE scores. This package should be submitted to the doctoral program office. The second application package, which contains the white copy of the application, the application fee, official GMAT or GRE scores, official transcripts and, for international students, official TOEFL and TSE scores and the certification of finances, should be submitted to the graduate admissions office. International students must submit official transcripts in the original language along with official English translations.

EXPENSES & FINANCIAL ASSISTANCE

All students admitted into the PhD program at the Smith School receive financial support in the form of either a graduate assistantship or fellowship. Graduate assistantships provide US$11,000–16,000 over a 10-month period, full tuition and university health insurance. In exchange, students are required to work between 10 and 20 hours a week as graduate assistants conducting research or teaching. Summer assistantships, which pay between US$2,000 and $5,000 over a two-month period, are also available.

Graduate School Fellowships offer 12-credit-hour tuition waivers and slightly higher stipends than graduate assistant appointments. Students may also compete for national awards offered by the International Association for Management Education (AACSB), the American Association of University Women (AAUW) and private foundations.

INTERNATIONAL STUDENT SUPPORT

There are currently 2,700 international students from 133 countries studying at UMCP.

The Office of International Education Services (IES) provides students with orientation, counseling on immigration concerns and cultural issues and advising on programs available to students interested in international study. IES also provides international students with a regular newsletter that provides information on campus clubs, lectures of interest to international students and information about orientations and volunteer possibilities.

ADMISSIONS AT A GLANCE

Minimum GMAT:	no set minimum
Minimum GPA:	3.0
Minimum TOEFL (paper):	575
Minimum TOEFL (computer):	–
Application Fee:	US$50 (dom& int'l)
Application Deadline:	US: Feb 1 (fall - preferred), Aug 1 (fall - final deadline) Int'l: Feb 1 (fall)

EXPENSES AT A GLANCE

Tuition:	
In State:	US$272 per credit hour
Out-of-State:	US$415 per credit hour
Int'l Students:	US$415 per credit hour
Books & Supplies:	US$300
Health Insurance:	–
Accommodation:	
University Residences:	US$775 per month (2 person apt)
Family Housing:	–
Private:	US$400–800 per month

PROGRAM FACTS

# of Full-time Students:	87
# of Part-time Students:	0
# of Applications per year:	450
# Accepted per year:	25
# Enrolled per year:	20
Average GMAT Score:	697
Average Age:	–
% Men/Women:	70%/30%
Work Experience (avg yrs):	–
# of Faculty:	100
% Faculty with Doctoral Degree:	100%
Annual Research Funding:	–

UNIVERSITY OF MARYLAND - COLLEGE PARK, THE ROBERT H. SMITH SCHOOL OF BUSINESS

UNIVERSITY AND LOCATION

Chartered in 1856 as the Maryland Agricultural College, the University of Maryland - College Park, is the flagship institution of the university system of Maryland. Over 32,000 undergraduate and graduate students can choose from more than 100 areas of study offered by 11 colleges and two schools. Students may also create their own program of individual study with the assistance of a faculty adviser.

The university has 350 buildings on 1,300 acres. Five on-campus libraries contain more than two million volumes and 11,000 periodicals. Computing facilities for research and education include UNIVAC and IBM mainframe systems with access to numerous IBM PCs.

Van Munching Hall, the home of the Smith School, is equipped with telecommunication technology, sophisticated computer labs and electronic classrooms. The Smith School houses outreach centers that provide unique learning and research opportunities including Dingman Center for Entrepreneurship and the Office of Executive Programs.

College Park, a community of 24,000, is situated close to a dynamic mix of historic towns and cities, rolling farmland, waterfront parks and modern urban centers. Located in the Baltimore-Washington corridor, residents have access to many educational, governmental, technological and cultural resources. Both major cities offer first-rate theater, concert performances, film, dance, art galleries and museums, as well as restaurants, clubs and sports events.

UMCP boasts close ties to the other educational institutions in the university system of Maryland as well as various governmental and private organizations such as the Goddard Space Flight Center of NASA, the US Department of Agriculture, the Smithsonian Institution, the National Institutes of Health, local school systems and many high-technology corporations.

City Population:	24,000
Cost of Living:	medium
Climate Range:	23° to 85°F
Campus Setting:	suburban
Total Enrollment:	32,925
Graduate Enrollment:	8,149
Students in Residence:	7,850

FACULTY

- Alavi, M. PhD, Ohio State
- Alt, F.B. PhD, Georgia Institute of Technology
- Assad, A.A. PhD, MIT
- Bailey, J.P. PhD, MIT
- Bakshi, G.S. PhD, Wisconsin-Madison
- Ball, M.O. PhD, Cornell
- Bartol, K.M. PhD, Michigan State
- Bedingfield, J.P. DBA, Maryland
- Biehal, G. PhD, Stanford
- Bodin, L.D. PhD, Berkeley
- Bolton, R. PhD, Carnegie Mellon
- Carroll, S.J. PhD, Minnesota
- Corsi, T.M. PhD, Wisconsin-Madison
- Draper, F.D. PhD, Catholic America
- Dresner, M. PhD, British Columbia
- Evers, P.T. PhD, Minnesota
- Faraj, S. PhD, Boston
- Frank, H. PhD, Northwestern
- Fromovitz, S. PhD, Stanford
- Fu, M. PhD, Harvard
- Gannon, M.J. PhD, Columbia
- Gass, S.I. PhD, Berkeley
- Geter, R.S. PhD, Pennsylvania
- Golden, B.L. PhD, MIT
- Gordon, L.A. PhD, Rensselaer Polytechnic Institute
- Greer, T.V. PhD, Texas
- Grimm, C. PhD, Berkeley
- Gupta, A.K. DBA, Harvard
- Haslem, J.A. PhD, North Carolina
- Ibrahim, H.A. PhD, George Washington
- Jolson, M.A. PhD, Maryland
- Kannan, P.K. PhD, Purdue
- Kolodny, R. PhD, New York
- Krapfel, R.E. PhD, Michigan State
- Lamone, R. PhD, North Carolina
- Leete, B.A. JD, American
- Lele, S. PhD, Michigan
- Lepak, D.P. PhD, Pennsylvania State
- Levine, M.J. PhD, Wisconsin-Madison
- Kim, O. PhD, Pennsylvania
- Locke, E.A. PhD, Cornell
- Loeb, M. PhD, Northwestern
- Loeb, S.E. PhD, Wisconsin-Madison
- Madan, D.B. PhD, Maryland
- Maksimovic, V. PhD, Harvard
- Mattingly, J.G. PhD, Maryland
- Morici, P. PhD, New York
- Nickels, W. PhD, Ohio State
- Olian, J.D. PhD, Wisconsin-Madison
- Palmer, J.W. PhD, Claremont Graduate
- Park, T. PhD, Purdue
- Peters, M.F. PhD, Indiana
- Phillips, G. PhD, Harvard
- Preston, L.E. PhD, Harvard
- Raghavan, S. PhD, MIT
- Reger, R.K. PhD, Illinois
- Riley, D.R. PhD, Purdue
- Senbet, L. PhD, New York
- Shaw, K.W. PhD, Wisconsin-Madison
- Sims, H.P. PhD, Michigan State
- Smith, K.G. PhD, Washington
- Stevens, C.K. PhD, Washington
- Taylor, M.S. PhD, Purdue
- Triantis, A.J. PhD, Stanford
- Venkatesh, V. PhD, Minnesota
- Wagner, J. PhD, Kansas State
- Widhelm, W.B. PhD, John Hopkins
- Windle, R.J. PhD, Wisconsin-Madison
- Zantek, P. PhD, Purdue

UNIVERSITY OF MASSACHUSETTS, AMHERST
PhD PROGRAM

Program Highlights

- *Recognized as one of the Best Business Schools in the US by the Princeton Review*
- *One of the oldest PhD business programs in New England*
- *Planning underway for a new US$12-million high-technology classroom wing*
- *Accredited by AACSB*

CONTACT INFORMATION
Eugene M. Isenberg School of
   Management
121 Presidents Drive, Box 34910
Amherst, Massachusetts USA 01003-4910
PH: 1-413-545-5608
FAX: 1-413-545-3858
EMAIL: gradprog@som.umass.edu
INTERNET: http://www.som.umass.edu

UNIVERSITY OF MASSACHUSETTS, AMHERST, PHD PROGRAM

PROGRAM OVERVIEW

Established in 1949, the Isenberg School of Management at the University of Massachusetts, Amherst (UMA) has been awarding doctoral business degrees since 1967. With over 60 students pursuing business studies at the PhD level, Isenberg is the largest doctoral business program at a public institution in New England.

The program emphasizes in-depth theoretical analysis of business issues with a focus on making original contributions to the field through rigorous research, detailed coursework and the interaction of PhD students with dedicated faculty, colleagues and business professionals.

The six areas of specialization are accounting, finance, marketing, management science, organization studies, and strategic management. Program requirements include coursework in one of these fields, a comprehensive exam, a dissertation, and at least one year of teaching. The typical amount of time for degree completion ranges from three to four years.

Accounting

The accounting option prepares candidates for rewarding academic careers by underscoring the importance of research, teaching and publication. The program includes coursework in research methods, major and minor areas of study, and economics and behavioral science. Majors offered by the department include behavioral research in accounting, introduction to financial research, security market research, and advanced readings in behavioral research.

Finance

The finance option offers advanced study in the field of modern financial economics to prepare students for careers in industry and academia. After a firm grounding in subjects including economics, statistics and mathematics, training in financial applications and theory is carried out in a series of finance seminars. One of the assets of the department is the Center for International Securities and Derivative Markets. This resource allows doctoral students access to sophisticated databases and software applications, and acts as coordinates initiatives involving investment management industry professionals.

Management Science

Management science is characterized by a innovative cross-disciplinary approach to learning. After pursuing core courses in linear algebra, data structures, numerical analysis, management science, probability and statistics, deterministic models, stochastic processes, and mathematical analysis, PhD students proceed with an individualized program of study under the faculty guidance.

Marketing

The option in marketing prepare candidates for careers as teachers and train them to produce research relevant to the field of business. The department offers courses in marketing theory, research methods and related disciplines.

Organization Studies

The organization studies program prepares students to work with and teach about, organizations and management in order to implement productive changes. Emphasis is on multidisciplinary problem-solving techniques.

Strategic Management

The program in strategic management is a cross-disciplinary study option that combines the fields of organizational theory with industrial organization economics. Within this diverse study area, students may pursue specializations in strategic resource allocation, leadership, entrepreneurship and organizational purpose, strategic decision processes or environmental analysis.

SELECTED RESEARCH AREAS

- Application of behavior decision theory in accounting and auditing contexts
- Aspects of accounting and tax compliance decisions
- Asset pricing
- Auditing in computer environments
- Business to business marketing
- Cognitive information processing
- Compensation and benefits
- Development of accounting standards
- Functioning of teams in applied settings
- Futures markets
- Gender effects in leadership
- Green marketing and environmental marketing
- History and theory of the corporation
- Impact of discrete decisions on individual income levels
- Industrial organization
- International business and finance
- Interpretive and critical approaches to organizing and theorizing
- Investigation of negative informational effects
- Japanese manufacturing techniques
- Management in turbulent environments
- Management of interest rate risk
- Management theory
- Marketing to an aging population
- Network optimization
- Nonprofit and social marketing
- Organizational renewal and change
- Organizational studies and international management through postmodern feminist and postcolonial conceptualizations
- Retail marketing strategy and patronage behavior
- Sports marketing
- Strategic management issues in professional service firms
- Supercomputing
- Technical support and analysis for management decisions

UNIVERSITY OF MASSACHUSETTS, AMHERST, PhD PROGRAM

ADMISSIONS CRITERIA & PROCEDURES

The Isenberg School has many program options but to keep enrollment deliberately small, accepts two to three students per year into each concentration. As a result, the admission process is highly selective.

Applicants must be graduates of an accredited American college or university (or equivalent). An MBA degree (or equivalent) is required for admission to the strategic management option, and is recommended for all other programs. Specific requirements for particular areas of specialization may be obtained by contacting the Isenberg School directly. In some instances these prerequisites require previous undergraduate- or graduate-level coursework, while in other cases self-study or work experience may satisfy specific program requirements.

The application package must include a completed application form, two official copies of transcripts from all undergraduate and graduate institutions attended, two letters of recommendation and an official GMAT score. In addition to the above information, international students must submit a financial statement and, in the case of applicants whose first language is not English, a minimum paper-based TOEFL score of 590.

Application information is available from the Graduate School at UMA. An application fee of US$25 (Massachusetts residents) or US$40 (all other applicants) must be included with each application. The deadline for receipt of all applications and supporting documentation is February 1 for fall term entry.

EXPENSES & FINANCIAL ASSISTANCE

Isenberg provides all doctoral candidates with financial support during the first four years of their studies. Teaching and research assistantships cover the cost of tuition and health insurance coverage for PhD students and are renewable for up to four years. These appointments typically involve 15 to 20 hours of work per week provide opportunities to teach and work closely with a faculty member on a particular study. In most instances, PhD students will have at least one year of experience as a teaching assistant and a second year as a research assistant.

To augment the income received through teaching assistantships, many doctoral students teach and/or research in the evening and during intersession periods. In addition, students with a superior academic record may be eligible for merit-based university fellowship awarded on a competitive basis. International students are eligible for a limited number of tuition waivers awarded through the Office of Foreign Students and Scholars (OFSS). Financial support for travel and research is also available through the Graduate School.

INTERNATIONAL STUDENT SUPPORT

UMA is committed to maintaining a diverse student population with substantial international representation. International students constitute 47 percent of the total PhD student enrollment at Isenberg. The OFSS acts as a coordinating body for students wishing to meet individuals from other countries, and provides an orientation program for all new international students.

Foreign students who have been offered teaching assistant positions may take advantage of UMA's Foreign Teaching Assistant Orientation program. This resource prepares students for the duties required of university instructors by offering assistance with English language communication skills, presentation techniques and teaching strategies.

Other resources for international students include the International Students Association, which organizes numerous social activities for non-domestic students, and an active Hospitality Program that brings international students and local families together. Special language and cultural programs are also available for spouses of international students.

ADMISSIONS AT A GLANCE

Minimum GMAT:	600
Minimum GPA:	3.0
Minimum TOEFL (paper):	590
Minimum TOEFL (computer):	–
Application Fee:	US$25 (Mass), US$40 (other)
Application Deadline:	Feb 1

EXPENSES AT A GLANCE

Tuition per year:
- In State: US$2,640
- Out-of-State: US$9,018
- Int'l Students: US$9,018

Books & Supplies: US$450 per year

Health Insurance: –

Accommodation:
- University Residences: US$4,538–4,986 per year
- Family Housing: US$3,789–5,580 per year
- Private: US$9,000 per year

PROGRAM FACTS

# of Full-time Students:	55
# of Part-time Students:	0
# of Applications per year:	100
# Accepted per year:	15
# Enrolled per year:	12
Average GMAT Score:	653
Average Age:	28
% Men/Women:	58%/42%
Work Experience (avg yrs):	–
# of Faculty:	44
% Faculty with Doctoral Degree:	100%
Annual Research Funding:	US$200,000

UNIVERSITY OF MASSACHUSETTS, AMHERST, PhD PROGRAM

UNIVERSITY AND LOCATION

The University of Massachusetts, Amherst was founded in 1863 as the first of five institutions in the University of Massachusetts system. UMA upholds principles of affirmative action, civility, equal opportunity and the free exchange of ideas.

With undergraduate and graduate programs offered across 10 schools, colleges and faculties, this comprehensive public university offers bachelor's degrees in 90 different areas of study, 70 master's programs and 50 doctoral study options.

Facilities for students include the W.E.B. DuBois Library, named after the African-American scholar and activist who co-founded the National Association for the Advancement of Colored People (NAACP). This resource houses more than five million items, including 16,000 magazines, journals and newspapers. Four computer labs are housed in the Isenberg School for exclusive use of business students, and computer classrooms and labs are strategically located around campus.

UMA's 1,400-acre campus includes 41 residence halls, making the university's residential system the fifth largest in the country. Student housing contains study areas, kitchenettes and fitness centers and dining facilities. The university also maintains an extensive off-campus housing data base and other aids for students seeking living quarters in the Amherst area.

Situated in the western part of the state of Massachusetts, approximately two hours from Boston, Amherst is a classic New England town with coffee houses, book stores and restaurants featuring different ethnic cuisine. The nearby mountain of western Massachusetts, New Hampshire and Vermont furnish skiing, camping and hiking opportunities for outdoor enthusiasts.

FACULTY

- Abranovic, W. PhD, Rensselaer Polytechnic
- Ali, A.I. PhD, Southern Methodist
- Asebrook, R. PhD, Wisconsin
- Barringer, M.W. PhD, Cornell
- Berkowitz, E.N. PhD, Ohio State
- Branch, B. PhD, Michigan
- Brashear-Alejandro, T. PhD, Georgia State
- Butterfield, D.A. PhD, Michigan
- Calas, M. PhD, Massachusetts
- Debevec Witz, K. PhD, Cincinnati
- Diamond, W. PhD, North Carolina
- Elgers, P. DBA, Maryland
- Gal, G. PhD, Michigan State
- Giacobbe-Miller, J. PhD, Cornell
- Hanno, D. PhD, Massachusetts
- Iyer, E. PhD, Pittsburgh
- Kapadia, N. PhD, New York
- Karren, R. PhD, Maryland
- Kazemi, H.B.. PhD, Michigan
- Kida, T. PhD, Massachusetts
- Lacey, N.J. PhD, Pennsylvania State
- Mangaliso, M. PhD, Massachusetts, Amherst
- Mannino, R. DBA, Colorado
- Manz, C. PhD, Pennsylvania State
- Marx, R.D. PhD, Illinois
- McComb, S. PhD, Purdue
- Milne, G.R. PhD, North Carolina
- Nagurney, A. PhD, Brown
- Nakosteen, R.A. PhD, Tennessee
- Nawalkha, S. PhD, Massachusetts
- Pfeiffer, R. PhD, North Carolina
- Porter, S. PhD, Univ of Washington
- Robinson, A.G. PhD, Johns Hopkins
- Sardinas, J. PhD, Pennsylvania State
- Schewe, C. PhD, Northwestern
- Schneeweis, T. PhD, Iowa
- Sharma, A. PhD, North Carolina, Chapel Hill
- Simpson, R. PhD, North Carolina
- Smircich, L. PhD, Syracuse
- Smith, J. PhD, Univ of Washington
- Swaminathan, V. PhD, Georgia
- Weinberger, M.G. PhD, Arizona State
- Wooldridge, W. PhD, Colorado
- Zacharias, L. JD, Columbia

City Population:	25,000
Cost of Living:	medium
Climate Range:	25° to 74°F
Campus Setting:	urban
Total Enrollment:	24,000
Graduate Enrollment:	6,600
Students in Residence:	12,720

UNIVERSITY OF MICHIGAN
PhD IN BUSINESS ADMINISTRATION

University
of Michigan
Business
School

Program Highlights

- *Eight areas of concentration*
- *Tailored specializations for interdisciplinary interests*
- *Limited enrollment for increased student-faculty interaction*
- *Accredited by AACSB*

CONTACT INFORMATION

Doctoral Studies Office Room D2254

University of Michigan Business School

701 Tappan Street

Ann Arbor, Michigan USA 48109-1234

PH: 1-734-764-2343

FAX: 1-734-647-8133

EMAIL: umbusphd@umich.edu

INTERNET: http://www.bus.umich.edu/

UNIVERSITY OF MICHIGAN, PHD IN BUSINESS ADMINISTRATION

PROGRAM OVERVIEW

The University of Michigan Business School (UMBS) offers a Doctor of Philosophy (PhD) in business administration with concentrations in accounting, computer and information systems, corporate strategy, finance, international business, marketing, operations management and organizational behavior. There is also an individualized program option which allows students to craft customized programs in other areas of study and interdisciplinary topics.

Fewer than 90 students at all stages of doctoral study are enrolled in the program ensuring close working relationships with the 130 full-time faculty members. Doctoral study requires full-time, year-round study and the average time required to complete the degree requirements is five years.

Areas of Concentration

Research in accounting focuses on business community concerns such as the impact of accounting information on capital markets and on the behavior of decision-makers within firms. Students majoring in accounting complete three courses in econometrics and statistics, two in economics, two in finance, four in accounting and two electives from finance, statistics or operations management.

Computer and information systems students take courses in three areas from telecommunications, database, expert or adaptive systems, systems analysis and design and user-centered design principles. They participate in seminars on information and knowledge management, behavioral aspects of information technology, quantitative modeling and software engineering.

Students concentrating in corporate strategy take four to five semesters to complete 16 to 20 core courses in economics and organizational theory, methods, strategy applications and cognate applications. Some of these courses are taken outside of the business school in departments such as economics, sociology and psychology.

In the finance program, students complete most coursework in the first two years. Classes in microeconomic theory, mathematical economics, statistics and finance are among the first-year requirements. Second-year courses include a minimum of six electives and two PhD-level finance courses. Students take two more seminars in finance during the third year and at least one course related to their research each term for the remainder of the program.

International business students must select a second area of concentration such as accounting, organizational behavior, business economics, finance or marketing. Students devote the first two years to meeting core and secondary requirements, including four seminars in international trade and foreign direct investment, international finance, current international business research and market environment, strategy and organization. Other requirements include one upper-level international business course, one upper-level course in the second area of concentration, four courses in research methods and two terms of doctoral seminars in the second concentration.

Students in the marketing concentration take a two-year sequence of courses in methodological foundations such as econometrics and multivariate statistics, theoretical foundations such as microeconomics and social psychology and relevant marketing literatures.

Operations management students focus on mathematical modeling and analysis tools courses in the first year. Second-year courses allow students to apply these tools to operations management topics, develop areas of specialization and round out their business education.

Organizational behavior and human resource management students spend the first two years in a sequence of four seminars on organizational behavior and theory and four terms of research methods courses, two of which must be quantitative. Students also take additional graduate courses in their areas of interest.

SELECTED RESEARCH AREAS

- Alternate dispute resolution
- Attitude theory and theory of action
- Bayesian inference and forecasting
- Behavior of Eurocurrency rates
- Business ethics
- Business survival
- Capital market research
- Corporate control
- Corporate finance
- Customer satisfaction and its measurement
- Employment law
- Financial accounting
- Financial statement analysis and firm valuation
- Global competition
- History and organizational theory
- Innovative capabilities of firms
- Insider trading
- International business in China
- International capital markets
- Intersection of environmentalism and globalism in relation to the behavior of industrial coporations
- Labor economics
- Management accounting
- Manufacturing performance measurement
- Markov decision models
- Mutual funds
- Organization effectiveness
- Performance measurement and control
- Production control
- Risk and return in land markets
- Stock market behavior
- Technology strategy and organizational change
- The role of emotion in advertising
- Top executive group perception

UNIVERSITY OF MICHIGAN, PHD IN BUSINESS ADMINISTRATION

ADMISSIONS CRITERIA & PROCEDURES

Criteria used to admit students include a distinguished academic record in undergraduate and/or graduate level studies, high scores on standardized tests, a strong record of research and/or relevant work experience demonstrating independence and initiative, and a close fit between student and faculty research interests. Applicants must have a working knowledge of college-level algebra, calculus and intermediate microeconomics. Applicants to accounting, finance and marketing must also know linear algebra and advanced calculus.

A bachelor's degree from an accredited college or university is the minimum academic requirement for admission. Applicants must provide two official transcripts from each university where they earned a degree and one copy from any other university or college attended. Other required materials include the US$55 application fee, official GRE or GMAT test scores, three letters of recommendation in sealed envelopes, a statement of purpose and official TOEFL results, if necessary. The minimum TOEFL score required for admission is 600 on the paper-based test or 250 on the computer-based test.

Applications from international students must be accompanied by transcripts which bear an official seal or stamp of the school and an official's signature, and a copy of the diploma. Transcripts in a language other than English must be accompanied by exact translations. Students whose native language is not English who have received a degree from a university in an English-speaking country do not have to submit TOEFL results.

The deadline for application for the fall term is January 15, 2001.

EXPENSES & FINANCIAL ASSISTANCE

Financial aid for up to four years is provided to all PhD students on a merit basis and no separate application is required. Assistance takes the form of fellowship stipends of US$7,500 per year and year-round research assistantships which provide a full tuition waiver and health insurance, as well as a stipend of approximately US$8,900 per year requiring 10 to 12 hours per week. During their third year, students are required to teach at least one semester for which they are paid as teaching assistants.

Fellowships for which eligible students are nominated can supplement other financial support.

INTERNATIONAL STUDENT SUPPORT

The International Center offers international students a week-long orientation including driver's license information and a test, seminars on communicating with academic advisors, immigration and visa information, and information technology. The center also provides campus housing information, a culture shock and survival series, and employment assistance.

The IC assists students with re-entry into the US after a temporary absence, verification of legal status, extensions of legal stay, changes of immigration status, social security card information and information about health resources and health insurance. English conversation classes are offered at the North Campus Office.

ADMISSIONS AT A GLANCE

Minimum GMAT:	no set minimum
Minimum GPA:	no set minimum
Minimum TOEFL (paper):	600
Minimum TOEFL (computer):	250
Application Fee:	US$55
Application Deadline:	Jan 15

EXPENSES AT A GLANCE

Tuition:	
In State:	US$21,574 for two terms
Out-of-State:	–
Int'l Students:	–
Books & Supplies:	–
Health Insurance:	–
Accommodation:	
University Residences:	US$550-800 per month
Family Housing:	–
Private:	US$650 per month

PROGRAM FACTS

# of Full-time Students:	80
# of Part-time Students:	0
# of Applications per year:	450-500
# Accepted per year:	30-35
# Enrolled per year:	15-18
Average GMAT Score:	710
Average Age:	27-28
% Men/Women:	–
Work Experience (avg yrs):	3
# of Faculty:	130
% Faculty with Doctoral Degree:	100%
Annual Research Funding:	–

UNIVERSITY OF MICHIGAN, PhD IN BUSINESS ADMINISTRATION

UNIVERSITY AND LOCATION

Founded in 1817, the University of Michigan is one of the oldest public universities in the US. It comprises 18 schools and colleges which encompass more than 200 fields of study in liberal arts, law, music, art, social work, medicine and the sciences. Total enrollment exceeds 50,000 students.

The university operates three campuses in Ann Arbor, Flint and Dearborn, Michigan. Over 30,000 students attend classes at the Ann Arbor campus in 211 major buildings on over 2,500 acres of land. The campus features 28 libraries and nine museums with special collections for advanced research..

The UMBS library can accommodate more than 600 readers in 19 group study rooms and open reading areas on three floors. The collection consists of more than 130,000 volumes, 420,000 microfilms, 5,000 working papers and 3,200 periodicals and serials.

Recreational facilities at the Ann Arbor campus include tennis courts, racquetball courts, swimming pools, weight rooms, golf courses and indoor and outdoor running tracks. The university hosts NCAA Division I Big Ten sports such as basketball, baseball, hockey, gymnastics and Wolverine football in Michigan stadium, the largest open-air college arena in the US.

The center of Michigan's booming high-tech industry, Ann Arbor is located less than an hour from Detroit and just five hours from Chicago and Toronto. It has a population of approximately 130,000 and combines urban conveniences such as shopping malls and entertainment centers with the intimacy of a small town supporting art galleries, theaters and museums.

City Population:	100,000
Cost of Living:	medium
Climate Range:	25° to 75°F
Campus Setting:	urban
Total Enrollment:	52,047
Graduate Enrollment:	15,247
Students in Residence:	30,000

FACULTY

- Anderson, E.W. PhD, Chicago
- Andrews, R.W. PhD, Virginia Polytechnic
- Ashford, S.J. PhD, Northwestern
- Bagozzi, R.P. PhD, Northwestern
- Baker, W.E. PhD, Northwestern
- Batra, R. PhD, Stanford
- Berkovitch, E. PhD, Northwestern
- Blair, D. PhD, Berkeley
- Brophy, D.J. PhD, Ohio State
- Cameron III, G.D. PhD, Michigan
- Capozza, D.R. PhD, Johns Hopkins
- Cox, T. PhD, Arizona
- Crocker, K.J. PhD, Carnegie Mellon
- Davis, G.F. PhD, Stanford
- Dechow, P. PhD, Rochester
- Duenyas, I. PhD, Northwestern
- Dufey, G. DBA, Washington
- Dutton, J.E. PhD, Northwestern
- Fornell, C. PhD, Lund
- Gladwin, T.N. PhD, –
- Gordon, M.D. PhD, Michigan
- Hanson, G. PhD, MIT
- Hines, J. PhD, –
- Imhoff, E.A. PhD, Michigan State
- Indjejikian, R. PhD, Pennsylvania
- Israel, R. PhD, Northwestern
- Jackson, J.E. PhD, Harvard
- Johnson, M.D. PhD, Chicago
- Karnani, A.G. DBA, Harvard
- Kaul, G. PhD, Chicago
- Kim, E.H. PhD, SUNY
- Kinnear, T.C. PhD, Michigan
- Lafontaine, F. PhD, UBC
- Lanen, W.N. PhD, Pennsylvania
- Lenk, P.J. PhD, Michigan
- Lewis, D.L. PhD, Michigan
- Lieberthal, K. PhD, Columbia
- Lim, L.Y.C. PhD, Michigan
- Lovejoy, W.S. PhD, Delaware
- Lundholm, R. PhD, Iowa
- Martin, C.L. PhD, Columbia
- Masten, S.E. PhD, Pennsylvania
- Mitchell, W. PhD, Berkeley
- Muir, D. JD, Michigan
- Nanda, V. PhD, Chicago
- Narayanan, M.P. PhD, Northwestern
- Olson, J.R. PhD, Michigan
- Oswald, L.J. JD, Michigan
- Prahalad, C.K. DBA, Harvard
- Price, R.H. PhD, Illinois
- Quinn, R.E. PhD, Cincinnati
- Ramaswamy, V. PhD, Pennsylvania
- Reece, J.S. CMA, Institute of Management Accounting
- Rogers, P. PhD, Michigan
- Ryan, M.J. PhD, –
- Sandelands, L. PhD, Northwestern
- Schipani, C.A. PhD, Chicago
- Schriber, T.J. PhD, Michigan
- Severance, D.G. PhD, Michigan
- Seyhun, H.N. PhD, Rochester
- Siedel III, G.J. JD, Michigan
- Skinner, D.J. PhD, Rochester
- Slemrod, J.B. PhD, Harvard
- Sloan, R. PhD, Rochester
- Stecke, K.E. PhD, Purdue
- Suslow, V.Y. PhD, Stanford
- Svejnar, J. PhD, Princeton
- Talbot, F.B. PhD, Pennsylvania State
- Taylor, J.R. PhD, Minnesota
- Terrell, K. PhD, Cornell
- Thakor, A.V. PhD, Northwestern
- Tichy, N.M. PhD, Columbia
- Walsh, J.P. PhD, Northwestern
- Weick, K.E. PhD, Ohio State
- Weiss, J.A. PhD, Harvard
- Welbourne, T.M. PhD, –
- Whitman, M. PhD, Columbia
- Wright, D.W. PhD, Michigan State
- Zald, M.N. PhD, Michigan

UNIVERSITY OF MINNESOTA - TWIN CITIES
PhD PROGRAM IN BUSINESS ADMINISTRATION

Ph.D. Program
Business Administration
CARLSON SCHOOL OF MANAGEMENT
UNIVERSITY OF MINNESOTA

Program Highlights

- *Six areas of concentration and several sub-fields*
- *US$15,000 in financial aid per year for all PhD students in addition to tuition waivers and paid health insurance*
- *Accredited by AACSB*

CONTACT INFORMATION
4 - 106 Carlson School of Management
321 19th Avenue South
Minneapolis, Minnesota USA 55455
PH: 1-612-624-0875 or 1-612-624-5065
FAX: 1-612-624-8221
EMAIL: ebronson@csom.umn.edu
INTERNET: http://www.csom.umn.edu/csom/phdprog/index.html

UNIVERSITY OF MINNESOTA - TWIN CITIES, PhD PROGRAM IN BUSINESS ADMINISTRATION

PROGRAM OVERVIEW

The Carlson School of Management (CSOM) at the University of Minnesota - Twin Cities (UMNTC) offers a Doctor of Philosophy (PhD) in Business Administration program with specializations in accounting, finance, information and decision sciences, marketing and logistics management, operations and management science, and strategic management and organization. While each concentration has its own course requirements, a typical degree program would consist of at least 40 semester credits, including required seminars, methodology courses, and minor or supporting field(s) classes.

Areas of Concentration

The accounting concentration increases the PhD student's understanding of accounting theory and accounting's relationship to other disciplines. The purpose and processes for conducting research are explored through methodology, coursework and seminars. Methods used to study accounting problems include mathematical modeling, empirical and econometric studies, and behavioral lab experiments.

The finance program at the CSOM is viewed as a field of applied economics. The program is thus most suited to individuals interested in economics, mathematics, or quantitative methods. Students spend their first year taking doctoral-level economics theory courses. Students without adequate quantitative backgrounds must take appropriate math or statistics courses. Finance doctoral seminars are generally taken during the second year in the program.

The information and decision sciences concentration delivers high quality research and instruction in the area of information management as well as decision-making science. The information management function is concerned with the problems that arise in the development and use of information/communication technology. Information/decision-making science is concerned with the methods, tools and approaches for acquiring, manipulating, retrieving, and presenting knowledge in support of individual or group activities.

The marketing and logistics management program is flexibly structured to provide doctoral students with both a common orientation to marketing or logistics issues as well as an opportunity to pursue areas of specialized study. Skills in theory building and empirical research in both private and public sectors are emphasized. Students acquire skills and knowledge through structured courses, doctoral seminars, and individual projects in marketing or logistics and related areas.

In the operations and management science concentration the focus is on the understanding and development of practices that enable manufacturing and service firms to utilize human resources, equipment, materials, and capital effectively. Minimal preparation for students entering this program would include coursework in differential, integral, and multivariable calculus, linear algebra, and probability and statistics.

The PhD concentration in strategic management and organization builds on three primary areas, each of which has a strong international focus: strategy - its formulation and implementation; organization structure and process; and business, government and society. Students emphasize only one of these three areas, but still take courses in all three to develop a broad understanding of the management field.

Examinations and Dissertation

Following the completion of all required coursework, students complete both written and oral preliminary exams intended to gauge the depth and breadth of expertise in major and minor or supporting field(s) areas. Following completion of these exams, students begin dissertation research. Both the dissertation proposal and final dissertation must be orally defended before a faculty committee.

SELECTED RESEARCH AREAS
- Accounting standards
- Advertising/false advertising
- Auditing
- Banking
- Brand management
- Business ethics
- Capital asset pricing
- Capital markets
- Computer technology
- Consumer behavior
- Contract theory
- Corporate finance
- Cost allocations
- Customer satisfaction
- Data warehousing
- Decision-making processes
- Distribution channels
- Efficient markets
- Electronic commerce
- Entrepreneurial studies
- Health care industry
- Information systems
- International finance & management
- Knowledge engineering
- Logistics management
- Manufacturing systems
- Marketing and pricing strategy
- New product development
- Operations management
- Organizational change & theory
- Quality control & management
- Risk management
- Strategic planning & management
- Supply chain management
- Taxation

UNIVERSITY OF MINNESOTA - TWIN CITIES, PHD PROGRAM IN BUSINESS ADMINISTRATION

ADMISSIONS CRITERIA & PROCEDURES

Admission to the PhD Program in Business Administration is based on the applicant's potential for research and teaching, commitment to an academic career beyond the PhD and ability to complete a rigorous program of study. Applicants must have a bachelor's degree or its equivalent from a recognized college or university.

The PhD program generally admits students in the fall semester only. Application materials for fall admission must be submitted by January 15 for fellowship consideration, or no later than March 31 for regular assistantship funding.

Complete application materials must be submitted to both the PhD Program Office and the Graduate School. This package should include the application for admission, the application fee (to Graduate School only) official transcripts from each college or university attended, a statement describing career objectives, research and teaching experience, three letters of recommendation from current or former professors or employers, and GMAT or GRE scores. TOEFL scores should also be submitted by all international applicants whose native language is not English, unless they have completed 24 quarter or 16 semester credits at a recognized US institution of higher education within the last two years.

EXPENSES & FINANCIAL ASSISTANCE

Every student admitted to the PhD in business administration program receives financial aid of at least US$15,000 for the academic year as well as a tuition waiver and paid health insurance benefits. Financial aid involves a combination of fellowships, graduate research and teaching assistantships. Student loan funds are also available from the university's Office of Student Financial Aid.

Fellowships include several university fellowship programs for new incoming students, disadvantaged and/or minority students and students working on doctoral dissertations.

PhD students are paid as half-time time research or teaching assistants and receive pay ranging from US$11.31 to US$15.78 per hour, depending on duties assigned.

INTERNATIONAL STUDENT SUPPORT

The International Student and Scholar Services (ISSS) includes a walk–in service for minor daily emergencies, advising for academic and career planning and assistance with various visa documents and application forms they may encounter.

The ISSS also provides programs such as the Culture Corps, through which international students become involved with the UMNTC campus community, discussion groups, an orientation program and an international friendship program that organizes various social outings for students.

ADMISSIONS AT A GLANCE

Minimum GMAT: 600
Minimum GPA:
　3.0 (undergrad), 3.5 (grad)
Minimum TOEFL (paper): 600
Minimum TOEFL (computer): 250
Application Fee:
　US$ 50 (dom); US$55 (int'l)
Application Deadline:
　Jan 15 for early consideration, or by Mar 31

EXPENSES AT A GLANCE

Tuition:
　In State:　waived with admission
　Out-of-State:
　　　　　　waived with admission
　Int'l Students:
　　　　　　waived with admission
Books & Supplies:
　　　　　　US$1,200 per year
Health Insurance:　paid by program
Accommodation:
　University Residences:
　　　　US$4,500 per year (approx)
　Family Housing:
　　　　US$300–500 per month
　Private:　US$4,200–9,000 per year

PROGRAM FACTS

# of Full-time Students:	81
# of Part-time Students:	0
# of Applications per year:	234
# Accepted per year:	34
# Enrolled per year:	24
Average GMAT Score:	697
Average Age:	30
% Men/Women:	62%/38%
Work Experience (avg yrs):	3
# of Faculty:	93
% Faculty with Doctoral Degree:	100%
Annual Research Funding:	US$1m

UNIVERSITY OF MINNESOTA - TWIN CITIES, PhD PROGRAM IN BUSINESS ADMINISTRATION

UNIVERSITY AND LOCATION

Founded as a preparatory school in 1851, the University of Minnesota came into formal existence in 1869 when it was reorganized as an institution of higher education. As such, it has consistently ranked among the top 20 public universities in the US. In addition, its library system ranks as the 17th largest among American universities, with over 48,000 subscriptions to periodicals and journals as well as 5.5 million volumes on the Twin Cities campus alone.

UMNTC is the largest of the four UMN campuses and is made up of 19 colleges that offer 161 bachelor's degrees, 218 master's degrees, 114 doctoral degrees, and five professional degrees. It has a total enrollment of approximately 40,000 students.

The UMNTC campus is divided into two separate campuses, one just east of downtown Minneapolis on the banks of the Mississippi River, and the other near the state fairgrounds in St. Paul.

Minneapolis, the largest city in the state, and St. Paul, the state capital, are the center of a metropolitan area with a population of over 2.3 million. The Twin Cities support many cultural and entertainment facilities such as the Guthrie Theater, the Minnesota Orchestra, the Science Museum and Omnitheater, the Walker Art Center, the Minnesota and Como zoos, and the Mall of America, as well as several major league sports teams. Outdoor enthusiasts can explore the region's 150 parks and 200 lakes or visit the Boundary Waters Canoe Area, an unsullied wilderness area just a few hours north by car.

FACULTY

- Adams, C.R. PhD, Purdue
- Ahlburg, D.A. PhD, Pennsylvania
- Albert, S. PhD, Ohio State
- Alexander, G.J. PhD, Michigan
- Amershi, A.H. PhD, British Columbia
- Anderson, J.C. PhD, Minnesota
- Anctil, R.M.. PhD, Minnesota

City Population: 2,300,000 (metro area)
Cost of Living: medium
Climate Range: 4° to 82°F
Campus Setting: urban
Total Enrollment: 39,595
Graduate Enrollment: 10,000 (approx)
Students in Residence: n/a

- Arvey, R.D. PhD, Minnesota
- Azevedo, R.E. PhD, Cornell
- Beier, F.J. PhD, Ohio State
- Benveniste, L.M. PhD, Berkeley
- Benzoni, L. PhD, Northwestern
- Bergen, M. PhD, Minnesota
- Bognanno, M.F. PhD, Iowa
- Bowie, N.E. PhD, Rochester
- Boyd, J.H. PhD, Pennsylvania
- Bromiley, P. PhD, Carnegie Mellon
- Cardozo, R.N. PhD, Minnesota
- Chakravarthy, B.S. DBA, Harvard
- Chang, C. PhD, Northwestern
- Chervany, N.L. DBA, Indiana
- Childers, T.L. PhD, Wisconsin
- Cuervo-Cazurra, A. PhD, MIT
- Curley, S.P. PhD, Michigan
- Davis, G.B. PhD, Stanford
- Dickhaut, J.W. PhD, Ohio State
- Duke, G.L. PhD, Georgia
- Erickson, W.B. PhD, Michigan State
- Everest, G.C. PhD, Pennsylvania
- Fossum, J.A. PhD, Michigan State
- Gibson, S. PhD, Boston College
- Hansen, R.A. PhD, Wisconsin
- Hill, A.V. PhD, Purdue
- Hoffmann, T.R. PhD, Wisconsin
- Houston, M.J. PhD, Illinois
- Ioffe, I. PhD, York
- John, D.R. PhD, Northwestern
- John, G. PhD, Northwestern
- Johnson, P.E. PhD, John Hopkins
- Joyce, E.J. PhD, Illinois at Urbana-Champaign
- Kanodia, C.S. PhD, Carnegie Mellon
- Kauffman, R. PhD, Carnegie Mellon
- Kidwell, D.S. PhD, Oregon
- Lenway, S.A. PhD, Berkeley
- Levine, R. PhD, California-Los Angeles
- Li, W.W. PhD, Waterloo
- Linderman, K. PhD, Case Western Reserve
- Loken, B. PhD, Illinois
- Maitland, I. PhD, Columbia
- March, S.T. PhD, Cornell
- Marcus, A.A. PhD, Harvard
- Mauriel, J.J. DBA, Harvard
- Meyer, S.M.. PhD, Ohio State
- Meyers-Levy, J. PhD, Northwestern
- Mukherji, A. PhD, Pittsburgh
- Murtha, T.P. PhD, New York
- Nachtsheim, C.J. PhD, Minnesota
- Nantell, T.J. PhD, Wisconsin
- Naumann, J.D. PhD, Minnesota
- Nichols, M.L. PhD, Kansas
- Park, J. PhD, Arizona
- Peteraf, M. PhD, Yale
- Polkovnichenko, V. PhD, Northwestern
- Povel, P. PhD, London School of Economics
- Prasad, B. PhD, Penn-Wharton
- Radhakrishna, B. PhD, Michigan
- Rao, A.R. PhD, Virginia Polytechnic Institute
- Rayburn, J. PhD, Iowa
- Roering, K.J. PhD, Iowa
- Rosko, P. PhD, Michigan
- Ruekert, R.W. PhD, Wisconsin
- Schnatterly, K. PhD, Michigan
- Schroeder, R.G. PhD, Northwestern
- Scoville, J.G. PhD, Harvard
- Seguin, P.J. PhD, Rochester
- Shah, P. PhD, Northwestern
- Shapiro, B. PhD, Minnesota
- Shroff, P. PhD, Columbia
- Singh, R. PhD, Carnegie Mellon
- Sinha, K.K. PhD, Texas at Austin
- Spero, A. PhD, Carnegie Mellon
- Subramani, M. PhD, Boston University
- Taaffe, M.R. PhD, Ohio State
- Van der Ven, A.H. PhD, Wisconsin-Madison
- Walker, O.C. PhD, Wisconsin
- Whitman, A.F. JD, Minnesota
- Winton, A.J. PhD, Pennsylvania
- Xia, W. PhD, Pittsburgh
- Zaheer, A. PhD, MIT
- Zaheer, S. PhD, MIT
- Zaidi, M.A. PhD, Berkeley
- Zellmer-Bruhn, M.E. PhD, Wisconsin-Madison

University of Mississippi
PhD Programs in Accountancy, Business Administration & Economics

Program Highlights

- *PhD programs in accountancy, business administration and economics*
- *Business administration offers specializations in finance, marketing, management or management information systems*
- *UM ranked as one of the top schools in the nation in Group Decision Support Systems*
- *Assistantships and fellowships include waivers of nonresident registration fees, as well as full and partial tuition scholarships*
- *Accredited by AACSB*

CONTACT INFORMATION

The Graduate School

University of Mississippi

University, Mississippi USA 38677

PH: 1-662-915-7474

FAX: 1-662-915-7577

EMAIL: gschool@olemiss.edu

INTERNET: http://www.olemiss.edu

UNIVERSITY OF MISSISSIPPI, PHD PROGRAMS IN ACCOUNTANCY BUSINESS ADMINISTRATION & ECONOMICS

PROGRAM OVERVIEW

The School of Business Administration (SBA) and the School of Accountancy (SA) at the University of Mississippi (UM) offer Doctor of Philosophy (PhD) degrees in accountancy, business administration and economics.

These programs are designed for students of exceptional ability who wish to do advanced work in preparation for careers in university teaching or research or as specialists in business, government or research organizations. Emphasis is placed on the development of students' ability to conduct significant research, which will ultimately be presented in the form of a scholarly dissertation.

To be awarded the PhD in any of the three fields named above, students must demonstrate that they have attained the high level of professional and academic competence expected of a person holding the doctoral degree.

Accountancy

The PhD in accountancy requires the completion of 30 credit hours of 600-level coursework beyond the master's degree and a dissertation. Two minor fields are required and at least one of these minors must be taken in the SBA. One modern foreign language or an approved alternative is also required, along with proficiency in quantitative methods. Students must also complete at least fifteen hours in research-tool courses.

The comprehensive examination in the major and each minor may not be taken until the student has satisfied the foreign language and has completed all coursework, or is in the last semester of coursework, for a particular major or minor field. Upon completion of the written comprehensive examinations, students take an oral examination covering both coursework and the doctoral dissertation proposal.

Business Administration

The doctoral program provides a deep understanding of business administration and in-depth study in a major field with emphasis in finance, management, management information systems, or marketing. A personalized program is designed for each student based upon the individual's background and needs.

Students must complete 60 credit hours of approved graduate courses beyond the bachelor's degree or at least 30 hours of approved courses above the 600-level beyond the master's degree. Each student must complete at least 12 credit hours in a major field beyond the master's degree and at least nine credit hours (preferably 12) in each of two minor fields beyond the bachelor's degree. Students must demonstrate proficiency in research methodology and satisfy a tool requirement.

Economics

The economics program encourages the development of the student's capacity to analyze economic problems and to do original research.

Students must complete at least 54 graduate credit hours beyond the bachelor's degree or at least 30 credit hours beyond the master's degree. To earn the PhD, students must choose a minimum of three fields. One field may be in an approved area outside of economics. Economics fields include managerial economics, labor economics, economic theory, econometrics, international economics, money and financial institutions and public economics. Proficiency in research methodology must be demonstrated and students must satisfy a departmental tool requirement.

Research & Facilities

In 1998, UM completed construction of a business & accountancy building complex with classrooms hardwired for the Internet, three computer labs, independent and group study rooms and lounges, and research facilities. The Hearin Center for Enterprise Science focuses on optimization technology, conducting prototype studies, fundamental and applied research, and executive development.

SELECTED RESEARCH AREAS
- Accountability
- Applied microeconomics
- Artificial intelligence
- Business cycles
- Capital budgeting
- Consumer behavior
- Cost estimation and analysis
- Cross cultural marketing
- Data warehousing
- Economic development
- Employee involvement
- Experimental economics
- Experimental markets
- Free enterprise
- Global transportation
- Household financial distress
- Industrial organization
- Information processing
- Intercultural communication
- International marketing
- Labor
- Leadership
- Learning in noncooperative games
- Macroeconomics and economic history
- Market pricing of risk
- Marketing ethics
- Marketing pharmaceuticals and health services
- Mergers and acquisitions
- Motivation
- Persuasive communication
- Production economics
- Production planning
- Public choice
- Public policy
- Real estate appraisal
- Research methodology
- Sales promotion
- Scheduling
- Software engineering
- Sports attendance
- Teamwork and team performance
- The Statute of Frauds

UNIVERSITY OF MISSISSIPPI, PHD PROGRAMS IN ACCOUNTANCY
BUSINESS ADMINISTRATION & ECONOMICS

ADMISSIONS CRITERIA & PROCEDURES

For admission to the accountancy program, applicants must present an acceptable score on the GMAT, including a score in the 60th percentile or better on the verbal portion, meet the requirements for a master's degree in accountancy or business and have demonstrated competence in the undergraduate areas of financial and managerial accounting, auditing and taxation. In addition, all students should hold some form of accounting certification such as CPA, CMA and/or CIA.

To be admitted to the program in business administration, applicants must achieve a score of at least 550 on the GMAT, have a minimum cumulative undergraduate GPA of 3.0 or of 3.1 or above on the last 60 credit hours of coursework at the undergraduate or graduate level. An alternative admission policy is available for students who do not meet quantitative standards.

Applicants to the PhD in economics must meet the admission requirements for the SBA's Master of Arts degree in economics and have a combined score of at least 1000 on the verbal and quantitative sections of the GRE general test, as well as a minimum 3.0 cumulative undergraduate GPA, a 3.25 GPA on the last 60 hours of undergraduate or graduate courses attempted, or a master's degree and at least one letter of recommendation from a faculty member at the school most recently attended.

International applicants must submit a minimum score of 550 on the paper-based TOEFL for admission. A score of 600 or better is required for the School of Accountancy.

EXPENSES & FINANCIAL ASSISTANCE

The SBA offers a limited number of graduate assistantships which are awarded on a competitive basis. Students holding assistantships and/or fellowships amounting to at least US$600 per semester who are not residents of Mississippi are not required to pay the nonresident registration fee. Those holding assistantships and/or fellowships amounting to at least US$1,125 per semester who are enrolled as full-time students are eligible to receive a full or partial tuition scholarship. The fee also applies to spouses of the enrolled student.

Fellowships are awarded by the Graduate School to incoming students of exceptional academic accomplishment. Students conducting research for a Hearin Chair may receive a research stipend. Summer teaching opportunities occasionally provide a means of earning additional income.

Applicants for teaching assistantships whose native language is not English must present acceptable scores on the TSE or the SPEAK.

INTERNATIONAL STUDENT SUPPORT

UM hosts over 650 international students and faculty from 65 nations.

The Office of International Programs (OIP) assists international students with arrival, orientation, personal counseling and immigration and academic advising. OIP also provides intercultural activities, nationality festivals, parties and a variety of other activities for international students.

UM's Host Friends & Families program places international students with local families who take students shopping, to the movies and to dinner. Several events are planned for the program, including a potluck dinner for all international students and their host families.

There are many student organizations at UM including the International Student Organization, which sponsors dinners to create awareness about different cultures and other social events for students.

ADMISSIONS AT A GLANCE

Minimum GMAT:	550
Minimum GPA:	3.0
Minimum TOEFL (paper):	
550 (business administration & economics)	
600 (accounting)	
Minimum TOEFL (computer):	–
Application Fee:	US$25
Application Deadline:	
Apr 1(fall admission); Oct 1 (spring admission)	

EXPENSES AT A GLANCE

Tuition:
  In State: US$170 per credit hour
  Out-of-State: US$342 per credit hour
  Int'l Students: US$342 per credit hour
Books & Supplies: US$1,000 per year
Health Insurance: –
Accommodation:
  University Residences: US$1,960 per year
  Family Housing: US$2,600–2,950 per year
  Private: US$2,940 per year

PROGRAM FACTS

# of Full-time Students:	56
# of Part-time Students:	7
# of Applications per year:	100-200
# Accepted per year:	25
# Enrolled per year:	25
Average GMAT Score:	565
Average Age:	27
% Men/Women:	68%/32%
Work Experience (avg yrs):	–
# of Faculty:	49
% Faculty with Doctoral Degree:	98%
Annual Research Funding:	–

UNIVERSITY OF MISSISSIPPI, PHD PROGRAMS IN ACCOUNTANCY
BUSINESS ADMINISTRATION & ECONOMICS

UNIVERSITY AND LOCATION

Founded in 1844, the University of Mississippi, also known as Ole Miss, is the oldest public institution of higher education in the state. UM has a total enrollment of approximately 11,000 students and is organized into the College of Liberal Arts and 11 academic schools including the schools of Accountancy, Business Administration, Education, Engineering, Pharmacy, Law, the Graduate School and the schools of Medicine, Nursing, Health Related Professions and Dentistry at the Medical Center campus. The university offers 120 majors in programs leading to bachelor's, master's, specialist and doctoral degrees.

The John Davis Williams Library houses 822,260 volumes, over one million microforms and more than 7,000 current periodical and serial subscriptions.

Ole Miss encompasses four campuses: Oxford (the original and main campus), Southaven, Tupelo and the UM Medical Center in Jackson. The 2,500-acre Oxford campus is noted for its natural beauty and its graceful elms, oaks, magnolias, poplars and dogwoods give it the appearance of a well-kept park. Most of the university buildings are Georgian or contemporary in design.

Known for its picturesque 19th-century town square, Oxford sits in the midst of the rolling, tree-covered hills of northern Mississippi. It is a small town with a rich southern culture and a variety of shops, restaurants and entertainment and residents are known for their warm hospitality. Despite its small size, Oxford and the surrounding area offer a cosmopolitan blend of music, literature and the arts along with a relaxed lifestyle, low cost of living, mild climate, a safe scenic environment and some of the state's best schools and hospitals. *USA Today* named Oxford a "thriving new south arts mecca" and one of the top six college towns in the nation. Live music is performed nearly every night at popular spots on and off the Square and the on-campus Union Unplugged series has won critical acclaim.

City Population:	10,000
Cost of Living:	low
Climate Range:	40° to 90°F
Campus Setting:	rural
Total Enrollment:	10,731
Graduate Enrollment:	1,540
Students in Residence:	3,188

FACULTY

- Aiken, M.W. PhD, Arizona
- Alidaee, B. PhD, Texas
- Barnes, J. PhD, Oregon
- Belongia, M.T. PhD, North Carolina State
- Blodgett, J.G. PhD, Indiana
- Burkett, H.H. DBA, Florida State
- Bush, V. PhD, Memphis
- Canty, A.L. PhD, Mississippi
- Cassidy, J. PhD, Texas Tech
- Chappell, W.F. PhD, South Carolina
- Christian, C. PhD, Florida State
- Conlon, J. PhD, Chicago
- Conlon, S. PhD, Illinois Institute of Technology
- Cook, D.O. PhD, Texas
- Cox, L.A. PhD, South Carolina
- Daigle, K. PhD, Clemson
- Davis, J.W. PhD, Mississippi
- Dorsey, J.H. PhD, Michigan
- Dula, J. PhD, Michigan
- Edmister, R.O. PhD, Ohio State
- Elam, R. PhD, Missouri
- Flesher, D. PhD, Cincinnati
- Flesher, T. PhD, Mississippi
- Frink, D.D. PhD, Illinois
- Gardner, W.L. DBA, Florida State
- Gilbert, F.W. PhD, North Texas
- Glover, F. PhD, Carnegie Mellon
- Hatfield, G.B. DBA, Louisiana Tech
- Hawley, D.D. PhD, Michigan State
- Hu, J. MS, Michigan
- Johnson, J.D. PhD, Texas A&M
- Kochenberger, G. PhD, Colorado
- Malone, R.P. PhD, Florida
- Martin, J. EdD, Memphis
- Metrejean, C. PhD, Texas A&M
- Moen, J.R. PhD, Chicago

- Nichols, D.L. PhD, Oklahoma State
- Paolillo, J.G.P. PhD, Oregon
- Payne, J. PhD, Florida
- Rayburn, W.B. DBA, Memphis
- Razzolini, L. PhD, Southern Methodist
- Reithel, B.J. PhD, Texas Tech
- Robinson, R.K. PhD, North Texas
- Rose, G.M. PhD, Oregon
- Schwab, A. PhD, Wisconsin
- Shughart, W. PhD, Texas A&M
- Sloan, H.J. PhD, Ohio State
- Smith, L.H. PhD, Tennessee
- Stocks, M.H. PhD, South Carolina
- Taylor, C. PhD, Texas
- Terasawa, K. PhD, Kentucky
- Tollison, R. PhD, Virginia
- Tosh, D.S. PhD, Georgia State
- Van Boening, M.V. PhD, Arizona
- Vitell, S.J. PhD, Texas Tech
- Wakefield, K.L. PhD, St.Louis
- Walker, C.H. JD, Mississippi
- Wiebe, F.A. PhD, Kansas
- Wilder, W.M. PhD, Florida State
- Wolcott, S. PhD, Stanford
- Womer, N.K. PhD, Pennsylvania State
- Zarzeski, M. PhD, Florida

UNIVERSITY OF OKLAHOMA
PhD IN BUSINESS ADMINISTRATION

Program Highlights

- *Major fields: accounting, finance, management, management information systems and marketing*
- *US$20 million gift from Michael F. Price will be used primarily to add distinguished faculty*
- *Ranked among the top 50 US business schools by Forbes magazine*
- *Assistantships & fellowships worth up to US$20,000 per year*
- *Support for student research & professional activities*
- *Accredited by AACSB*

CONTACT INFORMATION

Graduate Programs Office

Price College of Business

307 W. Brooks Room 105-K

Norman, Oklahoma USA 73019-4003

PH: 1-405-325-4107

FAX: 1-405-325-1957

EMAIL: ltullius@ou.edu

INTERNET: http://www.ou.edu/business

UNIVERSITY OF OKLAHOMA, PHD IN BUSINESS ADMINISTRATION

PROGRAM OVERVIEW

The Michael F. Price College of Business (PCOB) and at the University of Oklahoma (OU) awards Doctor of Philosophy (PhD) in business administration degrees with full-time study in accountancy, finance, management, management information systems and marketing. In addition to required coursework, programs are tailored to meet individual career objectives and research interests.

A breadth requirement is fulfilled through coursework in accounting, finance, management and marketing and by previous study or inclusion of specific courses in the program of study. Research expertise is obtained through study of microeconomic theory, statistics and research methodology courses. Most doctoral students are appointed to a research assistantship early in their program to establish close cooperation with faculty members. Courses in a major field provide students with literature overviews and research techniques.

Students follow completion of all coursework with a general examination, consisting of written and oral portions and covering material from the major and concentration areas.

A dissertation must be developed, written and defended within four calendar years of passing the general examination.

Accounting
PhD students majoring in accounting conduct original research in areas such as financial, managerial, tax or audit accounting by either analyzing available economic data or running behavioral experiments. The accounting department offers seminars in current accounting research, and training in statistics, economics, behavioral science and/or finance, depending on their chosen research specialization.

Finance
The finance major focuses on investments and/or corporate finance. A special feature of the major in finance is the research paper undertaken during the second summer of study, which gives students research experience prior to the beginning of dissertation work. The project is a full-time activity guided by a faculty member with corresponding research interests.

Management
The PhD program in management provides a foundation for research and teaching in the management areas of organizational behavior, human resources management, strategic management, and others. Students learn research methodology and current research practices and techniques applicable to management-related problems. Both the development of current theory and the application of concepts to pragmatic managerial issues are important parts of the program.

Management Information Systems
The major program in management information systems focuses on organization and management issues. Coursework provides the theory and research methodology needed for organizational and managerial research on management information systems-related phenomena.

Marketing
The marketing major focuses on marketing management, marketing theory, logistics, channel/institutional structure and management and social responsibility/marketing strategy and planning. Students also receive training in marketing research statistics and research methodologies. The major strengths of the faculty are in marketing channels, retail and wholesale distribution and logistics/supply chain management.

SELECTED RESEARCH AREAS
- Aggregate production planning
- Business ethics
- Business issues in telecommunications
- Business policy and strategy
- Commercial law
- Consumer behavior
- Corporate finance and investments
- Corporate financial reports
- Corporate retrenchment
- Distribution
- Electronic data processing auditing
- Employment law
- Financial, managerial and intermediate accounting
- Futures and options
- Impact of learning on risky asset prices
- Impact of taxes on business decisions
- Information systems
- Interest rate structure
- International diversification
- International pricing
- Interorganizational linkages
- Inventory management
- Judgment and decision-making
- Logistical trends
- Long-term performance measurement
- Municipal bonds
- Partnership
- Pension accounting
- Product liability law
- Quantitative analysis
- Real estate appraisal
- Securities markets
- Selection and development of organizational leaders
- Short-term financial management
- Small business development
- Social issues management
- Strategic management
- Transfer pricing
- Understanding of business processes
- Venture capital and entrepreneurial finance
- Work socialization

UNIVERSITY OF OKLAHOMA, PHD IN BUSINESS ADMINISTRATION

ADMISSIONS CRITERIA & PROCEDURES

Admission is based on undergraduate and graduate GPA and GPA for the last 60 hours of upper-level coursework (at least 3.5 on a 4.0 scale), GMAT scores of at least 640, employment history, letters of recommendation and the applicant's personal statement of goals. Applicants must demonstrate an aptitude for, and an interest in, advanced research in business. Previous study in business is not required.

International applicants whose first language is not English must have an official TOEFL score of 550 (or 213 on the computer based test) or higher and a verbal subscore from the GMAT at or above the 50th percentile. International applicants are also asked to submit official TSE scores.

New doctoral students are admitted in the fall semester only. The application deadline is April 1.

EXPENSES & FINANCIAL ASSISTANCE

Assistantships of 20 hours of research or teaching per week are awarded on the basis of demonstrated scholarly potential. Both teaching and research assistantships pay US$14,000 stipend for nine months, and are granted in-state tuition status.

Barnett Fellowships and OU Alumni Fellowships of up to US$5,000 per year are also available. Students who receive these awards normally receive research or teaching assistantships as well. The Rath Doctoral Fellowship in Strategic Management is a four-year package of support worth US$20,000 per year, including graduate assistantship and summer assistantship stipends.

Other financial aid includes tuition waiver scholarships, summer assistantships and health insurance subsidy.

INTERNATIONAL STUDENT SUPPORT

Over 1,700 international students from 101 nations including Korea, Japan, India, Venezuela, Canada, Peru, England, Malaysia, Italy, China, Bulgaria and Turkey attend OU.

The Office of International Student Services (OISS) conducts an orientation program to provide international students with information and assistance regarding enrollment procedures, academic programs and government regulations.

OU supports more than 200 student organizations, including some with an international character. Asian, Latin American, European, African and Arab student associations help new students adjust to life in the US. The OU Cousins program introduces American students to international students, bringing them together in on-campus social activities.

ADMISSIONS AT A GLANCE

Minimum GMAT:	640
Minimum GPA:	3.5
Minimum TOEFL (paper):	550
Minimum TOEFL (computer):	213
Application Fee:	US$25 (dom); US$50 (int'l)
Application Deadline:	Apr 1 (fall admission)

EXPENSES AT A GLANCE

Tuition per year:
- In State: US$2,058
- Out-of-State: US$5,460
- Int'l Students: US$5,460

Books & Supplies: US$800 per year
Health Insurance: US$485 per year
Accommodation:
- University Residences: US$400–700 per month
- Family Housing: US$360-590 per month
- Private: US$400–750 per month

PROGRAM FACTS

# of Full-time Students:	36
# of Part-time Students:	0
# of Applications per year:	51
# Accepted per year:	11–13
# Enrolled per year:	9–11
Average GMAT Score:	681
Average Age:	34
% Men/Women:	58%/42%
Work Experience (avg yrs):	10
# of Faculty:	59
% Faculty with Doctoral Degree:	100%
Annual Research Funding:	–

UNIVERSITY OF OKLAHOMA, PhD IN BUSINESS ADMINISTRATION

UNIVERSITY AND LOCATION

Created by the Oklahoma Territorial Legislature in 1890, 17 years before Oklahoma became a state, the University of Oklahoma has 25,000 students enrolled in 19 colleges on the Norman campus and at the Health Sciences Centers in Oklahoma City and Tulsa. The university offers 160 undergraduate degree programs, 127 master's degree programs, 79 doctoral programs, professional degrees in six areas and 47 dual professional/master's programs.

The OU library system, the largest in Oklahoma, consists of 2.5 million volumes, 1.6 million government documents, three million microforms and subscriptions to 17,000 periodicals. Special collections include the History of Science collection, the Western History collection, the Bass Business History collection and the Carl Albert Congressional Research and Studies Center.

OU's main campus occupies almost 900 acres in the city of Norman. On-campus housing options include residence halls and apartments. Recreation facilities offer a physical fitness center with an indoor track, weight room and basketball and tennis courts, a swimming complex with indoor, outdoor and diving pools and a university golf course.

The Norman campus is home to two of the southwestern US's premier museums. The Sam Noble Oklahoma Museum of Natural History, currently under construction, sits on a 40-acre site and will be the largest university-based museum of natural history in the US.

OU is located in the city of Norman, Oklahoma in the heart of the central US, halfway between the Pacific and Atlantic coasts. Norman has a population of over 90,000, a 10,000-acre lake and park area, a community theater, an art center and art league and many other amenities. It is the state's third largest city, with easy access to Oklahoma City, Tulsa and Dallas.

City Population:	80,000
Cost of Living:	medium
Climate Range:	25° to 95°F
Campus Setting:	urban
Total Enrollment:	25,000
Graduate Enrollment:	3,142
Students in Residence:	5,700

FACULTY

- Austin, J.R. PhD, Georgia
- Ayres, F.L. PhD, Iowa
- Barman, S. PhD, Clemson
- Bolton, R.N. PhD, Carnegie Mellon
- Buckley, M.R. PhD, Auburn
- Busenitz, L. PhD, Texas A&M
- Butler, S.A. PhD, Iowa
- Carte, T.A. PhD, Georgia
- Crain, T.L. PhD, Texas Tech
- Cuccia, A.D. PhD, Florida
- Dauffenbach, R.C. PhD, Illinois
- Daugherty, P.J. PhD, Michigan State
- Driver, R.W. PhD, Georgia
- Ederington, L.H. PhD, Washington
- Emery, G.W. PhD, Kansas
- Evans, R.E. PhD, Michigan State
- Ghosh, D. PhD, Pennsylvania State
- Griffith, D.A. PhD, Kent State
- Hamilton, H.A. MBA, Oklahoma
- Harvey, M.G. PhD, Arizona
- Hobbs, J.A. MLA, Oklahoma City
- Horrell, J.F. PhD, Colorado State
- Hoskisson, R.E. PhD, UC Irvine
- Jasperson, J. PhD, Florida State
- Jensen, K.L. PhD, Florida
- Kasulis, J.J. PhD, Northwestern
- Kenderdine, J.M. DBA, Indiana
- Knapp, M.C. PhD, Oklahoma
- Linn, S.C. PhD, Purdue
- Lipe, M.G. PhD, Chicago
- Lipe, R.M. PhD, Chicago
- Lusch, R.F. PhD, Wisconsin
- Megginson, W.L. PhD, Florida State
- Michaelsen, L.K. PhD, Michigan
- Moriarty, S.R. PhD, Illinois
- Myers, M.B. PhD, Michigan State
- Nayar, N. PhD, Iowa
- Ostas, D.T. PhD/JD, Indiana
- Payne, J.L. PhD, Florida
- Penn, D.A. PhD, Oklahoma
- Price, R.L. DBA, Oklahoma
- Ralston, D.A. MBA/DBA, Florida State
- Razook, N.M. JD, Oklahoma
- Roberston, T.D. PhD, Georgia
- Russell, C.J. PhD, Iowa
- Saunders, C.S. PhD, Houston
- Saunders, J.R. JD, Texas Tech
- Schwarzkopf, A.B. PhD, Virginia
- Shaft, T. PhD, Penn State
- Sharfman, M.P. PhD, Arizona
- Smith, F. MBA, Texas
- Stanhouse, B.E. PhD, Illinois
- Stanley, J.W. MBA, Oklahoma
- Stock, D.R. PhD, Ilinois
- Tersine, M.G. MBA, Old Dominion
- Van Horn, R.L. PhD, Carnegie Mellon
- Whitely, W.T. PhD, Minnesota
- Willinger, G.L. DBA, Florida State
- Wren, D.A. PhD, Illinois
- Zmud, R.W. PhD, Arzona

UNIVERSITY OF RHODE ISLAND
PhD PROGRAM IN BUSINESS ADMINISTRATION

UNIVERSITY OF RHODE ISLAND

Program Highlights

- *Four areas of concentration*
- *Research supported by several private and government funded centers,*
- *Four college-run research centers, including the PACAP Capital Markets and Financial Service Research Center, the Research Institute for Telecommunications and Information Marketing, and the Research Center in Business and Economics*
- *Accredited by AACSB*

CONTACT INFORMATION
Office of Graduate Business Programs
College of Business Administration
Kingston, Rhode Island USA 02881-0802
PH: 1-401-874-5000
FAX: 1-401-874-7047
EMAIL: clenshaw@uri.edu
INTERNET: http://www.cba.uri.edu

UNIVERSITY OF RHODE ISLAND, PhD PROGRAM IN BUSINESS ADMINISTRATION

PROGRAM OVERVIEW

The College of Business Administration (CBA) at the University of Rhode Island (URI) offers a PhD program in business administration with concentrations in finance and insurance, management, management science, and information systems and marketing.

The coursework phase of the program requires the completion of a minimum of 32 hours of advanced coursework in an area of specialization. During this phase, each PhD candidate is required to write at least three papers of publishable quality. The coursework phase concludes with written and oral comprehensive examinations in the candidate's specialization, research methods, statistics and other areas.

Following the comprehensive exam, candidates engage in research under the supervision of a faculty member. Research is expected to make a major contribution to the state of knowledge in the candidate's field. The PhD is awarded upon successful completion of all requirements, including an oral defense of the dissertation.

Finance and Insurance

The Department of Finance and Insurance undertakes research in global capital markets, with an emphasis on Asian and Pacific capital markets. The department and the Pacific-Basin Capital Markets Research Center creates and distributes capital markets databases for Asian and Pacific countries.

With access to the best databases available, PhD students have an advantage in carrying out research on Asian and Pacific capital markets.

Management

In the PhD in Management, students apply organizational theory and research methods to management-related problems in the workplace. The program is designed to help candidates structure organizational issues in ways conducive to the application of research and problem-solving methods. Specializations include technological impacts on management, environmental issues, leadership, negotiations and conflict resolution, strategic compensation, entrepreneurship, arbitration and gender issues in management.

Management Science and Information Systems

Management Science employs computer technologies for managerial decision-making as well as the modeling and resolution of business choices under conditions of risk and uncertainty. Four areas of specialization are offered: operations management, management information systems, managerial statistics or operations research. Students must complete at least two research seminars in the various management science fields. Choices of electives and research methods courses are based on students' interests.

Marketing

The marketing faculty at URI's CBA conducts research in the areas of telecommunications and information technology marketing, services marketing and macromarketing. This program has been created to strengthen understanding in the foundations of marketing. To develop future scholars, pedagogical and research skills are incorporated into the curriculum, and each candidate is expected to develop a customized area of specialization.

Computing Facilities

The CBA provides access to a wide spectrum of computing technologies through a network of computer laboratories. The Ballentine Hall Callaghan microcomputer lab houses 34 IBM microcomputers connected to a Novell local area network and the decision support lab provides microcomputing and access to URI's central computing facility through 20 networked IBM PCs. The CBA's general computing facility contains 70 office PCs.

SELECTED RESEARCH AREAS

- Asian banking environment
- Behavior of corporate grouping
- Cognitive adaptability in communications
- Communication competence
- Consumer behavior
- Consumer satisfaction
- Database management
- Demand forecasting
- Electronic business/electronic commerce
- Group cognitive style
- Health care management
- Interactivity and advertising
- International high-tech markets
- ISO9000
- Leaders' motivation and behavior influence
- Macro marketing
- New product development
- Operations management for service industries
- Organization culture theory
- Pacific basin financial institutions
- Process control
- Seasonal adjustment
- Stock return behavior
- Strategic decision making
- Supply chain
- Systems analysis and design
- Technological innovation
- Time series modeling
- Trading mechanism
- Work and family

UNIVERSITY OF RHODE ISLAND, PHD PROGRAM IN BUSINESS ADMINISTRATION

ADMISSIONS CRITERIA & PROCEDURES

The PhD program is small and highly selective. Admission is based on academic merit, research capabilities and the match of research interests between the applicant and the faculty in the indicated area of specialization. Applicants with diverse backgrounds are encouraged to apply.

A master's degree and results of a GMAT taken within the last five years are required of all applicants. Applicants must submit official transcripts for all undergraduate and graduate studies and three letters of reference from individuals who can attest to the applicant's intellectual capabilities and research aptitude. The submission of written work and either a campus or telephone interview between the applicant and faculty are strongly encouraged. International applicants are required to take the TOEFL.

Rhode Island residents must submit a US$30 nonrefundable fee with their applications and out-of-state residents must include a US$45 application fee.

Admissions are made on a rolling basis until June 1. Applicants who submit applications before the first cut-off date of March 1 will receive early notification if accepted.

INTERNATIONAL STUDENT SUPPORT

The Office of International Students and Scholars (OISS) provides assistance in the areas of social, personal, financial, housing and immigration. All communications from international scholars and faculty concerning nonimmigrant visas are handled by the OISS. A number of organizations provide opportunities for students to participate in cultural activities and the university's International Center serves as a meeting place for study, social events and other cocurricular activities.

EXPENSES & FINANCIAL ASSISTANCE

Rhode Island residents pay US$3,446 per year in tuition fees and out-of-state students pay US$9,850. Other mandatory fees include a registration fee, a student health services fee, a memorial union fee, a library and computing fee, a student services fee and a health insurance fee. Combined fees are about US$1,800 per year, though the US$514 health insurance fee may be waived for students with comparable coverage.

Various research and teaching assistantships, fellowships and other forms of financial aid are available to qualified students. Students who wish to apply for assistantships should submit the assistantship application forms along with other admission application materials directly to the CBA's Office of Graduate Programs.

Students awarded assistantships work up to 20 hours per week in instructional and research activity.

ADMISSIONS AT A GLANCE

Minimum GMAT:	60%
Minimum GPA:	
2.8 undergraduate; 3.2 graduate	
Minimum TOEFL (paper):	575
Minimum TOEFL (computer):	233
Application Fee:	
US$30 (in-state),	
US$45 (out-of-state)	
Application Deadline:	
Rolling admissions before Jun 1 with Mar 1 as the first cut-off date	

EXPENSES AT A GLANCE

Tuition:	
In State:	US$3,446 per year
Out-of-State:	US$9,850 per year
Int'l Students:	US$9,850 per year
Books & Supplies:	US$697 per year
Health Insurance:	US$514 per year
Accommodation	
University Residences:	n/a
Family Housing:	US$450-700 per month
Private:	US$300-700 per month

PROGRAM FACTS

# of Full-time Students:	43
# of Part-time Students:	0
# of Applications per year:	25–45
# Accepted per year:	6–12
# Enrolled per year:	6–10
Average GMAT Score:	625
Average Age:	35
% Men/Women:	73%/27%
Work Experience (avg yrs):	4 years
# of Faculty:	55
% Faculty with Doctoral Degree:	100%
Annual Research Funding:	–

UNIVERSITY OF RHODE ISLAND, PhD PROGRAM IN BUSINESS ADMINISTRATION

UNIVERSITY AND LOCATION

The University of Rhode Island is a medium-sized state university in southern Rhode Island. Founded as a land-grant college in 1892, URI has expanded to offer a wide range of educational programs. Because of its location near the ocean and six miles from Narragansett Bay, the university has developed strong marine programs and is designated as one of the National Sea Grant colleges.

The university comprises nine colleges – Arts and Sciences, Business Administration, Continuing Education, Engineering, Human Science and Services, Nursing, Pharmacy, Resource Development and University College – and the Graduate School, the Graduate School of Library and Information Studies, and the Graduate School of Oceanography.

The library collection of approximately 1.4 million bound volumes and of microforms equivalent to a million volumes is housed in the University Library in Kingston, at the College of Continuing Education in Providence and at the Claiborne Pell Marine Science Library on the Narragensett Bay campus. The University Library, which houses the bulk of the collection, has open stacks with direct access to books, periodicals, documents, maps, microforms and audiovisual materials.

The main campus is a spacious, rural site 30 miles south of Providence in the northeastern metropolitan corridor between New York and Boston. The center of the campus is quadrangle of old granite buildings surrounded by newer academic buildings, student residence halls and fraternity and sorority houses.

URI has three other campuses. The 165-acre Narragansett Bay campus is the site of the Graduate School of Oceanography and features academic and research buildings and docks for research vessels. The College of Continuing Studies main offices are located in Providence and the 2,300-acre W. Alton Jones campus in the western section of the state is the site of environmental education, research and conference facilities.

Kingston is located 30 miles south of Providence, 75 miles from Boston, and 160 miles from New York City.

City Population:	6,504
Cost of Living:	low
Climate Range:	18° to 81°F
Campus Setting:	rural
Total Enrollment:	14,319
Graduate Enrollment:	3,611
Students in Residence:	7,250

PARTIAL LIST OF FACULTY

- Beauvais, L. PhD, Tennessee
- Beckman, J. PhD, Texas Tech
- Budnick, F. DBA, Maryland
- Chen, S.K. PhD, Michigan
- Cooper, E. PhD, Akron
- Della Bitta, A.J. PhD, Massachusetts
- Dholakia, N. PhD, Northwestern
- Dholakia, R.R. PhD, Northwestern
- Dugal, S.S. PhD, Massachusetts
- Ebrahimpour, M. PhD, Nebraska
- Faught, J. PhD, Georgia State
- Geiger, M. PhD, Penn State
- Harlam, B. PhD, Pennsylvania
- Hazera, A. PhD, Kentucky
- Jarrett, J. PhD, New York
- Lai, G.C. PhD, Texas at Austin
- Lee, Y. PhD, Texas at Austin
- Lehrer, M. PhD, Berkeley & INSEAD
- Lloyd, S. PhD, Kent
- Mangiameli, P.M. PhD, Ohio State
- Mazze, E. LD, Penn State
- McLeavey, D.W. DBA, Indiana
- Oppenheimer, H.R. PhD, Purdue
- Randall, L. PhD, Massachusetts
- Rosen, D. PhD, Tennessee
- Scholl, R.W. PhD, California at Irvine
- Shroeder, J.E. PhD, Berkeley
- Suprenant, C. PhD, Wisconsin
- Vangermeesch, S. PhD, Florida
- Varki, S. PhD, Vanderbilt
- Westin, S.A. PhD, Massachusetts

UNIVERSITY OF SOUTH CAROLINA
THE DARLA MOORE SCHOOL OF BUSINESS

Program Highlights

- *One of only five US government grant recipients for the establishment of a Center for International Business & Research*

- *International business programs ranked first or second by US News & World Report since 1989*

- *One of the top 50 business schools in the US according to BusinessWeek magazine*

CONTACT INFORMATION

Graduate Admissions Office

The Darla Moore School of Business

University of South Carolina

Columbia, South Carolina USA 29208

PH: 1-803-777-4346

FAX: 1-803-777-0414

EMAIL: barbc@darla.badm.sc.edu

INTERNET: http://www.badm.sc.edu/

UNIVERSITY OF SOUTH CAROLINA, THE DARLA MOORE SCHOOL OF BUSINESS

PROGRAM OVERVIEW

Established in 1919, the Darla Moore School of Business (DMSB) at the University of Southern Carolina (USC) is committed to innovation. The DMSB is a comprehensive business school offering business administration and related programs for students engaged in bachelor's, master's and doctoral study options. The two PhD programs in business administration and economics require four years of full-time study for successful completion. The school is accredited by AACSB - The International Association for Management Education.

PhD in Business Administration

The PhD in business administration prepares students for careers in university teaching and research, business, and/or government. It combines training in business studies with instruction in business research methods.

Each individual in the business administration PhD program must select a major area of concentration and a minor field of cognate coursework. The major requires a minimum of 15 semester hours of study, while the cognate field is covered in nine semester hours. Students may select their specialization from accounting, business policy/strategic management, finance, international business, international finance, management information systems, marketing, operations research, organizational behavior, probability and statistics, or production/operations management. Cognate fields can be in one of these subjects or from related fields including insurance, personnel, economics, banking, real estate, tax or an area outside of the college's curricular offerings with departmental approval.

Students study the main principles and theories underlying their chosen field of specialization. In addition, they develop the critical skills required to evaluate and create new research pertaining to their area of concentration. Graduates will be prepared to assume teaching and research positions at academic institutions.

PhD in Economics

The PhD in economics provides students with a flexible business curriculum. Areas of specialization include human resources, international economics, and applied microeconomics. Graduates follow careers in the World Bank, the US Department of Health & Human Services, the Milliken Research Center and at various academic institutions across the country.

Doctoral students in economic complete fundamental coursework in advanced microeconomic and macroeconomic theory, and econometrics and regression. Students then embark on a program of study designed in consultation with a three-person advisory committee.

A Distinguished Faculty

The faculty at the DMSB are committed pedagogues and prolific researchers. In the past five years, DMSB faculty members have published more than 700 journal articles, books, monographs and other works. The college maintains a faculty editorial service for professional journals.

SELECTED RESEARCH AREAS

- Accounting systems
- Applied microeconomics
- Audit Committees
- Auditing
- Banking
- Behavioral accounting
- Business ethics
- Business process redesign
- Capital investment
- Computing technologies
- Corporate finance
- Econometrics
- Economic development
- Economic history
- Electronic markets
- Employment mandates
- Experimental design
- Financial markets in East Asia
- Group decision making
- Growth theory
- Human capital
- Industrial organization
- Information systems development
- Insurance
- International accounting
- International management
- International marketing
- International negotiations
- Labor economics
- Managerial accounting
- Market anomalies
- Political risk
- Political strategy
- Public finance
- Real estate
- Sales force management
- Scheduling
- Shop floor control
- Statistics
- Tax laws
- Top management decision making
- Trade theory
- Urban economics
- Value analysis
- Voting behavior
- Wage structure
- Worker participation

UNIVERSITY OF SOUTH CAROLINA, THE DARLA MOORE SCHOOL OF BUSINESS

ADMISSIONS CRITERIA & PROCEDURES

Applicants to the business administration program may apply for summer or fall entry, while applicants to the PhD in economics commence studies in the fall semester only. A background in the functional areas of business is recommended. Individuals interested in economics must have intermediate-level micro and macroeconomics courses and experience in calculus, statistics and probability. All applicants will have graduated from an accredited college or university with standing in the upper half of the class.

To be eligible for either program, applicants must submit to the USC Graduate School, the completed DMSB application forms, the application fee, official transcripts, two letters of recommendation, GMAT or GRE results, a resume and a statement of career objectives. Students whose native language is not English and have not completed a degree at a US institution will be required to provide a TOEFL score.

EXPENSES & FINANCIAL ASSISTANCE

Financial support is available through graduate assistantships and fellowships. Currently, assistantships are worth US$11,500 over 10 months and include a partial tuition waiver. Assistantship recipients work for 20 hours per week during the academic year and 12 hours per week during the summer session. For best consideration, students should submit application forms by February 1. International students vying for assistantships must also submit TOEFL and GMAT scores to the DMSB no later than the end of January.

A limited number of university-wide doctoral fellowships are available to incoming students. Worth US$8,000 per year for up to four years of academic study, these prizes are awarded in addition to money received through assistantship positions. Students must be nominated by their department in order to be eligible for such funding.

Financial support for African American students is also provided through USA's African American Professor's Program (AAPP), which awards scholarships of US$7,500 per year to admitted individuals who are interested in becoming college professors.

INTERNATIONAL STUDENT SUPPORT

There are 148 international graduate students enrolled at the DMSB, accounting for 28 percent of the student population. International students comprise 61 percent of the doctoral business students. Countries represented by this student body include Australia, Bulgaria, China, Germany, Russia, Brazil, Cyprus, Denmark and Costa Rica.

The International Programs for Students Office provides pre-arrival assistance, immigration counseling, and individual consultations to resolve challenges related to academic, personal and cultural adjustment issues. The office also organizes several cultural and social events throughout the year, including the International Festival. There are a number of student cultural organizations that meet on the USC campus, such as the International Student Association.

ADMISSIONS AT A GLANCE

Minimum GMAT:	570
Minimum GPA:	3.2
Minimum TOEFL (paper):	
625 (PhD in BA); 570 (PhD in Econ)	
Minimum TOEFL (computer):	
263 (PhD in BA); 230 (PhD in Econ)	
Application Fee:	US$35
Application Deadline:	Feb 1

EXPENSES AT A GLANCE

Tuition per semester:	
In State:	US$2,007
Out-of-State:	US$4,264
Int'l Students:	US$4,264
Graduate Assistants:	US$725
Books & Supplies:	US$800 per year
Health Insurance:	US$500 per year
Accommodation:	
University Residences:	US$375–548 per month
Family Housing:	US$402–644 per month
Private:	US$475-700 per month

PROGRAM FACTS

# of Full-time Students:	54
# of Part-time Students:	11
# of Applications per year:	125
# Accepted per year:	48
# Enrolled per year:	20
Average GMAT Score:	660
Average Age:	31
% Men/Women:	78%/22%
Work Experience (avg yrs):	4.5
# of Faculty:	105
% Faculty with Doctoral Degree:	86%
Annual Research Funding:	US$0.55m

UNIVERSITY OF SOUTH CAROLINA, THE DARLA MOORE SCHOOL OF BUSINESS

UNIVERSITY AND LOCATION

The University of South Carolina, founded in 1801, is one of the oldest public universities in the US. During the American Civil War, USC was temporarily converted into a hospital as its students left to join the ranks of the Confederate army. The university now boasts an enrollment of more than 36,000 students, and delivers more than 350 programs at the graduate and undergraduate levels through its 15 colleges and schools. Study at USC is supported by a library collection of nearly three million items and 21 research centers. In addition to the main campus in downtown Columbia, USC has four-year campuses in Aiken and Spartanburg, and five regional campuses offer mostly two-year programs.

Named after the explorer Christopher Columbus, Columbia was founded in 1786. The capital of the state of South Carolina, Columbia offers students a culturally diverse environment in which to live and study. Columbia is a progressive Southern city, and features several museums, the Riverbank Zoo and many local theater companies. The economy of South Carolina thrives because of a booming tourist industry and international trade. Students will enjoy the many recreational spots the region has to offer, including ocean resorts such as Myrtle Beach, and the Blue Ridge Mountains.

City Population:	500,000
Cost of Living:	medium
Climate Range:	33° to 92°F
Campus Setting:	urban
Total Enrollment:	36,680
Graduate Enrollment:	8,548
Students in Residence:	10,100

FACULTY

- Addison, J.T. PhD, London School of Economics
- Arpan, J.S. DBA, Indiana
- Bauerschmidt, A.D. PhD, Florida

- Bearden, W.O. PhD, South Carolina
- Blackburn, M. PhD, Harvard
- Boucher Breuer, J. PhD, North Carolina-Chapel Hill
- Brooks, L.D. PhD, Michigan State
- Carlsson, R.J. PhD, Rutgers
- Chappell, H.W. PhD, Yale
- Chewning, Jr, E.G. PhD, South Carolina
- Clower, R.W. PhD, Oxford
- Cohn, E. PhD, Iowa State
- Coller, M. PhD, Indiana
- Cotte, J. PhD, Connecticut
- DeZoort, F.T. PhD, Alabama
- Doerpinghaus, H.I. PhD, Pennsylvania
- Donohue, J.M. PhD, Virginia Polytechnic
- Doupnik, T.S. PhD, Illinois
- Feldman, D.C. PhD, Yale
- Fiedler, K.D. PhD, Pittsburgh
- Folks, W.R. DBA, Harvard
- Fry, T.D. PhD, Georgia
- Fryer, J.S. DBA, Indiana
- Grover, V. PhD, Pittsburgh
- Harrell, A.M. PhD, Texas
- Harrington, S.E. PhD, Illinois
- Harrison, G.W. PhD, UCLA
- Harrison, P.P. PhD, Arizona State
- Karwan, K.R. PhD, Carnegie Mellon
- Kettinger, W.J. PhD, South Carolina
- Kiker, B.F. PhD, Tulane
- Klaas, B.S. PhD, Wisconsin-Madison
- Koch, T.W. PhD, Purdue
- Korsgaard, M.A. PhD, New York
- Kostova, T. PhD, Minnesota
- Kuhlman, J.A. PhD, Northwestern
- Kwok, C.C.Y. PhD, Texas
- Leiblein, M.J. MBA, Rensselaer
- Leitch, R. PhD, Tennessee
- Logan, J.E. PhD, Columbia
- Luoma, G.A. DBA, Washington
- Madden, T.J. PhD, Massachusetts
- Malhotra, M.K. PhD, Ohio State
- Mann, S.V. PhD, Nebraska
- Markland, R.E. DBA, Washington
- Martin, R.C. PhD, Washington
- McDermott, J. PhD, Brown
- McInnes, M.M. PhD, Yale
- Meglino, B.M. PhD, Massachusetts
- Money, R.B. PhD, California-Irvine
- Moore, W.T. PhD, Virginia Polytechnic
- Niehaus, G.R. PhD, Washington
- Nigh, D.W. PhD, UCLA
- Oberhelman, D. PhD, Purdue
- Philipoom, P.R. PhD, Virginia Polytechnic
- Phillips, W. PhD, MIT
- Pritchett, S.T. DBA, Indiana
- Ravlin, E.C. PhD, Carnegie Mellon
- Reeves, G.R. DS, Washington
- Roenfeldt, R.L. DBA, Indiana
- Rogers, R.C. PhD, Ohio State
- Rolfe, R.J. PhD, Oklahoma
- Rose, R.L. PhD, Ohio State
- Roth, K. PhD, South Carolina
- Roth, M.S. PhD, Pittsburgh
- Rutstrom, E.E. PhD, Stockholm School of Economics
- Ryan, J.M. PhD, Missouri
- Sandberg, W.R. PhD, Georgia
- Sapienza, H. DBA, Maryland
- Schweiger, D.M. DBA, Maryland
- Sharma, S. PhD, Texas at Austin
- Shimp, T.A. DBA, Maryland
- Shuptrine, F.K. PhD, Texas
- Steele, D.C. PhD, Iowa
- Sweigart, J.R. PhD, Carnegie Mellon
- Teel Jr, J.E. PhD, North Carolina
- Teng, J.T.C. PhD, Minnesota
- Tuttle, B.M. PhD, Arizona State
- Ullman, J.C. PhD, Chicago
- Whitcomb, K.M. PhD, Minnesota
- White, R.A. PhD, Arizona State
- Wilder, R.P. PhD, Vanderbilt
- Wood, S.L. PhD, Florida
- Woodward, D. PhD, Texas at Austin
- Yi, M.Y. PhD, Maryland

UNIVERSITY OF TENNESSEE AT KNOXVILLE
COLLEGE OF BUSINESS ADMINISTRATION

Program Highlights

- *PhD areas of business administration, economics, industrial/organizational psychology and management science*
- *Departmental and university fellowships and assistantships*

CONTACT INFORMATION

Office of the Dean

722 Stokely Management Center

College of Business Administration

Knoxville, Tennessee USA 37996-0570

PH: 1-565-974-1642

FAX: 1-565-974-1766

EMAIL: not available

INTERNET: http://www.utk.edu

UNIVERSITY OF TENNESSEE AT KNOXVILLE, COLLEGE OF BUSINESS ADMINISTRATION

PROGRAM OVERVIEW

The University of Tennessee at Knoxville (UTK) offers Doctor of Philosophy (PhD) degree programs in business administration, economics, industrial/organizational psychology and management science through its College of Business Administration (CBA).

Business Administration

The business administration program has concentrations in accounting, finance, logistics and transportation, marketing, and statistics.

Students in accounting must complete 12 semester hours of accounting coursework, including nine semester hours each in doctoral seminars, a complementary area and research methods coursework, with six hours of statistics. Comprehensive examinations are required in the concentration and complementary areas, as is a dissertation based on original research.

Coursework in finance covers topics such as capital market imperfections, interest rate theory, financial market microstructure, dividend policy and recent theoretical and empirical developments in microfinance and macrofinance literature.

The program in logistics and transportation produces scholars capable of conducting and communicating significant, original research. Students must demonstrate understanding of the theoretical, conceptual and managerial foundations of logistics and transportation. Advanced study in research methods and analytical procedures provides the necessary tools for research development and implementation.

The curriculum for the concentration in marketing consists of coursework in core business disciplines, research methods, the marketing concentration and a minor or supporting field, such as psychology, communications or economics.

PhD students in statistics study computational methods in statistics, theory for developing new tools, advanced statistical process control and topics in experiment design. Students complete graduate seminars in experiment design, modeling, process control, regression or reliability, complementary coursework in business, engineering or science, an internship and a dissertation based on industrial applications-driven research.

Economics

The PhD in economics requires competence in microeconomic and macroeconomic theory, quantitative methods and the history of economic thought. Students undergo coursework and comprehensive exams in two fields of specialization and take two economics electives. Participation in departmental workshops help students develop their research skills and identify dissertation topics.

Industrial/Organizational Psychology

The program in industrial/organizational psychology requires a minimum of 51 semester hours of coursework, 15 semester hours of supervised field training and 24 semester hours of dissertation research. Students acquire a comprehensive background in industrial and organizational psychology and may tailor the program to fit their interests and academic needs.

Management Science

The PhD in management science educates in fundamental management science and operations research mathematical models and their uses, and provides tools to carry out original research. Individual programs of study suit academic background and future aspirations. Students complete 49 semester hours of coursework, qualifying exams in statistics and mathematics, a comprehensive exam in management science and 24 semester hours of dissertation research.

SELECTED RESEARCH AREAS
- Accounting education
- Accounting methods
- Applied statistics
- Asset Pricing
- Auditing
- Bank capital issues
- Business formation
- Capital market reactions
- Cohort influences
- Corporate finance
- Customer satisfaction
- Entity selection
- Financial accounting
- Financial market volatility
- Forecasting
- Global competitiveness issues
- Global logistics
- Information management
- Information needs for decision making
- Insurance cost disclosure
- International finance
- Interviewing methods
- Investments
- Lean manufacturing
- Linear models
- Management of information technology
- Managerial accounting
- Market opportunity analysis
- Market segmentation
- Marketing communications
- Organizational liability issues
- Personal taxation
- Process design
- Psychometrics
- Quality cost concepts
- Regression analysis
- Reliability
- Sales management
- Supply chain strategies
- Tax decision models
- Tax equity issues
- Technology in service delivery
- Third party logistics

UNIVERSITY OF TENNESSEE AT KNOXVILLE, COLLEGE OF BUSINESS ADMINISTRATION

ADMISSIONS CRITERIA & PROCEDURES

Admission to the business administration program is based on prior academic performance, GMAT scores, relevant extracurricular activities and work experience, letters of recommendations and a brief statement of career objectives and preparation for doctoral studies. Normally, successful applicants will have a GPA of at least 3.5 in the most recently completed 60 hours of academic coursework and a GMAT score in the top 20 per cent of examinees.

The Ph.D. program in economics evaluates applicants based on previous academic performance, scores achieved on the general portion of the GRE and recommendations.

Applicants to the industrial/organizational psychology program must have completed at least six semester hours of college mathematics and one course in statistics. Other requirements include a GPA of 3.5 or above and a combined score of 1200 on the verbal and quantitative sections of the GRE.

To be considered for admission to the PhD in management science, applicants must have a strong mathematical background, such as the completion of at least two years of college calculus, and proficiency in a computer language. Applicants also need three recommendation letters and should complete the aptitude portion of the GMAT or GRE.

International students whose native language is not English must submit TOEFL results unless they have completed a degree from an accredited US university within two years of the application. The minimum acceptable TOEFL score is 550 on the paper-based test.

Completed applications for the fall semester should be received by the CBA no later than March 1.

EXPENSES & FINANCIAL ASSISTANCE

State-funded assistantships for up to 20 hours per week of work over a 12-month period and awarded according to academic history, the strength of reference letters and GRE or GMAT scores. The stipend is approximately US$10,000 a year plus a tuition waiver. Students may also apply for summer teaching positions.

Fellowships are available from individual departments and students with GPAs of 3.7 or higher may apply for the Hilton A. Smith Graduate Fellowship, the UTK Graduate School Fellowship and the Herman E. Spivey Graduate Fellowship.

INTERNATIONAL STUDENT SUPPORT

International House at UTK sponsors several programs for new international students. An orientation to the campus and local community includes seminars on academic and cultural acclimation and a program to introduce international students to other UTK students for cultural exchange. There are regular coffee meetings, international film nights, cultural exchange nights, holiday celebrations, dinners and dances. International House also offers regular ESL conversation classes and cooking demonstrations.

ADMISSIONS AT A GLANCE

Minimum GMAT:	no set minimum
Minimum GPA:	2.7
Minimum TOEFL (paper):	550
Minimum TOEFL (computer):	–
Application Fee:	US$35
Application Deadline:	Mar 1

EXPENSES AT A GLANCE

Tuition:	
In State:	–
Out-of-State:	–
Int'l Students:	–
Books & Supplies:	–
Health Insurance:	–
Accommodation:	
University Residences:	–
Family Housing:	–
Private:	–

PROGRAM FACTS

# of Full-time Students:	75
# of Part-time Students:	40
# of Applications per year:	196
# Accepted per year:	53
# Enrolled per year:	24
Average GMAT Score:	–
Average Age:	–
% Men/Women:	64%/38%
Work Experience (avg yrs):	–
# of Faculty:	104
% Faculty with Doctoral Degree:	92
Annual Research Funding:	US$1,257,000

UNIVERSITY OF TENNESSEE AT KNOXVILLE, COLLEGE OF BUSINESS ADMINISTRATION

UNIVERSITY AND LOCATION

Founded in 1794, two years before Tennessee became a state, the University of Tennessee at Knoxville is the federal land-grant institute of the state, one of the oldest academic institutions west of the Appalachians and the only state-supported university in Tennessee classified as a Research I institute by the Carnegie Foundation.

One of the largest universities in the southern US, UTK delivers 297 bachelor's, master's and doctoral degree programs through 15 colleges and schools, with courses in agriculture and natural resources, architecture and planning, arts and sciences, business administration, communications, education, engineering, human ecology, law, nursing, social work, biomedical sciences, library and information science and veterinary medicine, among others. The total enrollment of approximately 26,000 students, includes 6,500 graduate and professional students.

UTK's Division of Information Infrastructure operates Internet-connected IBM and Macintosh computer labs, Sun workstations, a computer graphics lab and access to the National Center for Supercomputing Applications. The university's library system offers business students collections including US economic statistics, indexes for business and economics, investment analyses and statistics, international economic statistics, patents, trademarks and copyrights and US company and industry information.

The Knoxville metropolitan area, with a population of approximately 600,000, is the commercial hub of eastern Tennessee and a major center for science and technology. The area sustains a ballet, an opera house, numerous theaters and a symphony as well as a variety of restaurants, museums and arts and crafts festivals. Located 40 miles from the Great Smoky Mountains amid lakes and rivers, Knoxville residents participate in skiing and hiking and water sports.

FACULTY

- Anderson, K.E. PhD, Indiana
- Auxier, A.L. PhD, Iowa
- Barnaby, D.J. PhD, Purdue
- Behn, B. PhD, Arizona State
- Black, H.A. PhD, Ohio State
- Boehm, T. PhD, Washington
- Bohm, R.A. PhD, Washington
- Bozdogan, H.B. PhD, Illinois
- Bruce, D. PhD, Syracuse
- Cadotte, E. PhD, Ohio State
- Carcello, J.C. PhD, Georgia Tech
- Carroll, S.L. PhD, Harvard
- Chang, H. PhD, Vanderbilt
- Clark, D.P. PhD, Michigan
- Collins, M.C. PhD, Georgia
- Dabholkar, P.A. PhD, Georgia State
- Daves, P. PhD, North Carolina
- Davidson, P. PhD, Pennsylvania
- Davis, F.W. PhD, Michigan State
- Dean, T.J. PhD, Colorado
- DeGennaro, R.P. PhD, Ohio State
- Dewhirst, H.D. PhD, Texas
- Dicer, G.N. PhD, Indiana
- Ehrhardt, M. PhD, Georgia Institute of Tech
- Fisher, B.D. PhD, Michigan
- Foggin, J.H. PhD, Tennessee
- Fox, W.F. PhD, Ohio State
- Fryxell, G.E. PhD, Indiana
- Gardial, S. PhD, Houston
- Garrison, C.B. PhD, Kentucky
- Gauger, J. PhD, Iowa State
- Glustoff, E. PhD, Stanford
- Guess, F.M. PhD, Florida State
- Gunthorpe, D.L. PhD, Florida
- Hamparsum, B. PhD, Illinois
- Herring, H.C. PhD, Alabama
- Herzog, Jr. H.W. PhD, Maryland
- Holcomb, H.C. PhD, Tennessee
- Judge, W.Q. PhD, North Carolina
- Kahn, J.R. PhD, Washington; Lee
- Kahn, K. PhD, Virginia Tech

City Population:	200,000
Cost of Living:	medium
Climate Range:	29° to 89°F
Campus Setting:	urban
Total Enrollment:	26,046
Graduate Enrollment:	5,628
Students in Residence:	-

- Kiger, J.E. PhD, Missouri
- Langley, C.J. PhD, Penn State
- Leitnaker, M.G. PhD, Kentucky
- Leon, R. PhD, Florida State
- Maddox, R.C. PhD, Texas
- Mee, R.W. PhD, Iowa State
- Mentzer, J.T. Michigan State
- Miller, A. PhD, U of Washington
- Murphy, D.P. PhD, North Carolina
- Murray, M.N. PhD, Syracuse
- Parr, W.C. PhD, Southern Methodist
- Philippatos, G.C. PhD, New York
- Reeve, J. PhD, Oklahoma State
- Reizenstein, R. PhD, Cornell
- Renisch, J. PhD, Maryland
- Rentz, J. PhD, Georgia
- Roth, H.P. PhD, Virginia Tech
- Santoro, R. PhD, Ohio State
- Schlottman, A.M. PhD, Washington
- Schmidhammer, J.L. PhD, Pittsburgh
- Schumann, D.W. PhD, Missouri
- Seaver, W. PhD, Texas A&M
- Shrieves, R.E. PhD, UCLA
- Stagna, K.G. PhD, Louisiana State
- Stahl, M.J. PhD, Rensselaer Polytechnic Institute
- Stango, V. PhD, California
- Stanley, D. PhD, Wisconsin
- Stewart, S. PhD, New Mexico
- Sylvester, D. PhD, Stanford
- Thorpe, D.I. PhD, Tennessee
- Towsend, R.L. PhD, Texas, Austin
- Wachowicz, J.M. PhD, Illinois
- Walker, E. PhD, Virginia Tech
- Wansley, J.W. PhD, South Carolina
- Williams, J.R. PhD, Arkansas
- Woehr, D.J. PhD, Georgia Institute of Tech
- Woodruff, R.B. DBA, Indiana
- Younger, M.S. PhD, Virginia Polytechnic Institute

UNIVERSITY OF TEXAS AT AUSTIN
THE TEXAS PHD PROGRAM

Program Highlights

- *Ranked in the top tier of US business schools by BusinessWeek magazine*
- *More than thirteen research centers, bureaus and institutes affiliated with the GSB*
- *Behavioral research and computer laboratories for doctoral students*

CONTACT INFORMATION

Graduate School of Business

Austin, Texas USA 78712-1178

PH: 1-512-471-5921

FAX: 1-512-471-7725

EMAIL: adgrd@utrdp.dp.utexas.edu (dom)

adint@utrdp.dp.utexas.edu (int'l)

INTERNET: http://www.bus.utexas.edu/phd/

UNIVERSITY OF TEXAS AT AUSTIN, THE TEXAS PHD PROGRAM

PROGRAM OVERVIEW

The PhD program offered by the Graduate School of Business (GSB) at the University of Texas at Austin (UT at Austin) is designed to produce talented academics capable of contributing to and advancing the field of business knowledge. In BusinessWeek magazine's 1998 rankings, UT at Austin was the only institution in Texas to place in the top tier of US business schools. The quality of the GSB is enhanced through the school's 105 endowed chairs that permit the acquisition and retention of top professors.

The PhD program is available in one of five fields of study: accounting, finance, management, management science and information systems (MSIS) and marketing. The normal amount of time required for the successful completion of the program is three to five years of full-time study.

Accounting

Students in the accounting option possess academic and professional experience in fields such as auditing, corporate accounting, banking and law.

In the course of their PhD studies, individuals in this program complement their accounting acumen with a firm foundation in economics, statistics, business organizations and math. The selection of a lead specialization and two supporting specializations is a further feature of the program. Popular lead specializations include auditing, financial reporting, managerial accounting and tax policy.

Finance

Students in the finance option receive the analytical and empirical training required of university professors. Through a curriculum that emphasizes the theoretical foundations of modern valuation theory, finance students become proficient at recognizing how economic value is constructed in the contemporary marketplace.

Areas of specialization within the doctoral finance option include corporate finance, real estate, investments, financial intermediaries and international finance.

MSIS

The MSIS program offers four areas of specialization: management science, information systems, decision science/risk management and statistics. Within each of these options, the pedagogical emphasis is on application-driven theory.

All of the MSIS options prepare students for either academic or industrial careers. Program graduates have gone on to teach at US universities and to positions as research scientists or consultants with national corporations.

Management

The management option trains students in research, teaching and service. Program graduates are well-versed in research methodologies and possess the skills required to communicate empirical and theoretical findings.

Areas of specialization available to management students include organizations & strategy (with concentrations in organization science and strategic management) and operations management.

Marketing

GSB marketing majors receive instruction in business- and research-related concepts in preparation for careers in universities, businesses or government agencies and organizations. Major fields of study available within the program include buyer behavior, international marketing, marketing management and strategy, and analytical and quantitative methods.

The seminar series in marketing brings scholars from across the country to the university to discuss contemporary research projects with the department's PhD students.

SELECTED RESEARCH AREAS
- Accounting
- Auditing
- Buyer behavior/industrial behavior
- Capital markets
- Corporate finance
- Decision science
- Experimental economics
- Financial intermediaries
- Financial reporting
- Information economics
- Information systems
- International finance
- International marketing
- Investments
- Management science
- Management strategy
- Managerial accounting
- Marketing research
- Operations management
- Orgainzations
- Quantitative methods in marketing modeling
- Real estate
- Risk management
- Statistics
- Strategy
- Taxation

UNIVERSITY OF TEXAS AT AUSTIN, THE TEXAS PHD PROGRAM

ADMISSIONS CRITERIA & PROCEDURES

Admissions are coordinated through each of the GSB's five PhD granting departments. The accounting program admits three to four students per year and typically attracts individuals with above average GPAs and GMAT scores. The MSIS program admits eight to ten students per year out of more than 100 applicants. While a master's level degree is not required for admission into the PhD in management, it is preferred for the marketing option. Due to these variances, applicants are advised to check admission requirements with the department they desire to join.

While there is no minimum GPA, GMAT or TOEFL requirement for the GSB, successful applicants usually have a GPA of 3.5 (on a 4.0 scale) and a GMAT score of 700. All students are assessed on the basis of their entire admissions portfolio. In addition to test scores, this should include transcripts of all postsecondary terms of study, three letters of recommendation, a completed application for admission, application fees and a personal statement of goals. These materials should be sent to the Graduate & International Admissions Center, with copies also forwarded to the relevant department's Graduate Coordinator.

Application deadlines vary. MSIS students must apply by December 1, finance students by January 15, management and marketing students by February 1 and accounting students by late February.

EXPENSES & FINANCIAL ASSISTANCE

UT at Austin offers one of the lowest tuition fees in the US for Texas residents and international students alike. In addition, graduate students who hold positions as teaching assistants or classroom instructors, or who are the recipients of certain fellowships or scholarships are allowed to pay in-state tuition fees.

In the GSB doctoral program, financial assistance typically takes the form of departmental teaching and/or research assistantships (usually awarded to students who hold master's level degrees) or fellowships. Students should contact individual departments for more details. As funding is determined early in the admission cycle, students are encouraged to apply to the GSB as early as possible.

INTERNATIONAL STUDENT SUPPORT

The UT at Austin has an international student population of approximately 4,000 individuals who hail from over 115 countries worldwide. The university hosts between 150 to 500 visiting foreign scholars and lecturers every year.

In order to encourage potential students from nearby Mexico, UT at Austin offers a limited number of tuition waivers to applicants from this region. Services available to all international students include personal counseling, assistance with academic scheduling, management of finances, housing, job searches, insurance, regulations and filing U.S. income tax returns.

Prominent international clubs on campus include the Brazilian American Business Group, the German Alumni Group, the Mexican Business Networking Association and Pacific Ties, an organization that promotes cross-cultural exchange, alumni networking and Asian awareness. Over 50 other on-campus international student organizations are active on the UT Austin campus.

ADMISSIONS AT A GLANCE

Minimum GMAT: no set minimum
Minimum GPA: no set minimum
Minimum TOEFL (paper): no set minimum
Minimum TOEFL (computer): no set minimum
Application Fee: US$50 (dom), US$75 (int'l)
Application Deadline:
  Dec 1 (MSIS), Jan 15 (Finance),
  Feb 1 (Management, Marketing),
  Late Feb/early Mar (Accounting)

EXPENSES AT A GLANCE

Tuition per year:
  In State: US$2,800
  Out-of-State: US$6,700
  Int'l Students: US$6,700
Books & Supplies: –
Health Insurance: US$375 per year
Accommodation:
  University Residences: US$370 per month
  Family Housing: US$425–550 per month
  Private: –

PROGRAM FACTS

# of Full-time Students:	110
# of Part-time Students:	n/a
# of Applications per year:	337
# Accepted per year:	43
# Enrolled per year:	28
Average GMAT Score:	716
Average Age:	30
% Men/Women:	62%/38% (new students)
Work Experience (avg yrs):	4.6
# of Faculty:	110
% Faculty with Doctoral Degree:	100%
Annual Research Funding:	–

UNIVERSITY OF TEXAS AT AUSTIN, THE TEXAS PhD PROGRAM

UNIVERSITY AND LOCATION

The University of Texas at Austin was founded in 1883 and began with eight faculty members teaching 221 students. Today, it is one of the largest universities in the US, and is recognized worldwide as the flagship institution of the 15-member University of Texas system.

UT at Austin offers 97 undergraduate and 90 graduate degrees to almost 49,000 students from the US and around the world. These individuals are taught by more than 2,300 faculty members, including Pulitzer Prize winners, Nobel Laureates, and members of the National Academy of Sciences and the National Academy of Engineering. Notable alumni of the university include former First Lady Lady Bird Johnson, journalist Walter Cronkite and US Secretary of Energy Federico Peña.

The UT at Austin campus covers 350 acres. It hosts the Archer M. Huntington Art Gallery and the active Performing Arts Center. The Graduate School of Business, a four-building complex of 106,600 sq. feet, houses classrooms, offices, research centers and computer laboratories.

While most master's and PhD-level students live off-campus in residential areas bordering the campus, UT at Austin also maintains on-campus residence facilities reserved for graduate students. These range from one- to three-bedroom unfurnished apartments at competitive rates. Meal plan options are available to both on- and off-campus UT at Austin students.

Austin, the capital city of Texas, lies amid rolling hills and is surrounded by rivers and lakes. The city features urban hiking and bike trails along the Town Lake and adjoining Barton Creek. The landmark Barton Springs pool, 172 city parks, 26 golf courses, and nine wilderness areas offer quiet refuge in an area of approximately one million people. The moderate climate makes outdoor recreation a year-round possibility. Austin also offers many cultural opportunities, including citizen-supported drama and comedy groups, dance companies, theaters, museums and galleries.

City Population:	514,000
Cost of Living:	medium
Climate Range:	39° to 95°F
Campus Setting:	urban
Total Enrollment:	48,906
Graduate Enrollment:	10,191
Students in Residence:	–

FACULTY

- Beyer, J. PhD, Cornell
- Brockett, P. PhD, California at Irvine
- Brown, K. PhD, Purdue
- Butler, J. PhD, Northwestern
- Fredrickson, J. PhD, Washington
- Freeman, R. PhD, Texas at Austin
- George, E. PhD, Stanford
- Golden, L. PhD, Florida
- Hoyer, W. PhD, Purdue
- Huber, G. PhD, Purdue
- Jaillet, P. PHD, MIT
- Jarvenpaa, S. PhD, Minnesota
- Jennings, R. PhD, Berkeley
- Kinney, Jr, W. PhD, Michigan State
- Lasdon, L. PhD, Case Institute of Technology
- Magee, S. PhD, MIT
- Mahajan, V. PhD, Texas at Austin
- McAlister, L. PhD, Stanford
- Newman, P. PhD, Texas at Austin
- Peterson, R. PhD, Minnesota
- Robinson, J. PhD, Michigan
- Ronn, E. PhD, Stanford
- Schkade, D. PhD, Carnegie Mellon
- Starks, L. PhD, Texas at San Antonio
- Titman, S. PhD, Carnegie Mellon
- Whinston, A. PhD, Carnegie Mellon

UNIVERSITY OF UTAH
PhD Program in Business Administration

Program Highlights

- *Small enrollment optimizes faculty-student interactions*
- *Program can be tailored to individual interests*
- *Research or teaching assistantship with a US$12,000 stipend and tuition waiver for most students*
- *Accredited by AACSB*

CONTACT INFORMATION

David Eccles School of Business

1645 East Campus Center Drive Rm. 101

Salt Lake City, Utah USA 84112-9301

PH: 1-801-581-8625

FAX: 1-801-581-7214

EMAIL: phdbbs@business.utah.edu

INTERNET: http://www.business.utah.edu/phd

UNIVERSITY OF UTAH, PHD PROGRAM IN BUSINESS ADMINISTRATION

PROGRAM OVERVIEW

The David Eccles School of Business (DESB) at the University of Utah (Utah) offers a Doctor of Philosophy (PhD) program in business administration through its School of Accounting and departments of finance, management and marketing.

The major emphasis of the program of study is the development skills necessary to conduct scholarly research and teach. Four to five years of full-time study are generally required.

Accounting

The School of Accounting PhD program is tailored to the needs and interests of each student, and ensures the close attention of faculty. Students hone skills in teaching, research and communication.

Core seminars within accounting include financial accounting, management information systems and auditing. Students study related fields such as economics, statistics, psychology and organizational behavior, and participate in seminars presented by other departments in the DESB and other schools on campus.

Finance

The Department of Finance curriculum is composed of economic theory and appropriate empirical methodology. Students take nine seminars in finance, supplemented by courses in microeconomics, mathematics and a mathematical statistics/econometrics sequence. Research in the field is shared through departmental seminar series and the Utah Winter Finance Conference, an annual three-day conference that attracts internationally renowned scholars from every area of finance and economics.

Management

The management program offers human resource management/organizational behavior, strategic management/business policy and production/operations management. Student programs are designed according to specific experience, interests and career goals. In human resource management/organizational behavior, students may concentrate on topics such as reward systems, management/union relations, organization design, organization theory and negotiation strategies. Specializations in strategic management/business policy include global strategic management, entrepreneurship, executive succession and organizational economics. Production/operations management students may emphasize global operations management, inventory theory, labor scheduling, facilities location, project scheduling or operations strategy.

Marketing

The marketing program is flexible and allows students to follow a highly personalized curriculum designed to serve their interests and needs.

SELECTED RESEARCH AREAS

- Accounting theory
- Analytical Procedures
- Auditing
- Business ethics
- Business strategy
- Capital budgeting
- Career planning and development
- Conflict management
- Consumer behavior
- Corporate finance
- Derivatives and investments
- Dividend policy
- Empirical capital markets
- Financial accounting
- Human resource law and policy
- Income taxation of individuals, partnerships and corporations
- Information economics
- Information systems
- Interfirm collaborations
- International marketing
- Interpersonal competence
- Japanese equity markets
- Labor market analysis
- Leadership
- Market leadership
- Market microstructure
- Marketing law and public policy
- Marketing of arts
- Materials management
- Multi location audit risks
- Multinational firm behavior
- New product introduction
- Organizational change
- Organizational communication
- Personal selling
- Problem solving
- Quality management
- Risk management and insurance
- Small group behavior
- Statistical methods
- Statistics
- Tax accounting
- Technology adoption problems

UNIVERSITY OF UTAH, PHD PROGRAM IN BUSINESS ADMINISTRATION

ADMISSIONS CRITERIA & PROCEDURES

In reviewing applications for the PhD program, the admissions committee looks for indications of intellectual capacity, maturity and carefully considered personal objectives. An advanced degree is not necessary. Applicants must specify the department in which they intend to study.

Applicants should complete both the DESB and the Graduate School application forms. These must be accompanied by GMAT scores, TOEFL results, a personal statement of future objectives and three letters of recommendation from former professors or professional colleagues. Official college transcripts should be sent directly from issuing institutions to Utah's admissions office. Students applying to the finance area must have completed one year of calculus prior to application. Applicants to all other areas need to have completed college algebra.

International applicants whose native language is not English must take the TOEFL by January of the year they plan to enter the PhD program. Students who hold a degree from a US institution are exempt from this requirement.

Applications for admission to the PhD program in business administration are reviewed once a year for admission in the fall semester. The application deadline is January 15.

EXPENSES & FINANCIAL ASSISTANCE

All applicants are considered for research and/or teaching assistantships which include a full tuition waiver and living stipend worth US$12,000. Almost all admitted students receive assistantships, renewable for four years given academic standing is maintained. There may also be summer teaching opportunities.

Other sources of funding include external awards, such as grants and bursaries, some of which are designed to support full-time dissertion research. DESB students are provided with assistance in writing grant applications.

INTERNATIONAL STUDENT SUPPORT

Approximately 2,000 international students and scholars from more than 100 countries attend Utah.

The International Center (IC) provides information about stipends, tuition payments and fee collections, immigration services, work permits, student assistance, immigration information, advising for exchange students and news about student organizations and events.

All students are welcome to attend the IC orientation of the university and Salt Lake City, which includes an information session on American culture, a campus tour, a tour of downtown with time for shopping, a barbecue, and organized sports.

Students may also participate in a trip to Snowbird, a leading ski resort in Utah's Cottonwood Canyon.

ADMISSIONS AT A GLANCE

Minimum GMAT:	n/a
Minimum GPA:	3.0
Minimum TOEFL (paper):	500
Minimum TOEFL (computer):	–
Application Fee:	US$40 (dom); $60 (int'l)
Application Deadline:	Jan 15

EXPENSES AT A GLANCE

Tuition per year:
- In State: waived with admission
- Out-of-State: waived with admission
- Int'l Students: waived with admission

Books & Supplies: US$500 per year
Health Insurance: paid by dept
Accommodation (per month):
- University Residences: US$250
- Family Housing: US$320–600
- Private: US$600–750

PROGRAM FACTS

# of Full-time Students:	34
# of Part-time Students:	0
# of Applications per year:	61
# Accepted per year:	13
# Enrolled per year:	7
Average GMAT Score:	677
Average Age:	32
% Men/Women:	53%/47%
Work Experience (avg yrs):	4
# of Faculty:	56
% Faculty with Doctoral Degree:	99%
Annual Research Funding:	US$300,000

UNIVERSITY OF UTAH, PHD PROGRAM IN BUSINESS ADMINISTRATION

UNIVERSITY AND LOCATION

The University of Utah, founded in 1850 by Brigham Young, is a public, state-assisted university with a total enrollment of approximately 20,000 students. Its 15 schools and colleges offer bachelor's degree in 72 majors, 50 teaching majors and minors and graduate degrees in 92 disciplines including the professional law and medical schools. The campus consists of 280 buildings, 41 instructional labs and 1,198 research labs on 1,494 acres along the foothills of the Wasatch Mountains, near downtown Salt Lake City, the state capital of Utah.

The university has the state's largest computing capacity and the Utah Supercomputing Institute. It is a gateway to the National Science Foundation's NSFNET, and theUtah Library Network and links schools in Utah, Idaho and Arizona. On-site facilities include 2,000 workstations, 8,500 microcomputers, 4,000 networked computers and 900 microcomputers.

The Marriott Library houses over 2 million books, 14,000 periodical subscriptions, and has collections in Western Americana, the Middle East, and Mormon History. Marriott has served as a depository for publications from the US government since 1863. It is also an official depository for the United Nations, FAO and the European Union.

Recreational facilities at Utah include a 60,000-square-foot facility with a track, five tennis courts, two weight rooms, cardiovascular fitness equipment, 13 handball courts, jacuzzis and saunas, a complex with three pools, a nine-hole golf course, an indoor tennis stadium and a 10-lane bowling alley.

The Salt Lake City metropolitan area has a population of approximately 800,000 and is named for the salty inland desert lake located to the west of the city. The city's location makes it a major urban center in the American west. It has been selected to host the 2002 Olympic Winter Games. Seven world-class ski resorts are located within 45 minutes of the university campus and Utah's five national parks are less than a day's drive away. The vast outdoor areas surrounding Salt Lake City make it a haven for hikers, rock climbers, campers, cyclists, fishers hunters, wind surfers and wildlife photographers.

City Population:	820,000
Cost of Living:	medium
Climate Range:	13° to 93°F
Campus Setting:	urban
Total Enrollment:	20,000
Graduate Enrollment:	5,041
Students in Residence:	1,200

FACULTY

- Allen, R.D. PhD, Michigan State
- Baruch, S. PhD, Washington
- Belk, R.W. PhD, Minnesota
- Bentley, J.C. PhD, Minnesota
- Bhattacharya, N. PhD, Georgia
- Boardman, C.M. PhD, North Carolina
- Bollen, N.P.B. PhD, Duke
- Botosan, C. PhD, Michigan
- Chesteen, S.A. PhD, Utah
- Costa, J.A. PhD, Stanford
- Cushing, B.E. PhD, Michigan State
- Derr, C.B. EdD, Harvard
- Eining, M.M. PhD, Oklahoma State
- Fladmoe-Lindquist, K. PhD, Minnesota
- Gahin, F.S. PhD, Wisconsin
- Granzin, K.L. PhD, Illinois
- Grikscheit, G.L. PhD, Michigan State
- Hanni, K.J. JD, Utah
- Harline, N.L. PhD, Nebraska
- Hesterly, W.S. PhD, California
- Johnson, R.E. PhD, Wisconsin
- Kalay, A. PhD, Rochester
- Keele, R. PhD, Purdue
- Lease, R.C. PhD, Purdue
- Loebbecke, J.K. BS, California - Berkeley
- Loewenstein, U. PhD, New York
- Ma, T.S. PhD, Minnesota
- Madhok, A. PhD, McGill
- Mangum, G.L. JD, Utah
- Millington, P. PhD, Utah
- Moore, W.L. PhD, Purdue
- Morgan, L.O. PhD, Duke
- Morgan, R. PhD, Duke
- Morton, A.R. PhD, Georgia Institute of Technology
- Nelson, K. PhD, Texas at Austin
- Nelson, H.J. PhD, Colorado
- Pavia, T.M. PhD, Maryland
- Phene, A. PhD, Texas at Dallas
- Plumlee, M.A. PhD, Michigan - Ann Arbor
- Plumlee, R.D. PhD, Florida
- Randall, R.H. PhD, California - Berkeley
- Randall, T. PhD, Wharton
- Robson, R.T. MS, Utah State
- Scammon, D.L. PhD, California
- Schallheim, J.S. PhD, Purdue
- Searfoss, D.G. PhD, Indiana
- Semenik, R.J. PhD, Ohio State
- Sondak, H. PhD, Northwestern
- Stewart, S.S. PhD, Purdue
- Tashjian, E. PhD, Purdue
- Thomas, W. PhD, Oklahoma
- Wardell, D.G. PhD, Purdue
- Watson, C.J. PhD, Utah
- Woolley, J.W. PhD, Texas
- Young, S.T. PhD, Georgia State
- Zender, J.F. PhD, Yale

UNIVERSITY OF WASHINGTON
BUSINESS SCHOOL

Program Highlights

- *Eight different areas of specialization*
- *Up to four years of assistantships, fellowships and scholarships*
- *Ranked in the top 20 US business schools by the Gourman Report on business and management programs, 6th ed.*

CONTACT INFORMATION

PhD Program Office

102 Mackenzie Hall

Box 353200

Seattle, Washington USA 98195-3200

PH: 1-206-543-4111

FAX: 1-206-685-9392

EMAIL: baphd@u.washington.edu

INTERNET: http://depts.washington.edu/bschool

UNIVERSITY OF WASHINGTON, BUSINESS SCHOOL

PROGRAM OVERVIEW

The University of Washington (UW) Business School offers a Doctor of Philosophy (PhD) in business administration degree program through the five departments listed below, with majors in accounting, finance, human resource management and organizational behavior, information systems, marketing, operations management, operations research and strategic management.

PhD students select two or three minor areas including research methods and one or two other related areas. Students in four-area programs have minors from an outside department. Those in three-area programs take either an outside minor or at least four basic discipline courses from other units on campus.

Accounting

The PhD curriculum in accounting encompasses two major streams of research. The first stream examines the role of accounting information (both financial and managerial) in contracting and in capital markets. The second stream covers aspects of judgement and decision making in accounting.

During their first year, accounting majors spend the majority of their time developing skills in microeconomics, statistics and econometrics. Students write a summer paper at the end of the first year under the supervision of one or two faculty. At the end of the second year, in early summer, students are expected to take the major area written exam.

Finance and Business Economics

Finance majors at the UW business school typically pursue coursework that covers the basic tools, substantive theory, and empirical evidence necessary to give students a solid foundation.

During their first year, finance majors spend the majority of their time developing their skills in microeconomics, mathematics, statistics, and econometrics. Second-year finance doctoral seminars cover such topics as decision-making under uncertainty, information and capital market efficiency, asset pricing theory and empirical research in finance.

Management and Organization

The Department of Management and Organization offers two majors fields of study: human resource management & organizational behavior (HRMOB) and strategic management. HRMOB is usually a three-area program. In addition to the required research methods area, many student minor in psychology. While HRMOB majors take courses in both human resource management and organizational behavior, their dissertation work may specialize in either one.

Strategic management can be either a three- or a four-area program. In addition to the required research methods area, strategic management students minor in a variety of disciplinary areas, including economics and sociology.

Management Science

The Department of Management Science offers programs of study in the areas of information systems, operations management, and operations research. Information systems is usually a three area program. In addition to the required research methods area, students have typically minored in economics, computer science or math. The curriculum in operations management focuses on the development of manufacturing and service organizations in the past 15 years. The operations research program is concerned with the theory and application of quantitative and statistical tools in the modeling and analysis of diverse business problems.

Marketing and International Business

In order to develop students' ability to contribute to the state of knowledge about marketing, the PhD program emphasizes the integration of quantitative techniques and behavioral models as applied to academic research in marketing. The fields of specialization within marketing include the development and study of marketing science models, the analysis of consumer behavior, and the study of marketing strategy.

SELECTED RESEARCH AREAS
- Absenteeism
- Behavioral aspects of consumer choice
- Characteristics of high-performance organizations
- Communication network design
- Corporate governance
- Empirical evaluation of asset pricing models
- Evaluation of behavioral science improvement strategies
- Financial institutions
- Futures
- Global strategy
- Industry structure and competitive dynamics
- Interest rate models
- International investment and financial management
- Law and economics
- Leadership behavior
- Managerial decision making
- Market microstructure
- Marketing science models
- Mergers and acquisitions
- Motivation
- Multivariate and econometric techniques applied to marketing problems
- Operations strategy
- Option pricing
- Organizational design
- Organizational leadership
- Portfolio management
- Self management and social learning theory
- Strategic decision-making and planning systems
- Turnover and employee commitment
- Women in management

UNIVERSITY OF WASHINGTON, BUSINESS SCHOOL

ADMISSIONS CRITERIA & PROCEDURES

The UW Business School admits a class of 10 to 15 PhD students in the autumn quarter each year, with primary consideration given to academic potential and aspiration.

Applicants are evaluated by undergraduate and graduate courses and grades, past awards and honors, GMAT scores, relevant nonacademic experience, academic and other references, and a statement of objectives. Admission decisions are also influenced by the number of students already in the program and the availability of faculty and financial support in each major area.

The deadline for applications and financial aid is February 1. Applicants are advised to apply early to ensure consideration. Applicants should take the GMAT in January or earlier.

Applicants who are not citizens of the US and whose native language is not English must take the TSE and the TOEFL unless they have received a bachelor's degree or higher from a US institution or from an accredited institution in an English-speaking country. International applicants who want to apply for teaching assistantships must take the TSE.

EXPENSES & FINANCIAL ASSISTANCE

Washington residents enrolled full-time in the PhD program pay tuition fees of US$7,191 per year. Out-of-state residents and international students pay US$15,480 per year.

Financial aid takes the form of tuition waivers, teaching and research assistantships, fellowships and scholarships. The financial support package funds students' education and allows for supervised professional experience in both teaching and research. The UW Business School's goal is to provide financial support for four years to all PhD students who continue to make satisfactory progress toward the completion of the degree and maintain a high standard of performance as teaching and research assistants. The Business School also provides fellowships to support outstanding candidates engaged in dissertation research during the final phase of their program.

INTERNATIONAL STUDENT SUPPORT

The International Services Office (ISO) advises on matters ranging from immigration procedures to coping with culture shock. The ISO also serves as the primary information and referral center for international students in coordination with other university offices and community agencies.

The Foundation for International Understanding Through Students (FIUTS) is a community organization that has striven to develop mutual understanding between UW's international community and the people of the Pacific Northwest since 1948. FIUTS sponsors several programs to promote contact between international students and others who share experiences.

ADMISSIONS AT A GLANCE

Minimum GMAT:	no set minimum
Minimum GPA:	3.0
Minimum TOEFL (paper):	600
Minimum TOEFL (computer):	250
Application Fee:	US$50
Application Deadline:	Feb 1

EXPENSES AT A GLANCE

Tuition per year:
In State:	US$7,191
Out-of-State:	US$15,480
Int'l Students:	US$15,480
Books & Supplies:	US$1,200 per year
Health Insurance:	US$764 per year

Accommodation:
- University Residences: US$298–400 per month
- Family Housing: US$426–666 per month
- Private: –

PROGRAM FACTS

# of Full-time Students:	65
# of Part-time Students:	n/a
# of Applications per year:	215
# Accepted per year:	35
# Enrolled per year:	15
Average GMAT Score:	700
Average Age:	26
% Men/Women:	67%/33%
Work Experience (avg yrs):	5
# of Faculty:	77
% Faculty with Doctoral Degree:	100%
Annual Research Funding:	–

UNIVERSITY OF WASHINGTON, BUSINESS SCHOOL

UNIVERSITY AND LOCATION

Founded in 1961, the University of Washington is the oldest state-assisted institute of higher education on the Pacific coast of the US. UW comprises 17 colleges and schools — social work, architecture and urban planning, dentistry, law, medicine, nursing, pharmacy, public health and community, arts and sciences, education, engineering, forest resources and fishery sciences — which offer over 5,000 courses in 100 academic disciplines. The university is a public research institution with campuses in Seattle, Tacoma and Bothell and it is accredited by the Northwest Association of Colleges and Schools.

UW's main campus is located on 900 acres in Seattle's university district, a historic section of the city, and features classic architecture, quiet walkways and lush foliage. There are seven residence halls, each with large community areas, study rooms, lounges and recreation facilities.

The UW library system includes the Odergaard Undergraduate Library, the Health Sciences Library and Information Center, the East Asia Library and 15 branch libraries. Collections include over five million volumes, five million items in microform and more than 50,000 serials tiles. The law and horticulture libraries are administered separately.

The Foster Business Library houses the business collection and a 157-seat computer lab containing 99 PCs, 55 Macintosh computers and three x-terminals. One computer lab, of eight student labs in total, is reserved for business students and was recently upgraded by the addition of 20 233 MMX computers.

Overlooking the Olympics and Cascade mountain ranges, as well as Lake Washington, Seattle features many arts and recreational facilities that contribute to its citizens' relaxed attitude towards life. Seattle also supports an efficient public transit system.

City Population:	3,000,000
Cost of Living:	medium
Climate Range:	34° to 75°F
Campus Setting:	urban
Total Enrollment:	34,000
Graduate Enrollment:	8,000
Students in Residence:	730

FACULTY

- Boeker, W. PhD, California
- Bowen, R. PhD, Stanford
- Bradford, W.D. PhD, Ohio State
- Burgstahler, D.C. PhD, Iowa
- Butler, J.E. PhD, New York
- Chen, X. PhD, Illinois at Urbana-Champaign
- Dey, D. PhD, Rochester
- Dewan, S. PhD, Rochester
- Dewenter, K.L. PhD, Chicago
- Dukes, R.E. PhD, Stanford
- Erickson, G.M. PhD, Stanford
- Faaland, B.H. PhD, Stanford
- Ferson, W.E. PhD, Stanford
- Frost, P.A. PhD, UCLA
- Fuller, S. PhD, Wisconsin at Madison
- Gautschi, D. PhD, Berkeley
- Gist, M.E. PhD, Maryland - College Park
- Gupta, Y. PhD, Bradford
- Haley, C.W. PhD, Stanford
- Hansen, G.S. PhD, Michigan
- Hess, A.C. PhD, Carnegie Mellon
- Higgins, R.C. PhD, Stanford
- Hill, C.W.L. PhD, Manchester
- Hillier, M.S. PhD, Stanford
- Huber, V.L. DBA, Indiana
- Ingene, C.A. PhD, Brown
- Jacobson, R.L. PhD, Berkeley
- Jain, A. PhD, Purdue
- Jiambalvo, J. PhD, Ohio State
- Jones, T.M. PhD, Berkeley
- Kadous, K.K. PhD, Illinois
- Kamara, A. PhD, Columbia
- Karpoff, J.M. PhD, UCLA
- Kennedy, S.J. PhD, Duke
- Kienast, P.K. PhD, Michigan
- Klastorin, T.D. PhD, Texas
- Koski, J.L. PhD, Stanford
- Kotha, S. PhD, Rensselaer
- Lee, T.W. PhD, Oregon
- Louie, T.A. PhD, UCLA
- MacLachlan, D.L. PhD, Berkeley
- Malatesta, P.H. PhD, Rochester
- Mitchell, T.R. PhD, Illinois at Urbana-Champaign
- Moinpour, R. PhD, Ohio State
- Moinzadeh, K. PhD, Stanford
- Mookerjee, V.S. PhD, Purdue
- Moxon, R. DBA, Harvard
- Myers, J.N. PhD, Michigan
- Narver, J.C. PhD, Berkeley
- Noreen, E.W. PhD, Stanford
- Novaes, W. PhD, MIT
- Okada, E.M. PhD, Wharton
- Paperman, J.B. PhD, Cornell
- Pontiff, J. PhD, Rochester
- Ramanathan, K.V. PhD, Northwestern
- Rice, E.M. PhD, UCLA
- Rindova, V. PhD, New York
- Rajgopal, S. PhD, Iowa
- Roley, V.V. PhD, Harvard
- Sarasvathy, S. PhD, Carnegie Mellon
- Saxberg, B.O. PhD, Illinois
- Schall, L.D. PhD, Chicago
- Schmitt, T.G. DBA, Indiana
- Schulz, M. PhD, Stanford
- Sefcik, S.E. PhD, Illinois at Urbana-Champaign
- Shevlin, T.J. PhD, Stanford
- Shores, D. PhD, Stanford
- Siegel, A.F. PhD, Stanford
- Spratlen, T.H. PhD, Ohio State
- Sullivan, J.J. PhD, New York
- Sundem, G.L. PhD, Stanford
- Tamura, H. PhD, Michigan
- Turner, D. PhD, Northwestern
- Vesper, K.H. PhD, Stanford
- Wicks, A.C. PhD, Virginia
- Yalch, R.F. PhD, Northwestern

UNIVERSITY OF WISCONSIN-MADISON
PhD PROGRAMS IN BUSINESS

Program Highlights

- *One of 25 Centers for International Business Education & Research*
- *Recognized for outstanding international programs*
- *Ranked in the top 20 graduate business schools in the US for scholarly research by faculty*
- *Judged one of the world's top 50 business schools*
- *Accredited by AACSB*

CONTACT INFORMATION

School of Business, PhD Coordinator

2266 Grainger Hall,

975 University Avenue

Madison, Wisconsin USA 53706-1323

PH: 1-608-262-9817

FAX: 1-608-265-4192

EMAIL: uwmadphd@bus.wisc.edu

INTERNET: http://wiscinfo.doit.wisc.edu/bschool/

UNIVERSITY OF WISCONSIN-MADISON, PHD PROGRAMS IN BUSINESS

PROGRAM OVERVIEW

The School of Business at the University of Wisconsin–Madison (UW-Madison), established in 1900, was one of the first commerce programs in the US. A founding member of AACSB – The International Association for Management Education, the school has been an integral player in establishing standards for management programs and in 1990, the school received AACSB re-accreditation. In addition, the school is recognized as a founding member of the Beta Gamma Sigma national professional business honor society and the Consortium for Graduate Study in Management. National surveys frequently rank the UW-Madison School of Business among the top ten business doctoral programs at public universities in the US.

The school offers full-time PhD program with concentrations in eight areas: accounting and information systems; business statistics; finance, investment and banking; management and human resources; marketing; operations and information management; real estate and urban land economics; and risk management and insurance. An international business sub-major is available in accounting, finance, management and marketing. Within these broad subject areas, further specializations are available, such as options in management information systems, operations management, operations research, quality and productivity improvement, and transportation and public utilities.

Specific program requirements vary from one option to the next. General program requirements include completion of at least 32 credits in the doctoral program. Two semesters of part-time teaching are also required of all doctoral students, along with the successful completion of a comprehensive preliminary exam in the candidate's field of specialization.

Minor Fields of Study

Doctoral students are required to complete an external minor. Most colleges and departments at UW-Madison offer courses that complement studies in business and students enrolling in other subject areas require a minimum of 10 graduate credits in the secondary discipline to complete the external minor. Similarly, the School of Business offers minor study options for students pursuing doctoral programs in nonbusiness fields.

Faculty Advisers: A Commitment to Mentoring

The School of Business maintains a faculty advising system to assist students in the course of their PhD studies. New PhD candidates are paired with a faculty mentor from the department the student is majoring in. The mentor's responsibilities include counseling on course scheduling and degree requirements, and acting as a liaison between the student and various School of Business and university departments.

In instances where a rapport has developed between mentor and student, and research interests coincide, the adviser may become the student's dissertation supervisor.

A Diverse Student Body

The business school community at UW-Madison includes 1,500 undergraduates, 650 master's level students, and 73 full-time PhD candidates. Over one-third of the PhD business student population is made up of international students and the majority of participants in the program are over 29 years of age. Less than half of these individuals hold undergraduate business degrees, making for a rich, cross-disciplinary classroom setting.

SELECTED RESEARCH AREAS
- Advertising effects
- Auditing
- Business cycles
- Conflict resolution and negotiations
- Corporate governance
- Corporate taxation issues
- Cross-cultural organizational behavior
- Customer-focused improvement
- Demographics and housing development
- Environmental risk management
- Equal employment opportunity
- Financial reporting standards and issues
- Game theory
- Health insurance
- Japanese corporate finance
- Managerial accounting
- Market microstructure
- Mortgage finance
- Postmodern culture
- Psychology of financial markets
- Quality improvement
- Real estate valuation and investment
- Sales ethics
- Semiotics and symbolism
- Small business management
- Stochastic optimization
- Strategic management of multinational corporations
- Supply chain management
- Time-based competition
- Urban economics
- Workmen's compensation regulations

UNIVERSITY OF WISCONSIN-MADISON, PHD PROGRAMS IN BUSINESS

ADMISSIONS CRITERIA & PROCEDURES

Admission to UW-Madison's doctoral business program is competitive and possession of the minimum academic requirements does not guarantee entry to the program. Admissions officials in the School of Business take into account an applicant's past performance in undergraduate and postgraduate studies, GMAT scores, work history, and involvement in school and community activities. The application package must include a completed application form for both the Graduate School and the School of Business, official academic transcripts for all previous university studies, GMAT scores sent directly from ETS, a statement of purpose and a current resume. Three letters of recommendation from individuals in a position to comment on the applicant's potential for success at the doctoral level of study are also required.

International applicants must include certification of degrees granted, proof of financial resources and, where applicable, TOEFL results submitted directly from ETS. A minimum paper-based TOEFL score of 600 is required.

Applications must be accompanied by a US$45 nonrefundable application fee. Admission deadlines are February 1 for fall semester entry and October 15 for spring semester entry. To be considered for financial assistance, potential candidates should submit completed applications no later than January 2.

EXPENSES & FINANCIAL ASSISTANCE

Tuition for in-state residents pursuing full-time doctoral studies at UW-Madison is US$5,406 per year. The comparable fee for out-of-state and international students is US$17,109 per year. Under the Minnesota-Wisconsin Reciprocity Agreement, Minnesota students may be permitted to pay instructional fees comparable to those in effect at the University of Minnesota (Twin Cities).

For individuals interested in on-campus residence, the fee for one academic year of room and board at UW-Madison is US$6,765. Private accommodation and living expenses in the Madison area typically range from US$585-730 per month.

All doctoral applicants are provided with an application for financial assistance. Funding for PhD students includes university-wide and department-specific scholarships and are awarded on the basis of superior grade-point averages and exemplary GMAT scores. Within the School of Business itself, funding is allotted through graduate fellowships, scholarships and teaching or project/research assistantships. The value of these awards ranges from US$500 to US$17,000 per year.

INTERNATIONAL STUDENT SUPPORT

With approximately 10 percent of its student population comprised of international students, UW-Madison has one of the largest international campus communities in the US. A recent survey found that 36 percent of PhD candidates in UW-Madison's School of Business are international students.

There are a number of organizations on campus to assist international students. Madison Friends of International Students, Inc. is a volunteer organization offering hospitality to non-domestic students. International Student and Scholar Services (ISSS), a university-wide resource, provides information to new international students on a number of issues including visa advising and registration.

International PhD candidates with dependents should note that enrollment in Madison public schools is possible for children of visiting students. In addition, several preschools, daycare centers and family daycare facilities are available.

ADMISSIONS AT A GLANCE

Minimum GMAT:	no set minimum
Minimum GPA:	3.0
Minimum TOEFL (paper):	600
Minimum TOEFL (computer):	–
Application Fee:	US$45
Application Deadline:	
Feb 1 (fall semester)	
Oct 15 (spring semester)	
Jan 2 (for fellowship consideration)	

EXPENSES AT A GLANCE

Tuition per year:	
In State:	US$5,406
Out-of-State:	US$17,109
Int'l Students:	US$17,109
Books & Supplies:	US$700 per year
Health Insurance:	–
Accommodation:	
University Residences:	US$528–1,928 per month
Family Housing:	–
Private:	US$500-800 per month

PROGRAM FACTS

# of Full-time Students:	73
# of Part-time Students:	n/a
# of Applications per year:	246
# Accepted per year:	28
# Enrolled per year:	15
Average GMAT Score:	680
Average Age:	35
% Men/Women:	69%/31%
Work Experience (avg yrs):	5.5
# of Faculty:	80
% Faculty with Doctoral Degree:	100%
Annual Research Funding:	US$1.5m

UNIVERSITY OF WISCONSIN-MADISON, PhD PROGRAMS IN BUSINESS

UNIVERSITY AND LOCATION

The University of Wisconsin–Madison was established in 1849 as a public, land-grant institution. Past surveys have ranked UW-Madison in the top ten nationwide for the quality of its scholars, research funding and faculty publication. The university is known as well for its esteemed faculty and Nobel prize-winning research.

UW-Madison is committed to academic excellence, carries out diverse public service initiatives and maintains a commitment to the local community.

UW-Madison offers more than 4,500 courses in programs leading to undergraduate, master's and doctoral degrees. Master's degrees are granted in 182 areas of study and doctoral degrees can be earned in 125 different majors.

The university has a 900-acre main campus in Madison, Wisconsin, a 1,262-acre arboretum and 6,100 acres of experimental research stations, making UW-Madison the fourth largest campus in the US. The main campus, located on the shores of Lake Mendota in the south central part of the state, houses eight sports facilities, an arts museum, theaters, concert halls, and numerous jogging and biking trails. Ranked as the "#1 Best Place to Live in America" by Money magazine, Madison boasts several local attractions and amenities, including four lakes and over 200 parks.

City Population:	200,000
Cost of Living:	moderate
Climate Range:	0° to 90°F
Campus Setting:	urban
Total Enrollment:	40,000
Graduate Enrollment:	8,524
Students in Residence:	–

FACULTY

- Aldag, R.J. PhD, Michigan State
- Anderson, D.R. PhD, UW-Madison
- Arora, N. PhD, Ohio State
- Ashbaugh, H. PhD, Iowa
- Attari, M. PhD, Iowa
- Baker, T. PhD, North Carolina at Chapel Hill
- Boyd III, H.C. PhD, Duke
- Brown, D.P. PhD, Stanford
- Browne, M.J. PhD, Pennsylvania
- Buchan, N.R. PhD, Pennsylvania
- Carpenter, M.A. PhD, Texas at Austin
- Covaleski, M.A. PhD, Penn State
- DeBondt, W.F.M. PhD, Cornell
- Dickson, P.R. PhD, Florida
- Dunham, R.B. PhD, Illinois
- Eichenseher, J.W. PhD, Michigan
- Fedenia, M.A. PhD, UW-Madison
- Finster, M.P. PhD, Michigan
- Frees, E.W. PhD, North Carolina
- Frischmann, P.J. PhD, Arizona State
- Green, R.K. PhD, UW-Madison
- Hanson, E.I. DBA, Michigan State
- Harmatuck, D.J. PhD, UW-Madison
- Harms, B.L. JD, UW-Madison
- Hartman, L.P. JD, Chicago
- Hausch, D.B. PhD, Northwestern
- Heide, J.B. PhD, UW-Madison
- Heneman III, H.G. PhD, UW-Madison
- Hodder, J.E. PhD, Stanford
- Hurtt, K. PhD, Utah
- Inman, J.J. PhD, Texas (Austin)
- Ito, K. PhD, Michigan
- Jackwerth, J.C. PhD, Georgia-Augusta-Universitat
- Johannes, J.M. PhD, UW-Madison
- Johnstone, K. PhD, Connecticut
- Joseph, H.J. EdD, North Carolina State
- Kohlbeck, M. PhD, Texas
- Krainer, R.E. PhD, Michigan
- Krueger, C.A. MBA, Wisconsin-Oshkosh
- Lazimy, R. DBA, Harvard
- Liginlal, D. PhD, Arizona
- Malpezzi, S. PhD, George Washington
- Matsumura, E.M. PhD, British Columbia
- Matthews, R.J. JD, Harvard
- Mayhew, B.W. PhD, Arizona
- Mello, A.S. PhD, London
- Mick, D.G. PhD, Indiana
- Miller, R.B. PhD, Iowa
- Miner, A.S. PhD, Stanford
- Morris, J.G. PhD, UW-Madison
- Nair, R.D. PhD, Michigan
- Nevin, J.R. PhD, Illinois
- Odders-White, E.R. PhD, Northwestern
- Olson, C.A. PhD, UW-Madison
- Olsson, P. PhD, Stockholm
- Peter, J.P. DBA, Kentucky
- Policano, A.J. PhD, Brown
- Pollock, T. PhD, Illinois at Urbana-Champaign
- Pricer, R.W. PhD, Western Michigan
- Rappold, J.A. PhD, Cornell
- Ready, M.J. PhD, Cornell
- Reilly, P.R. BBA, UW-Madison
- Rittenberg, L.E. PhD, Minnesota
- Rosenberg, M.A. PhD, Michigan
- Rothschild, M.L. PhD, Stanford
- Ruckes, M. PhD, Mannheim
- Schmit, J.T. PhD, Indiana
- Schwab, D.P. PhD, Minnesota
- Seward, J.K. PhD, UW-Madison
- Shilling, J.D. PhD, Purdue
- Stajkovic, A.D. PhD, Nebraska
- Stevenson, R.E. PhD, Michigan State
- Thompson, H.E. PhD, UW-Madison
- Thompson, J.C. PhD, Tennessee
- Vandell, K.D. PHD, MIT
- Wade, J.B. PhD, Berkeley
- Warfield, T.D. PhD, Iowa
- Wemmerlov, U. PhD, Lund Institute of Technology
- Weng, Z.K. PhD, Purdue
- Weygandt, J.J. PhD, Illinois
- Wild, J.J. PhD, UW-Madison
- Young, V.R. PhD, Virginia
- Zariphopoulou, T. PhD, Brown

Vanderbilt University
PhD Program in Management

Program Highlights

- *Program's small size ensures students have opportunities for personal interaction with faculty members who share similar research interests*

- *Specializations in finance, marketing, operations management and organization studies available*

- *Accredited by AACSB*

CONTACT INFORMATION

Owen Graduate School of Management

401 - 21st Avenue South

Nashville, Tennessee USA 37203

PH: 1-615-343-1989

FAX: 1-615-343-7177

EMAIL:

maureen.writesman@owen.vanderbilt.edu

INTERNET: http://mba.vanderbilt.edu

VANDERBILT UNIVERSITY, PhD PROGRAM IN MANAGEMENT

PROGRAM OVERVIEW

Vanderbilt University's (Vanderbilt) Owen School of Graduate Management (Owen School) offers a Doctor of Philosophy (PhD) degree in management, with specializations in finance, marketing, operations management and organization studies.

The program prepares PhD students for a career in academic research and teaching. Students acquire core knowledge in functional business fields, economics, and analytical tools appropriate to their specialization. Prior graduate study can exempt some core requirements.

Students must pass a preliminary examination in a basic discipline (economics, quantitative methods, or one of the behavioral sciences), a preliminary examination in their specialization, and a qualifying examination which entails the defense of a dissertation proposal.

The PhD degree is awarded after completion of 72 semester credit hours of coursework and successful defense of the dissertation.

Finance

The PhD in finance is an intensive program involving finance workshops, special PhD seminars and research. Coursework in financial theory and empirical methods, economics, and econometrics is intended to broaden the student's understanding of current research in the field and provide them with in-depth knowledge of the latest analytical techniques. Electives may be chosen from graduate courses in economics, mathematics, engineering, management and from advanced MBA-level classes in finance.

In the first year of the program, students serve as research assistants to a finance faculty member or in the Financial Markets Research Center. Second- and third-year PhD students have an opportunity to work as teaching assistants in MBA-level finance courses.

Marketing

The PhD in marketing program is small and selective and offers close faculty supervision, so the program can be tailored to suit each student's interests and background. Marketing students learn to critically evaluate current marketing models, become proficient in the advanced statistical techniques of market analysis and learn to develop new research topics. They participate in seminars with nationally known marketing researchers and graduate from the program with a thorough grounding in the major disciplines of marketing.

Operations Management

Doctoral studies in operations management offer students the opportunity to conduct research in areas such as supply chain management, new product development and quality management. Program requirements include the completion of a publishable research paper by the end of the program's third semester, a preliminary examination in quantitative methods, a preliminary examination in the area of specialization, a qualifying examination on the thesis proposal, and the submission and defense of the doctoral dissertation.

Organization Studies

Organization studies include the interrelated fields of human resource management, organizational behavior and organizational theory. These disciplines are integrated in the doctoral program to prepare students for in-depth study and research. The small size of this program allows students to develop a course of studies to match their interests and career goals.

SELECTED RESEARCH AREAS

- Asset pricing
- Business ethics
- Consumer behavior in computer-mediated environments
- Consumer self-management
- Corporate finance
- Corporate strategy and global marketing
- Customer satisfaction psychology
- Derivatives
- Deterministic scheduling
- Dividend policy
- Electronic commerce
- Financial accounting
- Financial institutions
- Financial markets
- Human resource management and strategy
- International corporate finance
- International logistics
- Internet marketing
- Investment banking
- Negotiations and conflict management
- Management of innovation
- Manufacturing cells
- Market microstructure
- Marketing research
- Motivation
- New product development
- Nonprofit marketing management
- Operations management and management science
- Organization theory and design
- Organizational behavior
- Quality management
- Service marketing
- Social and moral consequences of new organizational forms
- Stochastic processes and statistics
- Supply chain management in high tech industries
- Team and workgroup composition and performance
- Technology in marketing

VANDERBILT UNIVERSITY, PHD PROGRAM IN MANAGEMENT

ADMISSIONS CRITERIA & PROCEDURES

The PhD program in management at Vanderbilt is highly selective and only seeks applicants with superior academic credentials and the motivation to excel in scholarly research in a management-related field. Due to the program's small size and the close collaboration between faculty and students, the PhD admissions committee favors applicants who can articulate their scholarly interests and demonstrate that these interests are similar to those of the faculty in the chosen area of specialization. Many qualified applicants are not offered admission because their applications do not meet these criteria.

Admission to the Owen School PhD program in management is based on undergraduate and, where applicable, graduate transcripts, scores on standardized tests, recommendations from former professors or employers who can speak to the applicant's ability and motivation to complete doctoral-level research, and the applicant's personal statement of purpose.

It is preferred that applicants submit GMAT scores, but the GRE is also accepted. In many ways, the statement of purpose is the most important part of the application. The admissions committee looks for evidence that the applicant understands the nature of the program, can articulate scholarly intentions that fit the current research interests of the faculty, and is academically prepared to undertake the demands of the program with a high probability of success.

EXPENSES & FINANCIAL ASSISTANCE

Tuition and fees for the PhD program are approximately US$22,900 per year. Living expenses for a single person, including room and board, books and supplies, medical insurance, and personal expenses are estimated to be about US$13,500 per year.

Students admitted to the PhD program are usually awarded Owen School fellowships that include full tuition waivers and US$15,000 stipends for a one-year period. Fellowship recipients are expected to work 12 hours per week as a research assistant, or engage in collaborative research with a faculty member. For outstanding candidates, the Graduate School awards a limited number of fellowships that provide US$3,000–5,000 in addition to the Owen School fellowship. Fellowship awards are typically renewable for up to four years.

INTERNATIONAL STUDENT SUPPORT

International Student & Scholar Services (ISSS) provides international students with advice, advocacy and counseling on matters pertaining to immigration, cross-cultural and personal matters, and supports a number of educational, social and cross-cultural programs.

Health insurance is mandatory for all international students, scholars and their dependents at Vanderbilt. International students are automatically enrolled in the Vanderbilt Health Insurance Plan unless they provide proof of alternative coverage.

The First Friends program matches international students at Vanderbilt with volunteers who offer friendship and promote cultural exchange. Volunteers who participate in First Friends help ease the cultural adjustment by providing both practical assistance and social support. Participants of the First Friends program generally meet on a monthly basis for dinner, museum visits, holiday celebrations and other activities.

ADMISSIONS AT A GLANCE
Minimum GMAT:	no set minimum
Minimum GPA:	3.0
Minimum TOEFL (paper):	620
Minimum TOEFL (computer):	–
Application Fee:	US$40
Application Deadline:	Jan 15

EXPENSES AT A GLANCE
Tuition:
In State:	US$22,900 per year
Out-of-State:	US$22,900 per year
Int'l Students:	US$22,900 per year

Books & Supplies: US$1,200 per year
Health Insurance: US$730 per year
Accommodation:
University Residences:	US$250-700 per month
Family Housing:	–
Private:	US$400–600 per month

PROGRAM FACTS
# of Full-time Students:	12
# of Part-time Students:	0
# of Applications per year:	83
# Accepted per year:	3–4
# Enrolled per year:	3–4
Average GMAT Score:	709
Average Age:	29
% Men/Women:	87%/13%
Work Experience (avg yrs):	4
# of Faculty:	45
% Faculty with Doctoral Degree:	95%
Annual Research Funding:	–

VANDERBILT UNIVERSITY, PhD PROGRAM IN MANAGEMENT

UNIVERSITY AND LOCATION

Established in 1873, Vanderbilt University is a private, comprehensive teaching and research university with an enrollment of approximately 10,000 students from all 50 states and almost 100 foreign countries. The university offers undergraduate, graduate and professional programs, including over 40 undergraduate majors, and employs approximately 1,800 full-time faculty members. Academic divisions at Vanderbilt include the Graduate School, which has an enrollment of 1,700 students, the College of Arts & Science, the schools of Divinity, Engineering, Law, Medicine and Nursing, Peabody College, the Blair School of Music and the Owen Graduate School of Management.

The university is accredited by the Commission on Colleges of the Southern Association of Colleges and Schools and is a member of the Association of American Universities.

Vanderbilt's Jean & Alexander Heard Library has a collection of over two million bound volumes, 1.8 million microform items and subscriptions to 16,000 periodicals.

The university's collegiate sports teams compete in the Southeast Conference of the NCAA.

The Vanderbilt campus, which has been designated as an arboretum, encompasses 330 acres in a park-like setting. It is located near the downtown business district of Nashville, within walking distance of Music Row, an international center for the music and recording industry.

Nashville, the capital city of Tennessee, is known as "Music City, USA" due to its many recording studios and entertainment events. It serves as a cultural, educational, financial and commercial center for the midsouth region and is a major center for several industries including printing, light manufacturing and tourism. The city's cultural activities include diverse popular music, the Nashville Symphony, a professional opera company, local and international touring dance companies, theater and a lively visual arts community.

Nashville is home to professional football, baseball and hockey teams and offers numerous facilities for indoor and outdoor activities as diverse as golf, boating, ice skating, polo, swimming and hiking. The surrounding region features wooded and hilly countryside offering year-round recreational opportunities for hiking, wildlife viewing and camping.

City Population:	550,000
Cost of Living:	medium
Climate Range:	26° to 90°F
Campus Setting:	urban
Total Enrollment:	10,300
Graduate Enrollment:	4,300
Students in Residence:	5,500

FACULTY

- Ball, C. PhD, New Mexico
- Barry, B. PhD, North Carolina at Chapel Hill
- Blackburn, Jr., J.D. PhD, Stanford
- Bonkoski, A. PhD, Pittsburgh
- Brown, A.O. PhD, Stanford
- Chordia, T. PhD, California
- Christie, W.G. PhD, Chicago
- Daft, R.L. PhD, Chicago
- Friedman, R.A. PhD, Chicago
- Gande, A. PhD, New York
- Gerhart, B. PhD, Wisconsin-Madison
- Gibbs, B.J. PhD, Chicago
- Hoffman, D.L. PhD, North Carolina at Chapel Hill
- Huang, R.D. PhD, Pennsylvania
- Hyer, N.L. PhD, Indiana
- LeBlanc, L.J. PhD, Northwestern
- Lewis, C.M. PhD, Wisconsin
- Mahoney, T.A. PhD, Minnesota
- Masulis, R.W. PhD, Chicago
- Novak, T.P. PhD, North Carolina at Chapel Hill
- Oliver, R.L. PhD, Wisconsin
- Oliver, R.W. PhD, SUNY, Buffalo
- Owens, D.A. PhD, Stanford
- Rados, D.L. PhD, California
- Rust, R.T. PhD, North Carolina
- Schlosser, A.E. PhD, Illinois at Urbana-Champaign
- Scudder, G.D. PhD, Stanford
- Stoll, H.R. PhD, Chicago
- Victor, B. PhD, North Carolina at Chapel Hill
- Weingartner, H.M. PhD, Carnegie Mellon

WASHINGTON UNIVERSITY PHD PROGRAM

Program Highlights

- *Tuition remission for all successful applicants*
- *Doctoral students carry out both teaching and research assistantships*
- *Limited enrollment ensures a high degree of faculty-student interaction*
- *Rigorous and rewarding PhD program*

CONTACT INFORMATION

John M. Olin School of Business

Campus Box 1133, One Brookings Drive

St. Louis, Missouri USA 63130-4899

PH: 1-314-935-6340

FAX: 1-314-935-4074

EMAIL: phdinfo@olin.wustl.edu

INTERNET: http://www.olin.wustl.edu

WASHINGTON UNIVERSITY, PHD PROGRAM

PROGRAM OVERVIEW

Fully accredited by AACSB, the John M. Olin School of Business (Olin) at Washington University (WU) offers a rigorous and rewarding PhD study option for highly motivated individuals. The program is kept small to ensure personal contact between students and faculty.

After completing a sequence of quantitative courses, including microeconomics and econometrics, students move into one of six areas of specialization.

Accounting
The options for PhD studies in accounting are wide-ranging, and include specializations in auditing, managerial accounting and taxation.

Accounting faculty at Olin are well-known for their scholarly productivity and many have published work in journals such as *The Accounting Review*, *Journal of Accounting & Economics* and *Journal of Accounting Research*.

Business Economics
Much of the research conducted by business economics faculty and PhD students is collaborative and interdisciplinary in nature. Recent projects include the development of methods of statistical inference based on simulation and research in both theoretical and applied game theory.

Research by business economics faculty appears in *Econometrica*, the *American Economic Review*, the *Journal of the American Statistical Association*, and the *Journal of Econometrics*.

Finance
The PhD in finance focuses on the allocation of capital, risk and rewards in the economy. Students explore issues using economic models and quantitative resources such as econometric and mathematical tools for empirical analysis. Faculty research is published in the *Journal of Finance*, *Review of Financial Studies* and the *Journal of Financial Economics*, among others.

Marketing
Faculty and students in marketing utilize methodolgies drawn from economics, probability, statistics, psychology and game theory to solve strategic problems in marketing. Faculty research papers have been published in *Marketing Science*, *Management Science*, *Journal of Business*, and the *Journal of Marketing Research*, among other scholarly publications.

Operations & Manufacturing Management
The operations and manufacturing management department provides answers to challenges faced by managers in manufacturing and service corporations. Many faculty have training in engineering; scholarly work produced by these individuals has been published in journals such as *Management Science* and *Operations Research*.

Organizational Behavior
Organizational behavior often focuses on how individuals and groups can affect and be affected by organizational issues. Faculty in this group approach the study of organizational issues with a foundation in various social sciences. Their work is published in such journals as the *Academy of Management Journal*, *Journal of Applied Psychology*, and *Organizational Behavior and Human Decision Processes*.

Strategy
Strategy is an interdisciplinary field that draws upon both economics and organizational theory to explore questions central to the general managers of organizations. Faculty research has been published in journals such as *Strategic Management Journal*, *Administrative Science Quarterly*, *Organizations Science*, *Journal of Law and Economics* and the *Journal of Law*.

SELECTED RESEARCH AREAS

Accounting
- Analysis and preparation of financial statements
- Auditing
- Managerial accounting
- Effects of taxes on investments and operating decisions
- Role of financial information in the operation of capital markets

Business Economics
- Public policy
- Environmental policy & risk analysis
- Econometrics
- Game theory
- Health care management & policy

Finance
- Theory & econometric testing of asset pricing models
- Investments, options & futures
- Theoretical corporate finance
- International investments

Marketing
- Supply chain coordination
- Assessing the competitive implications of information-intensive marketing
- Modeling consumer choice behavior
- Competitive strategies in new product development
- Private label strategies

Operations & Manufacturing
- Production planning & inventory control
- Assembly-line design
- Facility layout

Organizational Behavior
- The formation of coalitions in policy-making groups
- Determinants of workplace violence
- Multiple constituencies and negotiated settlements

Strategy
- Economics of organizations
- Horizontal and vertical boundaries of firms
- Models of competition
- Origins of competitive advantage

WASHINGTON UNIVERSITY, PHD PROGRAM

ADMISSIONS CRITERIA & PROCEDURES

In selecting candidates for the doctoral program at the Olin School of Business, admissions officials look for evidence of a strong quantitative background and a high degree of motivation. The minimum academic requirement for admission is a bachelor's degree and proficiency in quantitative areas such as matrix and linear algebra, advanced calculus, and statistics. While there is no minimum GMAT score or GPA required, successful candidates in the past have had an average GMAT score in the upper 600s.

Application forms can be obtained directly from Olin, or students can apply online via the university's website (http://www.olin.wustl.edu). Application packages must include a completed application form, US$75 nonrefundable processing fee, three letters of recommendation from academic referees, original GMAT or GRE score reports (GMAT preferred), and official transcripts from all undergraduate and graduate study. International applicants who do not have an academic degree from an American university must include a recent original TOEFL score to be eligible for admission.

Applications are accepted throughout the year; however, to be eligible for fall semester admission students must submit all application information (including test results and supporting documentation) by February 15. Individuals applying for university-wide fellowships should have their application package submitted to the university by late-January. Final admission decisions are typically made by mid-April.

EXPENSES & FINANCIAL ASSISTANCE

All students in the PhD program at the Olin School receive a combination of funding that includes a full tuition remission each year and a renewable cash stipend awarded over 12 months. In addition, students who complete degree requirements in a timely fashion may be eligible for a funding increase over the course of their doctoral program. In return for this financial assistance, most PhD candidates work as researchers or teachers after their first year of study.

There are two additional types of scholarship awards for new doctoral students: the Mr. and Mrs. Spencer T. Olin Fellowships for Women and the Chancellor's Graduate Fellowships. Olin Fellowships are four-year awards with generous stipends to outstanding female students entering doctoral programs at WU. The Chancellor's Graduate Fellowships are awarded to African-American students who have been admitted to a doctoral program and who plan to become college or university professors.

The application deadline for these awards is February 1 for Olin Fellowships and January 25 for Chancellor's Graduate Fellowships. Interested students should contact WU's Graduate School of Arts and Sciences for more details.

INTERNATIONAL STUDENT SUPPORT

Students in the PhD program at Olin come from all over the world, bringing with them a wealth of diverse experiences, background and training.

Services for international students at WU are offered through the International Office. These include an orientation program and English language courses ranging from intensive training for non-English speakers to conversational classes designed for individuals who want to perfect their communication skills.

The International Office serves as the hub of international activity on campus. Social and cultural events are held throughout the year, involving international students, faculty and community organizations.

ADMISSIONS AT A GLANCE

Minimum GMAT: no set minimum
Minimum GPA: no set minimum
Minimum TOEFL (paper): 600
Minimum TOEFL (computer): –
Application Fee: US$75
Application Deadline: Feb 15
(Jan 25 for Chancellor Fellowship; Feb 1 for Olin Fellowship)

EXPENSES AT A GLANCE

Tuition:
  In State: waived with admission
  Out-of-State: waived with admission
  Int'l Students: waived with admission
Books & Supplies: US$818 per year
Health Insurance: –
Accommodation:
  University Residences: US$8,640 per year
  Family Housing: US$8,640 per year
  Private: US$8,640 per year

PROGRAM FACTS

of Full-time Students: 32
# of Part-time Students: n/a
# of Applications per year: 204
Accepted per year: 18
Enrolled per year: 9
Average GMAT Score: upper 600s
Average Age: 29
% Men/Women: 75%/25%
Work Experience (avg yrs): 1.3
# of Faculty: 73
% Faculty with Doctoral Degree: 89%
Annual Research Funding: US$930,000

WASHINGTON UNIVERSITY, PHD PROGRAM

UNIVERSITY AND LOCATION

Established in 1853, Washington University is a medium-sized independent university internationally renowned for its commitment to excellence in learning. WU ranks among the top ten independent universities in the US in terms of doctoral degrees awarded per year, and has been recognized as a "best value" by US News & World Report.

Undergraduate and graduate programs, in 80 areas of study with almost 1,600 courses, are offered by the Schools of Architecture, Art, Arts and Sciences, Engineering and Applied Science, Law, Medicine, the John M. Olin School of Business and the George Warren Brown School of Social Work.

Approximately 12,000 full- and part-time students from all 50 states and 80 countries worldwide attend WU. The student population is about 50 percent men and 50 percent women, and multicultural and international students make up approximately 25 percent.

Faculty include many accomplished individuals and almost all full-time teaching staff hold a doctorate or the highest professional degree in their discipline. Twenty one Nobel laureates have been affiliated with WU, including nine who conducted most of their primary research on campus. These scholars teach both graduate and undergraduate courses at WU, giving all students an opportunity to learn under and work with experts in their chosen field of study.

WU is located in St. Louis, Missouri, a metropolitan city of more than 2.5 million people, recognized by Fortune magazine as one of the top 50 commercial centers in the world. St. Louis is home to the headquarters of nine Fortune 500 companies, making the city an excellent place for business professionals and entrepreneurs. A revamped waterfront area, complete with museums, antique stores and floating restaurants provides an example of the city's commitment to urban renewal and innovation.

Known as the "Gateway to the West", St. Louis boasts numerous cultural and recreational activities, such as live theater, jazz and a symphony orchestra. The Gateway Arch, a 630-foot stainless steel parabola spanning the Mississippi River in the heart of the city, is one of St. Louis' most recognizable landmarks.

City Population:	2,500,000
Cost of Living:	–
Climate Range:	0° to 90°F
Campus Setting:	urban
Total Enrollment:	12,035
Graduate Enrollment:	5,707
Students in Residence:	–

FACULTY

- Aviv, Y. PhD, Columbia
- Back, K.E. PhD, Kentucky
- Baloff, N. PhD, Stanford
- Bigelow, L. PhD, Berkeley
- Bottom, W.P. PhD, Illinois at Urbana-Champaign
- Boylan, R.T. PhD, California Institute of Technology
- Bunderson, J.S. PhD, Minnesota
- Carrillo, J.E. PhD, Georgia Institute of Technology
- Chib, S. PhD, California, Santa Barbara
- Dong, L. PhD, Stanford
- Dopuch, N. PhD, Illinois
- Durbin, E. PhD, Columbia
- Dybvig, P.H. PhD, Yale
- Erlebacher, S.J. PhD, Michigan
- Eynan, A. PhD, Washington
- Farnsworth, H. PhD, Washington
- Greenbaum, S.I. PhD, Johns Hopkins
- Griffith, T.L. PhD, Carnegie Mellon
- Gupta, M. PhD, Stanford
- Hamilton, B.H. PhD, Stanford
- Heilman, C.. PhD, Purdue
- Hesford, J. PhD, Southern California
- Hilgert, R.L. Phd, Washington
- Ho, V. PhD, Stanford
- Iyer, G. PhD, Toronto
- Jackson, S. PhD, Rice
- King, R.R. PhD, Arizona
- Kouvelis, P. PhD, Stanford
- Krolick, D.L. PhD, Chicago
- Kropp, D.H. PhD, Stanford
- Li, C.L. EngScD, Columbia
- Little, J.T. PhD, Minnesota
- Liu, H. PhD, Pennsylvania
- Loewenstein, M. PhD, Columbia
- Milner, J.M. PhD, MIT
- Moreton, P. PhD, Berkeley
- Narasimhan, C. PhD, Rochester
- Nickerson, J.A. PhD, Berkeley
- Owan, H. PhD, Stanford
- Padmanabhan, V. PhD, Texas at Dallas
- Panchapagesan, V. PhD, Southern California
- Parks, J.M. PhD, Iowa
- Pazgal, A.I. PhD, Northwestern
- Pirrong, S.C. PhD, Chicago
- Pollak, R.A. PhD, MIT
- Radas, S. PhD, Florida
- Rankin, F.W. PhD, Texas A&M
- Rao, A. PhD, U of Pennsylvania
- Rosenblatt, M.J. PhD, Stanford
- Schmeits, A. PhD, Amsterdam
- Schwartz, R. PhD, Northwestern
- Scruggs, J.T. PhD, Washington
- Seetharaman, P.B. PhD, Cornell
- Swinkels, J. PhD, Princeton
- Thomas-Hunt, M.C. PhD, Northwestern
- Zenger, T.R. PhD, UCLA
- Zhou, G. PhD, Duke

List of AACSB Accredited Institutions in the USA

This list (as of January 2000) appears courtesy of AACSB - The International Association for Management Education. Direct links with the websites of business schools at AACSB member institutions are available through the AACSB website: http://www.aacsb.edu.

"*" = institution has a doctoral program

University of Akron
College of Business Administration
Akron, Ohio 44325-4805 USA
institution type: Public

University of Alabama*
Culverhouse College of Commerce and
  Business Administration
Manderson Graduate School of Business
Box 870223
4 North Stadium Drive, 420 Alston Hall
Tuscaloosa, Alabama 35487-0223 USA
institution type: Public

University of Alabama at Birmingham*
School of Business
Graduate School of Management
1150 Tenth Avenue South
Birmingham, Alabama 35294-4460 USA
institution type: Public

University of Alabama in Huntsville
College of Administrative Science
301 Sparkman Drive
Huntsville, Alabama 35899-0001 USA
institution type: Public

University of Alaska Anchorage
College of Business and Public Policy
3211 Providence Drive
Anchorage, Alaska 99508-8244 USA
institution type: Public

University of Alaska Fairbanks
School of Management
P.O. Box 756080
Fairbanks, Alaska 99775-6080 USA
institution type: Public

**University at Albany, State University of
  New York***
School of Business
1400 Washington Avenue
Albany, New York 12222 USA
institution type: Public

Alfred University
College of Business
Saxon Drive
Alfred, New York 14802 USA
institution type: Private

American University
Kogod School of Business
4000 Massachusetts Avenue, N.W.
Washington, D.C. 20016-8004 USA
institution type: Private

Appalachian State University
John A. Walker College of Business
4135 Thelma C. Raley Hall
P.O. Box 32037
Boone, North Carolina 28608-2037 USA
institution type: Public

The University of Arizona*
Eller College of Business & Public Admin
Eller Graduate School of Management
McClelland Hall 417
Tucson, Arizona 85721-0108 USA
institution type: Public

Arizona State University*
College of Business
P.O. Box 873506
Tempe, Arizona 85287-3506 USA
institution type: Public

Arizona State University West
School of Management
4701 West Thunderbird Road
P.O. Box 37100, Mail Code 2451
Phoenix, Arizona 85069-7100 USA
institution type: Public

University of Arkansas*
Walton College of Business Administration
301 Business Administration Building
Fayetteville, Arkansas 72701 USA
institution type: Public

University of Arkansas at Little Rock
College of Business Administration
2801 South University Avenue
Little Rock, Arkansas 72204-1099 USA
institution type: Public

Arkansas State University
College of Business
P.O. Box 970
State University, Arkansas 72467-0970 USA
institution type: Public

Auburn University*
College of Business
Lowder Business Building, Suite 516
415 West Magnolia Avenue
Auburn University, Alabama 36849-5240 USA
institution type: Public

Auburn University Montgomery
School of Business
P.O. Box 244023
Montgomery, Alabama 36124-4023 USA
institution type: Public

Augusta State University
College of Business Administration
2500 Walton Way
Augusta, Georgia 30904-2200 USA
institution type: Public

Babson College
School of Management
Babson Park, Massachusetts 02457 USA
institution type: Private

Ball State University
College of Business
WB 100
Muncie, Indiana 47306-0325 USA
institution type: Public

List of AACSB Accredited Institutions in the USA

"*" = institution has a doctoral program

University of Baltimore
Robert G. Merrick School of Business
1420 North Charles Street
Baltimore, Maryland 21201-5779 USA
institution type: Public

**Baruch College-The City University
of New York***
The Zicklin School of Business
17 Lexington Avenue, Box E-0933
New York, New York 10010-5585 USA
institution type: Public

Baylor University
Hankamer School of Business
Box 98001
425 Speight
Waco, Texas 76798-8001 USA
institution type: Private

Bentley College
175 Forest Street
Waltham, Massachusetts 02154-4705 USA
institution type: Private

**Binghamton University, State University of
New York***
School of Management
Binghamton, New York 13902-6015 USA
institution type: Public

Boise State University
College of Business and Economics
1910 University Drive
Boise, Idaho 83725-1600 USA
institution type: Public

Boston College*
Carroll School of Management
140 Commonwealth Avenue
Chestnut Hill, Massachusetts 02467-3808 USA
institution type: Private

Boston University*
School of Management
595 Commonwealth Avenue
Boston, Massachusetts 02215 USA
institution type: Private

Bowling Green State University
College of Business Administration
371 Business Administration Building
Bowling Green, Ohio 43403-0260 USA
institution type: Public

Bradley University
Foster College of Business Administration
1501 West Bradley Avenue
Peoria, Illinois 61625 USA
institution type: Private

Brigham Young University
J. Willard and Alice S. Marriott School
of Management
730 TNRB
Provo, Utah 84602 USA
institution type: Private

Bryant College
1150 Douglas Pike
Smithfield, Rhode Island 02917-1284 USA
institution type: Private

**University at Buffalo, State University of
New York***
School of Management
160 Jacobs Management Center
P.O. Box 60400
Buffalo, New York 14260-4000 USA
institution type: Public

Butler University
College of Business Administration
4600 Sunset Avenue
Indianapolis, Indiana 46208-3487 USA
institution type: Private

University of California, Berkeley*
Haas School of Business
545 Student Services Building #1900
Berkeley, California 94720-1900 USA
institution type: Public

University of California, Davis
Graduate School of Management
AOB IV
Davis, California 95616-8609 USA
institution type: Public

University of California, Irvine*
Graduate School of Management 350
Irvine, California 92697-3125 USA
institution type: Public

University of California, Los Angeles*
John E. Anderson Graduate School
of Management
110 Westwood Boulevard, Suite F407
Los Angeles, California 90095-1481 USA
institution type: Public

**California Polytechnic State University,
San Luis Obispo**
College of Business
1 Grand Avenue
San Luis Obispo, California 93407-0300 USA
institution type: Public

**California State Polytechnic University,
Pomona**
College of Business Administration
3801 West Temple Avenue
Pomona, California 91768-4083 USA
institution type: Public

California State University, Bakersfield
College of Business and Public Administration
9001 Stockdale Highway
Bakersfield, California 93311-1099 USA
institution type: Public

LIST OF AACSB ACCREDITED INSTITUTIONS IN THE USA

"*" = institution has a doctoral program

California State University, Chico
College of Business
Chico, California 95929-0001 USA
institution type: Public

California State University, Fresno
The Sid Craig School of Business
5245 North Backer Avenue, P.B. 8
Fresno, California 93740-8001 USA
institution type: Public

California State University, Fullerton
School of Business Administration
  and Economics
P.O. Box 6848
Fullerton, California 92834-6848 USA
institution type: Public

California State University, Hayward
School of Business and Economics
25800 Carlos Bee Boulevard
Hayward, California 94542-3066 USA
institution type: Public

California State University, Long Beach
College of Business Administration
1250 Bellflower Boulevard
Long Beach, California 90840-8501 USA
institution type: Public

California State University, Los Angeles
School of Business and Economics
5151 State University Drive
Los Angeles, California 90032-8120 USA
institution type: Public

California State University, Northridge
College of Business Administration
  and Economics
18111 Nordhoff Street
Northridge, California 91330-8245 USA
institution type: Public

California State University, Sacramento
College of Business Administration
Sacramento, California 95819-6088 USA
institution type: Public

California State University, San Bernardino
College of Business and Public Administration
5500 University Parkway
San Bernardino, California 92407-2397 USA
institution type: Public

Canisius College
Richard J. Wehle School of Business
Buffalo, New York 14208 USA
institution type: Private

Carnegie Mellon University*
Graduate School of Industrial Administration
Frew and Tech Streets
Pittsburgh, Pennsylvania 15213-3890 USA
institution type: Private

Case Western Reserve University*
Weatherhead School of Management
10900 Euclid Avenue
Cleveland, Ohio 44106-7235 USA
institution type: Private

University of Central Arkansas
College of Business Administration
201 Donaghey Avenue
Conway, Arkansas 72035-0001 USA
institution type: Public

University of Central Florida*
College of Business Administration
P.O. Box 161991
4000 Central Florida Boulevard, BA 230
Orlando, Florida 32816-1991 USA
institution type: Public

Central Michigan University
College of Business Administration
ABSC Suite 250
Mt. Pleasant, Michigan 48859 USA
institution type: Public

Central Missouri State University
Harmon College of Business Administration
Dockery 212
Warrensburg, Missouri 64093-5016 USA
institution type: Public

Chapman University
The George L. Argyros School of Business
  and Economics
333 North Glassell Street
Orange, California 92866-1032 USA
institution type: Private

University of Chicago*
Graduate School of Business
1101 East 58th Street
Chicago, Illinois 60637-1563 USA
institution type: Private

University of Cincinnati*
College of Business Administration
Carl H. Lindner Hall
Cincinnati, Ohio 45221-0020 USA
institution type: Public

The Citadel
Department of Business Administration
171 Moultrie Street
Charleston, South Carolina 29409-0215 USA
institution type: Public

Claremont Graduate University
Peter F. Drucker Graduate School
  of Management
1021 North Dartmouth Avenue
Claremont, California 91711-6184 USA
institution type: Private

LIST OF AACSB ACCREDITED INSTITUTIONS IN THE USA

"*" = institution has a doctoral program

Clarion University of Pennsylvania
College of Business Administration
330 Still Hall
Clarion, Pennsylvania 16214 USA
institution type: Public

Clark University
Graduate School of Management
950 Main Street
Worcester, Massachusetts 01610-1477 USA
institution type: Private

Clark Atlanta University
School of Business Administration
223 Brawley Drive S.W.
Atlanta, Georgia 30314 USA
institution type: Private

Clarkson University
School of Business
Box 5765
Potsdam, New York 13699-5765 USA
institution type: Private

Clemson University*
College of Business and Public Affairs
P.O. Box 341301
Clemson, South Carolina 29634-1301 USA
institution type: Public

Cleveland State University*
Nance College of Business Administration
1860 East 18th Street
Cleveland, Ohio 44115-2440 USA
institution type: Public

Coastal Carolina University
Wall School of Business Administration
755 Highway 544
P.O. Box 261954
Conway, South Carolina 29528-6054 USA
institution type: Public

College of Charleston
School of Business and Economics
9 Liberty Street
Charleston, South Carolina 29424-0001 USA
institution type: Public

The College of New Jersey
School of Business
P.O. Box 7718
Ewing, New Jersey 08628-0718 USA
institution type: Public

College of William and Mary
School of Business Administration
P.O. Box 8795
Williamsburg, Virginia 23187-8795 USA
institution type: Public

University of Colorado at Boulder*
College of Business Administration and
Graduate School of Business Administration
Campus Box 419
Boulder, Colorado 80309-0419 USA
institution type: Public

University of Colorado at Colorado Springs
College of Business and Administration
Graduate School of Business Administration
P.O. Box 7150
1420 Austin Bluffs Parkway
Colorado Springs, Colorado 80933-7150 USA
institution type: Public

University of Colorado at Denver
College of Business and Administration and
Graduate School of Business and
   Administration
Campus Box 165
P.O. Box 173364
Denver, Colorado 80217-3364 USA
institution type: Public

Colorado State University
College of Business
Fort Collins, Colorado 80523 USA
institution type: Public

Columbia University*
Graduate School of Business
101 Uris Hall
3022 Broadway
New York, New York 10027-6902 USA
institution type: Private

University of Connecticut*
School of Business Administration U-41D
368 Fairfield Road
Storrs, Connecticut 06269-2041 USA
institution type: Public

Cornell University*
Johnson Graduate School of Management
207 Sage Hall
Ithaca, New York 14853-6201 USA
institution type: Private

Creighton University
College of Business Administration
2500 California Plaza
Omaha, Nebraska 68178-0130 USA
institution type: Private

Dartmouth College
Tuck School of Business Administration
100 Tuck Drive
Hanover, New Hampshire 03755-9040 USA
institution type: Private

University of Dayton
School of Business Administration
300 College Park
Dayton, Ohio 45469-2226 USA
institution type: Private

LIST OF AACSB ACCREDITED INSTITUTIONS IN THE USA

"*" = institution has a doctoral program

University of Delaware
College of Business and Economics
303 MBNA America Hall
Newark, Delaware 19716-2701 USA
institution type: Public

University of Denver
Daniels College of Business
2101 South University Boulevard
Denver, Colorado 80208-3411 USA
institution type: Private

DePaul University
College of Commerce and The Charles H. Kellstadt Graduate School of Business
1 East Jackson Boulevard
Chicago, Illinois 60604-2287 USA
institution type: Private

University of Detroit Mercy
College of Business Administration
4001 West McNichols Road
Detroit, Michigan 48219-0900 USA
institution type: Private

Drake University
College of Business and Public Administration
2507 University Avenue
Des Moines, Iowa 50311-4505 USA
institution type: Private

Drexel University*
Bennett S. Lebow College of Business
32nd and Market Streets
Philadelphia, Pennsylvania 19104-2875 USA
institution type: Private

Duke University*
The Fuqua School of Business
Box 90120
134 Towerview Drive
Durham, North Carolina 27708-0120 USA
institution type: Private

Duquesne University
A. J. Palumbo School of Business Administration
Graduate School of Business Administration
Room 709 Rockwell Hall
600 Forbes Avenue
Pittsburgh, Pennsylvania 15282-0180 USA
institution type: Private

East Carolina University
School of Business
Greenville, North Carolina 27858-4353 USA
institution type: Public

East Tennessee State University
College of Business
Room 210 Sam Wilson Hall
P.O. Box 70699
Johnson City, Tennessee 37614-0699 USA
institution type: Public

Eastern Illinois University
School of Business
600 Lincoln Avenue
Charleston, Illinois 61920-3099 USA
institution type: Public

Eastern Michigan University
College of Business
Ypsilanti, Michigan 48197 USA
institution type: Public

Eastern Washington University
College of Business and Public Administration
668 North Riverpoint Boulevard, Suite A
Spokane, Washington 99202-1660 USA
institution type: Public

Emory University
Goizueta Business School
1300 Clifton Road
Atlanta, Georgia 30322-2710 USA
institution type: Private

Fairfield University
School of Business
North Benson Road
Fairfield, Connecticut 06430 USA
institution type: Private

University of Florida*
Warrington College of Business
100 Bryan Hall
P.O. Box 117150
Gainesville, Florida 32611-7150 USA
institution type: Public

Florida Atlantic University*
College of Business
777 Glades Road
Boca Raton, Florida 33431-0991 USA
institution type: Public

Florida International University*
College of Business Administration
University Park Campus
Miami, Florida 33199 USA
institution type: Public

Florida State University*
College of Business
Tallahassee, Florida 32306-1110 USA
institution type: Public

Fordham University
Graduate School of Business Administration
113 West 60th Street, Room 624
New York, New York 10023 USA
institution type: Private

Fort Lewis College
School of Business Administration
1000 Rim Drive
Durango, Colorado 81301-3999 USA
institution type: Public

LIST OF AACSB ACCREDITED INSTITUTIONS IN THE USA

"*" = institution has a doctoral program

Francis Marion University
School of Business
4822 East Palmetto Street
Florence, South Carolina 29506 USA
institution type: Public

George Mason University
School of Management
Mail Stop 1B1
440 University Drive
Fairfax, Virginia 22030-4444 USA
institution type: Public

The George Washington University*
School of Business and Public Management
710 21st Street, N.W.
Washington, D.C. 20052 USA
institution type: Private

Georgetown University
The McDonough School of Business
207 Old North
37th and O Streets, N.W.
Washington, D.C. 20057-1008 USA
institution type: Private

University of Georgia*
Terry College of Business
Athens, Georgia 30602-6251 USA
institution type: Public

Georgia College & State University
School of Business
Campus Box 010
231 West Hancock Street
Milledgeville, Georgia 31061-0490 USA
institution type: Public

Georgia Institute of Technology*
The DuPree College of Management
755 Ferst Drive
Atlanta, Georgia 30332-0520 USA
institution type: Public

Georgia Southern University
College of Business Administration
P.O. Box 8002
Statesboro, Georgia 30460-8002 USA
institution type: Public

Georgia State University*
J. Mack Robinson College of Business
  Administration
University Plaza
35 Broad Street
Atlanta, Georgia 30303-3083 USA
institution type: Public

Gonzaga University
School of Business Administration
502 East Boone Avenue
Spokane, Washington 99202 USA
institution type: Private

Grand Valley State University
Seidman School of Business
Allendale, Michigan 49401-9403 USA
institution type: Public

Harvard University*
Graduate School of Business Administration
Soldiers Field
Boston, Massachusetts 02163 USA
institution type: Private

University of Hawaii
College of Business Administration
2404 Maile Way
Honolulu, Hawaii 96822 USA
institution type: Public

Henderson State University
School of Business
Box H-7801
1100 Henderson Street
Arkadelphia, Arkansas 71999-0001 USA
institution type: Public

Hofstra University
Frank G. Zarb School of Business
134 Hofstra University
Weller Hall
Hempstead, New York 11549 USA
institution type: Private

University of Houston*
College of Business Administration
#350 Melcher Hall
4800 Calhoun Street
Houston, Texas 77204-6283 USA
institution type: Public

University of Houston-Clear Lake
School of Business and Public Administration
2700 Bay Area Boulevard
Houston, Texas 77058-1098 USA
institution type: Public

University of Houston-Downtown
College of Business
One Main Street, Room 1009-N
Houston, Texas 77002-1001 USA
institution type: Public

Howard University
School of Business
2600 Sixth Street, N.W.
Washington, D.C. 20059 USA
institution type: Private

University of Idaho
College of Business and Economics
Moscow, Idaho 83844-3161 USA
institution type: Public

Idaho State University
College of Business
COB Building #202 Campus Box 8020
5th and Carter Streets
Pocatello, Idaho 83209-8020 USA
institution type: Public

LIST OF AACSB ACCREDITED INSTITUTIONS IN THE USA

"*" = institution has a doctoral program

University of Illinois at Chicago*
College of Business Administration M/C 075
601 South Morgan Street
Chicago, Illinois 60607-7122 USA
institution type: Public

University of Illinois at Urbana-Champaign*
College of Commerce & Business Admin
260 Commerce West
1206 South Sixth Street
Champaign, Illinois 61820-6980 USA
institution type: Public

Illinois Institute of Technology*
Stuart School of Business
565 West Adams Street
Chicago, Illinois 60661-3691 USA
institution type: Public

Illinois State University
College of Business
5500 College of Business
Normal, Illinois 61790-5500 USA
institution type: Public

Indiana University*
Kelley School of Business, Room 332
(Bloomington/Indianapolis)
1309 East 10th Street
Bloomington, Indiana 47405-1701 USA
institution type: Public

Indiana University-Northwest
Division of Business and Economics
3400 Broadway
Gary, Indiana 46408-1197 USA
institution type: Public

Indiana University-Purdue University at Fort Wayne
School of Business and Management Sciences
2101 Coliseum Boulevard East
Fort Wayne, Indiana 46805-1499 USA
institution type: Public

Indiana University South Bend
Division of Business and Economics
1700 Mishawaka Avenue
P.O. Box 7111
South Bend, Indiana 46634 USA
institution type: Public

Indiana University Southeast
Business & Economics
4201 Grant Line Road
New Albany, Indiana 47150-6405 USA
institution type: Public

Indiana State University
School of Business
Ninth and Sycamore Streets, Suite 1109
Terre Haute, Indiana 47809-5402 USA
institution type: Public

Iona College
Hagan School of Business
715 North Avenue
New Rochelle, New York 10801-1890 USA
institution type: Private

University of Iowa*
Henry B. Tippie College of Business
108 Pappajohn Business Building, Suite C120
Iowa City, Iowa 52242-1000 USA
institution type: Public

Iowa State University
College of Business
310 Carver Hall
Ames, Iowa 50011-2063 USA
institution type: Public

Jackson State University
School of Business
1325 J.R. Lynch Street
Jackson, Mississippi 39217-0960 USA
institution type: Public

Jacksonville State University
College of Commerce and Business Administration
100 Merrill Hall
700 Pelham Road North
Jacksonville, Alabama 36265-1602 USA
institution type: Public

James Madison University
College of Business
Zane Showker Hall, MSC 0207
Harrisonburg, Virginia 22807 USA
institution type: Public

John Carroll University
John M. and Mary Jo Boler School of Business
University Heights, Ohio 44118-4581 USA
institution type: Private

University of Kansas*
School of Business
203 Summerfield Hall
Lawrence, Kansas 66045-2003 USA
institution type: Public

Kansas State University
College of Business Administration
Calvin Hall
Manhattan, Kansas 66506-0501 USA
institution type: Public

Kennesaw State University
Coles College of Business
1000 Chastain Road
Kennesaw, Georgia 30144-5591 USA
institution type: Public

Kent State University*
College of Business Administration
P.O. Box 5190
Summit Street at Terrace Drive
Kent, Ohio 44242-0001 USA
institution type: Public

LIST OF AACSB ACCREDITED INSTITUTIONS IN THE USA

"*" = institution has a doctoral program

University of Kentucky*
Carol Martin Gatton College of Business and Economics
Lexington, Kentucky 40506-0034 USA
institution type: Public

Lamar University
College of Business
P.O. Box 10059
211 Redbird Lane
Beaumont, Texas 77100-0059 USA
institution type: Public

La Salle University
School of Business Administration
1900 West Olney Avenue
Philadelphia, Pennsylvania 19141-1199 USA
institution type: Private

Lehigh University*
College of Business and Economics
621 Taylor Street
Bethlehem, Pennsylvania 18015-3117 USA
institution type: Private

Longwood College
School of Business and Economics
103-1 Hiner Hall
201 High Street
Farmville, Virginia 23909-1899 USA
institution type: Public

Louisiana State University*
Ourso College of Business Administration
3304 CEBA, Nicholson Extension
Baton Rouge, Louisiana 70803-6302 USA
institution type: Public

Louisiana State University in Shreveport
College of Business Administration
One University Place
Shreveport, Louisiana 71115-2399 USA
institution type: Public

Louisiana Tech University*
College of Administration and Business
Ruston, Louisiana 71272-0046 USA
institution type: Public

University of Louisville
College of Business and Public Administration
Louisville, Kentucky 40292 USA
institution type: Public

Loyola University Chicago
School of Business Administration
Walter Tower Campus
820 North Michigan Avenue
Chicago, Illinois 60611 USA
institution type: Private

Loyola University New Orleans
Joseph A. Butt, S.J. College of Business Administration
6363 St. Charles Avenue
New Orleans, Louisiana 70118-6195 USA
institution type: Private

Loyola College in Maryland
Sellinger School of Business and Management
4501 North Charles Street
Baltimore, Maryland 21210-2699 USA
institution type: Private

Loyola Marymount University
College of Business Administration
7900 Loyola Boulevard
Los Angeles, California 90045-8395 USA
institution type: Private

University of Maine
Maine Business School
5723 Donald P. Corbett Business Building
Orono, Maine 04469-5723 USA
institution type: Public

Marquette University
College of Business Administration
Straz Hall
P.O. Box 1881
Milwaukee, Wisconsin 53201-1881 USA
institution type: Private

Marshall University
Lewis College of Business
400 Hal Greer Boulevard
Huntington, West Virginia 25755-2300 USA
institution type:

University of Maryland*
The Robert H. Smith School of Business
2416 Van Munching Hall
College Park, Maryland 20742-1815 USA
institution type: Public

University of Massachusetts-Amherst*
Eugene M. Isenberg School of Management
Amherst, Massachusetts 01003-4910 USA
institution type: Public

University of Massachusetts-Lowell
College of Management
Lowell, Massachusetts 01854-2882 USA
institution type: Public

Massachusetts Institute of Technology*
Sloan School of Management
50 Memorial Drive
Cambridge, Massachusetts 02142-1347 USA
institution type: Private

McNeese State University
College of Business
P.O. Box 92140
Lake Charles, Louisiana 70609-2140 USA
institution type: Public

LIST OF AACSB ACCREDITED INSTITUTIONS IN THE USA

"*" = institution has a doctoral program

The University of Memphis*
Fogelman College of Business and Economics
3675 Central, Room 432
Memphis, Tennessee 38152 USA
institution type: Public

University of Miami*
School of Business Administration
P.O. Box 248027
Coral Gables, Florida 33124-6520 USA
institution type: Private

Miami University
Richard T. Farmer School of Business Administration
500 East High Street
Oxford, Ohio 45056-9978 USA
institution type: Public

The University of Michigan*
University of Michigan Business School
701 Tappan
Ann Arbor, Michigan 48109-1234 USA
institution type: Public

The University of Michigan-Dearborn
School of Management
4901 Evergreen Road
Dearborn, Michigan 48128-1491 USA
institution type: Public

The University of Michigan-Flint
School of Mangement
303 East Kearsley
Flint, Michigan 48502-1950 USA
institution type: Public

Michigan State University*
The Eli Broad College of Business
The Eli Broad Graduate School of Management
520 North Business Complex
East Lansing, Michigan 48824-1121 USA
institution type: Public

Middle Tennessee State University
College of Business
P.O. Box 101
1301 E Main Street
Murfreesboro, Tennessee 37132-0001 USA
institution type: Public

Millsaps College
Else School of Management
1701 North State Street
Jackson, Mississippi 39210 USA
institution type: Private

University of Minnesota*
Carlson School of Management
321 19th Avenue South, Suite 4-300
Minneapolis, Minnesota 55455-0430 USA
institution type: Public

Minnesota State University, Mankato
College of Business
MSU Box 14
P.O. Box 8400
Mankato, Minnesota 56002-8400 USA
institution type: Public

University of Mississippi*
School of Business Administration
Holman Hall, Room 253
University, Mississippi 38677 USA
institution type: Public

Mississippi State University*
College of Business and Industry
Darden Avenue
P.O. Box 5
Mississippi State, Mississippi 39762-5288 USA
institution type: Public

University of Missouri-Columbia*
College of Business and Public Administration
106 Middlebush Hall
Columbia, Missouri 65211 USA
institution type: Public

University of Missouri-Kansas City
Henry W. Bloch School of Business and Public Administration
5110 Cherry Street
Kansas City, Missouri 64110-2499 USA
institution type: Public

University of Missouri-St. Louis
School of Business Administration
8001 Natural Bridge Road
St. Louis, Missouri 63121-4499 USA
institution type: Public

Monmouth University
School of Business Administration
West Long Branch, New Jersey 07764-1898 USA
institution type: Private

University of Montana
School of Business Administration
Missoula, Montana 59812 USA
institution type: Public

Montana State University
College of Business
412 Reid Hall
Bozeman, Montana 59717-0306 USA
institution type: Public

University of Montevallo
Michael E. Stephens College of Business
Station 6540
Montevallo, Alabama 35115-6540 USA
institution type:

Morehouse College
Department of Economics and Business Administration
830 Westview Drive, Southwest
Atlanta, Georgia 30314 USA
institution type:

LIST OF AACSB ACCREDITED INSTITUTIONS IN THE USA

"*" = institution has a doctoral program

Morgan State University
School of Business and Management
1700 East Cold Spring Lane
Baltimore, Maryland 21251 USA
institution type: Public

Murray State University
College of Business and Public Affairs
P.O. Box 9
Murray, Kentucky 42071-0009 USA
institution type: Public

University of Nebraska-Lincoln*
College of Business Administration
12th and R Streets
P.O. Box 880405
Lincoln, Nebraska 68588-0405 USA
institution type:

University of Nebraska at Omaha
College of Business Administration
Room 414
60th and Dodge
Omaha, Nebraska 68182-0048 USA
institution type:

University of Nevada, Las Vegas
College of Business
4505 Maryland Parkway
Las Vegas, Nevada 89154-6001 USA
institution type: Public

University of Nevada, Reno
College of Business Administration
1664 North Virginia Street
Mail Stop 024
Reno, Nevada 89503-0016 USA
institution type: Public

University of New Hampshire
Whitmore School of Business and Economics
McConnell Hall, 15 College Road
Durham, New Hampshire 03824-3593 USA
institution type: Public

New Jersey Institute of Technology
School of Management
CAB - Third Floor, University Heights
Newark, New Jersey 07102-1982 USA
institution type: Public

University of New Mexico
Robert O. Anderson School and Graduate
School of Management
1924 Las Lomas N.E.
Albuquerque, New Mexico 87131-1221 USA
institution type: Public

New Mexico State University*
College of Business Admin & Economics
Business Complex, Room 127
Box 30001 MSC 3AD
Las Cruces, New Mexico 88003-8001 USA
institution type: Public

University of New Orleans*
College of Business Administration
New Orleans, Louisiana 70148-1520 USA
institution type: Public

New York University*
Leonard N. Stern School of Business
Kautman Management Center, 11-160
44 West 4th Sreet
New York, New York 10012-1126 USA
institution type: Private

Nicholls State University
College of Business Administration
906 East First Street
P.O. Box 2015, NSU
Thibodaux, Louisiana 70310 USA
institution type: Public

Norfolk State University
School of Business
2401 Corprew Avenue
Norfolk, Virginia 23504 USA
institution type: Public

The University of North Carolina at Chapel Hill*
Kenan-Flagler Business School
CB 3490, McColl Building
Chapel Hill, North Carolina 27599-3490 USA
institution type: Public

The University of North Carolina at Charlotte
The Belk College of Busines Administration
9201 University City Boulevard
Charlotte, North Carolina 28223-0001 USA
institution type: Public

The University of North Carolina at Greensboro
Joseph M. Bryan School of Business and
Economics
P.O. Box 26165
Greensboro, North Carolina 27402-6165 USA
institution type: Public

University of North Carolina at Wilmington
Cameron School of Business
601 South College Road
Wilmington, North Carolina 28403-3297 USA
institution type: Public

North Carolina A & T State University
School of Business and Economics
1601 East Market Street
Greensboro, North Carolina 27411-1027 USA
institution type: Public

The University of North Dakota
College of Business and Public Administration
Centennial Drive
Grand Forks, North Dakota 58202-8098 USA
institution type: Public

LIST OF AACSB ACCREDITED INSTITUTIONS IN THE USA

"*" = institution has a doctoral program

University of North Florida
College of Business Administration
4567 St. Johns Bluff Road South
Jacksonville, Florida 32224 USA
institution type: Public

University of North Texas*
College of Business Administration
Denton, Texas 76203-1160 USA
institution type: Public

Northeast Louisiana University
College of Business Administration
700 University Avenue
Monroe, Louisiana 71209-0100 USA
institution type: Public

Northeastern University
College of Business Administration
101 Hayden Hall
360 Huntington Avenue
Boston, Massachusetts 02115-5096 USA
institution type: Private

Northern Arizona University
College of Business Administration
McConnell Circle, Building 70, Room 100
P.O. Box 15066
Flagstaff, Arizona 86011-5066 USA
institution type: Public

University of Northern Colorado
Kenneth W. Monfort College of Business
Greeley, Colorado 80639-0019 USA
institution type: Public

Northern Illinois University
College of Business
DeKalb, Illinois 60115 USA
institution type: Public

University of Northern Iowa
College of Business Administration
325 Business Building
Cedar Falls, Iowa 50614-0123 USA
institution type: Public

Northern Kentucky University
College of Business
Business/Education/Psychology Building,
Room 405
Highland Heights, Kentucky 41099-6008 USA
institution type: Public

Northwestern State University of Louisiana
College of Business
Natchitoches, Louisiana 71497-0002 USA
institution type: Public

Northwestern University*
J. L. Kellogg Graduate School of Management
Leverone Hall
2001 Sheridan Road
Evanston, Illinois 60208-2001 USA
institution type: Private

University of Notre Dame
College of Business Administration
Room 204
Notre Dame, Indiana 46556-5646 USA
institution type: Private

Oakland University
School of Business Administration
418 Varner Hall
Rochester, Michigan 48309-4493 USA
institution type: Public

The Ohio State University*
Max M. Fisher College of Business
201 Fisher Hall
2100 Neil Avenue
Columbus, Ohio 43210-1144 USA
institution type: Public

Ohio University
College of Business
Copeland Hall, Suite 614
Athens, Ohio 45701-2979 USA
institution type: Public

University of Oklahoma*
Michael F. Price College of Business
307 West Brooks, Room 208
Norman, Oklahoma 73019 USA
institution type: Public

Oklahoma State University*
College of Business Administration
Stillwater, Oklahoma 74078-0555 USA
institution type: Public

Old Dominion University*
College of Business and Public Administration
Graduate School of Business and Public
   Administration
49th Street and Hampton Boulevard
Norfolk, Virginia 23529-0218 USA
institution type: Public

University of Oregon*
Charles H. Lundquist College of Business
Undergraduate School of Business and
   Graduate School of Management
268 Gilbert Hall
1208 University of Oregon
Eugene, Oregon 97403-1208 USA
institution type: Public

Oregon State University
College of Business
200 Bexell Hall
Corvallis, Oregon 97331-2603 USA
institution type: Public

LIST OF AACSB ACCREDITED INSTITUTIONS IN THE USA

"*" = institution has a doctoral program

Pace University*
Lubin School of Business
Pace Plaza
New York, New York 10038 USA
institution type: Private

University of the Pacific
Eberhardt School of Business
3601 Pacific Avenue
Stockton, California 95211-0197 USA
institution type: Private

Pacific Lutheran University
School of Business
121st and South Park Avenue
Tacoma, Washington 98447-0003 USA
institution type: Private

University of Pennsylvania*
The Wharton School
3620 Locust Walk, Suite 1000
Philadelphia, Pennsylvania 19104-6364 USA
institution type: Private

The Pennsylvania State University*
The Mary Jean and Frank P. Smeal College
  of Business Administration
801 Business Administration Building
University Park, Pennsylvania 16802-3008 USA
institution type: Public

The Pennsylvania State University at Harrisburg
School of Business Administration
777 West Harrisburg Pike
Middletown, Pennsylvania 17057-4898 USA
institution type: Public

Pittsburg State University
Gladys A. Keke College of Business
1701 South Broadway
Pittsburg, Kansas 66762 USA
institution type: Public

University of Pittsburgh*
Katz Graduate School of Business
372 Mervis Hall
Pittsburgh, Pennsylvania 15260 USA
institution type: Private

University of Portland
School of Business Administration
5000 North Willamette Boulevard
Portland, Oregon 97203-5798 USA
institution type: Private

Portland State University
School of Business Administration
P.O. Box 751
Portland, Oregon 97207-0751 USA
institution type: Public

Purdue University*
School of Management and Krannert Graduate
  School of Management
1310 Krannert Building
West Lafayette, Indiana 47907-1310 USA
institution type: Public

Radford University
College of Business and Economics
Radford, Virginia 24142-6950 USA
institution type: Public

Rensselaer Polytechnic Institute*
Lally School of Management and Technology
Troy, New York 12180-3590 USA
institution type: Private

The University of Rhode Island*
College of Business Administration
7 Lippitt Road
301 Ballentine Hall
Kingston, Rhode Island 02881-0802 USA
institution type: Public

Rice University
Jones Graduate School of Management
MS 531, Box 1892
Houston, Texas 77005-1892 USA
institution type: Private

University of Richmond
E. Claiborne Robins School of Business
Richmond, Virginia 23173 USA
institution type: Private

Rider University
College of Business Administration
2083 Lawrenceville Road
Lawrenceville, New Jersey 08648-3099 USA
institution type: Private

University of Rochester*
William E. Simon Graduate School of Business
  Administration
Carol Simon Hall 2-202
Wilson Boulevard
Rochester, New York 14627 USA
institution type: Private

Rochester Institute of Technology
College of Business
107 Lomb Memorial Drive
Rochester, New York 14623-5608 USA
institution type: Private

Rollins College
Crummer Graduate School of Business
1000 Holt Avenue-2722
Winter Park, Florida 32789-4499 USA
institution type: Private

Rutgers-The State University of New Jersey
School of Business
Camden, New Jersey 08102 USA
institution type: Public

LIST OF AACSB ACCREDITED INSTITUTIONS IN THE USA

"*" = institution has a doctoral program

Rutgers-The State University of New Jersey*
Faculty of Management
111 Washington Street
Newark, New Jersey 07102 USA
institution type: Public

St. Cloud State University
College of Business
720 Fourth Avenue South
St. Cloud, Minnesota 56301-4498 USA
institution type: Public

St. John's University
College of Business Administration
8000 Utopia Parkway
Jamaica, New York 11439 USA
institution type: Private

Saint Louis University*
School of Business and Administration
3674 Lindell Boulevard
St. Louis, Missouri 63108-3397 USA
institution type: Private

St. Mary's University
School of Business and Administration
One Camino Santa Maria
San Antonio, Texas 78228-8607 USA
institution type: Private

Salisbury State University
Franklin P. Perdue School of Business
Holloway Hall-100
1101 Camden Avenue
Salisbury, Maryland 21801-6860 USA
institution type: Public

Sam Houston State University
College of Business Administration
P.O. Box 2056
Huntsville, Texas 77341-2056 USA
institution type: Public

Samford University
School of Business
800 Lakeshore Drive
Birmingham, Alabama 35229-2306 USA
institution type: Private

University of San Diego
School of Business Administration
5998 Alcala Park
San Diego, California 92110-2492 USA
institution type: Private

San Diego State University
College of Business Administration
San Diego, California 92182-8230 USA
institution type: Public

University of San Francisco
McLaren School of Business
2130 Fulton Street
San Francisco, California 94117-1080 USA
institution type: Private

San Francisco State University
College of Business
1600 Holloway Avenue
San Francisco, California 94132 USA
institution type: Public

San Jose State University
College of Business
One Washington Square
San Jose, California 95192-0065 USA
institution type: Public

Santa Clara University
Leavey School of Business
500 El Camino Real
Santa Clara, California 95053-0410 USA
institution type: Private

University of Scranton
The Arthur J. Kania School of Management
Scranton, Pennsylvania 18510-4602 USA
institution type: Private

Seattle University
Albers School of Business and Economics
900 Broadway
Seattle, Washington 98122-4340 USA
institution type: Private

Seton Hall University
W. Paul Stillman School of Business
400 South Orange Avenue
South Orange, New Jersey 07079-2692 USA
institution type: Private

Shippensburg University
John L. Grove College of Business
1871 Old Main Drive
Shippensburg, Pennsylvania 17257-2299 USA
institution type: Public

University of South Alabama
Mitchell College of Business
Mobile, Alabama 36688-0002 USA
institution type: Public

University of South Carolina*
The Darla Moore School of Business
1705 College Street
Columbia, South Carolina 29208 USA
institution type: Public

University of South Carolina, Spartanburg
School of Business Administration
and Economics
800 University Way
Spartanburg, South Carolina 29303-9395 USA
institution type: Public

LIST OF AACSB ACCREDITED INSTITUTIONS IN THE USA

"*" = institution has a doctoral program

University of South Dakota
School of Business
414 East Clark Street
Vermillion, South Dakota 57069-2390 USA
institution type: Public

University of South Florida*
College of Business Administration
4202 East Fowler, BSN 3403
Tampa, Florida 33620-5500 USA
institution type: Public

Southeast Missouri State University
Harrison College of Business
One University Plaza
Cape Girardeau, Missouri 63701-4799 USA
institution type: Public

Southeastern Louisiana University
SLU 10735
500 Western Avenue
Hammond, Louisiana 70402-0735 USA
institution type: Public

University of Southern California*
Marshall School of Business
Hoffman Hall 800
701 Exposition Boulevard
Los Angeles, California 90089-1421 USA
institution type: Private

Southern Illinois University-Carbondale*
College of Business and Administration
Mail Code 4619
Carbondale, Illinois 62901-4619 USA
institution type: Public

Southern Illinois University at Edwardsville
School of Business
Box 1051
Edwardsville, Illinois 62026-1051 USA
institution type: Public

University of Southern Indiana
School of Business
8600 University Boulevard
Evansville, Indiana 47712-3597 USA
institution type: Public

University of Southern Maine
School of Business
96 Falmouth Street
P.O. Box 9300
Portland, Maine 04104-9300 USA
institution type: Public

Southern Methodist University
Edwin L. Cox School of Business
6212 Bishop Boulevard
P.O. Box 750333
Dallas, Texas 75275-0333 USA
institution type: Private

The University of Southern Mississippi
College of Business Administration
200 North 31st Avenue, Box 5021
Hattiesburg, Mississippi 39406-5021 USA
institution type: Public

Southern University and A & M College
College of Business
P.O. Box 9723
Baton Rouge, Louisiana 70813-9723 USA
institution type: Public

Southwest Missouri State University
College of Business Administration
901 South National
Springfield, Missouri 65804-0094 USA
institution type: Public

Southwest Texas State University
School of Business
601 University Drive
San Marcos, Texas 78666-4616 USA
institution type: Public

University of Southwestern Louisiana
College of Business Administration
USL Box 40200
104 University Circle
Lafayette, Louisiana 70504-0200 USA
institution type: Public

Stanford University*
Graduate School of Business
518 Memorial Way
Stanford, California 94305-5015 USA
institution type: Private

State University of West Georgia
Richards College of Business
Carrollton, Georgia 30118 USA
institution type: Public

Stephen F. Austin State University
College of Business
1936 North Street 137 McGee
P.O. Box 13004
Nacogdoches, Texas 75962-3004 USA
institution type: Public

Stetson University
School of Business Administration
421 North Woodland Boulevard Unit 8398
DeLand, Florida 32720-3774 USA
institution type: Private

Suffolk University
Sawyer School of Management
Beacon Hill, 8 Ashburton Place
Boston, Massachusetts 02108-2770 USA
institution type: Private

Susquehanna University
Weis School of Business
514 University Avenue
Selinsgrove, Pennsylvania 17870-1001 USA
institution type: Private

LIST OF AACSB ACCREDITED INSTITUTIONS IN THE USA

"*" = institution has a doctoral program

Syracuse University*
School of Management
Syracuse, New York 13244-2130 USA
institution type: Private

The University of Tampa
College of Business and Graduate Studies
401 West Kennedy Boulevard
Tampa, Florida 33606-1490 USA
institution type: Public

Temple University*
School of Business and Management
111 Speakman Hall (006-00)
Philadelphia, Pennsylvania 19122 USA
institution type: Private

University of Tennessee at Chattanooga
School of Business Administration
615 McCallie Avenue
Chattanooga, Tennessee 37403-2598 USA
institution type: Public

University of Tennessee at Knoxville*
College of Business Administration
716 Stokely Management Center
Knoxville, Tennessee 37996-0570 USA
institution type: Public

University of Tennessee at Martin
School of Business Administration
Lovelace Avenue
Martin, Tennessee 38238-9998 USA
institution type: Public

Tennessee State University
College of Business
Nashville, Tennessee 37203-3401 USA
institution type: Public

Tennessee Technological University
College of Business Administration
P.O. Box 5025
Peachtree Street, Johnson Hall
Cookeville, Tennessee 38505-0001 USA
institution type: Public

The University of Texas at Arlington*
College of Business Administration
P.O. Box 19377
Arlington, Texas 76019-0377 USA
institution type: Public

The University of Texas at Austin*
College and Graduate School of Business
GSB 2.104
Austin, Texas 78712-1178 USA
institution type: Public

The University of Texas at El Paso
College of Business Administration
El Paso, Texas 79968-0545 USA
institution type: Public

The University of Texas-Pan American*
College of Business Administration
Edinburg, Texas 78539-2999 USA
institution type: Public

The University of Texas at San Antonio
College of Business
6900 North Loop 1604 West
San Antonio, Texas 78249-0631 USA
institution type: Public

The University of Texas at Tyler
School of Business Administration
3900 University Boulevard
Tyler, Texas 75799-6699 USA
institution type: Public

Texas A & M University*
Lowry Mays College and Graduate School of Business
413 Wehner Building
College Station, Texas 77843-4113 USA
institution type: Public

Texas A & M University-Commerce
College of Business and Technology
Commerce, Texas 75429-3011 USA
institution type: Public

Texas A&M University-Corpus Christi
College of Business
6300 Ocean Drive
Corpus Christi, Texas 78412-5599 USA
institution type: Public

Texas Christian University
Neeley School of Business
TCU Box 298530
Fort Worth, Texas 76129-3286 USA
institution type: Private

Texas Tech University*
College of Business Administration
Box 42101
15th Street and Flint Avenue
Lubbock, Texas 79409-2101 USA
institution type: Public

Thunderbird, The American Graduate School of International Management
15249 North 59th Avenue
Glendale, Arizona 85306-6000 USA
institution type: Private

University of Toledo*
College of Business Administration
Stranahan Hall
2801 West Bancroft
Toledo, Ohio 43606-3390 USA
institution type: Public

List of AACSB Accredited Institutions in the USA

"*" = institution has a doctoral program

Towson University
College of Business and Economics
Stephens Hall 218
8000 York Road
Towson, Maryland 21252-0001 USA
institution type: Public

Trinity University
Department of Business Administration
715 Stadium Drive
San Antonio, Texas 78212-7200 USA
institution type: Private

Truman State University
Division of Business and Accountancy
100 East Normal street
Kirksville, Missouri 63501-0828 USA
institution type: Public

Tulane University*
A. B. Freeman School of Business
7 McAlister Drive, Suite 440
New Orleans, Louisiana 70118-5669 USA
institution type: Private

University of Tulsa
College of Business Administration
Business Administration Hall, Room 216
600 South College
Tulsa, Oklahoma 74104-3189 USA
institution type: Private

Tuskegee University
College of Business, Organization and Management
Tuskegee, Alabama 36088 USA
institution type: Private

University of Utah*
David Eccles School of Business
1645 East Campus Center Drive, Room 101
Salt Lake City, Utah 84112 USA
institution type: Public

Utah State University
College of Business
Logan, Utah 84322-3500 USA
institution type: Public

Valdosta State University
College of Business Administration
Valdosta, Georgia 31698-0065 USA
institution type: Public

Valparaiso University
College of Business Administraiton
230 Urschel Hall
Valparaiso, Indiana 46383-6493 USA
institution type: Private

Vanderbilt University*
Owen Graduate School of Management
401 21st Avenue, South
Nashville, Tennessee 37203 USA
institution type: Private

University of Vermont
School of Business Administration
Kalkin Hall
Burlington, Vermont 05405-0157 USA
institution type: Public

Villanova University
College of Commerce and Finance
800 Lancaster Avenue
Villanova, Pennsylvania 19085-1678 USA
institution type: Private

University of Virginia, Darden*
Darden Graduate School of Business Administration
100 Darden Boulevard
Charlottesville, Virginia 22903 USA
institution type: Public

University of Virginia, McIntire
McIntire School of Commerce
#236 Monroe Hall
Charlottesville, Virginia 22903 USA
institution type: Public

Virginia Commonwealth University*
School of Business
1015 Floyd Avenue
P.O. Box 844000
Richmond, Virginia 23284-4000 USA
institution type: Public

Virginia Polytechnic Institute and State University*
Pamplin College of Business
1030 Pamplin Hall
Blacksburg, Virginia 24061-0209 USA
institution type: Public

Wake Forest University, Babcock
Babcock Graduate School
Box 7659
2114 Worrell Professional Center
Wake Forest Road
Winston-Salem, North Carolina 27109-7659 USA
institution type: Private

Wake Forest University, Calloway
The Wayne Calloway School of Business and Accountancy
Box 7285, Reynolda Station
Winston-Salem, North Carolina 27109 USA
institution type: Private

University of Washington*
School of Business Administration
Box 353200
Seattle, Washington 98195-3200 USA
institution type: Public

List of AACSB Accredited Institutions in the USA

"*" = institution has a doctoral program

Washington University*
Olin School of Business
Campus Box 1133
1 Brookings Drive
St. Louis, Missouri 63130-4899 USA
institution type: Private

Washington and Lee University
Williams School of Commerce, Economics and Politics
Lexington, Virginia 24450 USA
institution type: Private

Washington State University*
College of Business and Economics
Todd Hall Addition 570
Pullman, Washington 99164-4750 USA
institution type: Public

Wayne State University
School of Business Administration
226 Prentis Building
5201 Cass Avenue
Detroit, Michigan 48202-3930 USA
institution type: Public

Weber State University
John B. Goddard School of Business and Economics
3801 University Circle
Ogden, Utah 84408-3801 USA
institution type: Public

University of West Florida
College of Business
11000 University Parkway
Pensacola, Florida 32514-5752 USA
institution type: Public

West Virginia University
College of Business and Economics
University Avenue
P.O. Box 6025
Morgantown, West Virginia 26506-6025 USA
institution type: Public

Western Carolina University
College of Business
Cullowhee, North Carolina 28723-9033 USA
institution type: Public

Western Illinois University
College of Business and Technology
One University Circle
Macomb, Illinois 61455-1369 USA
institution type: Public

Western Kentucky University
Gordon Ford College of Business
1 Big Red Way
Bowling Green, Kentucky 42101-3576 USA
institution type: Public

Western Michigan University
Haworth College of Business
1201 Oliver Street
Kalamazoo, Michigan 49008-3801 USA
institution type: Public

Western Washington University
College of Business and Economics
Parks Hall 419
Bellingham, Washington 98225-9072 USA
institution type: Public

Wichita State University
Barton School of Business
1845 North Fairmount Avenue
Wichita, Kansas 67260-0048 USA
institution type: Public

Widener University
School of Business Administration
1 University Place
Chester, Pennsylvania 19013-5792 USA
institution type: Private

Willamette University
Atkinson Graduate School of Management
900 State Street
Salem, Oregon 97301-3922 USA
institution type: Private

Winthrop University
College of Business Administration
701 Oakland Avenue
Rock Hill, South Carolina 29733 USA
institution type: Public

University of Wisconsin-Eau Claire
College of Business
P.O. Box 4004
Eau Claire, Wisconsin 54702-4004 USA
institution type: Public

University of Wisconsin-La Crosse
College of Business Administration
1725 State Street
La Crosse, Wisconsin 54601 USA
institution type: Public

University of Wisconsin-Madison*
School of Business
5110 Grainger Hall
975 University Avenue
Madison, Wisconsin 53706 USA
institution type: Public

University of Wisconsin-Milwaukee*
School of Business Administration
P.O. Box 742
3202 North Maryland Avenue
Milwaukee, Wisconsin 53201-0742 USA
institution type: Public

University of Wisconsin-Oshkosh
College of Business Administration
800 Algoma Boulevard
Oshkosh, Wisconsin 54901-8675 USA
institution type: Public

LIST OF AACSB ACCREDITED INSTITUTIONS IN THE USA

"*" = institution has a doctoral program

University of Wisconsin-Parkside
School of Business and Technology
900 Wood Road, Box 2000
Kenosha, Wisconsin 53141-2000 USA
institution type: Public

University of Wisconsin-Whitewater
College of Business and Economics
800 West Main Street
Whitewater, Wisconsin 53190-1790 USA
institution type: Public

Wright State University
College of Business and Administration
3640 Colonel Glenn Highway
Dayton, Ohio 45435-0001 USA
institution type: Public

University of Wyoming
College of Business
P.O. Box 3275
Laramie, Wyoming 82071-3275 USA
institution type: Public

Xavier University
Williams College of Business
3800 Victory Parkway
Cincinnati, Ohio 45207-3230 USA
institution type: Private

Yale University
School of Management
Box 208200
135 Prospect Street
New Haven, Connecticut 06520-8200 USA
institution type: Private

List of AACSB Accredited Institutions Outside the USA

University of Alberta*
Faculty of Business
Edmonton, Alberta T6G 2R6 Canada

University of Calgary*
Faculty of Management
2500 University Drive, N.W.
Calgary, Alberta T2N 1N4 Canada

The Chinese University of Hong Kong
Shatin N.T.
Faculty of Business Administration
Hong Kong, China

Concordia University*
Faculty of Commerce and Administration
1455 de Maisonneuve Boulevard West
Montreal, Quebec H3G 1M8 Canada

Groupe ESSEC School of Management*
1, avenue Bernard-Hirsch, BP 105
95021 Cergy Pontoise France

The Hong Kong University of Science and Technology
School of Business and Management
Clearwater Bay
Hong Kong China

INCAE
P.O. Box 960-4050
Alajuela Costa Rica

Instituto Tecnológico Autónomo de México (ITAM)
Business School
Rio Hondo #1, Col.Tizapan San Angel
D.F., 01000 Mexico

Instituto Tecnológico y de Estudios Superiores de Monterrey (ITESM)
Graduate School of Business Administration and Leadership
Avenida Eugenio Garzo Sada 2501
Monterrey, N.L. 64849 Mexico

Université Laval*
Faculte des Sciences de l'Administration
Quebec City, Quebec G1K 7P4 Canada

University of Manitoba
Faculty of Management
Room 324, Drake Centre
181 Freedman Crescent
Winnipeg, Manitoba R3T 5V4 Canada

Queen's University*
Queen's School of Business
Kingston, Ontario K7L 3N6 Canada

Rotterdam School of Management*
Erasmus Graduate School of Business
PO Box 1738
Rotterdam, DR 3000 The Netherlands

University of Toronto
Rotman School of Management
105 St. George Street
Toronto, Ontario M5S 3E6 Canada

University of Warwick
Warwick Business School
Coventry, England CV4 7AL

List of AACSB Candidacy Status Institutions in the USA

This list (as of January 2000) appears courtesy of AACSB - The International Association for Management Education. "Candidacy" status signifies that the institution is demonstrating reasonable progress towards the attainment of accreditation. However, candidacy standing does not indicate "accredited" status nor does it guarantee eventual accreditation. Direct links to the websites of business schools at AACSB member institutions are available through the AACSB website: http://www.aacsb.edu.

"+" = in candidacy for accounting program   "*" = in candidacy for doctoral program

Abilene Christian University
College of Business Administration
Box 29301
Abilene, Texas 79699-9301 USA
institution type: Private

Albany State University
College of Business
504 College Drive
Albany, Georgia 31705 USA
institution type: Public

Alcorn State University
School of Business
1000 ASU Drive, #90
Alcorn State, Mississippi 39096 USA
institution type: Public

Alfred University
College of Business
Saxon Drive
Alfred, New York 14802 USA
institution type: Private

Andrews University
School of Business
Chan Shun Hall - Suite 201
Berrien Springs, Michigan 49104-0020 USA
institution type: Private

University of Arkansas at Pine Bluff
School of Business and Management
1200 North University Drive
P.O. Box 4976
Pine Bluff, Arkansas 71601 USA
institution type: Public
undergraduate enrolment: 525

Arkansas Tech University
School of Business
Russellville, Arkansas 72801-2222 USA
institution type: Public

Austin Peay State University
College of Business
681 Summer Street
Clarksville, Tennessee 37044 USA
institution type: Public

Barry University
Andreas School of Business
11300 North East Second Avenue
Miami Shores, Florida 33161-6695 USA
institution type: Private

Bellarmine College
W. Fielding Rubel School of Business
2001 Newburg Road
Louisville, Kentucky 40205-0671 USA
institution type: Private

Belmont University
College of Business Administration
1900 Belmont Boulevard
Nashville, Tennessee 37212-3757 USA
institution type: Private

Berry College
Campbell School of Business
P.O. Box 495024
Mount Berry, Georgia 30149-5024 USA
institution type: Private

Bethune-Cookman College
Division of Business
640 Mary McLeod Bethune Boulevard
Daytona Beach, Florida 32114 USA
institution type: Private

Bloomsburg University
College of Business
400 Second Street
Bloomsburg, Pennsylvania 17815-1301 USA
institution type: Public

Brigham Young University - Hawaii
School of Business
55-220 Kulanui Street, BYUH Box 1956
Laie, Hawaii 96762-1294 USA
institution type: Private

California State University, San Marcos
College of Business Administration
San Marcos, California 92096-0001 USA
institution type: Public

Christian Brothers University
School of Business
650 East Parkway South
Memphis, Tennessee 38104-5581 USA
institution type: Private

Christopher Newport University
School of Business
1 University Place
Newport News, Virginia 23606-2998 USA
institution type: Public

Columbus State University
Abbott Turner College of Business
Jordan Hall
4225 University Avenue
Columbus, Georgia 31907-5645 USA
institution type: Public

University of Dallas
Graduate School of Management
1845 East Northgate Drive
Irving, Texas 75062-4736 USA
institution type: Private

Eastern Illinois University+
School of Business
600 Lincoln Avenue
Charleston, Illinois 61920-3099 USA
institution type: Public

LIST OF AACSB CANDIDACY STATUS INSTITUTIONS IN THE USA

"+" = in candidacy for accounting program   "*" = in candidacy for doctoral program

Elon College
Spencer Love School of Business
Elon College, North Carolina 27244-2020 USA
institution type: Private

Emporia State University
School of Business
1200 Commercial Street
Emporia, Kansas 66801-5087 USA
institution type: Public

Fayetteville State University
School of Business and Economics
1200 Murchison Road
Fayetteville, North Carolina 28301-4298 USA
institution type: Public

Florida Institute of Technology*
School of Business
150 West University Boulevard
Melbourne, Florida 32901-6975 USA
institution type: Private

Grambling State University
College of Business
P.O. Box 848
Grambling, Louisiana 71245 USA
institution type: Public

University of Hartford
Barney School of Business and Public
   Administration
200 Bloomfield Avenue
West Hartford, Connecticut 06117-1599 USA
institution type: Private

University of Hawaii at Hilo
School of Business
200 West Kawili Street
Hilo, Hawaii 96720-4091 USA
institution type: Public

Hofstra University+
Frank G. Zarb School of Business
134 Hofstra University
Weller Hall
Hempstead, New York 11549 USA
institution type: Private

University of Illinois at Springfield
College of Business and Management, L-13
P.O. Box 19243
Springfield, Illinois 62794-9243 USA
institution type: Public

Indiana University of Pennsylvania
Eberly College of Business
401 Eberly Complex
Indiana, Pennsylvania 15705-1087 USA
institution type: Public

Kennesaw State University+
Coles College of Business
1000 Chastain Road
Kennesaw, Georgia 30144-5591 USA
institution type: Public

King's College
McGowan School of Business
133 North River Street
Wilkes-Barre, Pennsylvania 18711-0801 USA
institution type: Private

Lander University
School of Business Administration
320 Stanley Avenue
Greenwood, South Carolina 29649-2099 USA
institution type: Public

Le Moyne College
1419 Salt Springs Road
Syracuse, New York 13214-1399 USA
institution type: Private

Long Island University - C.W. Post Campus
College of Management
C. W. Post Campus/L.I.U.
Roth Hall 309
Brookville, New York 11548 USA
institution type: Private

Loyola University Chicago+
School of Business Administration
Walter Tower Campus
820 North Michigan Avenue
Chicago, Illinois 60611 USA
institution type: Private

Lynchburg College
School of Business and Economics
1501 Lakeside Drive
Lynchburg, Virginia 24501 USA
institution type: Private

Maine Maritime Academy
Loeb-Sullivan School of International
   Business and Logistics
Pleasant Street
Castine, Maine 04420 USA
institution type: Public

Manhattan College
School of Business
Riverdale, New York 10471 USA
institution type: Private

Marist College
School of Management
290 North Road
Poughkeepsie, New York 12601-1387 USA
institution type: Private

University of Maryland Eastern Shore
Department of Business
University Drive, Kiah Hall
Princess Anne, Maryland 21853-1299 USA
institution type: Public

LIST OF AACSB CANDIDACY STATUS INSTITUTIONS IN THE USA

"+" = in candidacy for accounting program   "*" = in candidacy for doctoral program

Maryville University-Saint Louis
John E. Simon School of Business
13550 Conway Road
St. Louis, Missouri 63141-0000 USA
institution type: Private

University of Massachusetts-Boston
College of Management
100 Morrissey Boulevard
Boston, Massachusetts 02125-3393 USA
institution type: Public

University of Massachusetts-Dartmouth
Charleton College of Business
Old Westport Road
North Dartmouth, Massachusetts 02747-2300 USA
institution type: Public

Mercer University-Macon and Atlanta Campuses
Eugene W. Stetson School of Business and Economics
1400 Coleman Avenue
Macon, Georgia 31207 USA
institution type: Private

Merrimack College
Division of Business Administration
North Andover, Massachusetts 01845-5800 USA
institution type: Private

Metropolitan State College of Denver
School of Business
MSCD Box 13
P.O. Box 173362
Denver, Colorado 80217-3362 USA
institution type: Public

Michigan Technological University
School of Business and Economics
1400 Townsend Drive
Houghton, Michigan 49931-1295 USA
institution type: Public

Middle Tennessee State University+
College of Business
P.O. Box 101
1301 E Main Street
Murfreesboro, Tennessee 37132-0001 USA
institution type: Public

University of Minnesota, Duluth
School of Business and Economics
Room 104 SBE
10 University Drive
Duluth, Minnesota 55812-2496 USA
institution type: Public

Montana State University-Billings
College of Business
1500 North 30th Street
Billings, Montana 59101 USA
institution type: Public

Montclair State University
School of Business
Upper Montclair, New Jersey 07043 USA
institution type: Public

Monterey Institute of International Studies
Robert L. and Marilyn J. Fisher Graduate School of International Business
425 Van Buren Street
Monterey, California 93940 USA
institution type: Private

Moorhead State University
College of Business and Industry
Center for Business 100
Moorhead, Minnesota 56563 USA
institution type: Public

Morehead State University
College of Business
Morehead, Kentucky 40351-1689 USA
institution type: Public

University of Nebraska at Kearney
College of Business and Technology
19th and University Drive
Kearney, Nebraska 68849-4450 USA
institution type: Public

University of New Haven*
School of Business
300 Orange Avenue
West Haven, Connecticut 06516 USA
institution type: Private

Niagara University
College of Business Administration
Niagara, New York 14109 USA
institution type: Private

The University of North Carolina at Asheville
Department of Management and Accountancy
Owen Hall, One University Heights
Asheville, North Carolina 28804-8507 USA
institution type: Public

North Carolina State University*
College of Management
Box 8614, 106 Nelson Hall
Raleigh, North Carolina 27695-8614 USA
institution type: Public

North Dakota State University
College of Business Administration
1301 12th Avenue North
Fargo, North Dakota 58105-5137 USA
institution type: Public

List of AACSB Candidacy Status Institutions in the USA

"+" = in candidacy for accounting program   "*" = in candidacy for doctoral program

Northeastern Illinois University
College of Business and Management
5500 North St. Louis Avenue
Chicago, Illinois 60625-4699 USA
institution type: Public

Northern Michigan University
Walker L. Cisler School of Business
Marquette, Michigan 49855-5359 USA
institution type: Public

Northern State University
School of Business
1200 South Jay Street
Aberdeen, South Dakota 57401-7198 USA
institution type: Public

Oswego State University
School of Business
101 Swetman Hall
Oswego, New York 13126 USA
institution type: Public

Ouachita Baptist University
Frank D. Hickingbotham School of Business
410 Ouachita - OBU Box 3760
Arkadelphia, Arkansas 71998-0001 USA
institution type: Private

The Pennsylvania State University at Erie, The Behrend College
School of Business
5091 Station Road
Erie, Pennsylvania 16563-1400 USA
institution type: Public

The Pennsylvania State University School of Graduate Professional Studies
Management Division
30 East Swedesford Road
Malvern, Pennsylvania 19355-1443 USA
institution type: Public

Pepperdine University
The George L. Graziadio School of Business and Management
400 Corporate Pointe
Culver City, California 90230-7615 USA
institution type: Private

University of Puerto Rico
College of Business Administration
Rio Piedras Campus
P.O. Box 23332
Rio Piedras, Puerto Rico 00931 USA
institution type: Public

Quinnipiac College
School of Business
Hamden, Connecticut 06518 USA
institution type: Private

Robert Morris College
Massey Hall
881 Narrows Run Road
Moon Township, Pennsylvania 15108-1189 USA
institution type: Private

Roger Williams University
Gabelli School of Business
One Old Ferry Road
Bristol, Rhode Island 02809-2921 USA
institution type: Private

Rowan University
College of Business Administration
201 Mullica Hill Road
Glassboro, New Jersey 08028-1701 USA
institution type: Public

Sacred Heart University
College of Business
5151 Park Avenue
Fairfield, Connecticut 06432-1000 USA
institution type: Private

Saginaw Valley State University
College of Business & Management
7400 Bay Road
University Center, Michigan 48710-0001 USA
institution type: Public

St. Bonaventure University
School of Business Administration
St. Bonaventure, New York 14778-2354 USA
institution type: Private

St. Cloud State University+
College of Business
720 Fourth Avenue South
St. Cloud, Minnesota 56301-4498 USA
institution type: Public

St. John Fisher College
Management Programs
3690 East Avenue
Rochester, New York 14618 USA
institution type: Private

Saint Joseph's University
Erivan K. Haub School of Business
Philadelphia, Pennsylvania 19131-1395 USA
institution type: Private

Salem State College
School of Business
352 Lafayette Street
Salem, Massachusetts 01970-4589 USA
institution type: Public

Savannah State University
College of Business Administration
P.O. Box 20359
Savannah, Georgia 31404 USA
institution type: Public

LIST OF AACSB CANDIDACY STATUS INSTITUTIONS IN THE USA

"+" = in candidacy for accounting program   "*" = in candidacy for doctoral program

Seattle University+
Albers School of Business and Economics
900 Broadway
Seattle, Washington 98122-4340 USA
institution type: Private

Seattle Pacific University
School of Business and Economics
3307 Third Avenue West, M/S 67
Seattle, Washington 98119-1997 USA
institution type: Private

Skidmore College
Department of Business
815 North Broadway
Saratoga Springs, New York 12866-1632 USA
institution type: Private

University of South Carolina-Aiken
School of Business Administration
471 University Parkway
Aiken, South Carolina 29801 USA
institution type: Public

South Carolina State University
School of Business
Box 7176
300 College Street, N.E.
Orangeburg, South Carolina 29117 USA
institution type: Public

Southern Arkansas University
School of Business Administration
100 East University
Magnolia, Arkansas 71753-5000 USA
institution type: Public

University of Southern Colorado
Hasan School of Business
2200 Bonforte Boulevard
Pueblo, Colorado 81001-4901 USA
institution type: Public

University of Southern Indiana+
School of Business
8600 University Boulevard
Evansville, Indiana 47712-3597 USA
institution type: Public

University of Southern Maine
School of Business
96 Falmouth Street
P.O. Box 9300
Portland, Maine 04104-9300 USA
institution type: Public

Southern Oregon University
School of Business
1250 Siskiyou Boulevard
Ashland, Oregon 97520-5022 USA
institution type: Public

Southern Utah University
College of Business, Technology and
   Communication
351 West Center Street
Cedar City, Utah 84720 USA
institution type: Public

State University of New York at New Paltz
75 South Manheim Boulevard
New Paltz, New York 12561-2499 USA
institution type: Public

State University of New York College at Brockport
Department of Business Administration and
   Economics
350 New Campus Drive
Brockport, New York 14420-2965 USA
institution type: Public

State University of New York College at Geneseo
Jones School of Business
Geneseo, New York 14454 USA
institution type: Public

State University of New York College at Oneonta
Department of Economics and Business
Ravine Parkway
Oneonta, New York 13820 USA
institution type: Public

The University of Texas at Brownsville
School of Business
80 Fort Brown
Brownsville, Texas 78520-4956 USA
institution type: Public

The University of Texas at Dallas*
School of Management
P.O. Box 830688 JO 52
Richardson, Texas 75083-0688 USA
institution type: Public

The University of Texas-Pan American*
College of Business Administration
Edinburg, Texas 78539-2999 USA
institution type: Public

Texas A & M University-Kingsville
College of Business Administration
Campus Box 182
1115 University Boulevard
Kingsville, Texas 78363-8203 USA
institution type: Public

Texas A & M International University
College of Business Administration
5201 University Boulevard
Laredo, Texas 78041-1900 USA
institution type: Public

LIST OF AACSB CANDIDACY STATUS INSTITUTIONS IN THE USA

"+" = in candidacy for accounting program   "*" = in candidacy for doctoral program

Texas Southern University
School of Business
3100 Cleburne Street
Houston, Texas 77004 USA
institution type: Public

University of Toledo+
College of Business Administration
Stranahan Hall
2801 West Bancroft
Toledo, Ohio 43606-3390 USA
institution type: Public

U.S. Air Force Academy
Department of Management
2354 Fairchild Drive, Suite 6H94
USAF Academy, Colorado 80840-5701 USA
institution type: Public

U.S. Coast Guard Academy
Department of Leadership and Management
15 Mohegan Avenue
New London, Connecticut 06320 USA
institution type: Public

Union College*
Graduate Management Institute
Lamont House Graduate Center
Schenectady, New York 12308 USA
institution type: Private

Virginia State University
School of Business
P.O. Box 9398
1 Hayden Drive
Petersburg, Virginia 23806-9398 USA
institution type: Public

Western Carolina University+
College of Business
Cullowhee, North Carolina 28723-9033 USA
institution type: Public

Western Connecticut State University
Ancell School of Business
181 White Street
Danbury, Connecticut 06810 USA
institution type: Public

Western New England College
School of Business
1215 Wilbraham Road
Springfield, Massachusetts 01119-2684 USA
institution type: Private

William Paterson University
College of Business
300 Pompton Road
Wayne, New Jersey 07470 USA
institution type: Public

Winona State University
College of Business
P.O. Box 5838
Winona, Minnesota 55987-5838 USA
institution type: Public

Winston-Salem State University
Division of Business and Economics
R.J. Reynolds Business Center
601 Martin Luther King, Jr. Drive
Winston-Salem, North Carolina 27110 USA
institution type: Public

Winthrop University+
College of Business Administration
701 Oakland Avenue
Rock Hill, South Carolina 29733 USA
institution type: Public

Worcester Polytechnic Institute
Department of Management
100 Institute Road
Worcester, Massachusetts 01609-2280 USA
institution type: Private

Youngstown State University
Williamson College of Business
One University Plaza
Youngstown, Ohio 44555-0001 USA
institution type: Public

List of AACSB Educational Institutions

This list (as of January 2000) appears courtesy of AACSB - The International Association for Management Education. The list consists of US and international institutions that are members of AACSB but are not AACSB accredited institutions or candidacy status institutions. Direct links to the websites of business schools at AACSB member institutions are available through the AACSB website: http://www.aacsb.edu.

The Aarhus School of Business
Academy of Entrepreneurship and Management
Adams State College
Adelphi University
Adolfo Ibanez University
Alabama A & M University
Alabama State University
Allentown College of St. Francis de Sales
Alverno College
The American College
The American College of Greece
American International College
American University of Beirut
The American University in Cairo
American University of Paris
Anna Maria College
Arab Academy for Science and Technology
University of Arkansas at Monticello
Armstrong University
Arthur D. Little School of Management
Ashland University
Ashridge
Asian Institute of Management
Assumption College
Athabasca University
Auckland Institute of Technology
Audrey Cohen College
Aurora University
Azusa Pacific University
Baldwin-Wallace College
Bar Ilan University
Barton College
Beaver College
Birmingham Southern College
Bond University
Brenau University
University of Bridgeport
University of British Columbia
Brock University
Bucknell University
Budapest University of Economic Sciences
University of California, Riverside
California Lutheran University
California State University, Dominguez Hills
California State University, Stanislaus
Cameron University
Campbell University
University of Cape Town
Capital University
Carlow College
Carson Newman College
Cedarville College
Central Connecticut State University
University of Central Oklahoma
Central State University
Central Washington University
Chaminade University of Honolulu
University of Charleston
Charleston Southern University
Chicago State University
University of Chile
Chulalongkorn University

City University
City University of Hong Kong
Clayton College and State University
The College of Insurance
College of Mount St. Joseph
College of Notre Dame
The College of St. Scholastica
Concordia College
Concordia University Wisconsin
Cranfield University
Cyprus College
Czech Management Center
Daemen College
David Lipscomb University
Delaware State University
Dominican University
Dowling College
Drury College
EAP-Ecole Europeenne des Affaires
EDC-Ecole des Dirigeants et Createurs d'entreprise
E. M. Lyon
ESC Rennes
Eastern College
Eastern Kentucky University
Ecole des Hautes Etudes Commerciales de Montreal
Ecole Superieure de Commerce et de Management (ESCEM)
University of Economics, Prague
Edgewood College
Elmhurst College
Embry Riddle Aeronautical University
Escuela de Administracion de Negocios Para Graduados (ESAN)
Escuela de Alta Direccion y Administracion (EADA)
Escuela Superior de Administracion y Direccion de Empresas (ESADE)
Escuela Superior Politecnica Del Litoral
European Business School
University of Evansville
Fairleigh Dickinson University
Ferris State University
Fisk University
Fitchburg State College
Florida A & M University
Fort Hays State University
Frostburg State University
Fundacao Getulio Vargas
Gannon University
Georgia Southwestern State University
Georgian Court College
Golden Gate University
Goldey-Beacom College
Governors State University
Greensboro College
University of Groningen
Groupe Ecole Superieure de Commerce de Rouen (ESC Rouen)
Groupe ESC Bordeaux
Groupe ESC Brest
Groupe ESC Clermont
Groupe ESC Grenoble
Groupe ESC Marseille Provence

Groupe ESC Nantes Atlantique
Groupe ESC Normandie
Groupe ESC Toulouse
Groupe ESCP
Groupe HEC
Groupe Sup De Co Montpellier
University of Guam
Hampton University
Hawaii Pacific University
Heidelberg College
Henley Management College
Higher School of Business-National Louis University
Holy Family College
The University of Hong Kong
Hood College
University of Houston-Victoria
Houston Baptist University
Humboldt State University
Husson College
IESE (International Graduate School of Management)
IMD International Institute
INSEAD
Illinois Wesleyan University
Indiana University Kokomo
University of Indianapolis
Institut d'Etudes Politiques de Paris-Sciences Po
Institut Quimic de Sarria
Institut Superieur du Commerce
Instituto de Altos Estudios Empresariales (IAE)
Instituto de Empresa
Instituto de Estudios Superiores de Administracion (IESA)
Instituto Panamericano de Alta Direccion de Empresa
Instituto Superior de Gestao
Instituto Tecnologico y de Estudios Superiores de Monterrey (ITESM-CEM)
International Executive Development Center (IEDC)
International Management Institute of St. Petersburg
International University of Japan
Ithaca College
Jacksonville University
The Johns Hopkins University
Kean University of New Jersey
Keio University
Keller Graduate School of Management
King Abdulaziz University
King Fahd University of Petroleum and Minerals
King Saud University
Kutztown University
Kuwait University
The Lake Forest Graduate School of Management
La Sierra University
Laurentian University
University of La Verne
Lebanon Valley College
University of Lethbridge
Lewis University
Lille Graduate School of Management
University of Ljubljana
London Business School
Long Island University
Luther College
Maastricht School of Management (MSM)

List of AACSB Educational Institutions

Macquarie University
Madonna University
Manchester Business School
University of Mannheim
Mars Hill College
Mary Washington
Marymount University
McGill University
McMaster University
Medgar Evers College of the City University of New York
Memorial University of Newfoundland
Meredith College
Mesa State College
Metropolitan State University
Midwestern State University
Millikin University
Minot State University
Mississippi College
Missouri Southern State College
Missouri Western State College
Moravian College
Morris Brown College
Mount Saint Mary College
Mount St. Mary's College
Muhlenberg College
National-Louis University
National University
National University of Singapore
Naval Postgraduate School
University of New Brunswick
New Hampshire College
University of New South Wales
New York Institute of Technology
Nichols College
Nijenrode University
North Carolina Central University
North Georgia College and State University
North Park University
Northwest Missouri State University
Norwegian School of Management
Nova Southeastern University
ORT University of Uruguay
Ohio Northern University
Oklahoma Christian University
Oklahoma City University
The Open University
Otterbein College
Our Lady of the Elms College
Pfeiffer University at Charlotte
Philadelphia University
University of Phoenix
Plattsburgh State University of New York
Polytechnic University of Puerto Rico
Pontificia Universidad Catolica de Chile
University of Pretoria
Providence College
University of Puerto Rico at Mayaguez
University of Puget Sound
Purdue University Calumet
University of Quebec at Montreal
The University of Queensland

Queensland University of Technology
Ramapo College of New Jersey
University of Redlands
Regents College
Richard Stockton College of New Jersey
University of Rio Grande
Rockhurst College
Roosevelt University
Ryerson Polytechnic University
St. Ambrose University
St. Edward's University
Saint Leo University
Saint Mary's College of California
Saint Mary's University
St. Norbert College
Saint Peter's College
University of St. Thomas
St. Thomas Aquinas College
University of Sao Paulo
University of Sarasota
University of Saskatchewan
Schiller International University
Seoul National University
Shenandoah University
Siena College
Simmons College
Simon Fraser University
Slippery Rock University
Sonoma State University
University of South Africa
Southern Connecticut State University
State University of New York at Stony Brook
State University of New York College at Old Westbury
State University of New York Institute of Technology at Utica/Rome
University of Stellenbosch
Stephens College
Stonehill College
University of Surrey
Tampa College
Taylor University
University of Technology-Sydney
Tel Aviv University
The University of Texas of the Permian Basin
Texas Wesleyan University
Texas Woman's University
Thammasat University
Tiffin University
Tilburg University
Troy State University
Troy State University at Montgomery
University of Turabo
United Arab Emirates University (UAEU)
United States International University
Universidad Catolica del Uruguay
Universidad de Los Andes
Universidad del Pacifico
Universidad ICESI
Universidad Pontificia Comillas
Universidad San Ignacio de Loyola
Universite Paris-Dauphine
Universiteit Maastricht

University College Dublin
University College of the Cariboo
University St. Cyril and Methodius
University of the Virgin Islands
Utah Valley State College
University of Victoria
Virginia Union University
Walsh College of Accountancy and Business Administration
Washburn University
Waynesburg College
Webber College
Webster University
West Chester University
West Liberty State College
West Virginia Institute of Technology
University of Western Ontario
Western Oregon University
University of Western Sydney
Whittier College
Wilfrid Laurier University
Wilkes University
University of Windsor
Wirtschaftsuniversitaet Wien
University of Wisconsin-Green Bay
University of Wisconsin-River Falls
Woodbury University
Worcester State College
Yeshiva University
Yonsei University
York University

FINAL NOTES

Additional Information for International Students
Destination – United States

Living in the US

The United States is an expansive, exciting country that boasts a distinct heritage, a blending of many interesting cultures and spectacular scenery.

A country famous for its "firsts"—the first light bulb was invented by Thomas Edison, the first aeroplane by the famous Wright brothers—the US is also the first choice of destinations for an increasing number of international students.

Country Facts

Though relatively young, the US is a nation rich in history and culture. International students studying and living in the US will have many opportunities to learn about its intriguing past — the establishment of colonial settlements, the American Revolution and the history of its native people. The ancestors of these first peoples, who now represent less than 1 percent of the population, arrived in North America 25,000 years ago.

The US boasts a widely varied landscape: expansive beaches, lush forests, fertile farmland, vast deserts, spectacular mountain ranges, tropical islands and subtropical wetlands. Hundreds of national and state parks offer unique geological and historic features.

Because of the size of the US — half the size of South America and slightly smaller than China — its climate varies dramatically, from tropical in Hawaii to arctic in Alaska. Summer months (June to August) are warm to hot in most places, and winter (November to February) can be cooler with rain and snow in many areas. Generally speaking, it is colder in the East and the Midwest than in the South; the West includes dry regions and rain forests. In summer, light clothing is sufficient, but warm clothes and raincoats are required in some places during winter months.

To provide a comprehensive description of all 50 US states would be impossible. The country can, however, be divided into four general regions: the East, Midwest, South and West. The

> **The US is the first choice of destinations for an increasing number of international students**

West ranges from the hot, arid, mostly desert lands of Arizona and New Mexico (the "wild" part of the West that spawned the genre of American films known as "Westerns") to the lush, forested Pacific Northwest. Mountain ranges divide the Midwest from the West. The Midwest is characterized by flat plains and fertile farmlands, though the northeastern states are heavily industrialized and are the automotive centre of the country. This region also features the Great Lakes. The East includes the New England states, where America's first immigrants, the Pilgrims, came ashore. The South is a vast geographical region stretching from Virginia, with its snowy, picturesque winters, to Florida, parts of which are just 300 kilometres from the Tropic of Cancer. Sometimes called "the sun belt," this region is characterized by its warmer climate and slower rhythm of life, especially in the Deep South.

The vastness of the country and the variations in climate offer opportunities to participate in virtually any physical activity, be it rock-climbing, downhill skiing, surfing or kayaking.

The population of the US is approximately 250 million people, nearly three-quarters of whom live in cities. Its multicultural society comprises people of mainly European, African American, Mexican and Latin American descent. Over 20 million people living in the US were born elsewhere.

The United States of America is a federal republic with a strong democratic tradition. The nation's capital, Washington, DC, is situated between Maryland and Virginia. The government is headed by the president and governed by Congress, which consists of the Senate and a House of Representatives.

The basic unit of currency in the US is the dollar, or "buck." All paper money is green, and its most widely used denominations are the $1, $5, $10, $20, $50 and $100 bills. Coins come in a variety of sizes and denominations including the 1-, 5-, 10-, and 25-cent coins. Banks throughout the US readily accept traveller's cheques and most foreign currency. The most widely accepted credit cards include Visa, MasterCard and American Express.

People and Culture

The American people have always placed a high value on individual rights, freedoms and responsibilities. Americans are renowned for taking great pride in their accomplishments as a nation. Often referred to as a melting pot, the US has been greatly influenced by the customs and cultures of the many immigrants who now call it home. International students will feel welcome and comfortable in multicultural, perspective-rich, American cities.

Sports are a major component of US culture and are an integral part of university and college life. Many students regularly attend their school's football and basketball games, and participate in a wide range of athletic endeavours themselves. Fraternities and sororities are also important to student life on US campuses. These student organizations, known as the "Greek" system, provide social activities, support and, in some cases, housing to students.

As with all multicultural societies, it

Most institutions have an international student office that provides an extensive range of services.

is difficult to generalize about US customs. Americans tend to treat others more informally than people in other countries, even given a difference in age or social standing, or while conducting business. This informality often extends into the classroom, though polite forms of address such as "Mr/Ms" or titles such as "Dr/Professor" are usually used. Americans are often outgoing, friendly and quite direct. A handshake and a smile are usually used to greet someone for the first time. Americans have never adopted the metric system; new arrivals will have to adapt to reading measurements in miles, feet, pounds, cups and Fahrenheit temperatures. Tipping about 15 per cent at hotels and restaurants is customary and usually expected.

Although hamburgers and French fries are known worldwide as American-style food, there is an enormous variety of foods available in the US. Not only is an exciting mix of international cuisine prominent in most places, regional dishes are often interesting eating—New England clam chowder, spicy Cajun and New Mexican dishes, and Pacific smoked salmon are some examples. Americans generally eat three meals a day: breakfast, lunch and dinner. Dinner, or supper as it is sometimes called, is the main meal. On weekends, many Americans enjoy brunch—a late breakfast. One popular menu item is Eggs Benedict—poached eggs with hollandaise sauce—a dish invented at the Waldorf Hotel in the 1890s.

Day-to-Day Living

American clothing is generally more casual than clothing in Europe. It is not unusual for women to wear skirts above their knees and sleeveless shirts.

Many schools have on-campus residences halls or dormitories, owing to the fact that American students usually travel long distances from home to attend college or university. Some schools offer separate residence halls or on-campus apartments for graduate students and families. Students may also choose to live in an apartment or shared house off campus, or through special arrangement with an American family. Most universities operate a housing office which can offer assistance and advice.

Most international airlines service the larger cities in the US, and many domestic airlines link major cities. When travelling throughout the US, overseas students should keep in mind the size of the country. Air travel has become quite common, and since the airlines were deregulated, air travel can be quite reasonably priced. Travel by train is not as popular as it once was, though it can still be a comfortable way to travel, offering students a unique opportunity to glimpse some of the more spectacular American landscape. One of the most extensive and least expensive means of travel is by coach (long-distance bus); the major international bus company is Greyhound-Trailways.

Although not as extensive as the European network, the Hostelling International-USA system offers substantial opportunities to make touring the country more economical. For travel within a city, buses and cars are the most common forms of transportation.

Studying in the US
Internationalization of Education

People from all over the world choose to study in the US. A recognition of the unique and important contributions international students make to education in the US has led many universities in recent years to begin offering courses with a global or multicultural focus.

In 1998, there were more than 481,000 international students studying in the US at over 3,000 colleges, universities, English language schools and postsecondary institutions.

To assist students who come to study in the US, most institutions have an international student office that provides an extensive range of social, academic and personal services. Often, institutions will offer an orientation program to familiarize new arrivals with the campus and US academics.

Overview of Education System

There is no national education system in the United States as in some other countries. Instead, education departments set guidelines for schools in their own states.

Universities are the largest and most complex of the country's higher education institutions. They comprise colleges, schools, departments and faculties, which deliver undergraduate, graduate and professional programs. Universities place a heavy emphasis on research, and most are publicly supported and funded by the state. Private institutions have more selective admission policies and often significantly higher fees. Some are affiliated with religious groups, and normally welcome all students regardless of whether or not they are church members. Colleges tend to be smaller and offer a more specific range of degree programs.

Master's programs normally take two years to complete; some schools offer accelerated, one-year programs and many offer part-time options. PhD degrees can take anywhere from three to seven years to complete. Professional programs can range from intensive weekend seminars to part-time, one- to four-year degree programs.

English as a Second Language, or ESL, courses are offered by all types of institutions. Some schools allow students with insufficient English language test scores to enroll conditionally in a program while upgrading their language skills through an ESL program.

US colleges and universities operate on one of three calendars: the semester, trimester or quarter system. Whatever the system, the academic year is approxi-

International students are advised to apply as early as possible

mately nine months long, from late August or September to May or June. Many schools operate year-long, offering some courses over the summer (May to August). International students are often advised to enter in the fall term, when many year-long classes start. By starting in the fall, new arrivals can participate in all the university's orientation programs. ESL programs offer many entry dates throughout the year.

General Admission Requirements for Graduate Students

Each school in the US sets its own entry requirements, which may vary depending on the degree of specialization of the program. Generally, students will be asked to supply official transcripts of all previous academic studies, letters of recommendation from previous professors or employers, an application fee, and scores from the Graduate Management Admission Test (GMAT), from the Graduate Record Examination (GRE) or from the Law School Admission Test (LSAT). Each has its own bulletin, a brochure explaining everything students need to know about the test, including cost and location of testing centres. Test bulletins are often available online or through the testing service.

International students are also required to meet the institution and program's minimum English language requirements. The most widely accepted test of proficiency is the Test of English as a Foreign Language (TOEFL), though some institutions also accept Michigan English Language Assessment Battery (MELAB) results or ELS Language Centers English proficiency recommendation. Generally, for admission to graduate programs, international students must have a minimum TOEFL score of 550 to 650.

Some schools also request students submit a current resume detailing relevant work experience and a personal statement outlining their goals and academic interests. Many schools require international students to provide proof of adequate financial resources to cover at least one entire year of study. Students should ensure that all documents are officially translated into English.

In the US, application for admission can only be made directly to the school itself. International students are advised to apply as early as possible to avoid potential delays from immigration procedures.

Fees and Cost of Living

Annual tuition fees for graduate degrees vary widely, ranging from just over US$4,000 to nearly $30,000. Many schools charge a higher rate to international students, and some require payment of a tuition deposit or of the entire year's fees in advance.

Depending on their lifestyle, students will require between US$9,000 and $13,000 yearly for living expenses. This will cover room and board, books and supplies, transportation, and other personal expenses. Living costs in large cities may be higher. Some schools also require students to have guaranteed, unlimited access to a personal computer for the duration of their studies.

Need-based financial assistance for international students is limited, but some international students may be eligible for merit-based scholarships, fellowships or assistantships.

> **International students may be eligible for merit-based scholarships, fellowships or assistantships.**

Health Insurance

Health care in the US is advanced, progressive — and potentially expensive for any individual who encounters an accident or illness requiring medical treatment. In the US, a visit to the doctor may cost US$100 and an overnight stay in the hospital is typically $1,000 per night.

Because of the expensive nature of US medical care, international students should be sure to obtain some form of health insurance to cover them for the duration of their stay in the US. Medical insurance is currently required for all J-1 visa holders and their spouses and dependents, and is expected to become mandatory for F-1 visa holders and their spouses and dependents as well.

Most colleges and universities in the US offer a health insurance plan for both domestic and international students. The cost for such insurance is approximately US$600 per year for the student, and coverage for spouses and dependents is available for an additional fee. Alternatively, students may choose to purchase or continue coverage from an insurance company in their home country. However, the terms of these agreements must match or exceed the specifications set by the university the student will attend. Most schools require students to provide proof of adequate medical coverage before enrolling.

While the exact terms of insurance plans can vary greatly from school to school, students should be aware that coverage does not always extend to dental and eye care and pre-existing conditions, such as pregnancy, that the student may have had prior to obtaining insurance. In addition, insurance usually covers approximately 80 percent of the cost of medical expenses and the remaining 20 percent must be paid by the student.

Visa Requirements

International students will require one of three types of student visas to study in the US. Most international students obtain an F-1 visa for full-time academic or language studies. A J-1 visa is required for students participating in an exchange program. An M-1 visa is necessary for individuals pursuing vocational studies.

To obtain a student visa, international students must submit an I-20 form (for an F-1 visa) or an IAP-66 (for a J-1 visa) to the US embassy or consulate in their home country. These forms are sent to students by US universities and colleges only after applicants have been accepted to a school and have demonstrated financial resources sufficient to cover the cost of studying in the US.

With few exceptions, US law generally prohibits students from outside the US from working. Students may be allowed to work part-time on campus after one year of study; outside employment generally requires government approval.

UNIVERSITY OF RHODE ISLAND
PhD Program in Business Administration

UNIVERSITY OF RHODE ISLAND

Please provide information

Last Name _____ First Name _____ Age _____ Sex _____
Address _____
City _____ Zip/Postal Code _____ Country _____
Telephone (___) _____ Fax (___) _____ Email _____
    Area Code   Area Code

DBM '00

WASHINGTON UNIVERSITY IN ST. LOUIS
John M. Olin School of Business

Washington WASHINGTON·UNIVERSITY·IN·ST·LOUIS

Please send information on

☐ Accounting   ☐ Marketing
☐ Business Econocics   ☐ Organizational Behavior/Strategy
☐ Finance   ☐ Operations & Manufacturing Management

Last Name _____ First Name _____ Age _____ Sex _____
Address _____
City _____ Zip/Postal Code _____ Country _____
Telephone (___) _____ Fax (___) _____ Email _____
    Area Code   Area Code

DBM '00

READER RESPONSE CARD

education international

To find out more about the programs that interest you, complete the form and send the card to the address on the back.

Arizona State University	☐ Florida State University	☐
Cornell University	☐ Illinois Institute of Technology	☐
Drexel University	☐ Kent State University	☐
Duke University	☐ Ohio State University, The	☐
Florida International University	☐ Pennsylvania State University, The	☐

Last Name _____ First Name _____ Age _____ Sex _____
Address _____
_____ Zip/Postal Code _____ Country _____
Telephone (___) _____ Fax (___) _____ Email _____
    Area Code   Area Code

Anticipated year of entry   2000   2001   2002 (please circle one)   DBM-00

| AIR MAIL | You can also fax the other side of this card to us at 1-401-874-4312 | ATTACH AIR MAIL POSTAGE |

PhD Program
College of Business Administration
UNIVERSITY OF RHODE ISLAND
7 Lippitt Road
Kingston, Rhode Island 02881-0802 USA

| AIR MAIL | You can also fax the other side of this card to us at 1-314-935-4074 | ATTACH AIR MAIL POSTAGE |

WASHINGTON UNIVERSITY IN ST. LOUIS
John M. Olin School of Business
Doctoral Program, Campus Box 1133
1 Brookings Drive
St. Louis, Missouri 63130-4899 USA

| AIR MAIL | You can also fax the other side of this card to us at 1-250-658-6285 | ATTACH AIR MAIL POSTAGE |

EI EDUCATION INTERNATIONAL LTD
PTSGE CORP./5000 Columbia Center
701 5th Avenue
Seattle, Washington
USA 98104-7078

education international

READER RESPONSE CARD

To find out more about the programs that interest you, complete the form and send the card to the address on the back.

Purdue University	☐	Universitiy of Arkansas	☐
Stanford University	☐	University of California - Irvine	☐
Syracuse University	☐	University of Central Florida	☐
Temple University	☐	University of Chicago	☐
Texas A & M University	☐		

Last Name _____ First Name _____ Age _____ Sex _____

Address _____

_____ Zip/Postal Code _____ Country _____

Telephone (____) _____ Fax (____) _____ Email _____
Area Code   Area Code

Anticipated year of entry   2000   2001   2002   (please circle one)

DBM-00

---

education international

READER RESPONSE CARD

To find out more about the programs that interest you, complete the form and send the card to the address on the back.

University of Cincinnati	☐	University of Illinois at Urbana-Champaign	☐
University of Connecticut	☐	University of Kansas	☐
University of Florida	☐	University of Maryland - College Park	☐
University of Georgia	☐	University of Massachusetts, Amherst	☐
University of Illinois at Chicago	☐	University of Michigan - Ann Arbor	☐

Last Name _____ First Name _____ Age _____ Sex _____

Address _____

_____ Zip/Postal Code _____ Country _____

Telephone (____) _____ Fax (____) _____ Email _____
Area Code   Area Code

Anticipated year of entry   2000   2001   2002   (please circle one)

DBM-00

---

education international

READER RESPONSE CARD

To find out more about the programs that interest you, complete the form and send the card to the address on the back.

University of Minnesota, Twin Cities	☐	University of Texas at Austin, The	☐
University of Mississippi	☐	University of Utah	☐
University of Oklahoma	☐	University of Washington	☐
University of South Carolina	☐	University of Wisconsin - Madison	☐
University of Tennessee at Knoxville	☐	Vanderbilt University	☐

Last Name _____ First Name _____ Age _____ Sex _____

Address _____

_____ Zip/Postal Code _____ Country _____

Telephone (____) _____ Fax (____) _____ Email _____
Area Code   Area Code

Anticipated year of entry   2000   2001   2002   (please circle one)

DBM-00

| AIR MAIL | You can also fax the other side of this card to us at 1-250-658-6285 | ATTACH AIR MAIL POSTAGE |

EI EDUCATION INTERNATIONAL LTD
PTSGE CORP./5000 Columbia Center
701 5th Avenue
Seattle, Washington
USA 98104-7078

| AIR MAIL | You can also fax the other side of this card to us at 1-250-658-6285 | ATTACH AIR MAIL POSTAGE |

EI EDUCATION INTERNATIONAL LTD
PTSGE CORP./5000 Columbia Center
701 5th Avenue
Seattle, Washington
USA 98104-7078

| AIR MAIL | You can also fax the other side of this card to us at 1-250-658-6285 | ATTACH AIR MAIL POSTAGE |

EI EDUCATION INTERNATIONAL LTD
PTSGE CORP./5000 Columbia Center
701 5th Avenue
Seattle, Washington
USA 98104-7078

Additional Resources

BUSINESS ORGANIZATIONS

AACSB - The International Association for Management Education
Suite 300, 600 Emerson Road
St. Louis, Missouri 63141-6762 USA
phone: 1-314-872-8481
fax: 1-314-872-8495
email: webmster@aacsb.edu
internet: http://www.aacsb.edu

Founded in 1916 as the American Assembly of Collegiate Schools of Business, AACSB adopted its new name (AACSB - The International Association for Management Education), more than 80 years later, to better reflect the changing vision and scope of the organization. With a membership consisting of corporations, educational institutions and other organizations, AACSB - The International Association for Management Education acts as the primary international accreditation body for business administration and accounting programs at all levels of postsecondary study.

Academy of Management (AOM)
PO Box 3020, 253 Elm Road
Briarcliff Manor, New York 10510-8020 USA
phone: 1-914-923-2607
fax: 1-914-923-2615
email: aom@academy.pace.edu
internet: http://www.aom.pace.edu

The Academy of Management (AOM) was created in 1936 to further the development of management research and teaching. AOM represents 10,000 members from around the world, including professors, doctoral students and executives.

Accounting Firms Associated Inc (AFAi)
2811 NW 41st Street, Building C
Gainsville, Florida 32606 USA
phone: 1-352-375-2324
fax: 1-352-375-4187
email: afai@afai.com
internet: http://www.afai.com

Established in 1978, the Accounting Firms Associated Inc (AFAi) is an international association of independent CPA firms with global affiliations. AFAi produces educational resources, and supports courses, professional training, conferences and other services for its members.

American Accounting Association (AAA)
5717 Bessie Drive
Sarasota, Florida 34233-2399 USA
phone: 1-941-921-7747
fax: 1-941-923-4093
email: aaahq@packet.net
internet: http://www.aaa-edu.org

The American Accounting Association (AAA), founded in 1916, is a voluntary organization of individuals dedicated to promoting accounting education, research and practice. AAA offers discounted associate memberships to full-time students in the USA and in Canada.

American Marketing Association (AMA)
250 South Wacker Drive, Suite 200
Chicago, Illinois 60606 USA
phone: 1-312-648-0536
fax: 1-312-993-7542
email: info@ama.org
internet: http://www.ama.org

The American Marketing Association (AMA) is a nonprofit organization active in promoting education, assisting in career development and advancing the science and ethical practice of marketing disciplines. Student members receive AMA's newspaper and gain access to many AMA career resources and publications.

American Risk & Insurance Association (ARIA)
c/o Chase Communications
PO Box 9001
Mount Vernon, New York 10552-9001 USA
phone: 1-800-951-2020
fax: 1-914-699-2025
email: aria@pipeline.com
internet: http://www.aria.org

Established in 1932, the American Risk & Insurance Association (ARIA) represents academics, industry representatives and institutional sponsors. ARIA's goals include expanding and improving academic instruction to students.

ADDITIONAL RESOURCES

Association for Information Systems (AIS)
PO Box 2712
Atlanta, Georgia 30301-2712 USA
phone: 1-404-651-0258
fax: 1-404-651-4938
email: ais@gsu.edu
internet: http://www.aisnet.org

The Association of Information Systems (AIS) is a professional organization that serves academics in the field of information systems and technology. AIS provides members with many services, including discounts on industry journals; the association also hosts an annual AIS Americas Conference.

Business Professionals of America (BPA)
5454 Cleveland Avenue
Columbus, Ohio 43231-4021 USA
phone: 1-614-895-7277
fax: 1-614-895-1165
email: bpa@ix.netcom.com
internet: http://www.bpa.org

The Business Professionals of America (BPA) is a national organization for students enrolled in business, office administration and technology education programs. BPA members participate in cocurricular programs to enhance their business and leaderships skills, and to develop important business contacts.

Decision Sciences Institute (DSI)
Georgia State University, University Plaza
Atlanta, Georgia 30303 USA
phone: 1-404-651-4073
fax: 1-404-651-2804 or 4008
email: dsi@gsu.edu
internet: http://dsi.gsu.edu

The Decision Sciences Institute is an international, nonprofit, professional organization of over 3,500 researchers, managers, educators, students and institutions. Through its annual meetings, competitions and publications, DSI acts as an international forum for research in the study of decision processes.

Graduate Management Admissions Council (GMAC)
Suite 750, 8300 Greensboro Drive
McLean, Virginia 22102 USA
phone: 1-703-749-0131
fax: 1-703-749-0169
email: gmacmail@gmac.com
internet: http://www.gmat.org

Best known for its role in administering the Graduate Management Admission Test (GMAT), the Graduate Management Admissions Council (GMAC) is a nonprofit association of graduate business schools from around the world. The organization aims to make graduate business education globally accessible by providing a variety of services and products, including self-study GMAT guides and MBA educational programs.

Institute for Operations Research & the Management Sciences (INFORMS)
PO Box 64794
Baltimore, Maryland 21264 USA
phone: 1-800-4INFORMS
fax: 1-410-684-2963
email: informs@informs.org
internet: http://www.informs.org

The Information for Operations Research & the Management Sciences (INFORMS) publishes journals and organizes professional conferences to serve the needs of OR/MS professionals, educators and students. Student members of INFORMS receive OR/MS TODAY magazine and half-price journal subscriptions, and may participate in online job placement services, meetings and student advice sessions.

Institute of Management Accountants (IMA)
10 Paragon Drive
Montvale, New Jersey 07645-1759 USA
phone: 1-201-573-9000
fax: 1-201-573-8438
email: feedback@imanet.org
internet: http://www.rutgers.edu/Accounting/raw
   ima/ima.htm

The Institute of Management Accountants (IMA) is a professional organization devoted to management accounting and finance management. IMA keeps its members current on relevant issues, and offers guidance to professionals.

ADDITIONAL RESOURCES

Institute of Management Consultants - USA (IMC)
521 5th Avenue, 35th Floor
New York, New York 10175-3598 USA
phone: 1-212-697-8262
fax: 1-212-949-6571
email: office@imcusa.org
internet: http://www.imcusa.org

Founded in 1968, the Institute of Management Consultants (IMC) is a national, nonprofit association which sets professional and ethical standards for the management consulting profession. Every year, IMC delivers over 200 workshops, seminars and conferences, and is a member of the International Council of Management Consulting Institutes.

MBA Career Services Council (MBA CSC)
The Wharton School, University of Pennsylvania
Suite 50 McNeil, 3718 Locust Walk
Philadelphia, Pennsylvania 19104-6209 USA
email: mbacsc@mbacsc.org
internet: http://www.mbacsc.org

Formed in 1994, the MBA Career Services Council (MBA CSC) is an international association for individuals involved in the field of MBA career services. MBA CSC strives to create a forum of open communication among members and provide operating procedure standards.

Network of International Business Schools (NIBS)
Project Management Group
Salisbury State University
Power Professional Building, Room 141
Salisbury, Maryland 21801-6860 USA
phone: 1-410-548-5353
fax: 1-410-219-2848
email: slparker@ssu.edu
internet: http://www.nibsnet.org

The Network of International Business Schools (NIBS) is a worldwide organization committed to the globalization of business education programs. To this end, NIBS supports student and faculty exchanges, advocates the practice of foreign languages, and promotes the study of business and management techniques on a comparative basis.

Securities Industry Association (SIA)
120 Broadway, 35th Floor
New York, New York 10271-0080 USA
phone: 1-212-608-1500
fax: 1-212-608-1604
email: info@sia.com
internet: http://www.sia.com

The Securities Industry Association (SIA) was founded in 1972, after the merger of the Association of Stock Exchange Firms (1913) and the Investment Banker's Association (1912). SIA represents approximately 800 securities firms across North America and draws membership from investment banks, broker-dealers, specialists and mutual fund companies.

INTERNATIONAL STUDENT RESOURCES

Association of International Educators (NAFSA)
1875 Connecticut Avenue, NW, Suite 1000
Washington, DC 20009-5728 USA
phone: 1-202-462-4811
fax: 1-202-667-3419
email: inbox@nafsa.org
internet: http://www.nafsa.org

The Association of International Educators (NAFSA) is an association of over 7,000 members who promote international student exchanges to and from the USA. NAFSA provides a variety of resources for international students on topics such as income tax, health, living with host families, and the services of the international offices at universities and colleges.

ADDITIONAL RESOURCES

Educational Testing Service (ETS) - TOEFL
Corporate Headquarters, Rosedale Road
Princeton, New Jersey 08541 USA
phone: 1-609-921-9000
fax: 1-609-734-5410
email: etsinfo@ets.org
internet: http://www.ets.org/body.html

Educational Testing Services is the administrative body responsible for managing the Test of English as a Foreign Language (TOEFL) under the guidance of the TOEFL Policy Council, a group of 15 members from independent academic organizations and government agencies. The service's online network (ETS Net) provides information on a range of subjects from financial aid to teacher certification. Sample TOEFL questions and hints about test preparation and registration are also available on ETS Net.

Hostelling International - American Youth Hostels (HI-AYH)
PO Box 37613
Washington, DC 20013-7613 USA
phone: 1-202-783-6161
fax: 1-202-783-6171
email: hiayhserv@hiayh.org
internet: http://www.hiayh.org

Hostelling International-American Youth Hostels (HI-AYH) is a nonprofit membership organization that promotes educational travel by operating nearly 5,000 hostels in over 70 countries worldwide. HI-AYH provides low-cost accommodation for student travellers, operates a reservations service and an international booking network, and offers a variety of books and maps.

Institute of International Education (IIE)
809 United Nations Plaza
New York, New York 10017-3580 USA
phone: 1-212-883-8200
fax: 1-212-984-5442
email: info@iie.org
internet: http://www.iie.org

Founded in 1919, the Institute of International Education (IIE) develops programs worldwide to promote international education. IIE also maintains a reference library with a variety of materials about scholarships and study opportunities in the USA.

National Council for International Visitors (NCIV)
1420 K Street, NW, Suite 800
Washington, DC 20005 USA
phone: 1-202-842-1414
fax: 1-202-289-4625
email: profexchg@iie.org
internet: http://www.nciv.org

The National Council for International Visitors (NCIV) is a national network of nonprofit agencies and organizations that implement programs for international visitors. The NCIV provides assistance with home hospitality, city tours, hotel bookings, language translation and many other services.

More on Education International

Education International (EI) provides high-quality information on postsecondary study opportunities in the USA and Canada. A global leader, EI provides comprehensive, in-depth information on academic programs through print guides, the Internet and student fairs.

EI guides cover a wide range of academic areas:

- ✔ business
- ✔ teacher education
- ✔ science
- ✔ distance learning
- ✔ secondary schools
- ✔ engineering
- ✔ nursing & health
- ✔ fine arts
- ✔ intensive English language
- ✔ universities and colleges

Accessible around-the-clock and around-the-world, EI publishes postsecondary study opportunities via eight state-of-the-art websites:

www.SchoolsinCanada.com
profiles undergraduate academic programs in Canada

www.SchoolsintheUSA.com
profiles undergraduate academic programs in the USA

www.GraduateBusiness.com
profiles graduate management programs

www.GradSciEng.com
profiles graduate engineering and science programs

www.GradFineArts.com
profiles graduate fine arts programs

www.GradEducation.com
profiles graduate teacher education programs

www.DistanceStudies.com
profiles distance learning degree and diploma programs

www.GraduateHealth.com
profiles graduate nursing and health programs

EI also produces annual student fairs featuring US academic institutions:

★ Latin American tour of US institutions
★ Mexican tour of US institutions
★ Hong Kong fair for US institutions

www.USEducationFairs.com
profiles education fairs of US institutions

Whether you are looking for an undergraduate or graduate program, we know that choosing the program suited to your unique needs is the key to your success. Our mission is to help make that process easier.

▪▪ education international
Guiding Students to Success

PTSGE CORP./5000 Columbia Center, 701 5th Avenue, Seattle, Washington USA 98104-7078
phone: 1-250-658-6283 fax: 1-250-658-6285 email: service@educationinternational.com

Glossary

Accelerated MBA – an intensive MBA program, usually taking one year or less to complete; students generally must have significant work experience (usually at least two to five years) and often have recently completed an undergraduate degree (so they are familiar with core business principles); accelerated MBAs are often offered in conjunction with undergraduate degree programs, enabling students to achieve two degrees in five years

Accredit – to approve or authorize; programs are often accredited by regional and/or general bodies, ensuring that specific curricular standards are met

Advanced Standing (Advanced Placement, Accelerated Study) – direct entry into more advanced levels in the program (bypassing initial components), based on performance on advanced placement tests, previously earned academic credit or previous work experience (see "waive")

Assistantship – a paid position offered by many universities to graduate students; students assist the professor with advising, laboratory supervision, marking and teaching, usually in return for payment of partial or complete tuition fees

Baccalaureate – a bachelor's degree level of study

Case Study – the application of management principles to simulated or real-life business situations to give students practice in applying their analytical and presentation skills as well as theoretical knowledge

Cohort – a group of students or colleagues who work or study together for the duration of a project or program

Concentration – a focus undertaken within a degree program; for example, students completing an MBA degree may pursue a concentration in one area, such as entrepreneurship (see "specialization" or "stream")

Consortium – an association of several business companies or corporations; plural: consortia

Consulting – the practice of serving as an outside adviser for a company; providing guidance and expertise to solve specific business problems through research and implementation

Cooperative or Co-op Program – education program that combines theoretical learning and practical experience; generally achieved by alternating periods of classroom study with paid or unpaid industrial or business work placements; can be mandatory or optional depending on the program

Co-signatory – a person signing a document jointly with others; students from overseas are sometimes required to have a co-signatory who is a US citizen or permanent resident

Core Courses – courses forming the basis of a degree progam; required courses that address the main components of a program; usually required for program completion

Curriculum – subjects included in a course of study; plural: curricula

Distance Education – education program that allows students to complete all or part of a degree program in a different geographical location from the degree-granting university/institution, with the final award conferred being equivalent in standard and content to a degree completed on campus; often makes use of communications technology (Internet, email) to increase the distance education student's contact with the institution

Dossier – a package of information about a person; a student's application package containing all relevant documents

Elective Courses – optional courses that complement the core components of a degree program

Entrepreneurship – the undertaking of an enterprise or business with chance of profit or loss; a common specialization in graduate management programs; program participants study the traits of successful entrepreneurs as well as what is needed to establish a new business

Exchange Program – an agreement between institutions that permits the movement of students from one to the other for short or long periods of study or employment that are credited to a degree earned at the original institution

Glossary

Fortune 500 (Company) – annual ranking published by Fortune magazine, consisting of the 500 largest manufacturing corporations in the US, based on annual revenue

Foundation (Studies/Year/Courses) – preliminary general or specific course of study that forms the basis of subsequent education; frequently offered as a qualifying year for candidates who require skills/knowledge upgrading for entry into a desired degree program

GMAT – Graduate Management Admission Test; a standardized test that measures general verbal, quantitative and analytical skills; often used by postsecondary institutions to determine an applicant's aptitude for its graduate management program

GMAT CAT – GMAT Computer-Adaptive Test; a recently developed form of the GMAT that has the same basic structure and content as the original GMAT but that is conducted in a computer-adaptive mode; offered at various testing centres in North America, Europe, Asia and Latin America, the new format of the GMAT enables the test to be offered much more frequently, making it more convenient for candidates

GPA – Grade Point Average; the average grade achieved by a student during the course of an educational program, calculated on various scales determined by individual institutions; the most common scales used by universities in this guide are a 4.0 scale and a 9.0 scale; many universities use average percentages and letter grades in place of a formal GPA

Interdisciplinary (Management Curriculum) – study of all aspects of management education; a common attribute of contemporary graduate management programs, interdisciplinary curricula give students—even those specializing in one functional area—a broad education; for example, students undertaking an accounting concentration may also study human resources and marketing; also referred to as "cross-disciplinary"

Internship – a concentrated period of degree-related industrial or business work for which the participant may or may not be remunerated

Ivy League – an association of eight independent colleges and universities in the northeastern US, established in 1954; due to the high quality of scholarship at member institutions, it has come to represent education of the highest standard

Joint Degree – degree combining two or more subject areas; for example, students may pursue a joint degree in business and law

Matriculation – qualifying by examination or otherwise for admission to a university

Practicum – a paid or unpaid period of work experience organized during an academic program; allows students to apply theoretical learning to practical situations; plural: practica

Prerequisite – course required as preparation for entry into a more advanced academic course or program

Qualitative – concerned with quality; elements that cannot be measured in concrete terms; qualitative disciplines in management include human resources, labour relations and strategic management

Quantitative – concerned with quantity; of or to do with elements that can be measured; quantitative disciplines in management studies include accounting, finance, statistical analysis and computer science

Recruiter – a company representative who visits university and college campuses to interview students and graduates as potential employees

Reference (Recommendation) – a commendation from a former teacher, counsellor or employer in the form of a letter attesting to the student's academic, professional and/or personal merits

Rolling Admissions – admissions policy by which there is no set deadline for application submission

Glossary

Specialization – a focus undertaken within a degree program; for example, students completing an MBA degree may specialize in one area, such as international business

Stream – as above, a focus of a graduate degree program; also called a specialization or track; certain programs offer several possible streams; for example, a student may choose between a human resource or an international commerce stream

Student Authorization – a visa issued by the United States government permitting international students to study at an institution in the US for an extended period

Study-Abroad Program – an agreement between institutions in different geographical locations facilitating the movement of students from one to the other for short- or long-term periods of study within a single degree program; see Exchange Program

TOEFL – Test of English as a Foreign Language; a test that measures a candidate's aptitude in English; frequently required by English-speaking postsecondary institutions for applicants whose first language is not English

Track – a focus taken during a graduate degree program; also variously called a specialization or a stream

Transcript – official academic records detailing place and time of study, courses completed and grades achieved

Videoconference – a conference conducted through the use of video technology, allowing individuals to participate from separate locations; frequently used by distance education programs

Waive – to bypass courses required for program completion; students with appropriate backgrounds may be allowed to waive foundation or prerequisite courses

Work Term – a period of industrial or business work placement that forms part of cooperative education programs

Acronyms

AACSB	The International Association for Management Education		Evaluators	IS	Information Systems
		EDP	Executive Development Programs	IT	Information Technology
AAU	Association of American Universities			LAN	Local Area Network
		EMAIL	Electronic Mail	LSAT	Law School Admissions Test
AICPA	American Institute of Certified Public Accountants	ESL	English as a Second Language	MELAB	Michigan English Language Assessment Battery
		ETS	Educational Testing Services		Management Information Decision Systems
AMAI	American Management Association International	FAFSA	Free Application for Federal Student Aid	MIS	Management Information Systems
CA	Chartered Accountant	FPS	Frames Per Second	NASA	National Aeronautics & Space Administration
CAD	Computer-Aided Design	GMAC	Graduate Management Admissions Council		
CBT	Computer-based Test (TOEFL)	GMAT	Graduate Management Admissions Test	NASPAA	National Association of Schools of Public Affairs & Administration
CD-ROM	Compact Disk-Read Only Memory	GMAT CAT	GMAT-Computer Adaptive Test	ORBH	Organizational Behaviour
CEO	Chief Executive Officer			PBT	Paper-based Test (TOEFL)
CFO	Corporate Financial Officer	GPA	Grade Point Average	PC	Personal Computer
CGA	Certified General Accountant	GRE	Graduate Record Examination	TOEFL	Test of English as a Foreign Language
CIO	Chief Information Officer	GST	Goods & Service Tax	TOEIC	Test of English for International Communication
CMA	Certified Management Accountant	HR	Human Resources		
		IA	Investment Adviser		
CPP	Certified Professional Purchaser	IB	International Baccalaureate	TSE	Test of Spoken English
		IELTS	International English Language Testing System	TWE	Test of Written English
CV	Curriculum Vitae			WWW	World Wide Web
ECE	Education Credentials				

Index

A

AACSB – The International Association for Management Education
   Accredited Institutions in the USA — 187
   Accredited International Institutions — 204
   Candidate Institutions — 205
   Member Institutions — 211
Opportunities & Challenges in Management Education (AACSB) — 3
   Dynamics of Graduate Education — 3
   Choosing a School — 4
   Other Considerations — 4
Additional Resources — 219
Arizona State University — 23

C

Choosing a School — 4
Computer-Adaptive GMAT — 5
Cornell University — 27

D

Destination USA — 215
Country Facts — 215
Day-to-Day Living — 216
Fees and Cost of Living — 217
General Admission Requirements for Graduate Students — 217
Health Insurance — 218
Internationalization of Education — 216
Living in the US — 215
Overview of Education System — 217
People and Culture — 215
Studying in the US — 216
Visa Requirements — 218
Drexel University — 31
Duke University — 35

F

Florida International University — 39
Florida State University — 43

G

Glossary — 224
Graduate Management Admission Test, The (GMAC) — 5
   Benefits of the GMAT — 5
   Computer-Adaptive GMAT — 5
   Cost of the GMAT — 6
   Future of the GMAT — 6
   Preparing to Take the GMAT — 6
   Scheduling an Appointment — 6
   Strategies for Taking the GMAT — 5

H

Health Insurance — 218

I

Illinois Institute of Technology — 47
International Students, Information for — 215

K

Kent State University — 51

L

List of Profiled Universities and Colleges — 13
Living in the USA — 215

M

Management Education — 3
Map of the USA — 8

N

Notes on Reading the Profiles — 11

O

Ohio State University, The — 55
Opportunities & Challenges in Management Education — 3

P

Pennsylvania State University, The — 59
Program Profiles — 21
Program Quick Facts — 14
Purdue University — 63

S

Stanford University	67
Studying in the USA	216
Syracuse University	71

T

Temple University	75
Texas A & M University	79

U

University of Arkansas	83
University of California – Irvine	87
University of Central Florida	91
University of Chicago	95
University of Cincinnati	99
University of Connecticut	103
University of Florida	107
University of Georgia	111
University of Illinois at Chicago	115
University of Illinois at Urbana-Champaign	119
University of Kansas	123
University of Maryland – College Park	127
University of Massachusetts, Amherst	131
University of Michigan – Ann Arbor	135
University of Minnesota, Twin Cities	139
University of Mississippi	143
University of Oklahoma	147
University of Rhode Island	151
University of South Carolina	155
University of Tennessee at Knoxville	159
University of Texas at Austin, The	163
University of Utah	167
University of Washington	171
University of Wisconsin – Madison	175

V

Vanderbilt University	179
Visa Requirements	218

W

Washington University	183